A POLITICAL BIOGRAPHY OF
JONATHAN SWIFT

EIGHTEENTH-CENTURY POLITICAL BIOGRAPHIES

Series Editor: *J. A. Downie*

TITLES IN THIS SERIES

Daniel Defoe
P. N. Furbank & W. R. Owens

FORTHCOMING TITLES

Delarivier Manley
Rachel Carnell

Alexander Pope
Pat Rogers

Henry Fielding
J. A. Downie

Richard Steele
Charles Knight

John Toland
Michael Brown

www.pickeringchatto.com/politicalbiographies

A POLITICAL BIOGRAPHY OF JONATHAN SWIFT

BY

David Oakleaf

LONDON
PICKERING & CHATTO
2008

Published by Pickering & Chatto (Publishers) Limited
21 Bloomsbury Way, London WC1A 2TH

2252 Ridge Road, Brookfield, Vermont 05036-9704, USA

www.pickeringchatto.com

BRITISH LIBRARY CATALOGUING IN PUBLICATION DATA

Oakleaf, David
A political biography of Jonathan Swift. – (Eighteenth-century political biographies)
1. Swift, Jonathan, 1667–1745 – Political and social views 2. Swift, Jonathan, 1667–1745 3. Novelists, Irish – 18th century – Biography 4. Satirists, Irish – Biography 5. Politics and literature – Great Britain – History – 18th century
I. Title
823.5

ISBN-13: 9781851968480

This publication is printed on acid-free paper that conforms to the American
National Standard for the Permanence of Paper for Printed Library Materials.

Typeset by Pickering & Chatto (Publishers) Limited
Printed in the United Kingdom at Athenaeum Press Ltd., Gateshead, Tyne & Wear

CONTENTS

For Anne

ACKNOWLEDGEMENTS

A scholar writing about Swift's life in politics finds himself perched on the shoulders of giants. I have relied throughout on the heroic labours of those who have edited massive collections or individual texts by Swift, on Irvin Ehrenpreis's monumental biography, on the political interpretations of Swift by J. A. Downie, F. P. Lock, and Ian Higgins. My own work has increased my respect for their accomplishments. For my perch on their shoulders, I am grateful to one of them, the general editor of this series, for his invitation to contribute this volume, and to Christopher Fox for his prior invitation to write on Swift's English politics for *The Cambridge Companion to Jonathan Swift*. To Patricia Brückmann of Trinity College, University of Toronto, I owe a debt of gratitude I can never repay: her infectious enthusiasm and inspired teaching made me a Swiftian and a Scriblerian.

Year in and year out, the often beleaguered but invariably courteous and efficient staff of the MacKimmie Library at the University of Calgary have supported my research. I am grateful too to the staffs of the Thomas Fisher Rare Book Library and the Robarts Library at the University of Toronto, the Bodleian Library, Oxford, and especially the British Library. Without librarians, we could have no scholars.

Directly and indirectly, my colleagues in the Department of English at the University of Calgary have shaped my approach to Swift. Completing this book, I am especially aware of my gratitude to a warm, steady colleague, the late Richard Wall. A scholar of the Irish Literary Revival, Dick made it impossible to forget that Swift was Irish. For their encouragement during the writing of this book, I would also like to thank Jay Macpherson, Beth McKittrick and Norm Wellington. Pam Perkins and the organizers of the Canadian Society for Eighteenth-Century conference in Winnipeg and Clara Joseph of the Postcolonial Research Group at the University of Calgary provided welcome opportunities to air my views of Swift and war. For warm hospitality during bookish sojourns in the UK, I thank James McWhir and Becky Gibby; Andrew McWhir and Naja Felter, who tolerated both solo and familial visits, generously sharing Liva and Melthe as well as themselves. In Canada but far from Calgary, John Oakleaf and Kathy Oakleaf,

Jane Oakleaf Spanton and John Spanton sustained and encouraged me. Much closer to home, Stephen Oakleaf and Catherine Oakleaf showed unfailing interest and support. My deepest obligation, recorded in the dedication, is to my wife and colleague, Anne McWhir. This book owes its virtues to many; its regrettable errors are solely my own.

LIST OF ABBREVIATIONS

Correspondence	*The Correspondence of Jonathan Swift*, ed. H.Williams, 5 vols (Oxford: Clarendon Press, 1963–5).
CW	*The Correspondence of Jonathan Swift, D.D*, ed. D. Woolley, 4 vols in 5 (Frankfurt am Main: Peter Lang, 1999–).
Discourse	J. Swift, *A Discourse of the Contests and Dissentions Between the Nobles and the Commons in Athens and Rome With the Consequences They Had Upon Both Those States* (1701), ed. F. H. Ellis (Oxford: Clarendon Press, 1967).
IE	I. Ehrenpreis, *Swift: The Man, His Works, and the Age*, 3 vols (Cambridge, MA: Harvard University Press, 1962–83).
Intelligencer	J. Swift and T. Sheridan, *The Intelligencer*, ed. J. Woolley (Oxford: Clarendon Press, 1992).
JS	J. Swift, *Journal to Stella*, ed. H. Williams, 2 vols [vol. 1: pp. 1–368; vol. 2, pp. 369–801] (Oxford: Clarendon, 1948).
ODNB	*Oxford Dictionary of National Biography* (Oxford: Oxford University Press, 2004).
Poems	J. Swift, *The Complete Poems*, ed. P. Rogers (New Haven, CT, and London: Yale University Press, 1983).
PW	J. Swift, *Prose Works*, ed. H. Davis and others, 14 vols. (Oxford: Blackwell, 1939–74).
Swift Vs. Mainwaring	F. H. Ellis (ed.), *Swift Vs. Mainwaring: The Examiner and The Medley* (Oxford: Clarendon Press, 1985).
Tale	J. Swift, *A Tale of a Tub; To Which is Added The Battle of the Books and the Mechanical Operation of the Spirit* (1710), ed. A. C. Guthkelch and D. N. Smith, 2nd edn (Oxford: Clarendon Press, 1958).

INTRODUCTION: "'THE CHURCH HAD NEVER SUCH A WRITER'"[1]

Swift's political life presents a number of paradoxes, some genuine, some only apparent. Attracted to the figure of Cato, the classical example of principled retirement from public life, he found his political mentor in a contemporary version of the type, Sir William Temple. He approached the emergence of modern partisan politics by fixing his eyes firmly on the past – on a church that tried to emulate primitive Christianity and on the exemplary models of constitutional balance provided by classical antiquity. Opposed to the very idea of political parties and contemptuous of turncoat writers, he himself wrote on behalf of first one and then the other of the dominant political parties of his day. An Anglo-Irishman eager for English preferment, he regarded his return to Ireland as an exile but was eventually celebrated as an Irish patriot. Although he did not see a contradiction, his simultaneous commitment to an authoritarian state church and the principle of liberty baffles modern readers. Because they try to align him with one of these impulses or the other, they disagree about whether he was 'really' a Whig or a Tory. They disagree, that is, about the primary political convictions of an eloquent writer who spent his life writing political pamphlets. Remarkably, this historically remote and elusive pamphleteer nevertheless enjoys the esteem of politically engaged modern writers, who find him oddly current. They hear in him a voice that speaks directly to their own experience of totalitarian regimes and colonial oppression. Indeed, readers who praise or condemn Swift for his agreement or disagreement with our standards have provoked an indignant backlash designed to place Swift back where he properly belongs. The campaign will be informative, but it seems about as likely to succeed as the attempt to fix his political identity unambiguously. These disputes might amuse Swift, and they would probably also inspire a familiar feeling of exasperation. When he contemplated his own posthumous fame in *Verses on the Death of Dr. Swift*, after all, he anticipated interested and obtuse uses of it. The hardest won lesson of his political life was his recognition that the price he paid for his effectiveness was his inescapable vulnerability to misunderstanding, misappropriation, and (in the early eighteenth-century sense of 'Mistaken or unjust suspicion') misprision.[2] He would certainly have relished the fact that disputes over the nature of his importance take that importance for granted, as he too tended to do.

To take these contradictions in turn. Swift's political mentor, Sir William Temple, provided an ambiguous model of political rectitude by largely avoiding politics. A retired Whig diplomat, he took a transparently vain delight in the fact that King William offered him political positions, which he then declined. In London after Temple's death, Swift defended Whig Lords impeached by the House of Commons in *A Discourse of the Contests and Dissentions between the Nobles and the Commons in Athens and Rome* (1701). Hoping for preferment, he dedicated his controversial early satire, *A Tale of a Tub* (1704), to Baron Somers, a powerful member of the Whig Junto. Although *A Tale* satirized self-serving political hacks who wrote for more than one faction, Swift himself achieved the patronage that had eluded him by becoming, after the Whigs fell, chief propagandist for a Tory ministry headed by Robert Harley. Harley too provided an ambiguous model. Educated at dissenting academies, he had himself begun his career as a Country Whig. Since he had also been speaker of the House of Commons that impeached the Junto Whigs, the effort that Swift had targeted in his *Discourse*, Swift's apostasy seemed complete. His friend Lord Peterborough (another former Whig) thought that his services deserved the reward of 'a Lean Bishoprick, or a fatt Deanery'.[3] Although Swift would gladly have stayed in England, the reward for his English service was an Irish place, and he became Dean of St Patrick's Cathedral, Dublin. Having cut his teeth writing for an English ministry, this reluctant Irishman spent the rest of his career savaging English administrations – and Irish ones he thought too pro-English. A discontented exile to his native land, he won an enduring reputation as an Irish patriot.

To modern readers (though not to Swift), his political commitments seem contradictory. He boasted that 'Fair LIBERTY was all his cry',[4] and throughout his life he defended the constitutional settlement reached at the Glorious Revolution, the settlement that ensured a Protestant rather than a Catholic held the throne and that limited the King's power. Yet he invariably also defended the privileges of the (Anglican) Church of Ireland, the church by law established, even though he felt that loyal servants like himself were unfairly denied promotion in the church hierarchy. He accepted religious toleration; that is, he accepted that Protestant dissenters from the established church had a right to worship. But he aggressively resisted any suggestion that dissenting Protestants had any more right than other infidels to hold civic or military office. Throughout his career, in fact, Swift greeted threats to the established church with a savage rhetoric that harks back to sixteenth-century religious persecutions and the seventeenth-century civil wars. His characteristic sectarian intolerance is all the more striking because it seems unnecessary. In 1688–9, adherents of the Church of England had successfully forced King James II from the throne for promoting Roman

Catholics to key positions in the civil and military administration. Commercial and military rivalry with Catholic and absolutist France kept alive the threat of Catholicism, which was reinforced by Louis XIV's recognition of the Catholic Stuart claimants to the English (soon British) throne. Domestically, though, there was little reason for the English to fear religious minorities. Despite high local concentrations of dissenters, those outside the established church made up less than 10 per cent of the population, and Protestant dissenters (unlike Roman Catholics) lacked foreign backing.[5] Swift, however, wrote from an Irish perspective. In Ireland, he enjoyed a position within the small but constitutionally privileged Church-of-Ireland (Anglican) community, which amounted to somewhere between one in ten and one in eight of the population of Ireland. The Protestant dissenters whose civic participation he opposed were about as numerous, and the thoroughly oppressed Roman Catholics were four or five times as numerous as the combined Protestant population.[6] When Swift spoke for the oppressed, he did so from a beleaguered but remarkably privileged position.

Late seventeenth-century English works that we still value include, to confine the list to a trio of famous writers, John Milton's *Paradise Lost* (1667) and *Paradise Regained* (1671); Isaac Newton's *Philosophiae naturalis principia mathematica* (1687) and *Opticks* (1704); John Locke's *Two Treatises of Government* and *An Essay Concerning Human Understanding* (1690). Yet Swift looked not to the present but the past. He thought his episcopalian established church came as close as was now possible to the perfection of the primitive church. Like Sir William Temple, he was an Ancient; that is, someone who rejected the notion that modern accomplishments rivalled those of the ancient world. Classical Greek and Roman models of political and literary excellence were sacrosanct. Swift viewed historical change not as development but as degeneration from the past. Yet this intolerant and backward-looking writer produced imaginative works that still have a powerful hold on our imaginations. *Gulliver's Travels* and *A Modest Proposal*, probably the two of his works most read today, strike many readers not only as profoundly political but as uncannily current.

That Swift seems current is unexpected. A numerous school of readers regards him as inescapably conservative in temperament and in politics. Employing a common verbal slippage that elides political position with personality, for example, George Orwell credits Swift with a 'reactionary cast of ... mind'. Considering Swift and his fellow satirists, Louis Bredvold coined a long-lived phrase, 'the gloom of the Tory satirists', which combines a temperament (gloomy) and a partisan position (Tory) with a literary kind (satire). Edward Said associates Swift with what he calls 'Tory anarchy'.[7] Even in F. P. Lock's *Swift's Tory Politics*, one of the best extended studies of Swift's political thought, the language of political ideology slides into an idiom of personality:

This is a 'Tory' interpretation of Swift, arguing that he was by no means the political liberal, the unequivocal champion of 'liberty' that some of his modern admirers would like him to have been. If Swift is read out of context, he can indeed sound deceptively liberal and libertarian. But taken as a whole and in context, his writings reveal a deeply conservative, even reactionary, political thinker.

Although Lock provides an important corrective to careless equations of the 'conservative' with the Tory, his investigation of Swift's political principles too elides ideology with personality. Swift's 'fundamental political values (order, hierarchy, stability)', he initially argues, are 'those of a "natural" Tory of his day'. Later, the self-conscious quotation marks vanish. Swift was '[a]lways a natural tory, for he was by temperament authoritarian'; he displays 'the natural toryism of a churchman'. Sunderland was 'not a "party" man but a "royal servant"' (in other words, a natural Tory) in the ministerial tradition of Clarendon and Danby, and subsequently of Godolphin and Harley'.[8] And so on. For Ian Higgins, who explores Swift's connections not just with the Tories but with the Jacobites, Swift again somehow seems Tory in essence: 'Despite the Whig associations and influences of his period in the household of Sir William Temple, and of his early political career and intellectual inheritance, Swift may be recognized as, *ontologically*, a "naturalized" Tory of the Queen Anne and Hanoverian period'.[9] Higgins is certainly right to stress Swift's complexity, but it is hard to understand how Swift can be both essentially Tory and an immigrant from the Whigs now naturalized as a Tory.

Higgins is challenging an orthodoxy that locates Swift's political ideas close to the political centre. Sensing something extremely radical in Swift, he nudges him toward a radical extreme. Unfortunately (and paradoxically), by associating Swift with one particular extreme, Jacobitism, he acknowledges his radicalism at the cost of conferring on it a reassuring degree of predictability. Higgins's antagonist is J. A. Downie, whose *Jonathan Swift: Political Writer* remains the most influential and thorough study of Swift as a political writer. Challenging the view that Swift is essentially Tory, Downie argues, in a position now orthodox, that Swift consistently remained Old Whig. Swift, that is, consistently if not always enthusiastically adhered to the principles of the Revolution Settlement, which brought William III and Mary II to the throne in 1689. Although he avoided party labels when he could, he called himself a Whig, usually an Old Whig, when he had to label himself. He even argued that there was no difference between Tory positions under Queen Anne and Old Whig positions. Such an argument usefully presents Swift's defection from the Whigs to a Tory administration as a display of consistency, of course, but it remains a fact that Swift did not call himself a Tory. Even as a Tory, he worked best and most closely with Old Whigs like Harley, resisting the commitment to a more thoroughly partisan politics that characterized the slightly younger generation of Henry St John and Robert Walpole. No one has yet improved on Swift's description of himself to Lord Somers as a Whig 'in politics' but a High-Churchman 'as to religion'. In politics, he was backward-looking but not thoroughly retrograde, locating his political commitments in the values of the Exclusion Crisis and Glorious Revolution, notably frequent parliaments and the Protestant succession.[10] A satirist as well as a polemicist, he shared animosities rather than principles with those at the political extremes. His radicalism is unpredictable, a matter of the destructive intensity with which he exploited any available means to discredit opponents.

Swift was a political writer during the rage of party, then, but modern scholars disagree about his party position. 'Fair liberty', Swift claimed, 'was all his cry', but he spoke most confidently and persuasively when he spoke for the privileged few. In England, he represented a ministry to an audience of country squires. In Ireland he opposed a ministry, but he still defended the privileges of the small Anglican elite. The unprecedented opportunities of his historical moment allowed him to become a political writer, but he turned for inspiration to the recent and, more profoundly, the remote past. Yet the number of modern writers who find something good to say about Swift, however much he troubles them, is impressive. W. B. Yeats, for example, has been recognized as an early example of what Edward Said calls 'the indisputably great *national* poet who during a period of anti-imperialist resistance articulates the experiences, the aspirations, and the restorative vision of a people suffering under the dominion of an offshore power'.[11] Yet he found a precursor in a fellow Anglo-Irish writer who would not have welcomed the Irish nation that Yeats inhabited – a republic independent of England and insistently Roman Catholic:

> Swift haunts me; he is always just round the next corner. Sometimes it is a thought of my great-great-grandmother, a friend of that Archbishop King who sent him to England about the 'First Fruits,' sometimes it is S. Patrick's, where I have gone to wander and meditate, that brings him to mind, sometimes I remember something hard or harsh in O'Leary or in Taylor, or in the public speech of our statesmen, that reminds me by its style of his verse or prose. Did he not speak, perhaps, with just such an intonation?[12]

Explaining to his Irish audience why he wrote a play about Swift, *The Words upon the Window-Pane*, Yeats obviously finds him a formidable presence. His snobbish reminder that his own ancestors were connected not with Swift but with his superior in the Church-of-Ireland hierarchy is perhaps defensive, an assertion of his own deep roots in the Anglo-Irish community. Archbishop King's complicated relationship with his unruly minion perhaps models Yeats's own. Nevertheless, Swift's presence anticipates and affirms his own quest to define his role as a modern national poet. The enormous differences between them notwithstanding, Yeats feels that he is treading in the footsteps of an earlier and remarkably effective defender of his nation.

In his seminal essay, 'Politics vs. Literature: An Examination of *Gulliver's Travels*', Orwell too engaged in a complex debate with Swift, treating him as if he were a contemporary who faced the same totalitarian enemies. A political writer but no party propagandist, Orwell is returning to the subject of his wartime script of an imaginary radio interview with Swift.[13] There Swift simply 'materialised after all' at the beginning and faded out at the end, a device comparable to the séance of Yeats's play. For Orwell as for Yeats, Swift is not just a writer recollected: he is a haunting presence. Despite celebrating Swift's enduring appeal to a man who first read *Travels* as an eight-year-old boy – '*Gulliver's Travels*, in particular, is a book which it seems impossible for me to grow tired of" – Orwell has trouble disentangling Swift from their mutual enemy. He condemns him for a 'reactionary cast of ... mind' and 'a world-view which only just passes the test of sanity'. Nevertheless, he also recognizes a fellow-combatant in the struggle that most mattered to him:

> Swift's greatest contribution to political thought, in the narrower sense of the words, is his attack, especially in Part III, on what would now be called totalitarianism. He has an extraordinarily clear prevision of the spy-haunted 'police State', with its endless heresy-hunts and treason trials, all really designed to neutralize popular discontent by changing it into war hysteria. And one must remember that Swift is here inferring the whole from a quite small part, for the feeble governments of his own day did not give him illustrations ready-made.[14]

On this front, a more or less modern reason explains Swift's apparent modernity. Swift was an outspoken critic of a government he thought corrupt and tyrannical, and although Orwell seems unaware of it, we should always remember that Swift had his imagination sharpened by the experience of having his correspondence read by the government of the day. That government, which seemed anything but feeble to Swift, suspected him and his friends of a capital crime – treasonous involvement with the outlawed Jacobite movement. Still, Orwell seems never to doubt that his fellow master of the gloomy political beast fable is a political writer of his own peculiarly modern kind. It would even be possible to argue that the endings *Animal Farm* and *Nineteen Eighty-Four* are Swiftian in their pessimism. Despite their affinity, however, Orwell's populist sympathies lead him to denounce Swift for taking an overly jaundiced view of human nature.

The twentieth-century dictatorships that Orwell opposed now seem historically remote, however, and one of my colleagues recently had the disconcerting experience of discovering that nobody in her undergraduate class had heard of *apartheid*, the oppressive South African system that fell far more recently than Nazism or Stalinism. To those involved in that struggle too Swift seemed strangely relevant. Consider this letter written in Gujarati before the outbreak of World War I:

Gulliver's Travels contains so effective a condemnation, in an ironic vein, of modern civilization that the book deserves to be read again and again. It is a very well-known book in the English language. Children can read it with enjoyment, so simple it is; and the wise ones get dizzy trying to comprehend its hidden significance. In Brobdingnag, Gulliver tumbled as low as he had risen high in Lilliput. Even in Lilliput, he has represented the tiny people as possessing a few powers which were superior to his own, that is to say, to those of normal people.[15]

This reader of Swift is Mahatma Gandhi, then an Indian lawyer and activist opposed to South African racism. Less guarded than Yeats or Orwell, Gandhi shows more sense of how much fun Swift is. Apparently delighting as much in Swift's wide accessibility as his irony, he recognizes a subversive empathy in Swift's representation of the occasional superiority of the 'little people', a phrase that encompasses the powerless as well as children.

Gandhi is recommending a favourite in familiar correspondence, not analyzing a classic, of course, but his empathy gives him a point of contact with Swift, who shared it. When Orwell criticizes Swift's misanthropy and resents his failure to imagine a political role for ordinary people, he speaks with a rare and admirable sympathy for society's least privileged. But few of Swift's contemporaries imagined a direct political role for the middling and the poor, about whom Swift sometimes had harsh words. Yet empathy with the least fortunate is even rarer than sympathy for them. In Swift, it appears not just in the physical humour of *Gulliver's Travels* but in his fondness for demotic phrases and literary forms. His characteristic verse everywhere reveals the pronounced influence of popular ballads and street cries. This empathy made possible his later masquerade as M. B. Drapier, the role largely responsible for his standing as a Anglo-Irish patriot. It is one of Swift's paradoxes that he combined his empathy for the life of the streets with his authoritarian role in the church.

The struggle against oppression is not purely a matter of the past, of course. Said too addresses Swift's continuing pertinence. Said enjoyed a position of privilege from which he spoke for the less well situated, his position at Columbia University perhaps providing an analogy to Swift's office as Dean of St Patrick's Cathedral. A modern scholar with his own keenly felt experience of exile and powerless communities, he finds in Swift a model for his own position as a politically engaged intellectual:

> From a class standpoint, then, Swift was a traditional intellectual – a cleric – but what makes him unique is that unlike almost any other major writer in the whole of English literature (except possibly for Steele) he was also an extraordinarily important organic intellectual because of his closeness to real political power.[16]

For Said, the major issues raised by Swift involve 'anything connected with human aggression or organized human violence': he is especially impressed by

Swift's refusal to glamorize war.[17] This too doubtless forms part of Swift's appeal to so many modern writers.

Taken together, these modern readers offer formidable testimony to Swift's enduring appeal and apparent modernity. They are obviously 'interested' readers of Swift, however, in the eighteenth-century sense of having a stake in the outcome of their discussion. They are looking for a mirror that will reflect their own commitments and commonly find instead a distorting glass. Consider the historian, Linda Colley. In her brilliant book, *Captives*, she tries to dissociate the early British Empire from the modern assumption that empire is the result of overwhelming technological and military superiority.[18] In her view, 'Two parables exist about the making and meanings of the British empire'. One is *Robinson Crusoe*. Colley reminds her reader that even this protagonist, in a point central to her thesis, has himself been a captive before he subordinates an island colony with the aid of a slave. Still, Daniel Defoe's novel has offered generations of readers a triumphal version of empire: 'Empire-making in this parable ... involves being a warrior and taking charge. I mean seizing land, planting it, and changing it'. Her second parable, anything but triumphal, is *Gulliver's Travels*:

> The hero of [this] second parable about British Empire ... sets sail from Bristol, centre of transatlantic commerce and slaving, bound for successive zones of European imperialism: Spanish America, the West Indies, coastal India. He never reaches them. Instead, his voyages are aborted, time and time again, by events and beings beyond his control. First, an apparently puny tribe, the Lilliputians, capture him, tie him down and reduce him to their will. Then a people much larger in stature than himself, the Brobdingnags, overwhelm him, sell him like a commodity, turn him into a spectacle, and sexually abuse him. But it is his last captivity that is most devastating. Confined on the island of the Houyhnhnms, creatures utterly unlike himself and far superior, he becomes so caught up in their society that he succumbs to its values. Forced at length to return to Britain, he can barely tolerate the stench of his one-time countrymen or the ugliness, as it now appears to him, of his own family. For this man, overseas venturing brings no conquests, or riches, or easy complacencies: only terror, vulnerability, and repeated captivities, and in the process an alteration of self and a telling of stories.[19]

Swift is certainly alert to the English traveller's vulnerability to capture and humiliation. Colley's 'interested' retelling of *Gulliver's Travels* suggests Swift's relevance to current views of empire as well as eighteenth-century ones, unsettling some cultural clichés as it does so. A historian who can tell a good story, Colley has the virtue of remembering that Swift sometimes writes not with the confidence of the metropolitan centre but from his experience of imperial subjugation.

Colley's argument is inevitably partial. The disparity in scale between European captivity overseas and the Atlantic trade in African slaves, which she briefly acknowledges,[20] reveals a discrepancy in economic if not military power between Europe's empires and others'. Swift's sensitivity to the vulnerability of English travellers seems not to have interfered with his willingness to see Englishmen like himself profit from the slave trade. As part of the treaties ratifying the Peace of Utrecht, the principal accomplishment of the Tory government for which Swift was a propagandist, Britain won the *Asiento*, the coveted right to sell slaves to Spanish Caribbean colonies. The ministerial policy that Swift defended in his brilliant pamphlet, *The Conduct of the Allies*, looks treacherous and self-serving in a retelling remote from the partisan quarrels of the 1710s.[21] A sometime spokesman for the Irish or for the oppressed, Swift (as Said acknowledged) spent some heady years near the very centre of political power. He unsettlingly speaks for both the oppressed and their oppressors, with and against those who engaged his sympathies. He resists a tidy alignment with modern parables of power.

That may be why the best reading of Swift's connection to the destructive impulses at the heart of modern history is C. J. Rawson's *God, Gulliver, and Genocide: Barbarism and the European Imagination, 1492–1945*, a contribution to the important strand of recent Swift scholarship that reads *Gulliver's Travels* from the perspective supplied by the Holocaust and modern totalitarianism:[22]

> My hope is to open up this topic in a way that will uncouple Swift from the indignant diatribes of self-righteous post-colonial censors, as well as from the well-intentioned ministrations of 'liberal' sensibilities ... performing the opposite irrelevance of refashioning Swift into a benign upholder of favourite causes: democracy, the denunciation of slavery, anti-war protest, anti-colonialism, and doubtless also affirmative action, racial and sexual equality, and sensitive speech. He spoke eloquently on some of these subjects, but the revisionist rectitudes of both groups are often as uncomprehending as the dismal colonial discourses they purport to replace.[23]

Swift's readers share his fondness for strong statements, and this one reads like a set-piece polished in oral delivery. Rawson's goal is laudable. He wants to demonstrate that Swift is inescapably *different* as well as complex. Praising Swift when he shares one of our views, like disparaging him when he fails to do so, diminishes a complex and often infuriating writer. Emphasizing only his distance from the present would also diminish him, however, slighting the interested, perceptive readers who provide irrefutable evidence that Swift's contemporaneity is as striking as his historical remoteness. His politics still matter.

A master of public opinion, Swift knew first-hand that political texts were appropriated for conflicting causes. He began his career like his Tale-Teller, looking for an elevation from which to address the crowd. He characteristically found it in the classical past or in the insider's air of unshakable authority. A confidant of the ministers, Mr Examiner at times sounds as if the earth never soiled the soles of his shoes. Even then, however, Swift was misread and attacked. He was caricatured. He was accused of godlessness or Jacobitism. Writing with extreme intemperance, he sometimes offended even powerful allies. Queen Anne resolved never to prefer him in the English church and at one point her government – the one for which he helped to polish the speech from the throne – put a price on his head for something he said in print. Exiled to Ireland and suspected of Jacobitism after the fall of the Tory ministry, Swift learned even harsher lessons about the vulnerability of his character as a writer to condemnation and misinterpretation. He resented this, of course, but he learned to trust himself to the contentious world of opinion. As the Drapier, he trusted to the mob rather than to the ministry for protection from yet another government that had put a reward on his head. Late in his political career, that is, an authoritarian Dean devoted to an ideal past at last found a voice in which future colonial and postcolonial readers would also hear themselves. That he was still a counter in the struggle between contending and clearly interested parties would not surprise him. For Swift, the only imaginable alternative would be to be forgotten. He could probably not imagine a better fate than our still lively contest over the Dean of St Patrick's, Dublin.

Swift's mastery of political pamphleteering and satire is hardly coincidental. Surely no two literary forms are more closely allied. They both make a home for caricature and vituperation. Hostility animates both of them. Swift is most famous today as the author of what we regard as imaginative works, notably *A Tale of a Tub*, *Gulliver's Travels*, *A Modest Proposal* and a substantial body of accomplished but not especially dignified verse. Anger gives its energy to all of them, and they all reflect the experience of a highly political writer. Most of the modern political responses cited above begin with the recognition that *Gulliver's Travels* in particular, remarkably appealing even to children as it is, is inescapably political. To a considerable degree, the diatribes about Swift's reactionary or enlightened politics, and the diatribes against them, turn on strong views of how to read *Gulliver's Travels*. Indeed, it seems to be a law of Swift scholarship that debates about Swift's politics become readings of *Gulliver's Travels*. As long as Swift's masterpiece forms part of the small canon of essential works of literature in English, we will continue to debate Swift's politics because we will all have an interest in the outcome.

This book is a political life of Swift. It emphasizes his career as a political writer from his first approach to the Whigs until his triumph as an unlikely Irish patriot in the 1720s, when he also published *Gulliver's Travels*. His time with Sir William Temple formed many of his attitudes and allowed him to test his constitutional positions in conversation with the great. It was while he was working with Temple that he developed the intimate practical knowledge of printers and book production that served him well as a propagandist. He continued to write about Irish affairs well after the publication of *A Modest Proposal* in 1729. But he wrote his most brilliant works, grappled most profoundly with the implications of party and partisan writing, and was most effective as a propagandist between his approach to the Whigs and his triumph as the Drapier. Between the publication of *A Discourse of the Contests and Dissentions between the Nobles and the*

Commons in Athens and Rome (1701) and *A Tale of a Tub* (1704) and the time he interrupted the writing of *Gulliver's Travels* (1726) to write *The Drapier's Letters* (1724–5), he had an unrivalled impact on the actual outcome of political events. Swift's gift for impersonation – hostile in *A Tale of a Tub*, playful in the *Bickerstaff Papers* – serves him well in the *Drapier's Letters*, a literary and political triumph that marks a significant development in Swift's conception of his relationship with his readers.

The primary concern of these chapters is to locate Swift's writing in his historical context. All politics is local, we are now told, and Swift's political writings all spring from his immediate involvement with a particular place at a particular moment. He reacted to pressing occasions, not to theoretical questions about the origins and nature of legitimate power. Arguably, he displayed a post-Revolution Anglo-Irish willingness to support a strong effective leader who was clearly in charge, leaving more speculative treatments of authority to others. Only because he involved himself so effectively in the affairs of his day – an attempt to impeach a former ministry, the struggle to negotiate a good end to a long war, resisting a badly flawed proposal to mint copper coins for Ireland – does he speak to readers today. His appeal to Gandhi and Yeats, to Orwell and Said, is an important but secondary fact about his writing. It is impossible to think about Swift's political writing without worrying that bone, too, but the foreground of attention has to be Swift and what he thought he was doing in the face of particular provocations. It was as a member of the English interest in Ireland, after all, that he wrote what came to seem statements of a nascent Irish nationalism or even condemnations of colonialism itself. Only because our society too had its origins in the warlike and expansionist society of his day do we feel so compelled to carry his principles to lengths he would have repudiated.

This book argues that the pervasive, brutal fact of war was central to all of Swift's writing. Like many in his society, Swift was haunted by the cultural memory of war, by experience of current war, and by anticipation of imminent wars. That is probably why he betrays so many affinities with Hobbes, a thinker whose absolutism he utterly rejected. War had radically transformed the communities to which he was most deeply attached, the Anglo-Irish community and the Church of Ireland. Seventeenth-century Irish history, with its bloody conquests, rebellions, and reconquests, was nasty and brutish even by English standards, and the English bore the scars of their extremely bloody civil wars. Sectarian conflict had left its mark on the Church of Ireland, too, the spiritual home of a privileged but beleaguered community. Roman Catholicism and Protestant dissent both made vigorous attacks on Swift's church, and if his High-Church rhetoric often sounds intransigent, it does so because he felt vulnerable in a way that someone in the Church of England would find it hard to imagine. That Swift always takes an Irish perspective on English affairs is a truism, as is the fact that he always writes as a minister of the church by law established. But we still probably underestimate the extent to which Swift was formed by his life in Ireland. We likewise underestimate how much war shaped cultural attitudes and, during Swift's lifetime, transformed England into the fiscal-military state that he opposed in the *Examiner*.[24] It is an not accident that Swift came closest to having a comfortably stable party-political identity when he wrote on behalf of a ministry dedicated to negotiating the end to a protracted war, the War of the Spanish Succession.

This book tries not to become another reading of *Gulliver's Travels*. An examination of Book IV in Chapter 1 clinches, I hope, the case that the twin facts of war and Ireland set the limits even to Swift's ability to imagine a utopian society. The final chapter returns to *Gulliver's Travels*, not for the dense texture of allusions to contemporary politics, the subject of many studies and annotations, but for a comic pattern solidly grounded in Swift's political career. This pattern that might be called Swift's satire of the first-person plural. A solitary who returns home only because he despairs of finding a desert island, Gulliver awkwardly and often inappropriately represents his membership in a variety of communities even though he fits well in none of them, not even England. He proudly celebrates his standing as a nardac of Lilliput, makes England contemptible by defending it in Brobdingnag and, after his last voyage, trots and whinnies to assert his presumed Houyhnhnm superiority. In such places, *Gulliver's Travels* reflects as comedy the question at the centre of his political life. From his days conversing with Baron Somers until his triumph as the Drapier and beyond, his circumstances posed a single question for the emphatically independent political writer. Was he a clergyman or playfully indecorous satirist? Was he a Whig or a Tory? Was he English or Irish? To which group did he belong? With which group did he identify himself? Since every *I* implies a *we*, these questions work variations on the question of identity: 'Who are you?' Since Swift's experience was invariably more complex than the binary logic of such questions allowed, he avoided simple answers. *Gulliver's Travels* shows us that he could laugh while also taking the question seriously. Swift's ability to keep posing the basic question of personal identity in political terms perhaps suggests why topical allusions to the politics of his day seem incidental rather than central to the ways in which his playful literary masterpiece forms part of the political life of Jonathan Swift.

1 SWIFT, WAR AND IRELAND: 'AN HEAP OF CONSPIRACIES, REBELLIONS, MURDERS, MASSACRES, REVOLUTIONS, BANISHMENTS'

War lay at the root of Swift's thought about human nature. Indeed, many readers respond primarily to his characteristic, and characteristically negative, view of war. George Orwell finds it disturbingly unpatriotic:

> Part I of *Gulliver's Travels*, ostensibly a satire on human greatness, can be seen, if one looks a little deeper, to be simply an attack on England, on the dominant Whig Party, and on the war with France, which – however bad the motives of the Allies may have been – did save Europe from being tyrannised over by a single reactionary power. Swift was not a Jacobite nor strictly speaking a Tory, and his declared aim in the war was merely a moderate peace treaty and not the outright defeat of England. Nevertheless there is a tinge of quislingism in his attitude ... which comes out in the ending ...[1]

Orwell reads England's eighteenth-century struggle with France in terms of Britain's recent war against a totalitarian and reactionary power, Nazi Germany. His Swift misses the vital nature of the struggle, fails to take an appropriately patriotic view of war. Scarred by his struggle against communists as well as fascists, Orwell also condemns the Houyhnhnms as totalitarian. But it is Swift's attitude to war itself that provokes Orwell's antagonism to a writer he otherwise admires. His Swift is not simply opposing the government of Walpole, he is attacking England itself and thereby collaborating with its worst enemies.

A gifted writer of political fables, Orwell is in many ways an exemplary reader of *Gulliver's Travels*. He brings profound political commitments to bear on a story over two centuries old. He recognizes that few writers engage as passionately as Swift with what Nadine Gordimer, herself a political writer, calls 'this other great theme in human existential drives – politics'.[2] But Orwell's passionate response shows us how easy it is to distort Swift's actual political terrain. Under

Queen Anne, Swift did serve a Tory government that ended a long war with France on favourable terms. By the time Swift published *Gulliver's Travels* well into the reign of George I, the Tories had been proscribed and Walpole had consolidated a Whig regime that largely avoided war. Although the effort has bedevilled readings ever since, it is not easy for even the most ingenious modern reader of *Gulliver's Travels* to align *Travels* with both Swift's career as a Tory propagandist and with his opposition to Walpole – let alone to engage simultaneously with modern politics.[3] The highly specialized subject of modern historical scholarship, the party politics of late Stuart and early Hanoverian England can seem not just irrelevant to a politically engaged modern reading but troublingly at odds with it. Yet they form the ground of Swift's enduring appeal, the arena within which a deliberately backward-looking humanist achieved his impressive modernity.

Consider Said, who also finds Swift's writing strangely current. Approaching Swift from a point of view very different from Orwell's, he celebrates the attitude toward war that Orwell deplores:

> What are the major issues ... that Swift's work defined? Principally, I would say anything connected with human aggression or organized human violence. Under this heading Swift was able to place such disparate things as war itself (about which he never had a good word to say: a remarkable fact), conquest, colonial oppression, religious factionalism, the manipulation of minds and bodies, schemes for projecting power on nature, on human beings, and on history, the tyranny of the majority, monetary profit for its own sake, the victimization of the poor by a privileged oligarchy.[4]

In addition to *Gulliver's Travels* on human pride in the destructiveness of war, Said cites *The Conduct of the Allies* on the frequently mercenary causes of war and on a great power's subsequent dependency on its nominally subordinate allies. Himself displaced and stateless as a consequence of imperial warfare and colonialism, Said admires Swift for the things that offend Orwell. He regards war not as a patriotic necessity but as self-serving and enormously destructive; like the King of Brobdingnag, he cannot share Gulliver's admiration for the technology of modern warfare. Said finds in Swift a fellow-writer whose view of war has also been shaped by his experience of colonization by a military power. Despite their striking differences, though, Orwell and Said are both responding to Swift's sense of war.

Swift does not imagine human society without war. Like Hobbes, he accepted that war was humanity's natural state, that there must be a war of all against all 'during the time men live without a common Power to keep them all in awe'.[5] Unlike Hobbes, he did not conclude from this fairly common assumption that only an absolutist state could impose social order. Born after the mid-seventeenth-century civil wars that ravaged the British isles, he found a way to reject absolutism while remaining authoritarian:

> Where any one *Person*, or *Body* of Men, who do not represent the *Whole*, seize into their Hands the Power in the last Resort; there is properly no longer a Government, but what *Aristotle*, and his Followers, call the *Abuse* and *Corruption* of one. This Distinction excludes arbitrary Power, in whatever Numbers; which, notwithstanding all that *Hobbes*, *Filmer*, and others have said to its Advantage, I look upon as a greater Evil than *Anarchy* it self; as much as a *Savage* is in a happier State of Life, than a *Slave* at the Oar.[6]

A political philosophy based on war is driven by fear. When Swift tells Archbishop King that 'the World is divided into two Sects, those that hope the best, and those that fear the worst',[7] he reluctantly places himself in the second sect. He feared the tyranny of the autocratic ruler. He feared the tyranny a group, be it small or large. But since he was passionately committed to social order, he also feared anarchy.

When push came to shove, however, anarchy frightened Swift less than 'arbitrary Power'. A respectable person who sincerely disagreed with him had obviously, he assumed, overlooked something obvious. He reconciled his love of order with his distrust of absolute power by treating absolutism as a form of literal-mindedness. It wrongly interpreted as 'a *single Person*', he argued, the '*Supreme Magistrate*' to whom absolute obedience was indeed due. By this mistake, 'the Obedience due to the *Legislature* was ... misapplied to the *Administration*'. Since this was such an easy error to make, those clergy who preached passive obedience to the monarch alone could be forgiven: 'this Error ... deceived *Hobbes* himself so far, as to be the Foundation of all the political Mistakes in his Book; where he perpetually confounds the *Executive* with the *Legislative* Power'.[8] Since he believes that there is indeed a supreme power in the state that commands absolute obedience, Swift remains authoritarian. But he positions himself among those who responded to late seventeenth-century political developments by arguing that they owed their absolute obedience not to the monarch personally but to a composite entity, the Crown-in-Parliament.

Notwithstanding his respect for the scruple of those fellow-clergyman who preached passive obedience to the monarch, Swift himself never expressed sympathy for the political pedantry that Alexander Pope later called, in *The Dunciad*, '"The RIGHT DIVINE of Kings to govern wrong"'.[9] Even in *The Sentiments of a Church-of-England Man*, where he explicitly writes as a clergyman, Swift lumped Sir Robert Filmer, who grounded his absolutist state on divine sanction, with Hobbes, whose apparently atheistic analysis alarmed many of his contemporaries. He evidently found the former no more attractive than – fundamentally no different from – the latter. In a 1713 tract, he ironically impersonates a free thinker who objects to Hobbes's '*High-Church* Politicks' but not to his apparent atheism. When he writes about politics, he feels no compulsion distinguish himself from Filmer, the bulwark of patriarchalist Toryism, with whom he has little in common and in whom he has little interest. Instead, he feels compelled to distinguish himself from the apparently free-thinking Hobbes. He preens himself on his grasp of 'this easy Distinction' between absolute loyalty to the King and that same loyalty to the legislature. In his memoir 'On the Death of Mrs. Johnson', he recalls with pleasure that Stella, his pupil and friend, 'understood the nature of government, and could point out all the errors of Hobbes, both in that and religion'.[10] As the Yahoos in *Gulliver's Travels* demonstrate, he agrees with Hobbes that mutual conflict is the natural state of humanity. He agrees, in Hobbes's famous wording, that people in a state of nature – people outside civil society – live in 'continuall feare, and danger of violent death, and the life of man, solitary, poore, nasty, brutish, and short'.[11] He just draws different conclusions.

Nevertheless, war was as central to Swift's imagination as to Hobbes's. 'MOST Kinds of Diversion in Men, Children, and other Animals', he reflected, 'are an Imitation of Fighting'.[12] For much of his life, his society was recovering from a recent war, actively engaged in a current war, or anticipating an imminent war. Recent experience of civil war and destabilizing experiments with republicanism, martial rule, and dictatorship kept war vivid in English memories. Resisted by one army, the Restoration itself had been mediated by another: General Monck had led his army south from Scotland to support Parliament and arrange a peaceful transition back to monarchy. Although James II easily crushed the Monmouth rebellion, bitter opposition to his attempt to impose absolutist rule coalesced around his son-in-law, William of Orange, who invaded England at the head of a Dutch army. Although these transfers of authority – to Charles II, then to William and Mary – went relatively smoothly in England, war had threatened.[13] Many regarded William III as a second William the Conqueror, a ruler *de facto* rather than *de jure*. Fear that England and Scotland would otherwise fall to different, potentially hostile kings – renewing their long history of warfare – provided the incentive for England to negotiate the Act of Union with Scotland that became law in 1707.

Born in the year that saw the end of the Second Anglo-Dutch War (1665–7), Swift lived through several foreign wars: the Third Anglo-Dutch War (1672–4); the inconclusive War of the League of Augsburg, also called the War of the Grand Alliance (1689–97); its renewal as the War of the Spanish Succession (1702–13); and the War of the Quadruple Alliance against Spain (1718–20). It would hardly have surprised him that the Seven Years War (1756–63) would eventually renew the imperial struggle with France on an even grander scale and at an even greater cost than the exhausting wars that lived in popular memory as King William's War and Queen Anne's War. The Country analysis that inspired the *Examiner's* attacks on the Whigs generally and on the Duke of Marlborough in particular actually prefigure a dominant theme of modern historiography. What was emerging, as Swift saw, was what John Brewer calls 'the fiscal-military state'; that is, a centralized state with the financial, civil, and political resources to wage effective warfare. Because he opposed the growing power of the administration (or Court) with respect to Parliament, however, Swift would find less to celebrate than the historians who chronicle the birth of imperial Britain under titles like *The Sinews of Power* (Brewer) and *Albion Ascendant* (Prest).[14]

Swift could probably not agree with a sardonic extension of this position, the argument that 'a fundamental reason why Britain was not torn apart by civil war after 1688 was that its inhabitants' aggression was channelled so regularly and so remorselessly into war and imperial expansion abroad'.[15] For Swift the line between a foreign war and war at home was much finer than this argument concedes. Internal dissension invited foreign invasion, he believed; hence his consistent hostility to factions in the state and sects in religion. After 1689, the existence of Jacobites – supporters at home and abroad of James II and his heirs in exile – kept open the threat (for some, the hope) that a combination of rebellion and invasion might undo the Glorious Revolution by repeating it, this time with the support of a French rather than a Dutch army. Sir William Temple, Swift's patron and King William's friend, argued in his *An Introduction to the History of England* (1695) that this had been the pattern of British history since the days of Julius Caesar: 'And here began the Fate of *Britain*, to make way for Foreign Conquests by their Divisions at home'.[16] Although it is possible to argue that William the Conqueror had, as George Berkeley phrased it in 1709, '"the same title to the crown that a highwayman has to your purse"',[17] Temple represents him as a benevolent invader who courted the consent of those he governed. In this, Temple is following a line of anti-absolutist argument that claimed for England an ancient constitution dating back to Anglo-Saxon times, a constitution that balanced other claims, notably parliament's, with royal authority. Just as it had justified Magna Carta's rejection of later Norman encroachments, so it had justified seventeenth-century resistance to Charles I's absolutism. Those sharing this view found it convenient to argue that William I like William III had simply asserted his claim to a disputed throne.[18] Temple is obviously trying to discourage a subsequent (read *Jacobite*) invasion from abroad by consolidating domestic support behind William.[19]

Unfortunately, fierce partisan divisions continued to mark English politics, encouraging supporters of James II and, subsequently, his son James Edward (the Old Pretender). There were major though unsuccessful Jacobite rebellions in 1715 and 1745 in addition to 'a series of military-style conspiracies' under William and Anne, most notably in 1691–2, 1695–6, and 1708, this last a threatened invasion of Scotland. Combined with the Atterbury Plot of 1720–2 and the Cornbury plot of 1734–5, these events kept alive the prospect that political turmoil at home could encourage an invasion.[20] The threat seemed real. These domestic concerns may well account for England's (later, Britain's) striking transformation into a European power. 'Ponder the question', Brewer asks rhetorically, 'of how many

English victories over continental powers you can name between the battles of Agincourt (1415) and Blenheim (1704)'. Between the historic victory celebrated by Shakespeare in *Henry V* and the victory for which Joseph Addison was commissioned to write *The Campaign* (1705), that is, England had played only a marginal role in European wars. What made the difference, Brewer argues, was the conversion of a foreign war into a domestic threat. By recognizing the Old Pretender as James III when James II died in 1701, Louis XIV converted the War of the Spanish Succession into 'a war of the English succession, fought to preserve a Protestant regime'.[21] For Swift and his contemporaries, war was never remote.

So it makes sense for Swift to emphasize war. When Gulliver gives the King of Brobdingnag 'a brief historical Account of Affairs and Events in *England* for about an hundred Years past',[22] for example, he ensures that civil war – 'that horrid *Rebellion*'[23] – will occupy centre stage. The King's appalled response is, approximately, Swift's own:

> He was perfectly astonished with the historical Account I gave him of our Affairs during the last Century; protesting it was only an Heap of Conspiracies, Rebellions, Murders, Massacres, Revolutions, Banishments; the very worst Effects that Avarice, Faction, Hypocrisy, Perfidiousness, Cruelty, Rage, Madness, Hatred, Envy, Lust, Malice, and Ambition could produce.[24]

This is a thoroughly reasonable response to seventeenth-century English history. Yet Gulliver 'artfully eluded many of his Questions; and gave to every Point a more favourable turn by many Degrees than the strictness of Truth allow',[25] which means that the King is spared the worst even though he hears enough to 'conclude the Bulk of your Natives, to be the most pernicious Race of little odious Vermin that Nature ever suffered to crawl upon the Surface of the Earth'.[26]

It is painful to imagine how the King would have responded to a similar account of Irish history. That history intensified Swift's sensitivity to the inevitability, and the horrors, of war. People in Ireland had learned even grimmer lessons than the English about their vulnerability to rebellion and invasion, lessons that simultaneously illuminate and test Swift's appeal to modern critics of colonialism and starkly mark his difference from them. Swift belonged to a group whose place in Ireland had been secured by English armies and that depended on a continuing military presence. Consider a passage in Swift's *A Letter to the Lord Chancellor Middleton*, a late-published addition to the *Drapier's Letters* that combines Swift's compelling modernity with early eighteenth-century Anglo-Irish particularities. Considering the passage in detail, Said detects familiar colonial stereotypes lurking behind 'the logic that gave rise to *A Modest Proposal*'; 'similar caricatures of African and Asian peoples', he observes, 'exist even today':[27]

> There is a Vein of Industry and Parsimony, that runs through the whole People of *England*; which, added to the Easiness of their Rents, makes them rich and sturdy.

> As to *Ireland*, they know little more than they do of *Mexico*; further than that it is a Country subject to the King of *England*, full of Boggs, inhabited by wild *Irish Papists*; who are kept in Awe by mercenary Troops sent from thence: And their general Opinion is, that it were better for *England* if this whole Island were sunk into the Sea: For, they have a Tradition, that every Forty Years there must be a Rebellion in *Ireland*. I have seen the grossest Suppositions pass upon them; that the *wild Irish* were taken in Toyls; but that, in some Time, they would grow so tame, as to eat out of your Hands: I have been asked by Hundreds, and particularly by Neighbours, your Tenants, at *Pepper-hara*; whether I had come from *Ireland* by Sea: And, upon the Arrival of an *Irish-man* to a Country Town, I have known Crouds coming about him, and wondering to see him look so much better than themselves.[28]

Swift's caricature of colonial disdain for the colonized has kept its bite. The natives are variously savages, animals to be tamed, or a nuisance best eliminated, perhaps by destroying their whole country. Simultaneously, the same natives are a hostile population subdued only by the expensive presence of a paid army, an army whose cost suggests that they are worth subduing! Swift's caricature of English ignorance is also telling: how could he travel from one island to another but by sea?

Said's influential postcolonial reading of this passage called attention to an often overlooked aspect of Swift. To call attention to the Irishman who embodies Swift's exasperated counter-recognition of English ignorance, I quote more of the passage than Said did.[29] The Irishman man who looks so much better than the amazed English crowd is obviously not one of the caricatured wild Irish – bog-dwelling, Gaelic speaking, Roman Catholic, poor, rebellious, and therefore savage. He is an Irishman like Swift himself, a member of the English settler community that their fellow Englishmen (as they saw them) insist on viewing as savages due to the accident of their birth across the Irish Sea. That Swift associates such ignorance with neighbours of the Lord Chancellor of Ireland on his family's estate at Peper Harow, Surrey, perhaps slanders the Whig politician for absenteeism. That Swift too had been eager to subordinate his Irish origins to his English ambitions may complicate and intensify some of the ironies at work, but most of the energy in this passage originates in unavoidable historical contradictions. Speaking from an English perspective, the Anglo-Irish colonist disparages the native Irish but gallingly finds that the English in turn disparage him as Irish.[30]

Like the horrors of war, these contradictions originated in the repeated experience of ethnic, sectarian, and political conflict that Swift invokes: 'For, they have a Tradition', Swift writes, 'that every Forty Years there must be a Rebellion in *Ireland*'. Swift emphasizes three conflicts that assured English domination and the ascendancy of a Protestant minority over Ireland. He begins his count with the Nine Years War, a rebellion against the last expansion of the Tudor plantations in Ireland. Led by Hugh O'Neill, second Earl of Tyrone, the bloody conflict ended only when Tyrone, just after the death of Elizabeth I in 1603 – he was unaware of it as he negotiated – submitted to English authority in the treaty of Mellifont.[31] Best known to literary scholars as the rebellion in which Edmund Spenser and his family fled the burning of his castle at Kilcolman,[32] this rebellion also proved fatal to the career of Elizabeth's courtier, the Earl of Essex, who led an ill-equipped and unsuccessful campaign against the rebels. Since the rebels counted on Spanish support, this struggle, too, was both domestic and international. Charles Blount, Lord Mountjoy, succeeded where Essex had failed by resorting systematically to 'an established procedure in Irish warfare' – the wholesale of destruction of crops.[33] Famine and disease ensured that the war proved disastrous for soldiers and civilians alike. Tyrone emerged from the rebellion with his power and his lands, but the submission of Tyrone completed the subjection of Gaelic Ireland to the English crown.[34] A reader of Edward Said's *Culture and Imperialism* who wanted to locate the point at which colonial and imperial expansion started leaving its imprint on canonical English literature could well begin with this conflict. Spenser was a reluctant participant. James Shapiro explores the impact of this colonial engagement and apprehension of possible disaster on Shakespeare's *Henry V, Julius Caesar, As You Like It* and *Hamlet*.[35]

This war was the first of the three rebellions and reconquests that decisively changed the face of Irish society. At roughly forty-year intervals, as Swift says, it was followed by two others. The first of these, the Rising of 1641, led to a Catholic Confederacy that was suppressed only by the Cromwellian Conquest of 1649–53. Called the Glorious Revolution in England, the second is remembered in Ireland as the War of the Two Kings, a conflict that ended only with the Treaty of Limerick in 1691.[36] For the Glorious Revolution was glorious in the sense of being largely bloodless – to the enormous relief of everyone who recalled the mid-century civil wars – only in England. Ireland experienced a bloody and international war: one modern account begins by introducing the *three* kings involved, treating France's Louis XIV as an important participant by proxy in the war between James II and William III.[37] Appealing to a much larger Catholic population and less encumbered by Parliament than he was in England, James with his agent the Earl of Tyrconnell had in Ireland been able push much further with the project of Catholicizing civil and, crucially, military offices.[38] By the end of January 1689, Swift fled to England from Trinity College, Dublin, which was feeling the impact of James and Tyrconnel's policy of appointing Jesuits to teaching positions in state endowed educational institutions.[39] In the event, William had to reconquer Ireland in a three-year war. David Dickson estimates death in battle at about 25,000, with many more dying of disease. Financially, the cost may have been more than twice the value of the land held by Irish Catholics, a problem since appropriation and redistribution of rebel land was meant to pay for the war.[40]

This catastrophic war recapitulated, decisively but only in miniature, the mid-century trauma of rebellion and conquest that had laid the foundation for the Protestant Ascendancy in Ireland.[41] Initially a widespread and mixed expression of discontent, the uprising that began in October 1641 lived in Protestant memory as the 'black legend' of a deliberate, carefully orchestrated massacre of Protestants. In fact, there seems to have been little coherent leadership to discipline the rebels, and disease took a higher toll than outraged Catholics of the Protestants who fled to crowded refuges. Symbolic acts, too, horrified the refugees who flocked to the north or to England to plead for support: ejected Protestants were sometimes stripped of their clothes, churches were desecrated, and bodies were exhumed from cemeteries and further desecrated. Highly mythologized accounts of atrocities outraged public opinion in England and Scotland, where estimates of the dead at times greatly exceeded the number of Protestants in all of Ireland.[42] Swift had direct connections with not only communal memories of this rebellion but with a principal mythologist of it, his patron's father, Sir John Temple. Described by Swift as 'a great Friend to the [Swift] Family',[43] John Temple wrote *The Irish Rebellion; or, An History of the Beginnings and First Progresse of the General Rebellion Raised within the Kingdom of Ireland, upon the Three and Twentieth Day of October, in the Year, 1641* (1646), a militant text that marks a return to an Elizabethan policy, advocated by Edmund Spenser, to subjugate Ireland by force.[44] Temple's immediate task was to fan the flames of Protestant retaliation, a retaliation that was delayed by political events in England but all the more savage when it came. Cromwell's zealous troops gave no quarter when they captured Drogheda and Wexford; after 1649, disease and famine combined with combat to kill perhaps a fifth of the total population.[45] It was through this earlier struggle that Catholics and Protestants alike viewed James II's Catholicization and William III's reconquest.

Resistance and reconquest – internal dissension followed by invasion – had decisively shaped Irish society. In Tudor and earlier seventeenth-century Ireland, the English interest had often been asserted by the Old English; that is, the Roman Catholic descendants of earlier English settlers. By the end of the century, the sectarian distinction between Catholic and Protestant had become more significant than the ethnic distinction between Irish (that is, Gaelic) and English, a decisive sectarian transformation that some historians compare not with events in England and Scotland but with the religious wars on the Continent through which, for example, Catholics displaced Protestants in Bohemia.[46] Through a Cromwellian Conquest that had seen itself as something like a crusade, members of a once-powerful elite had been disenfranchised and, to a considerable extent, dispossessed of their land:

> the importance of the Cromwellian land settlement in creating the substructure on which Protestant dominance was based is entirely justified. It is shown most clearly in the simple statistic that, whereas in 1641, 59 per cent of the profitable lands in

Ireland had been owned by Catholics, the Catholic share had dropped to 22 per
cent. An incipient Irish Protestant ascendancy came into being during the 1650s.[47]

Undermined by Charles II and directly challenged by James II, this nascent
Protestant ascendancy was restored by William, but land tenure was thrown
into doubt at each stage.[48] The winners were vengeful although, as Toby Barnard
puts it, 'the mood led not to massacres but to measures' – the penal laws that
largely excluded Catholics from public life. Catholic share of land dropped again,
to about 14 per cent, property being once more redistributed to the victorious
Protestants. But the experience of twice nearly losing their land and their new
ascendancy taught those Protestants that their position in Ireland depended on
England's military support. Their triumph went hand in hand with the recognition of their subordination.

Loyalties were consequently complex, memories troubled. To win their support for the Restoration, Charles II had to respect the claims of the Protestant
community established in Ireland by Cromwellian rebels against his father rather
than the Catholic Old English, whose rebellion in 1641 had in part expressed
support for the royalist cause in the struggle between King and Parliament.
Dispossessed Old English planters complained of the injustice in print: 'It is
indeed a most wonderful conveniency to dispossess the ancient Proprietour who
fought for the king and give his Estate to a Fanatique Soldier who fought for
Cromwel.'[49] King and Court were aware of the irony:

> From an English Protestant point of view the massive Cromwellian expropriations,
> confirmed for the most part by Charles II, were no less than justice for the rebellion
> and associated atrocities committed by Irish Catholics in 1641 and after. But the
> atrocities were almost impossible to investigate until many years later, and in any
> case they were not exclusively the work of those expropriated, many of whom were
> quite innocent. As for the alleged act of 'rebellion' at a moment (October 1641)
> when Charles I was facing the veritable insurrection of his House of Commons, it
> was partially actuated by feelings of loyalty to the crown. As Charles II confided
> to Clarendon at a Privy Council meeting in late 1661, 'rebel for rebel, I had rather
> trust a papist rebel than a presbyterian one.' Clarendon's somewhat trimming reply
> was, 'The difference is that you have wiped out the memory of the rebellion of the
> one, whilst the other is liable to all the reproaches.'
>
> Charles II and James II never lost sight of this irony, and the new proprietary
> class could never forget that its title to Irish land required that the irony be over-
> looked.[50]

Thirty years later, of course, William III defeated James II and his supporters in
battle, regaining Protestant Anglo-Irish loyalty to the English crown in Ireland
by restoring the threatened Cromwellian land settlement. This did little to lessen
the historical ironies.

Not surprisingly, related ironies inform the passage in which Swift repeats English caricatures of the wild Irish. He resents these caricatures because they type as Irish even members of the seventeenth-century English plantation of Ireland, to which he belonged. Free to visit England and comment on his reception there, Swift's spokesman here is not one of 'wild *Irish Papists*; who are', in Swift's Hobbesian phrase, 'kept in Awe by mercenary Troops'. The reference is to a professional army rather than a militia. Swift's spokesman would be familiar with such English troops firsthand. The English government avoided popular aversion to a peacetime standing army, widely regarded as a threat to liberty, by garrisoning much of its peacetime army in Ireland. This kept it out of English sight and paid for it out of the pockets of Anglo-Irish taxpayers who had been thoroughly schooled in their dependency on English arms.[51] So it was especially insulting to treat an Anglo-Irish Protestant whose taxes supported that army as if he were one of the natives it was meant to subdue. An indignant English settler, Swift is unavoidably implicated in the extremes he condemns: associated with the Irish natives, he distinguishes himself from them by identifying himself as English, like the very people who cannot be bothered to make that distinction.

Swift's role in articulating an Anglo-Irish identity is familiar but, given the recurrent experience of invasion and conquest that seemed normative to Temple, historians dispute the extent to which Irish experience actually was colonial. To some, Ireland is a kingdom like England (later Britain), dominated by waves of invaders but eventually becoming a nation. In these terms, Defoe had caricatured English enemies of their foreign king, William III, as mongrel descendants of waves of foreign soldiers, 'a compounded Breed', 'the most Scoundrel Race that ever liv'd'.[52] To others, however, Ireland is instead like the overseas plantations that characterize the British Empire. J. G. A. Pocock, for example, suggests that the English interest in Ireland had much in common with English settler communities across the Atlantic:

> Communities of settlers, it may be suggested, face the problem of establishing the cultural and political identity they have brought with them in a new environment; they claim both to have remained what they were, and to have taken root where they are and derive identity from it. Tensions with their community of origin may equal or exceed tensions with the indigenous community among whom they have settled; they may find themselves claiming both to continue part of the original community and to assert themselves against it.[53]

From this point of view, Swift's complex identifications and resentments are hardly unique. To judge by most of his Irish political writing, he did not feel threatened by the Catholic population, which had been thoroughly subjugated by English arms. He felt threatened by Protestant dissenters and by the English government that, in the end, governed Ireland.

The debate over whether to view Ireland as a kingdom or a colony has deep roots.[54] But Swift and other members of his community in Ireland did not regard themselves as colonists: "Anglo-Irish political thinking ... held no brief for the idea that they were colonists, or that Ireland was in any respect like Virginia or Maryland".[55] Even some in England agreed. In *Mac Flecknoe*, for example, MacFlecknoe is assigned an empty kingdom: 'Heavens bless my son, from *Ireland* let him reign / To far *Barbadoes* on the Western main'.[56] John Dryden slyly distinguishes the disorder symbolized by the Atlantic Ocean from an ordered plenitude centred geographically on London and historically on imperial Rome. He then subdivides his imperial order into a familiar here and an alien there. He shows no doubt, however, that Ireland marks not the near edge of there – the colonial hinterland – but the far edge of here, the metropolitan centre.

Dissenting voices point out colonial features but do not always carry the day. By 1720, the anonymous author of *The Jamaica Lady*, an explicitly racist and misogynist short novel, represented Ireland and Jamaica as parallel island possessions sure to corrupt the English visitor: "'tis as impossible for a Woman to live at *Jamaica* and preserve her Virtue, as for a Man to make a Voyage to *Ireland*, and bring back his Honesty'.[57] Colonial standing is further suggested by the fact that the assimilation to dominant structures that characterized English relationships with the Welsh or even the Scottish highlanders failed to occur in Ireland, where Protestant plantations were too small to assimilate or dominate numerically the native population.[58] Nevertheless, S. J. Connolly's impressive study of Protestant Ireland challenges the appropriateness of colonialism as a model for Irish settlement. According to Connolly, Ireland resembles other areas of *ancien régime* Europe that were dominated by foreign rulers. While he acknowledges that a 'history of conquest followed by plantation and the expropriation of native proprietors gave Ireland some features of a colony', he argues that geographic proximity and the lack of a racial difference between settlers and natives distinguish Ireland from England's colonial possessions: 'the barrier created by the penal laws could be crossed, in a way that no barrier based on colour could ever be, by a change of religious allegiance'. Although this difference from other colonies must indeed be acknowledged, such an analysis unfortunately takes race as a given and equates it with colour.[59] Such an assumption neglects the extent to which settlers themselves actually racialize the people they conquer and displace. In *God, Gulliver and Genocide*, Claude Rawson explores the ways the English associated the Irish with stereotypes of the savage, many of them incorporating features of the African or the American.[60] *Savage* is not directly a racial category, and *race* itself only gradually came to perform the cultural tasks familiar to us. Yet the characterizations of the Irish to which Swift responds do mark the native or wild Irish as savages who are physically as well as culturally other.[61] The analogy between Irish and colonial experience nevertheless offers a fruitful basis for modern engagements with Swift provided that it is suitably qualified by Connolly's careful attention to historical particularities.

Connolly does convincingly challenge the notion that Swift and his class felt insecure about their title of the island their ancestors had occupied since the seventeenth century, the idea that features of Irish ruling-class life reflect 'the identity crisis of the conquistador'.[62] Swift commonly expresses indignation at English obtuseness, not personal insecurity. He inhabited Ireland confidently, and as Irvin Ehrenpreis observed, 'there is always a first-handedness in his experience of his native country which his life in England lacked'.[63] Most people knew that their social stability required what Hobbes called a common power to keep all in awe, and Swift shared with his Protestant countryman a pragmatic conviction that effective government mattered more than theoretical elaboration of political principle.[64] He may have inhabited a heavy-drinking provincial society fond of lavish hospitality and quarrels of honour, but he commonly presents – I quote Connolly's description not of Swift but of his countryman Alan Brodrick, later Lord Midleton! – 'the other face of the early eighteenth-century Protestant élite: sober, restrained, and ... possessed of a proper sense that prosperity was partly at least the reward of industry and self-discipline'.[65] Even Swift's proud conviction that he had a right to engage as an equal with anyone reflects, it has been argued, 'a kind of aristocratic egalitarianism' characteristic of a society in which a 'sense of a common superiority to the Roman Catholic masses tended to weaken the force of class divisions within the dominant group'.[66] In accord with the Hobbesian principle that mankind's bleak prospects in a state of nature stem from a fundamental equality,[67] visitors observed within that group 'less an exaggerated concern with the niceties of personal honour than a murderous aggression', 'a general disposition toward aggression and ready violence'.[68] Quoting John Dunton's account of a visit to Dublin, Connolly observes that 'in such loud, boisterous, competitive company, where men were expected to jostle for attention and esteem, it is hardly surprising that trivial disputes could be magnified into points of honour and verbal aggression could give way suddenly to physical violence.'[69] Although nothing predicts a writer as distinctive as Swift, it is perhaps not surprising that a satirist nourished by this society should in *A Tale of a Tub* imagine Grub Street as the quasi-Lucretian site of chaotically colliding egos. Nor that Swift should challenge his fellow-writers with such aggressive intensity. No dueller, Swift displays a striking 'disposition toward aggression and ready violence' not in his daily behaviour but in his style: 'Last Week I saw a Woman *flay'd*, and you will hardly believe, how much it altered her Person for the worse.'[70] On many levels, he speaks as an assured member of the society of his birth.

In many ways, then, not all of them typical, Swift writes not as an Englishman but as a member of the English interest in Ireland. And it is undeniable that this clergyman of the Protestant church 'by law established' as the national church of Ireland vividly articulates an experience that speaks directly even to postcolonial readers as astute as Said. Some readers actually hear not just the voice of his anomalous settler community but the voice of all the colonized. Quoting the passage from *A Letter to the Lord Chancellor Middleton* that Said also considers, Carole Fabricant argues that Swift finds a voice that speaks for all oppressed Irish people:

> In passages such as the ones I've cited from *The Drapier's Letters*, the arrogant but insecure self-assertion and the injured pride of the scorned Anglo-Irish settler has moved into another register; it has crossed over, blended, and transformed into the frustration and anger of the native Irish population, with their deep sense of victimization not only by British armaments and unjust laws but also by a network of falsifying myths.[71]

Fabricant's reading obscures the undeniable fact that I have been emphasizing. Swift speaks not for the abject Irish but rather on behalf of, and as one of, the Anglo-Irish settlers whose greatest fear was that the Catholic population, native Irish and Old English alike, might somehow reassume their lands and the social authority they had once held in their hands, 'put[ting] the new proprietary at risk of annihilation' as Karl S. Bottigheimer words it.[72] So it is very hard to imagine him as simply and patriotically Irish, harder still to imagine him as a spokesman for the Catholic population. Still, nations are imagined communities,[73] and by resisting English stereotypes Swift's voice has, as Fabricant argues, contributed to the ways the peoples of Ireland came to imagine their nation.

It would be misguided to treat Swift as simply and representatively Anglo-Irish, however, in part because his society was divided on both sides of the sectarian divide. Catholics included Old English as well as Gaels. Protestants divided ethnically too, into English and Scots. Unless qualified, the term Protestant typically referred to the official church 'by law established', but the English as well as the Scots included members of a variety of dissenting Protestant denominations. In the absence of an external threat, sectarian animosities marked relations among these denominations, but shared experience fostered some common attitudes. Irish responses to William III's assumption of the throne and his subsequent reconquest of Ireland, S. J. Connolly suggests, reveal some features less common in England. They show 'both a marked concern with effective authority as opposed to legitimacy, and a notably greater willingness than their English counterparts to discuss the whole episode in terms of war and of the breakdown and reconstitution of the political order'. Ability to defend the beleaguered Irish Protestant minority mattered more than finer points of constitutional interpretation.[74] Crudely speaking, they seem, as Swift often does, more Hobbesian than Filmerian or Lockian. Swift certainly writes pragmatically about royal power: 'every *limited* Monarch is a King *de jure*, because he governs by the Consent of the *Whole*; which is Authority sufficient to abolish all precedent Right'.[75] He devotes little intellectual sophistication to rationalizing his support for replacing one king by another:

> And if such a King as I have described, cannot be deposed but by his own Consent in Parliament, I do not well see how he can be *resisted*; or what can be meant by a *limited* Monarchy ... I desire no stronger proof that an Opinion must be false, than to find very great Absurdities annexed to it; and there cannot be greater than in the present Case ...[76]

A threat to social standing and property abundantly justifies the resistance. The Glorious Revolution needs no fuller justification than its restoration of the orderly rule of law after internal dissension had led to war.

Central to Swift's appeal to modern readers, then, are widespread contemporary attitudes given a characteristic personal inflection by his Irish experience. Swift believed that war was inevitable, inevitably horrific, and (in what it achieved) deeply ironic. This belief links his commitment to liberty, which is often regarded as Whig, with his High-Church conviction, often regarded as Tory, that a strong national church was necessary to maintain a stable social and moral order. Even at his most utopian, war shapes his thought. In *Gulliver's Travels*, his most popular work, war is central even to the rational Houyhnhnm society he imagines in Book IV. The Houyhnhnms embody an idealized version of the independent landed gentry to whom he had addressed his *Examiner* papers. They live independently and frugally with their families, raising and consuming their own crops instead of relying on imports. They divide into gentry and servants, a feature of social structure that almost everyone took for granted, but – remarkably – they make do without an aristocracy and without a monarch. In the terms of Swift's *Sentiments of a Church-of-England Man*, they make do without an administration distinct from the legislature, the source of '*Abuse* and *Corruption*' in government. There is no Court and no prime minister: subservience to a leader figures, repulsively of course, only among the Yahoos.[77] This bucolic society nevertheless does have a legislature, 'a Representative Council of the whole Nation, which meets in a Plain ... and continueth about five or six days'.[78] Since the Houyhnhnms are frugal and rational, the assembly has little to do apart from adjusting regional inequities. Inevitably, though, it must also attend to 'the only Debate that ever happened in their Country'; that is, 'Whether the *Yahoos* should be exterminated from the Face of the Earth'.[79]

Even this apparently stable society of horses, so to speak, maintains itself with nervous vigilance:

> He ['One of the *Members* for the Affirmative'] took Notice of a general Tradition, that *Yahoos* had not been always in their Country: But, that many Ages ago, two of these Brutes appeared together upon a Mountain; whether produced by the Heat of the Sun upon corrupted Mud and Slime, or from the Ooze and Froth of the Sea, was never known. That these *Yahoos* engendered, and their Brood in a short time grew so numerous as to over-run and infest the whole Nation. That the *Houyhnhnms* to

get rid of this Evil, made a general Hunting, and at last inclosed the whole Herd; and destroying the Older, every *Houyhnhnm* kept two young Ones in a Kennel, and brought them to such a Degree of Tameness, as an Animal so savage by Nature can be capable of acquiring; using them for Draught and Carriage.[80]

The Houyhnhnms are not, as Orwell thought, 'creatures without a history'.[81] They preserve an oral history that turns on a decisive act of violence whose consequences haunt the present. On what to do, even they can reach no consensus.

Even their phrase puts the Houyhnhnms in strange company. A 'general hunting' oddly connotes a lordly, even splendidly barbaric gathering accompanied by a massive slaughter of game.[82] In a homely travel narrative contemporary with *Travels*, however, a general hunting kills forty scrawny goats but sadly yields only four or five pounds of the tallow that a stranded narrator needs to stanch his boat.[83] It rarely suggests the extermination of a pest, although in a jocular early eighteenth-century text 'APOLLO appoints a general Hunting, to destroy, if possible, the Species of Ants and Tortoises, as Animals of ill Example to Mankind'.[84] Application to a manhunt or a lynching is figurative and unusual, but not unprecedented, and the thought must cross the mind of readers who see themselves in the hunted Yahoos.[85] At the very least, Swift's use of the phrase suddenly presents the Houyhnhnms as socially organized hunters distinct from their hapless animal prey.

The Houyhnhnm speaker, like most Enlightenment Englishmen, takes brutality for granted. Roy Porter describes an English culture of frequent thrashings, blood sports, and public punishments that should probably frame our readings of Swift: 'Work-animals were driven relentlessly: England was notoriously "hell for horses"'.[86] No wonder the Houyhnhnms are appalled by the treatment of English horses! But Gulliver waxes more eloquent than the Houyhnhnm debater on the possibility of counter-violence:

> The *Houyhnhnms*, indeed, appear not to be so well prepared for War, a Science to which they are perfect Strangers, and especially against missive Weapons. However, supposing myself to be a Minister of State, I could never give my Advice for invading them. Their Prudence, Unanimity, Unacquaintedness with Fear, and their Love of their Country would amply supply all Defects in the military Art. Imagine twenty Thousand of them breaking into the Midst of an *European* Army, confounding the Ranks, overturning the Carriages, battering the Warriors Faces into Mummy, by terrible Yerks from their hinder Hoofs ...[87]

Central to an anti-colonial tirade, Gulliver's 'sadistic fantasy'[88] serves as an act of historical reconstruction. Any confrontation with European invaders will repeat the past, for the Houyhnhnms insist that the Yahoos are invaders, not '*Ylnhniamshy* (or *Aborigines* of the Land)'.[89] The general hunting of the Yahoos must have ended like this. Unruly but unarmed, the Yahoos lack 'missive Weapons' like the arrow that wounds Gulliver when he meets a more conventional example of natural humanity.[90] They would have posed a far less formidable threat than the hapless European army Gulliver imagines. Since Houyhnhnms too lack weapons, 'destroying the Older' Yahoos before taming some of the younger presumably means, as Gulliver here imagines, beating them to 'Mummy' with blows of their hooves. We are not directly told this, but alternatives like confining them and leaving them to starve would add the European refinement of siege warfare to the Houyhnhms' meagre list of military strategies. It would not make this passage more palatable to the imagination.

Coolly deliberate, the Houyhnhnms treat the Yahoos not as vermin but as enemies. Since they keep cats on which the Yahoos occasionally prey, presumably to control mice in their granaries, they understand the difference. It explains why they have to exile Gulliver:

> For, they alledged, That because I had some Rudiments of Reason, added to the natural Pravity of those Animals, it was to be feared, I might be able to seduce them into the woody and mountainous Parts of the Country, and bring them in Troops by Night to destroy the *Houyhnhnms* Cattle, as being naturally of the ravenous Kind, and averse from Labour.[91]

To use an Irish phrase, the Houyhnhnms are afraid that Gulliver might persuade the Yahoos to turn tory. He might, that is, lead groups of them to pillage the Houyhnhnm community, as did the rapparees or tories who periodically raided the English settler community in Ireland – and supplied the derogatory nickname for the English political party Swift himself served after he left the Whigs and turned tory in politics. As late as 1707, the Irish Parliament passed 'An Act for the more effectual suppression of tories, robbers, and rapparees'.[92] Any Irish reader of this passage in *Travels* would surely detect an analogy with Irish history.

I do not want to argue that the invading Yahoos *are* the Irish Catholics dispossessed by Protestant settlers, a position that has been hotly debated.[93] As Claude Rawson shrewdly observes, 'the tension created by Swift rests on the opposite and contending perceptions of difference of species and racial difference within the same species'. Gulliver may identify himself with the lordly Houyhnhnms, but he resembles their prey. When Rawson adds that, 'Strictly, a Houyhnhnm plan to exterminate the Yahoos most closely resembles some hygienic undertaking to exterminate a farmyard pest, except of course that in the reader's perspective the Yahoos resemble humans', he slights the extent to which Swift positions the Yahoos as enemies rather than as vermin.[94] On this issue, I am content to observe that Swift keeps in play the analogy to war. He refuses to imagine even a utopian society of rational animals without grounding it on a historical act of violence that his all-too-human protagonist gleefully imagines as an act of bloody war. Since Swift reveals in *The Drapier's Letters* that he both is and is not Irish, both is and is not English, I will also conjecture that the most Anglo-Irish feature of *Gulliver's Travels* is an astonishing act of simplification. Swift imagines that the despised and subjugated labourers are invaders, the rational landowners natives.[95] It seems that he can imagine a cause for a just war that is not already corroded by irony. He just cannot imagine even a utopian society that was free from war itself.

Swift's fable provokes thought about issues that are in the broadest sense political, questions about the foundations of civil authority and the legitimate exercise of power. In part because the perennial question of war informs Swift's own thought, it still arouses passions in thoughtful readers. Yet it grows out of Swift's involvement in the practical politics of a day that seems remote from our own. Seeing himself as a champion of liberty, he served as an emissary for a state church that wanted to confine all civil office to its members. Offering his services to a new political party, he then became chief propagandist – media manager may suggest his role more accurately to modern readers – for a ministry whose goal was to end a prolonged and expensive war. Following the death of Queen Anne, the party that dominated that ministry remained out of office until long after Swift's death, disabled by its own internal divisions and tainted by the compromises it had made in pursuit of the peace. Despite his ambition to live in England, Swift spent the rest of his life as Dean of St Patrick's Cathedral, Dublin. There a reluctant exile from England and native of the English settlement in Ireland returned to politics in opposition to the English government. There he came to champion Anglo-Irish liberties, often through corrosive satire of the Anglo-Irish establishment. Despite writing political works of undoubted brilliance in England – essays in the *Examiner*; *The Conduct of the Allies* – and in Ireland – *The Drapier's Letters*, *A Modest Proposal* – he became famous for satires whose precise political import eludes modern readers even though they provoke intensely political speculation about human nature itself: *A Tale of a Tub* and *Gulliver's Travels*. The political life of Swift that occupies the following chapters will at times engage with Swift when he seems most remote from, or least appealing to us. But these political struggles commanded his interest. Apart from playful poems to friends, Swift wrote little that was not political. He published *A Tale of a Tub* to display his talents for the Whig Junto he hoped to serve. Like Daniel Defoe, he turned to imaginative fiction only after the Septennial Act and Walpole's firm hold on power had rendered opposition political writing ineffective.[96] We increasingly understand that the professional imaginative writing we now value emerged from forms of political intervention that puzzle us.[97] Reading Swift in his political context may illuminate not only his best-known works but our own paradoxical relationship to the war-torn, politically factious age that shaped them.

2 COURTING THE FAVOUR OF THE GREAT: *A DISCOURSE* AND *A TALE OF A TUB*

Following Sir William Temple's death, Swift scrambled for a position while publishing Temple's works, a demanding but modestly lucrative enterprise that allowed him to call attention to himself as the protégé of a respected and uncommonly well connected former patron. Once he secured a modest independence as vicar of Laracor, he began to demonstrate his considerable abilities by also publishing, at a significant interval, two substantial works of his own. These shows of strength displayed the wide reading and the literary mastery that would, he hoped, attract the favour of the recently fallen Whig Junto. Since he was busy establishing himself in Ireland, a task that included getting his friends Esther Johnson and Mrs. Dingley settled in Dublin, he could visit England only briefly. So he probably regarded these bids for attention as an investment in the future, stepping stones to future advancement within the learned profession he had chosen. Despite its title, *A Discourse of the Contests and Dissentions between the Nobles and Commons in Athens and Rome* is a topical and partisan pamphlet. In it, Swift intervenes in the paper war that accompanied the attempt by the House of Commons to impeach the Whig lords who had dominated the earlier ministry, and he unabashedly sides with the Court Whigs who were under attack. *A Tale of a Tub*, on the other hand, was apparently largely written during his years with Temple but subsequently revised to keep it current. Swift dedicated it to Baron Somers, chief of the Junto lords, and timed its publication in 1704 for a moment when it seemed Somers might return to power.

In this brilliant, unruly satire of abuses in learning and religion, Swift makes what is probably the oddest bid for preferment in the history of English political writing. Yet *A Tale* shares many features with the more straightforward *Discourse* that preceded it. Each proceeds by analogy to link distinguishable realms – the personal and the political, quotidian experience and affairs of state, national events and international, and (in *A Tale*) religion with learning. Although Swift's allegiance to the Crown-in-Parliament marks a decisive step from imagining political loyalties as purely personal, each work assumes an intimate connection between affairs of state and the ordinary human passions, assumed to be universal, of political agents. *A Tale of a Tub*, published later but largely completed earlier, satirizes a personality that Swift sees at the root of all forms of instability, political as well as social, that substitute personal ambition for common concerns. This is a personality undisciplined by the classically-oriented education reserved for the land owning classes. Each, that is, flaunts Swift's uncompromising mastery of classical literature, and each therefore addresses the question of cultural as well as political authority in a way that aligns Swift with Temple as a champion of the ancients rather than the moderns. In terms of Swift's own ambition for advancement, however, these works had opposite effects. *A Discourse* won him the acquaintance of the great, notably Baron Somers. *A Tale*, on the other hand, created a reputation for irreligion that dogged him as he worked to secure preferment within the English rather than the Irish church. But both staked his claim to the attention of the powerful.

Independence and liberty were personal before they were political. As the posthumous son of a professional man in Dublin, Swift had never been able to take his own independence for granted as a landowner or his heir might do. He had depended on the modest resources of his family for his education, and although his family had commendably supported him at Kilkenny School and then Trinity College, Dublin, Swift bitterly recalled that 'by the ill Treatment of his nearest Relations, he was so discouraged and sunk in his Spirits, that he too much neglected his Academical Studyes'.[1] After he fled 'the Troubles' in 1689, he depended on Temple, an Irish connection of the family. The temporary rift with Temple, during which he was ordained in Ireland and assumed responsibility for the parish of Kilroot, shows how galling he found his prolonged dependency. 'It is a miserable Thing to live in Suspence', he memorably wrote; 'it is the Life of a Spider'.[2] But Kilroot, his parish in the heavily Presbyterian north of Ireland, would not do, and Temple urged him back to Moor Park. Swift felt that his display of independence had earned respect and a better prospect of advancement: 'I am once more offered the advantage to have the same acquaintance with greatness that I formerly enjoyed', he wrote to Jane Waring in 1696, 'and with better prospect of interest'.[3] He continued to hope for more, putting his faith in Temple's friend the second Earl of Sunderland, who resigned as Lord Chamberlain a few months after accepting the position and just after Swift formally resigned Kilroot: 'My Ld Sunderland fell and I with Him'.[4] With Temple, he read prodigiously, wrote much, and published little. Wry self-reflection informs his comment, in *A Tale of a Tub*, that there are 'three wooden Machines, for the Use of those Orators who desire to talk much without Interruption'.[5] A writer who wants to make a figure in the world, he knew, first needs a place from which to speak. The machine Swift found was the pulpit. His modest but secure independence as Vicar of Laracor and prebendary of St Patrick's Cathedral, Dublin, freed him at last from complete dependence on the whims of his patrons. But it failed to gratify ambition. Independence secured, he published a partisan political pamphlet, calling public attention to the talents through which he hoped to win greater rewards.

The story is familiar. Temple died in January 1699, leaving Swift still unprovided for apart from a small legacy of £100 and 'the care and trust and Advantage of publishing his posthumous Writings'. Swift's sister's letter no doubt reflects her brother's views:

> My poor brother has lost his best friend Sir William Temple, who was so fond of him whilst he lived, that he made him give up his living in this country to stay with him at Moor-Park, and promised to get him one in England; but death came in between, and has left him unprovided both of friend and living.[6]

A friend in this sense is a supporter, someone who can further Swift's advancement: his patron had let him down, leaving him without either an advocate or the church living he had hoped for. Swift promptly went to London, hoping for 'a Prebend of Canterbury or Westminster' but settling for a place as domestic chaplain to Temple's friend Lord Berkeley, one of the Lords Lieutenant of Ireland. This disappointment proved fortunate in the event, but the resentment that colours Swift's memoir, written a quarter of a century later, provides the measure of his fierce ambition. The King himself, he recalled, had promised Sir William Temple that he would give Swift the prebend. Yet when he applied, the Earl of Romney failed to second the petition: 'he was an old vitious illiterate Rake without any sense of Truth or Honor, [who] said not a word to the King'. When the Deanery of Derry fell vacant, Berkeley could and should have awarded it to Swift, 'Yet things were so ordered that the Secretary having received a Bribe, the Deanry was disposed of to another, and Mr Swift was put off with some other Churchlivings not worth above a third part of that rich Deanry, and at this present time, not a sixth'.[7] Years after these events, Swift's resentment is palpable.

Still, Swift's direct appeal to the King reveals less naive vanity (or desperation) than we might think. William III had visited his friend Temple at Sheen. Temple's diplomatic triumph – quickly repudiated by Charles II – had been the negotiation of the Triple Alliance, the Protestant alliance against France that was the central object of William's foreign policy. He had also helped negotiate William's marriage to James II's daughter, Mary. He had written an admiring, frequently reprinted account of the Dutch, *Observations upon the United Provinces of the Netherlands* (1673). (This is one of the few areas in which Swift, consistently biased against the Dutch, utterly resisted his patron's influence.) When William was opposing Parliament's desire for triennial parliaments – a measure to keep the monarch from excessive power, partly by limiting the term of sinecures that might allow the Court to buy Members' loyalties by awarding them places – Swift 'was sent to Kensington [Palace] with the whole account of the matter, in writing, to convince the King and the Earl' of Portland to drop their opposition to the bill.[8] Trusted by Temple to support his constitutional position on a pressing legislative matter, Swift had personally discussed policy with the King and, at greater length, Portland. His arguments failed at the time, but William eventually bit the bullet, accepting a Triennial Act in 1694. Although the political world was sometimes remote from Swift, it was never impersonal. He lived in retirement with Temple but not in isolation from public affairs. His interactions with the powerful were face-to-face. He felt that he could make his claims for preferment to anyone.

Modern scholarship tells a tale less soured by anger, a tale more alert than Swift seems to have been to the ways patrons juggle competing claims on their favour.[9] However far short of his merit he thought it, Swift had in fact gained something significant. Still dependent when he accompanied Berkeley to Ireland in August 1699, he had been instituted vicar of Laracor by March 1700. He had thus done well. As a contemporary worded the realities of professional ambition in the late 1690s, "'in the law, talk and acquaintance carry it; and in divinity, interest'".[10] Swift had too little interest to claim a deanery. Derry was a plum that required not only more active patronage but also stronger claims on it than he could make. He benefited anyway, for he was presented to the rectory of Agher and the vicarages of Laracor and Rathbeggan, which were vacated by John Bolton, the man preferred to Derry. Although the new Dean kept the valuable parish of Ratoath, formerly combined with Laracor, Swift – 'possibly to compensate him'[11] – was in September presented to the Prebend of Dunlavin in St Patrick's Cathedral, gaining valuable contact with the Church hierarchy whose emissary he would eventually become. That Derry appealed so little to the man who vacated Laracor – Ratoath had to sweeten the pot before he accepted – suggests the advantages of even the reduced grouping that Swift gained. Combined with the prebend, Swift enjoyed about £230 a year. This sum distinguished him from the poorer clergy who despite their education, as Toby Barnard puts it, lacked 'the means to blend easily into the gentry or squirearchy ... The kind of living that they craved was described [in 1737] by Archbishop Hoadley of Dublin: "a very pretty preferment in my church, of near £200 and a good fine, ready money, as it were in hand, fit for any gentleman as it is the perfect sine cure"'.[12] Of course, Swift did not want to blend in. He wanted to distinguish himself. But he had made a good start. Now in his thirties, Swift was securely established in a good parish close to Dublin and attached to the cathedral.

As Temple's literary executor, Swift had also been working diligently to publish his patron's works, and thus to begin making a name for himself. His task was not complete until the third volume of Temple's *Memoirs* appeared in 1709, after those it mentioned critically had died, but two volumes of Temple's *Letters* appeared promptly in November 1699, 'Published by *Jonathan Swift Domestick Chaplain to his Excellency the Earl of Berkeley*, one of the Lords Justices of Ireland'. Although Swift's dedication to the King has been read as evidence of the ineptness with which he sought preferment, the exalted choice likely reflects his imminent departure for Ireland with Berkeley, which would leave him unable to cultivate

English preferment. It would recall his retired patron's friendship with William while usefully suggesting the potential value to patrons of the deferential editor who was presenting to the public the works of a baronet with a solid reputation as a diplomat, an honest man, and a polished writer.[13] Swift returned to England with Berkeley in April 1701, and Temple's *Miscellanea. The Third Part* appeared in October, 'Published by Jonathan Swift, A.M. Prebendary of St Patrick's, Dublin'.[14] The title pages to his editions of Temple's works record his gradual advance in dignity as well as his industry. He was becoming a more public figure than he could have been when he shared Temple's retirement.

Since Temple was a respected retired diplomat and an esteemed writer, his editor was making a valuable and suitably deferential contribution to contemporary letters. To put one's name on a title page, as Swift did with these works, was not a neutral act. So Swift, in his edition of Temple's *Letters*, deferentially praises the 'Perfection' of Temple's style and, despite his ambition to write history, asserts the superiority of participants' letters to history: 'it is certain, that nothing is so capable, of giving a true Account of Story, as Letters are; which describe Actions, while they are alive and breathing; whereas all other Relations are of Actions past and dead'.[15] It was also to enter contemporary political debate, for contemporaries were always alert to parallels with the contemporary situation. 'In its humblest form', Ehrenpreis suggests, '"parallel history" was merely the reprinting of a historical work in circumstances which made the affairs related seem parallel to recent events, as, for example, the reappearance of Sir John Temple's *Irish Rebellion* at the time of the Popish Plot'.[16] That Swift gave 'Of Popular Discontents' pride of place in *Miscellanea* III suggests its contemporary importance.[17] Since Swift claims in 'The Publisher to the Reader' that it was 'written many Years before the Author's Death'[18] – internal evidence suggests during the factional strife attending the Exclusion Crisis – it perhaps represents a form of parallel history that is humbler still because covert; that is, the essay written at one political moment but published only when another gives it renewed currency.[19] The subject was certainly topical when Swift was preparing the essay for the press during the controversy, also addressed in his *Discourse*, over the attempt to impeach the Junto lords. Slightly later, Swift uses the final volume of Temple's letters to do the same thing. He was forced to hasten this work, he complains, under pressure from a rival (and less authoritative) edition: 'I daily hear, that new Discoveries of Original LETTERS are hasting to the *Press*; To stop the Current of which, I am forced to an earlier Publication than I designed'.[20] *Letters to the King, the Prince of Orange, the Chief Ministers of State, and Other Persons* (1703) consequently appeared sooner, and as a smaller volume, than he had intended. Yet he adds – his only substantial contribution apart from the nearly invisible labours of editing – an anecdote, attributed to Temple, explaining why even Charles II, who was notoriously pro-French, indignantly refused a French bribe to limit his standing army to eight thousand troops. The note calls attention to the opinion

Temple records, 'That nothing could be more evident than that *France* intended a Universal Monarchy, and nothing but *England* could hinder it'.[21] Like the placement of 'Of Popular Discontents', Swift's note aligned Temple (and Swift himself) with a primarily Whig ministry that supported the King's (and then Queen Anne's) desire to maintain a strong army and to wage a vigorous continental campaign rather than relying, as the Tories preferred, on a largely naval war. Even before he published a tract of his own, Swift was positioning himself to earn the favour of the Court Whigs and doing so in ways that assumed that different historical moments ran parallel with one another.

Swift's first independent political tract elaborates more learnedly, through appeal to a classical past, this impulse to see current events as repetitions of past events. And it continues his appeal to the Whigs. Someone who wanted to design an appropriate occasion for Swift's first tract could not improve on the alarming political situation Swift encountered in London when he arrived in London in April 1701. It involved popular unrest and a paper war between the champions of the rival sides, both elements that recalled calamitous seventeenth-century divisions. Parties had adopted stances at odds with ideals professed earlier, suggesting that passion rather than principle drove the combatants. Rival assertions about the limits of monarchical and parliamentary authority – a constitutional issue – hampered effective government by delaying supply for a government at war. A response to the House of Commons' resolution to impeach members of the fallen Whig Junto, *A Discourse of the Contests and Dissentions Between the Nobles and the Commons in Athens and Rome* – the title does not disguise the fact that this is a topical pamphlet – appeared in the same month as the third volume of Temple's *Miscellanea*; that is, a little too late to influence the course of events. In it, Swift addresses the destructive effects of internal dissension that, he thought, threatened to subvert the balanced constitution on which English liberties depended, leading in this case to what Swift thought of as a tyranny of the many. War – more accurately, the likelihood of yet another war – provided its international context. William III had committed England to the international struggle to maintain, in the face of French expansion, a balance of power in Europe. The issues were domestic but far from insular, at once constitutional and directed at the pragmatic administration of affairs.

In conflict with the House of Lords, the House of Commons was attempting to impeach the most prominent members of the recently fallen administration. The immediate justification for impeachment was that they had helped William negotiate the so-called Partition Treaties, secret treaties with France and the Netherlands; that is, treaties not discussed with Parliament or the Privy Council. Negotiating treaties and declaring war were traditional areas of royal prerogative, but the high cost of modern war left the King dependent on the Commons, which alone could raise the taxes needed to wage effective war. Treaties commit nations to consequences, sometimes to war, so the keepers of the public purse demanded to be informed. The resulting struggle pitted the Court – the King and his ministers, who enjoyed a majority in the House of Lords – against the opposition, who dominated the elected House of Commons.

Although it retained significant traces of the split between Court and Country that had blurred party lines early in William's reign, in large measure it expressed a partisan struggle for power by a Tory majority dominant in the Commons but frustrated that a primarily Whig administration continued to hold office and control the patronage that went with it. Although party divisions themselves went back to the Exclusion Crisis, positions had changed since 1699, and the issue of a standing army in peacetime had recently stirred up party passions. When the Treaty of Ryswick ended the War of the League of Augsberg, Louis XIV surrendered most of his conquests and acknowledged William III (rather than James II) as King of England. Nevertheless, the fear that started the war remained. When Carlos II of Spain died, the vagaries of dynastic inheritance might give the Spanish Empire to France, creating a combined power that could dominate Europe. With his eye on this prospect, William had tried to retain a strong army after Ryswick. To an opposition consisting mostly of Tories but including radical Whigs like John Trenchard, however, a standing army in peacetime could lead only to tyranny. It therefore challenged an administration that was primarily Whig but also bipartisan.

William and his allies wanted to partition the Spanish inheritance so that most of it went to a claimant other than the heir to the French throne. Hoping to do so diplomatically, William in 1698 had negotiated, in secret in Holland, a treaty with France and the Netherlands that settled the succession of Spain on the Electoral Prince of Bavaria but ceded some Italian possessions to the Dauphin of France. When Joseph Ferdinand predeceased Carlos II, the parties to the first Partition Treaty negotiated a second, ceding Lorraine and parts of Italy to France but leaving the bulk of the Spanish Empire to the Archduke of Austria. In the event, Carlos II died in October 1700, leaving his inheritance to one of Louis's grandsons, Philip, Duke of Anjou. Betraying a conservative reluctance to interfere with inheritance of property, even a throne, the Tories also suspected that French gains in Italy could threaten English trade with the Levant and remained unworried when Louis ignored the treaty, welcoming his grandson's inheritance. A foreign war came closer to home, though, when James II died and Louis, again preferring dynastic inheritance to negotiated settlements, defied the Treaty of Ryswick and recognized James Edward as James III of England. A dynastic struggle on the Continent exacerbated the dynastic struggle between Protestant and Roman Catholic Stuarts for the English throne. When William died in March 1702, his successor Queen Anne promptly entered the war he had anticipated. The partition treaties had solved nothing.

The cry for impeachment in 1700 thus had deep roots in Country hostility to William III's foreign policy. Still it was primarily a Tory attempt to destroy the former administration so that it could never again thwart their ambition for power.[22] It was headed by the Speaker of the House, Robert Harley, a moderate opposition Whig hostile to the Court Whigs of the Junto and dependent on Tory support in the Commons. He had formed his political ties in the commissions of public accounts scrutinizing, with both Whigs and Tories, the use the administration made of the funds voted by the Commons.[23] Events would soon find him the head of a Tory party that absorbed much of his former Country alliance, and he would eventually lead a Tory administration. Although he has been seen as helpless before back-bench frenzy, he vigorously opposed the Junto leader (and Court Whig), Lord Somers.[24] Once the Tories recognized that they had been too optimistic about Louis's intentions, Parliament unanimously agreed to honour treaty obligations to support the United Provinces (Holland) against renewed French aggression by supplying troops and ships.

A sufficiently grave danger could temporarily curb these divisive energies or channel them constructively. When Anne's only surviving child, the Duke of Gloucester, died in July 1700, it seemed likely that neither William nor his successor Anne would produce an heir to the throne. It was necessary to reopen the question of succession, a necessity that William urged on the Parliament that met in February 1701. Passed unanimously during this turbulent session, the Act of Succession ensured the Protestant succession by settling the Crown on the Electress Sophia of Hanover and her Protestant heirs. But even in this debate, the Commons continued its attack on William by extending the 1689 Bill of Rights to limit the powers of the crown after the deaths of William and Anne. The Act for the further Limitation of the Crown, and the better securing of the Rights and Liberties of the Subject – its formal title – secured a Protestant succession, as William desired. At the same time, it continued the opposition assault on him, limiting the powers of any subsequent foreign monarch. Hostile to William's reliance on Dutch advisers, it ensured that foreigners would be excluded from the Privy Council, Parliament, and civil or military office under Anne's successor, for example. It imposed the first constitutional limit on the crown's power to wage war: the monarch would no longer be able, without parliamentary approval, to declare war in defence of foreign possessions of the crown. Opposition hostility to the court shaped even this expedient, bipartisan legislation.

The Act of Settlement achieved, the Commons promptly returned to its partisan agenda, delaying a vote to supply the war. To many observers, it seemed that the government was collapsing. Continuing its opposition to the King, the Commons resolved to impeach three members of the Junto – Lords Somers, Orford, and Montagu. By urging the King to remove them from his councils and presence forever, it assumed their guilt. This affronted the House of Lords, jealous of its prerogative to determine judicial matters. An ugly quarrel divided the nation while a foreign enemy was arming for war. Parliament divided between the Commons, which insisted on its right to punish those who had not properly consulted it, and the Lords, which insisted on its judicial role in cases of impeachment. The House of Commons divided internally, pitting the opposition (a majority of the house, including some dissident Whigs as well as the Tories) against the government (a predominantly but not exclusively Whig ministry). The nation itself divided. Responding to a Whig-orchestrated propaganda campaign, the populace agitated in the streets. A series of petitions asked the House to vote timely supply: people were demanding to be taxed! Resenting the affront to its authority, the Commons high-handedly imprisoned five Kentish petitioners. It successfully passed a motion censuring the King's Dutch favourite, the Earl of Portland, but government supporters rallied to defeat, narrowly, a preliminary motion censuring the Junto leader, Somers. William was offended that his ministers would not save his favourite and, perhaps at his instigation, Members learned that Somers had affixed the Great Seal to a blank treaty largely negotiated by foreigners – the originally unsuspected first Partition Treaty.[25] When William resolved on a snap election in November, indignation at the treatment of the Kentish petitioners led to Whig gains, producing an evenly divided House that was even more likely to be fractious.[26]

Adding to the confusion, this chaos caught both parties acting at odds with their original principles. Experience of power after 1689 had led Court Whigs to moderate many radical Whig positions, while experience of opposition had driven Tories to oppose royal initiatives. So, although the Tories were nominally the party supporting royal prerogative, they were leading a furious onslaught on William's foreign policy, a traditional area of that prerogative, and – admittedly led by a former though moderate Whig – had introduced an act to further limit monarchy when the Hanoverians came to the throne. Originally a party of popular opposition to royal prerogative, the Whig administration was eagerly defending that prerogative against the House that could claim to embody the wishes of the people. Voters in turn shifted more clearly to support the King and the Lords against the encroachments of the Commons. Appropriately enough, the impeachment effort proved feckless. It ended inconclusively, even comically, when the Commons' demands for collaboration were rejected by an indignant Lords. (In fact, the demands probably represented the Commons' desire to delay a trial in the wake of popular indignation at treatment of the Kentish petitioners.) Charges were dismissed when the Lords judged that they had not been presented in a timely manner. The Kentish petitioners were released on the dissolution of Parliament. The furor that alarmed the nation failed in its objective. Members of the Junto were not removed from the King's council and person forever. Primarily a partisan parliamentary manoeuvre, the struggle clarified no prerogatives and set no constitutional precedents.

While it lasted, however, this tempest in a teacup looked like a serious storm, and Swift contributed his pamphlet to the paper war. Authoritarian but not absolutist, he sided with the Whig Junto that he hoped would eventually prefer him.

He spoke as the voice of impartial reason articulating certain obvious truths. 'It is agreed', he says here as well as in his later reflections as a Church-of-England man, 'that in all Government there is an absolute unlimited Power'.[27] This falls far short of a radical Whig emphasis on the contractual basis of government, but Swift's support of Revolution principles and his Protestant Irish pragmatism, scarcely distinguishable here, led him to defend the ability of a monarch and his administration to lead the nation effectively in war. Committed to a balanced constitution that located an absolute authority in the King-in-Parliament, he resisted what he saw as a power grab by the least stable element of a tripartite government: 'I THINK it is an universal Truth, that the People are much more dextrous at pulling down , and setting up, than at preserving what is fixed'.[28] In a series of historical parallells, he outlines the disaster provoked when one part of the balanced constitution upsets the balance by enlarging its power. He takes the metaphor of the balance very literally – vivid, often reductive images recur throughout Swift's writing – but it allows him to establish an analogy between internal and external relations of the state:

> Now consider several States in a Neighbourhood: In order to preserve Peace between these States, it is necessary they should be formed into a Ballance, whereof one, or more are to be Directors, who are to divide the rest into equal Scales, and upon Occasions remove from one into the other, or else fall with their own Weight into the lightest: So in a State within it self, the Ballance must be held by a third Hand, who is to deal the remaining Power with the utmost Exactness into each Scale.[29]

Swift inhabits his system of analogies easily, turning it against opposition writers (primarily Charles Davenant) who supported impeachment and English strength in Europe:

> those Reasoners, who employ so much of their Zeal, their Wit, and their Leisure for upholding the Ballance of Power in *Christendom*, at the same time that by their Practices they are endeavouring to destroy it at home; are not such might Patriots, or so much in the true Interest of their Country, as they would affect to be thought; but seem employed like a Man, who pulls down with his right Hand what he has been building with his left.[30]

Balance is central to Swift's conception of the constitution, and he easily pairs the external struggle with France and the internal quarrel with a self-aggrandizing House of Commons. That internal dissension exacerbates the threat posed by external war provides a refrain in *Discourse*. Property is best secured 'by preparing against Invasions from Abroad, and maintaining Peace at Home':[31]

> In short, to be encompassed with the greatest Dangers from without; to be torn by many virulent Factions within; then to be secure and senseless under all this, and to

make it the very least of our Concern: These and some others that might be named, appear to me to be the most likely Symptoms in a State of a *Sickness unto Death*.[32]

The stakes in the current contest seemed very high, all the higher to someone alert to recent Anglo-Irish history and in agreement with Temple's analysis of William's role.

For Swift, the state, when it functions appropriately, imposes political order by imposing order on individuals. In the *Discourse*, he closely follows Temple, whom he 'seems unconsciously to include', Frank H. Ellis suggests, 'in the phrase "the Historians of those Ages"'.[33] Written in conjunction with Swift's editorial tasks, the *Discourse* also echoes the most important essay that Swift edited for *Miscellanea*, 'Of Popular Discontents', which he may also have published to comment on current affairs.[34] According to Temple, who goes on to cite ancient governments, 'the true natural and common Source of such personal Dissatisfactions, such Domestick Complaints, and such Popular Discontents as afflict not only our private Lives, Conditions and Fortunes, but even our Civil States and Governments' is a feature of human nature, 'a certain Restlessness of Mind and Thought, which seems universally and inseparably annexed to our very Natures and Constitutions'.[35] The same humanist vision of human restlessness forms the basis of Samuel Johnson's *Rasselas* (1759), but in Temple and Swift the principle aligns the personal and the domestic with the political in the widest sense. Swift attributes the current broil not to a clash of political principles but to the leaders of the House, who act 'upon the Score of *personal Piques*; or *to employ the Pride they conceive in seeing themselves at the Head of a Party*; or *as a method for Advancement*'.[36] When the governors divide, they leave private men without a common power to keep them in awe. Swift locates that common power in a balanced constitution rather than in an absolute monarch, but he has no doubt that human nature requires such a power.

For Swift, such passions form the basic ground of human nature. Only the rational discipline of the state and the church can contain them. Fundamentally authoritarian and paternalistic, Swift's attitude is in accord with his functions as a clergyman in an established church, charged with disciplining the passions and behaviour of his parishioners:

> For, I think, the Ambition of private Men, did, by no Means, begin, or occasion this War, although Civil Dissentions never fail of introducing, and spiriting the Ambition of private Men; who thus become, indeed, the great Instruments for deciding of such Quarrels, and at last are sure to seize on the Prize. But no Man, who sees a Flock of Vultures hovering over two Armies ready to engage, can justly charge the Blood drawn in the Battle to them, although the Carcasses fall to their Share. For, while the Ballance of Power is equally held, the Ambition of private Men, whether Orators or great Commanders, gives neither Danger nor Fear, nor can possibly enslave their Country; but, That once broken, the divided Parties are

forced to unite each to its Head; under whose Conduct, or Fortune, one Side is, at first, victorious, and, at last, both are Slaves.[37]

Swift's stance as an impartial observer of the conflict leads him to this characteristic, vulture's-eye view of war. Conflict is basic to human nature, and war reduces people to carrion on which vultures feast. His immediate target here is Robert Harley, called 'orator' because Speaker of the House, but Swift will later attack Marlborough, England's greatest military commander, in similar terms. Just as characteristically, Swift also assumes that the routine selfishness of private men, no matter how able, poses a danger only when the constitutional order that normally contains them breaks down.

Self-aggrandizing private men who exploit civil dissension are not soldiers but scavengers who exploit the ruin left when public men – the natural (landed) governors of society – fail to act for the common good. For Swift the recent 'Distinction between the *personal* and the *political* Capacity' has a pernicious impact on legislators because common sense gives way to eccentricity:

> For, I think, there is hardly to be found, through all Nature, a greater Difference between two Things, than there is between a representing Commoner, in the Function of his publick Calling, and the same Person, when he acts in the common Offices of Life. Here, he allows himself to be upon a Level with the rest of Mortals: Here, he follows his own Reason, and his own Way; and rather affects a Singularity in his Actions and Thoughts, than servilely to copy either from the wisest of his Neighbours. In short, here his Folly, and his Wisdom, his Reason, and his Passions, are all of his own Growth; not the Eccho, or Infusion of other Men. But when he is got near the Walls of his Assembly, he assumes, and affects an entire Set of very different Airs; he conceives himself a Being of a superior Nature to those *without*, and acting in a Sphere where the vulgar Methods for the Conduct of human Life, can be of no Use. He is listed in a Party, where he neither knows the Temper, nor Designs, nor perhaps the Person of his Leader; but whose Opinions he follows and maintains, with a Zeal and Faith as violent, as a young Scholar does those of a Philosopher, whose Sect he is taught to profess. He hath neither Thoughts, nor Actions, nor Talk, that he can call his own; but all conveyed to him by his Leader, as Wind is through an Organ. The Nourishment he receives hath been not only *chewed*, but *digested*, before it comes into his Mouth. Thus instructed, he followeth his *Party*, right or wrong, through all its Sentiments; and acquires a Courage, and Stiffness of Opinion, not at all congenial with him.[38]

At home, the Member of Parliament, like the country squire of Restoration comedy, is an image of sturdy if occasionally foolish independence. By contrast, the partisan Member resembles the would-be fashionable wit of the same comedy. To cite the familiar embodiments of these stereotypes in William Congreve's *The Way of the World*, a Sir Wilful Witwoud at home dwindles into a Tony Witwoud in town. Adherence to party reduces the independent squire to infantile dependence. His food first chewed by another, his voice becomes the echo of another's. In an image more fully elaborated in the Aeolism of *A Tale of a Tub*, he becomes an empty vessel through which another's spirit passes like wind through an organ.

Given Swift's hostility to party itself, it makes some sense to argue, as Ehrenpreis does, that the *Discourse* is not a partisan document.[39] Maintaining the constitutional balance, Swift feels, depends on Members of Parliament acting independently, refusing to wander out of what *A Tale* will call common forms:

> Because, this must be said in Behalf of human Kind; that common Sense, and plain Reason, while Men are disengaged from acquired Opinions, will ever have some general Influence upon their Minds; Whereas, the Species of Folly and Vice are infinite, and so different in every Individual, that they could never procure a Majority, of other Corruptions did not enter to pervert Mens Understandings, and misguide their Wills.[40]

Party can only subvert the operation of common sense in individuals. The stakes seem alarmingly high because Swift sees in the encroaching Commons a parallel with the events leading to the seventeenth-century civil wars. Throughout his life, Swift blamed 'a Faction in *England*', which, under the Name of *Puritan*' gradually upset the ideal Elizabethan balance of nobles and commons, eventually overthrew the constitution, 'and, according to the usual Course of such Revolutions, did introduce a Tyranny, first of the People, and then of a single Person.'[41] Although an Irish example has no place in this English tract, Irish experience intensifies Swift's reaction to the House of Commons' drive to impeach ministers of the Crown. Swift believed that 'that wicked English parliament' was also responsible for the Irish Rebellion. Encouraged by 'that rebellious spirit in the English House of Commons', 'the leaders in the Irish Popish massacre' reckoned that the King would be unable to aid 'his Protestant subjects' in Ireland: 'we may truly say that the English parliament held the King's hands, while the Irish Papists here were cutting our grandfathers throats.'[42] In the 'wild confusion'[43] that follows the breakdown of order, the warlike nature of man finds full scope, creating food for vultures. The strife of party he encountered in London fed some of Swift's deepest fears.

Unfortunately for Swift, there is no non-partisan way to take sides in a partisan quarrel. Despite Swift's stated opposition to party itself, it also makes no sense, as Ehrenpreis also recognizes,[44] *not* to read the *Discourse* as a partisan tract. Swift is siding with a partisan group, the Court Whigs who had dominated the previous administration. He is pitting himself against an equally partisan, predominantly Tory opposition. But it is important to observe that he does so in a way that maximizes his own independence, his freedom to manoeuvre on this contested terrain. He never professed primary allegiance to a political party – hardly surprising since he denied the validity of political parties. When he supported or opposed a particular administration, he thought of himself as expressing the views of the majority of the political nation, and he imagined his opponents, when he could not think of them as misguided potential allies, as self-serving devotees of a destructive faction. He had clear political principles, but by identifying himself as an Old Whig, as he habitually did, he announced his support for the Glorious Revolution and a constitutional monarchy while preserving his independence of a particular party label. The crown typically did the same thing, avoiding a monopoly on positions by a single party to preserve its independence. The *Discourse* argues no principle that is unequivocally Whig rather than Tory. Such principles identify only party extremes. The doctrine of non-resistance to royal authority, for example, continued to identify extreme Tories, many of them Jacobites. Strong assertions of the people's right to resist, to resume the contract by which they were governed, similarly identified radical Whigs. But neither of these positions was typical of a full range of party opinion. By the turn of the century, many Tories as well as most Whigs accepted that England had a mixed government in which the King governed in cooperation with Lords and Commons. Many Tories and most Whigs also accepted the Revolution, which many indeed regarded as primarily Tory. Swift positions himself on a broad middle ground which pro-Revolution Tories could share with constitutionally conservative Whigs who appealed by preference to constitutional precedents rather than the popular right to refashion the contract on which the state was based.

Many of those who shared this terrain reached it from different directions, and in other situations they could be pulled apart instead of falling together. Swift's classically-oriented parallel history positions him in an existing building; he has no interest in developing fashionable suburbs. Neither disinterested nor impartial, Swift devoted his energies to 'preserving what is fixed'. He represents change as iconoclasm ('pulling down') and idolatry ('setting up'), his language associating the current House of Commons with the seventeenth-century assault on monarchy and episcopacy that he persistently equated with the idolatry condemned in the Old Testament. His chosen literary form carries an ideological freight. Classicism was the property of no single party, for the language of classical republicanism had supplied the idiom of political debate over issues like the standing army.[45] Parallel history, however, embodies a cast of mind that aligns Swift with Temple as an Ancient. On one level, Swift simply appeals to Greek and Roman historical parallels to shed the light of past history on the strife of the moment. Many Englishmen regarded England as the current home of ancient liberty; hence the custom of regarding London, like ancient Rome, as a reborn Troy. William Shakespeare had investigated contemporary political currents by exploiting parallels in Roman as well as English history, no doubt hoping (like Swift) to evade the censoring eye of a watchful government as he did so. The Augusta of Dryden's *Mac Flecknoe* assumes this heritage to condemn (like *A Tale of a Tub*) contemporary bad writing.

According to this habit of mind, political structures are, in one of Swift's favourite terms, 'fixed' rather than fluid and open to change. In the *Discourse*, the current parliamentary squabble reveals not political tensions produced by the unique economic and social pressures of a distinctive historical moment but rather the fundamental and consequently recurrent patterns of human nature. What always happens will happen yet again, Swift warns. He consequently challenges Davenant's thoroughly conventional statement that the balanced constitution is not timeless but a Gothic (that is, feudal) invention: 'a mixt Government partaking of the known Forms received in the Schools, is, by no Means, of *Gothick* Invention, but hath Place in Nature and Reason'.[46] If the English do not listen to reason (and recollect their history), England will foolishly repeat what Athens and then Rome just as foolishly did before them: 'THUS was the most powerful Commonwealth of all *Greece* ... utterly destroyed by that rash, jealous and inconstant Humour of the People'.[47] As a parallel history, Swift's *Discourse* resists historical change. As Pocock characterizes adherents of this strand of Augustan thought, 'they were looking to a past, and seeking to defend virtue against innovative forces symbolized as trading empire, standing armies, and credit'.[48] For Swift, change is degeneration.

Swift is also, of course, displaying his own intellectual power. Drawing on his years of reading with Temple, he exploits the foundational texts of literate political discussion to champion an inherited political order threatened with corruption. He quotes a dizzying array of parallels from classical Greek and Roman history, and he deploys this vast repertoire with the 'effortlessness' of a master. In a paradox typical of him, Swift flaunts his own authority by making a bid to speak with the impersonal authority of inherited tradition.[49] The point of the classical training at the core of the education shared by aristocracy and gentry was not an accurate historical grasp of the ancient past. What counted was the ability to apply one's reading to current situations. Swift takes what a modern classicist would call liberties with his text, but to say that 'he was only concerned, as Shakespeare had been, to make literature out of Plutarch' or to judge that 'Unscrupulousness in a scholar is rightly called "economy" in an artist'[50] obscures the nature of the exercise. Parallel history may be an art, but it is an applied art. Interpreting a present crisis in the light of an exemplary classical past demands flexibility. It also requires readers who share this flexible command of the past with the writer, as a reader like Somers certainly did. Swift was also an Anglican clergyman, and committed Protestants still make a similar – on occasion, a similarly tendentious – use of scripture. Much as the Protestant appeal to the practices of the primitive church serves to identify and remove corruptions in the church, so Swift's political appeal to the practices of the ancients is intended to identify corruptions in the state so that it too can be restored as close as possible to the perfection of its primitive simplicity. The impulse behind Swift's *Discourse* is authoritarian. The question is less 'Does this reading interpret accurately a unique past event?' than 'How does my reading of that authority inform my understanding of the present?' Since even disagreement provokes renewed engagement with an acknowledged common authority, there is no wonder that Swift so often satirizes his opponents as narrowly literal-minded or self-indulgently fanciful readers. No wonder he so often raises the questions of how to read, of what kinds of authority writers can legitimately demand.

As a timely intervention in a present crisis, Swift's *Discourse* failed. By playing a delaying game, the Commons kept the issue alive but avoided a decision they seemed likely to lose in the Lords. But although it looked for a time as if proceedings would drag on interminably, relations between Commons and Lords broke down in June. The Lords staged a hearing at which no one appeared to present the charges against the impeached ministers, whom they acquitted.[51] Swift seems to have been caught short by the abrupt end of the crisis. The acquittal of the Junto lords could now owe nothing to his arguments. Rather than abandon his work, he seems to have added the final chapter to the *Discourse* in order to generalize it for publication after the fact.[52] When he returned to Ireland in September 1701, he left the *Discourse* to appear anonymously in October, when he was safely out of the way. His anonymity was not timidity. To publish in his own name would have been presumptuous, a public assertion that he as a private man possessed the authority to judge the Commons. It was common to float such tracts anonymously, relying on the impersonal authority of argument. Where a pamphlet succeeded, the author could decorously acknowledge authorship after the fact.

That is what Swift did. As he had hoped, the *Discourse* attracted attention. It was read: two editions appeared in 1701. A Tory writing to Harley noted its partisan thrust: the "'author pretends to much reading and great sincerity, but towards the end there are pretty bold reflections'".[53] More important, as Swift later boasted, some readers assumed that it came from the pen of a powerful polemicist:

> This discourse I sent very privately to the press, with the strictest injunctions to conceal the author, and returned immediately to my residence in Ireland. The book was greedily bought, and read; and charged some times upon my Lord Sommers, and some times upon the Bishop of Salsbury ...

These are flattering comparisons: Somers was the Whig leader; Gilbert Burnet, the bishop of Salisbury, a formidable Whig polemicist. Swift could confidently acknowledge authorship:

> Returning next year for England, and hearing the great approbation this piece had received, (which was the first I ever printed) I must confess, the vanity of a young man prevailed with me, to let myself be known for the author: Upon which my Lords Sommers and Hallifax, as well as the Bishop above mentioned, desired my acquaintance, with great marks of esteem and professions of kindness: Not to mention the Earl of Sunderland, who had been of my old acquaintance. They lamented that they were not able to serve me since the death of the King, and were very liberal in promising me the greatest preferments I could hope for, if ever it came in

their power. I soon drew domestic with Lord Hallifax, and was as often with Lord Sommers, as the formality of his nature (the only unconversable fault he has) made it agreeable to me.[54]

Swift is bragging. He is also justifying himself, looking back at his connection with the Whigs after his defection to the Tories in 1710. Stressing their esteem for him and his own sturdy independence, he recollects promises that remained unfulfilled even when the Whigs once more were in a position to gratify his wishes. To judge by his past performance, Swift could easily exaggerate what he had been promised. In fact, his belated contribution to the debate marked him as someone worth keeping an eye on, but it merited nothing more substantial.

Swift relished his acquaintance with the great. In addition to whetting his ambition for preferment in England, access to this powerful in-group appealed to his love of masculine society animated by competitive emulation. The Whig lords' power kept him in a peripheral role, but their attention was flattering. Swift justly preens himself on the story that his *Discourse* was attributed to a writer as influential as the Bishop of Salisbury.[55] A quarter of a century his senior, Burnet had declined bishoprics earlier in his life. He owed his preferment as Bishop of Salisbury to his intimacy with William III, whom he had known in Holland. He was also a writer, a theologian and historian then known for, *inter alia*, the first two volumes of his *History of the Reformation in England* (1679, 1681; volume III would follow in 1714) and now famous for his posthumous *History of My Own Times* (1724–34).[56] An apologist for the Glorious Revolution, he was derided for opportunism by some contemporaries, for like many churchmen, he had once preached the necessity of obedience to the sovereign, only later accepting the allegiance to Crown-in-Parliament that Swift took for granted. Latitudinarian where Swift was High Church, he was nevertheless proof that a churchman and man of letters could play an influential role in the state. Although he lost influence under Anne, it was she who adopted his proposal, originally made to William, to set aside the first fruits and tenths to create a fund for the poorer clergy, the grant eventually known as Queen Anne's Bounty.

The Junto lords Swift mentions were an uncommonly impressive lot. Charles Spencer, third Earl of Sunderland, was the son of the second Earl whose fall had dashed Swift's hopes, an 'acquaintance' because he had visited Moor Park. A widely read man with a good command of languages, he was an energetic and partisan Whig. A promising opposition politician, he would eventually become Secretary of State when the Junto assumed power in 1706, returning to high office after the fall of Harley's ministry and the death of Queen Anne. A former Chancellor of the Exchequer, Charles Montagu, Baron Halifax, was a poet as well as a politician, having with Matthew Prior written *The Hind and the Panther Transvers'd to the Story of the Country Mouse and the City Mouse* (1687), a parody of John Dryden's apology for his conversion to Roman Catholicism, *The Hind and The Panther.* In Parliament, he had distinguished himself as Chancellor of the Exchequer and First Lord of the Treasury during the period that saw the founding of the Bank of England in 1694 and the great recoinage of 1696, the latter necessitated by the drastic debasement of earlier coins as the price of the bullion needed to pay foreign troops soared. Most impressive of all was John, Baron Somers, the dominant politician of his day, who, after Swift's experience of Temple, must have seemed to possess everything a talented writer on the make could want in a patron. He had the trust of the King. He had long wielded considerable power and seemed likely to do so again. He was a formidable jurist who had successfully defended the seven bishops imprisoned for seditious libel when they opposed James II's second Declaration of Indulgence – one of whom was William Sancroft, the Archbishop of Canterbury to whom Swift had written an early ode. He was a writer on political and constitutional topics who had played an important role in the Convention Parliament and had served as Lord Keeper and Lord Chancellor under William.[57]

These men espoused Whiggish principles at odds with Swift's classicist vision of the state, but as a jurist, Somers is most closely associated with arguments cast in 'the characteristic historical-legal language of political debate' rather than 'arguments derived from reason and nature'. In the Convention Parliament, according to one historian, he worked for compromise with the 'Williamite whigs' who, to win over Tory support 'deliberately emasculated the document [the Declaration of Rights], stripping it of all its proposals and leaving a half-hearted assertion of 'ancient' liberties'.[58] In his defence of the Kentish Petitioners, *Jura Populi Anglicani; or, The Subject's Power of Petitioning Set Forth* (1701), for example, Somers deployed both conservative arguments likely to appeal to Tories and more emphatically Whiggish arguments.[59] If we regard Tories not as divine-right absolutists but as primarily conservative legal-constitutionalists committed to the rule of law, as Tim Harris presents them,[60] then Somers, the definitive Court Whig comfortable in the exercise of power, was clearly a Whig with whom Swift, as a self-described Old Whig of a conservative bent, could find common ground. More extreme Whig thought appalled him, but he also distinguished himself carefully from the extreme of Tory thought that clung to the obligation of passive resistance and the indefeasible right of royal inheritance. Such convictions found no place for the Glorious Revolution, which Swift defended, threatening to restore the Catholic Stuart heir currently in exile on the Continent.

In this heady environment, as the figures of Halifax and Somers perhaps attest, there was little if any distinction between intellectual and political spheres. The competition for distinction among the powerful took forms unfamiliar today:

> At the Revolution probably the leading library was that formed by Sir Robert Cotton early in the seventeenth century and maintained by his heirs. A major collection of around 30,000 volumes was created by John Moore, the Bishop of Ely

... Robert Harley, the politician, began collecting voraciously in 1705 and soon amassed 6,000 manuscripts and 40,000 books. Thomas Rawlinson, the son of a Lord Mayor of London, had reputedly collected 200,000 volumes by his death in 1725. Around the turn of the [seventeenth] century a number of peers, including Lord Somers, the Duke of Devonshire, and the Earl of Sunderland, began to form major libraries as a signal of their intellectual and financial virility.[61]

This account by Julian Hoppit lists Swift's eventual political master ahead of the Whigs he was courting, but it aptly captures something of the energetic and intellectually engaged society of the powerful into which Swift's first political tract had opened a door. A learned jurist and occasional polemicist, Somers took the world of letters seriously. He had encouraged Jacob Tonson to bring out a folio edition of *Paradise Lost* in 1688. Although Swift did not in the end benefit, he became an important patron of letters.[62] In November 1709, Swift wrote to Halifax – hoping for further support – that Somers had supported his bid for the bishopric of Waterford.[63] Finally, Somers was one of the first politicians to court writers, recognizing their value in managing public opinion.[64]

Once Swift found a home with the Tories, he inevitably disparaged the men he had once courted. They were in opposition to the ministry it was his job to defend. By magnifying differences, Swift could also make his own shift of allegiance seem principled rather than opportunistic. He retained some affection for Halifax, but looking back even on his service to ministry in *History of the Last Four Years of the Queen*, he caustically dismissed Sunderland – the able politician who would contest leadership of the Whigs with Walpole! – as a heterodox mediocrity. His 'ungovernable temper'[65] was an obstacle in his relations with the queen, as even his friends recognized. He was guilty of both pernicious youthful principles and apostasy from them: 'he hath much fallen from the Height of those Republican Principles with which he began'. Little commands respect: 'His Understanding is at best of the middling Size; neither hath he much improved it either in reality, or, which is very unfortunate, even in the Opinion of the World, by an overgrown Library'.[66]

Somers, on the other hand, Swift would criticize but not diminish. He is capable but swayed by Whig extremism:

> That Accident which first produced him into the World, of pleading for the Bishops whom King *James* had sent to the Tower, might have proved a Piece of Merit as honourable, as it was fortunate: But, the old Republican Spirit, which the Revolution had restored, began to teach other Lessons: That, since we had accepted a new King from a Calvinistical Commonwealth, we must likewise admit new Maxims in Religion and Government: But, since the Nobility and Gentry would probably adhere to the Established Church, and to the Rights of Monarchy as delivered down from their Ancestors; it was the Practice of these Politicians to introduce such Men, as were perfectly indifferent to any or no Religion; and who were not

> likely to inherit much Loyalty from those to whom they owed their Birth. Of this Number was the Person I am now describing ...[67]

This is the routine Tory charge that the Whigs were godless republicans. In the same spirit, Swift will dryly refer in the *Examiner* for 26 April 1711 to 'Those among the *Whigs* who believe a GOD'.[68] Here it frames his character of an otherwise admirable statesman: 'I have hardly known any man with Talents more proper to acquire and preserve the Favour of a Prince'. In the *Letter to the Lord Chancellor Middleton*, written in his own person during the Drapier's campaign against Wood's pence, he will refer to Somers as 'the greatest Man I ever knew of your Robe'.[69] Acquaintance with Somers remained a privilege that years later still dignified Swift himself.

Swift admired highly literate men connected to circles of power. Somers succeeded Temple as the object of Swift's hopes for acknowledgment and preferment; he was succeeded in turn by Robert Harley, government leader, remarkable book collector, and adept master of writers through the power of whose pens he could manage popular opinion. When his critique of Somers returns to the complaint of an 'extreme Civility ... universal and undistinguished' in private as in public, Swift no doubt registers a disappointed longing for greater intimacy. He also reveals feelings of affinity. Somers may be overly conscious of humble origins – exaggerated by contemporaries but likely a point of contact for Swift – or perhaps, Swift speculates, 'being sensible how subject he is to violent Passions, he avoideth all Incitements to them, by teaching those he converses with from his own Example, to keep a great way within the bounds of Decency and Respect'.[70] The contrast is with Sunderland, who could not manage his passions even with the queen. Given the resentment that colours Swift's recollections of his quest for preferment, the parallel with Swift himself – fond of deadpan humour and guarded witty play but quick to resent a slight – is just as obvious if perhaps not as deliberate. Courting the great, Swift too guarded his passions and hoped to make his way, like Somers, through a conspicuous display of his ability.

Convinced that people were inevitably and destructively quarrelsome, Swift distinguished himself as a writer in adversarial forms fuelled by hostility – satire and political writing. Satire elaborates in literature the primitive impulse to curse an enemy, an impulse often, in Swift, displaced only slightly in the direction of rational argument. His best political writing likewise mounts a memorable attack – on Marlborough, on Britain's allies, on Anglo-Irish complacency, on British interference in Ireland. The 'peculiar emotional intensity' that F. R. Leavis long ago defined as 'the disturbing characteristic of [Swift's] genius' and condemned as 'directed negation' that was 'purely destructive' should probably be named as anger.[71] So it is suggestive that Swift detected the same quality in the Whig statesman he most admired: 'his Breast hath been seen to heave, and his Eyes to sparkle with Rage, in those very moments when his Words and the Cadence of his Voice were in the humblest and softest manner'. Of Swift it could never be said as he said of Somers that 'With an excellent Understanding adorned by all the polite Parts of Learning, He hath very little Taste for Conversation; to which he prefers the pleasure of Reading and Thinking'.[72] But the violent passion that Somers is said to have governed with difficulty in social situations is the same passion that, channelled into his writing, made Swift a valuable political ally.

When Swift first encountered the Junto lords, then, he was impressed by powerful men he recognized as worth impressing in turn. Dedicated to Somers, *A Tale of a Tub* is not a political tract. It is a bravura display of Swift's learning and literary craft, also of the emotional energies behind it. It is literature on the attack, and in it, as has been noticed, Swift delights in his own power to attack enemies: 'the only thing in the nature of a positive that most readers will find convincingly present is self-assertion – *superbia*. Swift's way of demonstrating his superiority is to destroy, but he takes a positive delight in his power'.[73] This is entirely appropriate. As Michael DePorte shrewdly observes, 'The *Tale*, for its part, is *entirely* about power'.[74] It is also smart, literate, and even more aggressively classical than *Discourse*, the aggression being as much to the point as the learning. What could better display Swift's power to demolish opponents in print?

A Tale's political import was genuine. Linking abuses in learning with abuses in religion, as *A Tale of a Tub* does, was hardly a far-fetched stratagem by a writer trying hard to be clever. It was the stuff of contemporary politics. Although dissent posed a much greater threat to the Church of Ireland than it possibly could to the Church of England, English political quarrels early in Anne's reign loudly echoed many of Swift's Anglo-Irish sectarian animosities.[75] The deliberate lapse of the Licensing Act in 1695 had permitted the publication of heterodox works, for example, leading many alarmed churchmen to conclude that the Church really was in danger. The works of the Scottish-educated Irishman, John Toland, provide a revealing example. A Whig who defended the Parliament of 1640 and served Harley's Country opposition by writing against the standing army, he also helped edit the works of such foundational Whig thinkers as Algernon Sidney, Edmund Ludlow, James Harrington, and John Milton, whose defence of the regicide places him in this political tradition.[76] In some of this, Toland was supported by Robert Harley, who had led the impeachment attempt Swift had opposed in print. Toland owed his notoriety, however, to a deistic tract, *Christianity not Mysterious, or, A Treatise Shewing that there is Nothing in the Gospel Contrary to Reason, nor above it* (1696). This book was condemned to be burned by the public hangman in England, condemned too by the House of Commons in Ireland. *A Tale of a Tub* invents neither the intellectual challenge nor the perfervid High-Church response.

A more practical challenge to the Church's authority invited a legislative response. The practice of occasional conformity convinced many that the Church was in danger. Although the sacramental test – the requirement that office holders take communion in the established church – was intended to exclude non-Anglicans from office, some dissenters evaded this restriction by practising what was called occasional conformity. By taking communion in the Church of England often enough to meet the letter of the law, they could qualify for public office even though they continued to participate publicly in their dissenting congregations. High-Churchmen found the sight of prominent dissenters in office, notably as Lord Mayor of London, especially provocative, and they took aim at a practice that threatened Anglican hegemony when Convocation, recalled for the first time since 1689, met in 1701. The bishops in the upper house were more likely to be latitudinarians like Burnet, willing to defend the practice because it united moderate Protestants in a common cause and perhaps tended toward comprehension of many dissenters within the established church. The High-Churchmen who dominated the lower house of convocation, by contrast, saw barbarians at the gates of the holy city. In a famous sermon preached in May 1702 in the University Church of St Mary's, Oxford, for example, the extreme High-Church polemicist, Henry Sacheverell, urged members of the Church not to accommodate dissenters but rather to '"hang out the bloody flag and banner of defiance"'![77] The Tory-dominated House of Commons responded with two bills against occasional conformity in 1702–3, but they were narrowly defeated in the House of Lords, where the bishops held the balance of power. In 1704, the Commons controversially tried 'tacking' the measure onto a money bill so that the Lords could not reject it. By the end of 1704, the Tack had failed. Popular opinion turned against the Tories for subordinating the serious business of supply to sectarian divisions, and the Whigs gained seats in the following election.

In this context, *A Tale of a Tub*'s satire of dissent could hardly have seemed extreme. Swift seems in fact to have remained aloof from the heated political quarrel. In London at the defeat of the second Occasional Conformity Bill in December 1703, he was amused by 'the warmest reign of party and faction that I ever knew or read of':

> the very night before the bill went up, a committee of Whig and Tory cats had a very warm and loud debate upon the roof of our house. But why should we wonder at that, when the very ladies are split asunder into High Church and Low, and, out of zeal for religion, have hardly time to say their prayers? The masks will have a crown more from any man of the other party ...[78]

He himself seems not to have feared that occasional conformity was destroying the Church he served. He was concerned enough to consult the great: he names Somers and Peterborough as well as Burnet. But with their reassurance that the Church was not in danger, he wrote against the bill 'but it came too late by a day: so I would not print it'.[79]

No ardent partisan, Swift especially disliked the conspicuous public involvement of private persons in affairs of state and the consequent corrosion of private relationships:

> But Whig and Tory has spoild all that was tollerable here, [he wrote to John Temple from Dublin several years later], by mixing with private Friendship and Conversation, and ruining both; tho it seems to me full as pertinent to Quarrell about Copernicus and Ptolemee, as about My Ld Treasurer, and Ld Rochester: at least for any Private man, and especially in our remote Scene; I am sorry we begin to resemble England onely in its defects ...[80]

Mere partisan difference simply alarmed Swift. He disdained public opinion and had apparently not yet learned that one of his great gifts was his ability to appeal to it.

Nevertheless, *A Tale* speaks directly to the concerns of the moment. It appeared in May 1704, shortly before Swift's return to Ireland and well before the outcome of the dispute over occasional conformity was clear. When Swift shows Jack in his tatters constantly being mistaken for Peter in his elaborate finery, the sectarian jibe is rooted in historical memory. Dissenters had seemed to form a common cause with Catholics when they supported James II's Toleration Acts, and resentment of their treachery, still vivid when *A Tale* appeared, gives it an intolerant edge that can offend a modern reader:

> Of Jack we are told, 'nor could all the world persuade him, as the common phrase is, to eat his victuals like a Christian'. It is characteristic of Swift that he should put in these terms, showing a complete incapacity even to guess what religious feeling might be, a genuine conviction that Jack should be made to kneel when receiving the Sacrament.[81]

Shrewd about the emotions in play, this judgment takes as personal and religious something that is first political. The criterion of 'religious feeling' wrenches *A Tale* from context, relegating religion to the realm of the personal and private. But private religious feeling is irrelevant to an allegory addressing the question of public authority. For Swift, the church by law established was an essential and public institution. Dissenters wanted publicly to reject worship according to the forms of the legally established church while nevertheless participating in public office. That is why Swift has Jack become Lord Mayor of London. The genuine feeling relevant to *A Tale* is Swift's conviction that the Church played an indispensable role in public affairs.

Such satire can hardly have appealed to the Junto Whigs. Their supremacy depended in part on lucrative ties with the dissenting community in the City, an important source of loans to the government. This marriage of convenience between money and power offended opposition Whigs like Robert Harley, a devout man of dissenting background who broke with the dissenters over it.[82]

Dissent was the issue on which Swift too was furthest from his new acquaint-
ances, as he recognized and apparently even acknowledged:

> It was then I first began to trouble myself with the difference between the principles
> of Whig and Tory; having formerly employed myself in other, and, I think, much
> better speculations. I talked often upon this subject with Lord Sommers; told him,
> that, having long been conversant with the Greek and Roman authors, and there-
> fore a lover of liberty, I found myself much inclined to be what they called a Whig
> in politics; and that, besides, I thought it impossible, upon any other principle, to
> defend or submit to the Revolution: But, as to religion, I confessed myself to be an
> High-churchman, and that I did not conceive how any one, who wore the habit of
> a clergyman, could be otherwise ...[83]

Swift's assertive independence and his commitment to classical models are as evident here as his skepticism about parties. As a clergyman, he has 'observed very
well with what insolence and haughtiness some Lords of the High-church party
treated not only their own chaplains, but all other clergymen whatsoever', but he
concedes that 'this was sufficiently recompensed by their professions of zeal to
the church'. He also notices that 'the Whig Lords took a direct contrary measure, treated the persons of particular clergymen with great curtesy, but shewed
much ill-will and contempt for the order in general', a necessity if they were to
attract 'all denominations of Protestants'. Writing well after popular support for
Sacheverell's later intransigence had provoked the change to a Tory ministry, he
claims to have warned the Whigs that the anti-clerical pamphlets of the extreme
Whigs 'would unite the church, as one man, to oppose them'.[84]

Since late Stuart party positions reflected the interplay of constitutional and
religious commitments,[85] Swift's position as a High-Church defender of the
Revolution settlement is hardly anomalous even in England, anything but in his
native Ireland. Publishing *A Tale* was undoubtedly an odd way to curry favour
with a ministry that needed to establish a broad bottom, as Swift concedes, but
its political principles certainly did not themselves position him on the fringes of
debate. More problematic is his satire of modern personality. In his Tale-Teller
– the term both William Wotton and Edmund Curll use[86] – Swift impersonates
a writer of a characteristically modern sort. Originally liberating, critical recognition of this hack's centrality eventually proved limiting: 'The Hack, then, is not
a fully developed fictional character, but a rhetorical device'.[87] From Swift's point
of view, the centrality and the inconsistency of the Tale-Teller together make the
crucial point. It is now usual to observe that *A Tale* is neither an inconsistent
proto-novel nor a satire unrelated to the novel but rather, like *Gulliver's Travels*
after it, an anti-novel: 'Given the opportunity', Brean S. Hammond conjectures,
'Swift would have stopped the developing novel in its tracks'.[88] The Tale of the
three brothers, Michael McKeon points out, manages a scathing critique of not
only of Peter's aristocratic corruption but also of the progressive narrative of Jack,

that *arriviste* who parlayed his asserted piety into worldly success as the Lord Mayor of London.[89] *A Tale* deliberately subverts those narratives recounting, often in the first person, the adventures of a desiring self; that is, with *self*-assertive writing of the kind that shapes the emerging commercial form we now call the novel.[90] Swift's narrative satires – *Gulliver's Travels* counts with *A Tale* here – embody his sustained, anti-novelistic demonstration that the first-person singular pronoun cannot on its own organize either a self or a narrative; hence the uncanny proto-postmodernity of *A Tale*, its weird premonition of texts that self-consciously deconstruct the novelistic self and its author.

Through the *book*-ishness of *A Tale*, Swift also satirizes the professional author and the concomitant commodification of writing that was challenging aristocratic patronage. First, *A Tale* smells of the lamp: it is deliberately and laboriously learned. (Borrowing a later Swift persona, Sir Richard Steele made the same kind of point with playful self-deprecation when he called the collected *Tatler* papers *The Lucubrations of Isaac Bickerstaff, Esq.*) More profoundly, *A Tale of a Tub* is a parodic example of what we now call material culture, an object containing the requisite parts of books – an elaborate title page with three epigraphs; a list of other works by the same author; an Apology [added in only 1710]; a Bookseller's [we would say, Publisher's] Dedication to a Lord; a Bookseller's note to the reader; a parodic Epistle Dedicatory from the nominal author to a second potential patron, Prince Posterity; a Preface by the nominal author; Section I of the Tale proper, which turns out to be 'The Introduction'; and finally, in 'Section II', a tale beginning 'Once upon a Time'.[91] What more does a book require? Yet Swift adds a second work that signals his intellectual context in the quarrel of the Ancients and Moderns while he parodically appeals in the same title to the market for up-to-date, gossipy coverage of court scandal, *A Full and True Account of the Battel Fought Last Friday, Between the Antient and the Modern Books in St. James's Library*. He also adds *A Discourse concerning the Mechanical Operation of the Spirit. In a Letter to a Friend. A Fragment*, appealing to the materialist explanations that characterize modern heterodoxy, the characteristically modern intimacy of private intercourse made public, and the fragmentariness of such self-advertising. In this book of books, a protégé of Temple scourges the modern by impersonating it.[92]

Swift's emphases are now familiar. *A Tale* is anomalous only in its concerted typicality. In contrast to ancient art, modern art is local and temporary:

> Such a Jest there is, that will not pass out of *Covent-Garden*; and such a one, that is no where intelligible but at *Hide-Park* Corner. Now, tho' it sometimes tenderly affects me to consider, that all the towardly Passages I shall deliver in the following Treatise, will grow quite out of date and relish with the first shifting of the present Scene: yet I must need subscribe to the Justice of this Proceeding: because, I cannot imagine why we should be at Expence to furnish Wit for succeeding Ages, when the former have made no sort of Provision for ours ...[93]

Modern writing is a commodity unlikely to travel well or last. Literature like any other item of expense is governed by fashion: 'as human Happiness is of a very short Duration, so in those Days were human Fashions, upon which it entirely depends'.[94] The Tale-Teller's short memory and detachment from tradition form the private and public sides of his modernity. Lacking the leisure to write – a sign he lacks the authority to write – he lives in poverty in a garret:

> as far as brevity will permit, I have recollected, that the shrewdest Pieces of this Treatise, were conceived in Bed, in a Garret: At other times (for a Reason best known to my self) I thought fit to sharpen my Invention with Hunger; and in general, the whole Work was begun, continued, and ended, under a long Course of Physick, and a great Want of Money.[95]

For an Ancient like Swift, *A Tale of a Tub* is a call to order. When the Tale-Teller sought evidence that modern writers are prolific, he has 'enquired in vain, the *Memorial of them was lost among Men, their Place was no more to be found*: and I was laughed to scorn, for a *Clown* and a *Pedant*, without all Taste and Refinement, little versed in the Course of *present* Affairs'.[96] Swift expects his reader to recognize Ecclesiasticus 44:9[97] and recollect that the chapter begins, 'Let us now praise famous men, and our fathers that begat us'.[98] The church – Ecclesiasticus means 'the book of the church' – draws its order from recollection and celebration of an ordered past, in direct contradiction to the Tale-Teller who celebrates Peter and Jack, allowing Martin to drop out of his tale.

The analogy between a church corrupted from its primitive purity and the corruption of classical scholarship supplies *A Tale of a Tub* with its organizing principle or, more accurately perhaps, its principle of disorganization. The title page tells the tale of *A Tale*. It self-importantly announces that this tale is 'Written for the Universal Improvement of Mankind' and adds a claim, in Latin, that people have long been wanting this book: '*Diu multumque desideratum*'. A further pair of epigraphs establishes the egregious Tale-Teller's heterodox modernity. The epigraph attributed to Irenaeus announces religious error, for it quotes not the father of the church but, as William Wotton noted at the time, the heretics he meticulously refuted.[99] That from the epicurean author Lucretius announces the writer's ambition while asserting his intellectual and religious error: he wants to be crowned by the muses for novelty.[100] Such intellectual and religious novelty, Swift shows, is not in fact novel. Even in his modernizing heterodoxy, the modern writer is inevitably just recapitulating past error. To Swift, modern free thinkers like Anthony Collins and Matthew Tindal belong to the school of Lucretius, who provides 'a compleat System of Atheism'.[101] In his hostile notes on Tindal's *Rights of the Christian Church Asserted, against the Romish and all Other Priests, Who Claim an Independent Power Over It* (1706), Swift says of Tindal that 'the Subject as unpromising as it seemeth at first View, is no less than that of *Lucretius*, to free Men's Minds from the Bondage of Religion'.[102] For both epigraphs, as for *A Tale of a Tub* itself, context is all. Swift expects the reader to know that St Irenaeus wrote *Adversus Hæreses* to refute the Gnostic heresies from which the Tale-Teller quotes as if they not the saint were authoritative. Lucretius announces his anti-religious goal just after the passage quoted on the title page, and Lucretius's atomism shapes *A Tale's* picture of jarring atoms and jostling crowds of fractious, self-assertive individuals. The ancient world too contained forms of the religious and intellectual error – gnosticism, godless epicureanism – that endanger those who cannot recall their history. (The Tale-Teller repeatedly refers to his shortness of memory.) By implication, Swift's characteristic modern is anything but as novel as he fancies himself, as the reader informed by appropriate reading and the disciplined memory it stocks will recognize. Peter and Jack, like modern materialist philosophy, express the timeless intellectual arrogance that invariably leads to error.

Lacking discipline, such moderns arrogantly pronounce on affairs of state as well as matters of faith and intellect. Swift's brothers – three Western theological traditions – are fashionable modern coffee-house politicians:

> Above all, they constantly attended those Committees of Senators who are silent in the *House*, and loud in the *Coffee-House*, where they nightly adjourn to chew the Cud of Politicks, and are encompass'd with a Ring of Disciples, who lye in wait to catch up their Droppings.[103]

This is the emergent world of public opinion, a force in political contexts and an affront to those who thought that social subordinates should not meddle in affairs of state.

Peter and Jack in particular develop their innovations in religion from the fashionable society that also corrupts learning. They share their self-importance with the Tale-Teller himself, whom Swift views not as an accomplished professional but as an emblem of modern venality:

> THESE Notices may serve to give the Learned Reader an Idea as well as a Taste of what the whole Work is likely to produce: wherein I have now altogether circumscribed my Thoughts and my Studies; and if I can bring it to a Perfection before I die, shall reckon I have well employ'd the poor Remains of an unfortunate Life. This indeed is more than I can justly expect from a Quill worn to the Pith in the Service of the State, in *Pro's* and *Con's* upon *Popish Plots*, and *Meal-Tubs*, and *Exclusion Bills*, and *Passive Obedience*, and *Addresses of Lives and Fortunes*; and *Prerogative*, and *Property*, and *Liberty of Conscience*, and *Letters to a Friend*: From an Understanding and a Conscience, thread-bare and ragged with perpetual turning; from a Head broken in a hundred places, by the Malignants of the opposite Factions, and from a Body spent with Poxes ill cured, by trusting to Bawds and Surgeons, who, (as it afterwards appeared) were profess'd Enemies to Me and the Government, and revenged their Party's Quarrel upon my Nose and Shins. Four-score and eleven Pamphlets have I written under three Reigns, and for the Service of six and thirty Factions. But finding the State has no farther Occasion for me and my Ink, I retire willingly to draw it out into Speculations more becoming a Philosopher, having, to my unspeakable Comfort, passed a long Life, with a Conscience void of Offence.[104]

For Swift, the writer's self-pity goes hand in hand with the self-importance that pronounces on affairs of state. The imagination of this hireling or hackney writer is in no better shape than a hackney horse: 'even, I my self, the Author of these momentous Truths, am a Person, whose Imaginations are hard-mouth'd and exceedingly disposed to run away with his *Reason*, which I have observed from long Experience to be a very light Rider, and easily shook off'.[105]

Heterodoxy, religious or intellectual, is an illness of the body politic. It was a cultural cliché that the 'Scandalous' professions of '*Whoring*' and '*Pamphleteering*' were analogous. Likely driven by poverty, the venal writer like the prostitute commodified for sale what properly embodied a more disinterested leisure exchange. 'The only difference between us', confesses the Grub-Street writer Ned Ward, 'is, in this particular, wherein the *Jilt* has the Advantage, We do our Business First, and stand to the Courtesie of our Benefactors to Reward us After; whilst the other, for her Security, makes her *Rider* pay for his *Journey*, before he mounts the *Saddle*.'[106] Hence the imagery of sexual disease and bodily decay that links Swift's prostitute writer with the disintegrating streetwalkers of some of his most vivid poems. The Tale-Teller's venal pamphleteering harks back to the emergence of political parties in the Exclusion Crisis. No writer could in good conscience support, say, the principle of passive obedience to the monarch (originally a touchstone of Tory loyalty) and an exclusion bill (the original Whig assertion of the people's right to resist). The phrase 'But to return' is a refrain marking the Tale-Teller's short-lived returns from his self-indulgent digressions. It eventually reaching its logical climax: 'BUT to return to *Madness*.'[107]

Although *A Tale of a Tub* expresses Swift's humanist vision of a timeless model from which modernity degenerates, it engages much more compellingly with that modernity than *Discourse*. It says a lot about Swift's high esteem for Somers in particular that he appealed to him in this way. He flaunts his High-Church antagonism toward dissent. Although Somers relied on writers to coordinate opinion out of doors – that is, to marshal popular opinion in support of his party – *A Tale* boldly mocks the self-aggrandizing venality of the writers paid to serve what Swift dismisses as factions. Yet Swift's dizzying command of his tumultuous historical moment makes the appeal to Somers's judgment even more flattering than the gracefully back-handed dedication. Swift was implicitly placing his pen at the service of party, and the energies that enliven his representation of his Grubaean sage suggest how exhilarating he found the possibilities available to him. Equally obviously, he scented danger as well as opportunity in the paper wars that had powerful statesmen courting the pens of sufficiently able writers. No modern, he trusted the forms of the Church and the traditional forms of classical learning to discipline the unruly passions of private men.

Although it has a zany energy as much beyond Temple's abilities as his desires, *A Tale* observes giddy modernity from a characteristically Ancient point of view. Swift's literary form insists that the reader supply from textual hints the constraining context discarded by the Tale-Teller. The dedication to Somers mocks a bookseller who employs no writer with the small Latin it takes to translate *Detur dignissimo*, locating the supplicant writer and the statesman within a privileged circle. As appropriately educated gentlemen, they are members of the political nation. Unlike the vacuous would-be's of the coffee house, they belong among the few who can legitimately comment on affairs of state. On a more intimate level of the compliment implied in the impersonal dedication, Somers and Swift are ambitious, uncommonly able gentleman following the road to preferment opened by sister learned professions, the clergy and the law, but the narrow vision of the political nation implicit in *Discourse* and *A Tale* is crucial to Swift's politics. Less staid than *Discourse* but not at odds with it, *A Tale* savages by impersonating the restless personality at the heart of political dissension.

This emergent personality type figures within current political debates. Its immediate context was the development of a fiscal-military state that was supporting imperial and commercial expansion by deploying increasingly large professional armies. The forces opposing stable agrarian values, as Pocock characterizes them, are largely forces that liberate elements of the modern personality elaborated in *A Tale of a Tub*:

> [Conservative Augustans] were seeking to defend virtue against innovative forces, symbolized as trading empire, standing armies, and credit. The second stood for specialization and the alienation of one's capacities; the last for fantasy, fiction, and social madness, the menace of a false consciousness which would engulf men in a sort of political Dunciad; both stood for corruption, and minds of this persuasion shared to the full the tendency to see corruption as irreversible.

Discussing the threat posed by mobile property in a landed society increasingly at the mercy of credit, Pocock evokes Swift's later ally Pope and, immediately following this passage, the patriot rhetoric of Bolingbroke.[108]

A Tale too surely diagnoses by displaying it just this phenomenon, the modern mind's definitive preference for 'fantasy, fiction, and social madness' over realities less volatile:

> Those Entertainments and Pleasures we most value in Life, are such as *Dupe* and play the Wag with the Senses. For, if we take an Examination of what is generally understood by *Happiness*, as it has Respect, either to the Understanding or the Senses, we shall find all its Properties and Adjuncts will herd under this short Definition: That, *it is a perpetual Possession of being well Deceived.* And first, with Relation to the Mind or Understanding; 'tis manifest, what might Advantages Fiction has over Truth; and the Reason is just at our Elbow; because Imagination can build nobler Scenes, and produce more wonderful Revolutions than Fortune or Nature will be at Expence to furnish. Nor is Mankind so much to blame in his Choice, thus determining him, if we consider that the Debate meerly lies between *Things past* and *Things conceived*; and so the Question is only this; Whether Things that have Place

> in the *Imagination*, may not as properly be said to *Exist*, as those that are seated
> in the *Memory*; which may be justly held in the Affirmative, and very much to the
> Advantage of the former, since This is acknowledged to be the *Womb* of Things, and
> the other allowed to be no more than the *Grave*.[109]

Swift is not offering a considered analysis of credit, although his later attacks on
the monied interest show how capable he was of presenting one. He is show-
ing how acutely attuned he was to an environment within which the volatility of
credit and the imagined rewards it promised was fostering passions that moralists
had traditionally devoted their energies to checking. The issue was topical. In the
following year, Bernard Mandeville published *The Grumbling Hive*, a doggerel
poem defending the morally troubling paradox that public prosperity depended
not on virtue but on private vices. But *The Fable of the Bees*, as Mandeville's
shrewdly ironic beast fable was called in later editions, lacks the vivid intensity
with which Swift impersonates and condemns the political personality unleashed
by modern society.[110]

Swift's embodiment of modernity exaggerates one pole of a debate, one perhaps no more common than an unreflecting confidence in the total superiority
of the ancients would be. For more thoughtful contemporaries, these attitudes
were likely to take the form of an ambivalence that made some concession to both
sides:

> If money and credit had indeed dissolved the social frame into a shifting mobility of
> objects that were desired and fictions that were fantasized about, then passion, opin-
> ion, and imagination were indeed the motors of human behaviour and the sources of
> human cognition. It is clear ... that this was strong meat even for the tough-minded
> Defoe; he busied himself, especially when challenged by Swift, to show how opinion
> and passion might be grounded upon experience rather than imagination ...[111]

Even a writer considerably more Whiggish than Swift, that is, could feel nervous
about the apparent instability of the modern world. That Pocock's exaggeration
verges on Swift's caricature is all the more suggestive because he seems oblivious
to *A Tale of a Tub*, unaware of its pertinence to his themes.[112] Although Swift and
Defoe would at times serve the same political master, they came at the volatility
of speculative investment from different directions.

Despite his evident hypersensitivity to the dangerous impulses of his historical moment, Swift unlike the Court Whigs remained convinced 'that there is a
formulaically balanced constitution whose principles are fundamental to government'.[113] His *Discourse* takes that balance for granted, and it is implicit in *A Tale*'s
aggressive but covert appeal to the classically disciplined reader. Although Swift
did not write *A Tale* like an Ancient, he wrote it as an Ancient. As the inclusion
of the *Battel of the Books* in the *Tale* volume reveals, his appeal to Somers and the
Whig Junto hearkens back to the formative influence of Temple. Swift may have

consciously identified a subversive new kind of property only later, under the pressure of new polemical demands.[114] He nevertheless heard the siren song of the new order, for the debate over credit supplied the milieu within which professional (that is, commercial) writers were struggling to establish their own kind of paper credit.[115] Since his days with Temple, moreover, he had enjoyed an exceptionally close connection with the world of publishing and book production.[116] Impersonating a Grub-Street pamphleteer, he located *A Tale of a Tub* at the fraught intersection of private and confessional with public and political, of traditional and classical with innovative and original, of patronage and disinterested service of the public good with commercial commodification and self-promoting venality.[117] For that was where he too would have to succeed by his pen. Indeed, *A Tale of a Tub* takes the ambition it expresses as one of its themes: 'WHOEVER hath an Ambition to be heard in a Crowd, must press, and squeeze, and thrust, and climb with indefatigable Pains, till he has exalted himself to a certain Degree of Altitude above them'.[118] It would be hard to write a more self-conscious work.

The results of Swift's self-conscious display were mixed. Like his *Discourse*, which appeared too late to benefit him, *A Tale of a Tub* did well without serving him well. It was eagerly read: there were three editions in 1704, two more in 1705, one of them Irish.[119] Of his brilliance and his ability to catch the taste of the fashionable town, there could now be no doubt. Although he was a conscientious clergyman, however, he met a Whiggish fate. Thanks to the success of *A Tale*, a reputation for profanity and godlessness dogged him for the rest of his career, marring the chance of preferment he was trying to mend.[120] In a letter written to a friend in July 1704, Francis Atterbury shrewdly assessed the accomplishment and the hazards:

> The author of *A Tale of a Tub* will not yet be known; and if it be the man I guess, he hath reason to conceal himself, because of the prophane strokes in that piece, which would do his reputation and interest in the world more harm than the wit can do him good ... Nothing can please more than that book doth here at London.[121]

To those who differentiated less sharply between the Church of England and its rivals, Roman Catholicism and Dissent, Swift's satire seemed to target Christianity itself, as Wotton pointed out: 'he discovers an equal mixture of Lewdness and Irreligion. Would any Christian compare a *Mountebank*'s *Stage*, a *Pulpit*, and a *Ladder* together?'[122] Such jesting was inconsistent with the character – the appropriate public demeanour – of a clergyman.

Swift added an Apology to the fifth edition (1710), blaming the occasional indecorous passage on his youth and (a favourite ploy) lack of access to his papers: 'He acknowledges there are several youthful Sallies, which from the Grave and the Wise may deserve a Rebuke'.[123] His long self-justification did little to mollify those who thought his popular book was blasphemous. Shaped by Irish experience of a Church threatened by a numerous and prosperous dissenting population, Swift felt that only aggression could defend the established Church, which was threatened by 'heavy, illiterate Scriblers, prostitute in their Reputations, vicious in their Lives, and ruin'd in their Fortunes': 'If the Clergy's Resentments lay upon their Hands, in my humble Opinion, they might have found more proper Objects to employ them on: *Nondum tibi defuit Hostis*'.[124] It offended him to see a Church with external enemies succumb to internal dissension by attacking its friends; that is, himself. Unfortunately, as Wotton's comment suggests, his critics were not champions of dissent. Swift may have been blinded to his larger audience by his eagerness to impress the formidably intelligent circle of readers centred on Somers. The rowdy indecorum that offended critics of *A Tale* perhaps reflects, as well, the norms of the provincial society described by Connolly, a society abandoning early modern customs for polite constraint more slowly than the metropolitan centre in which Swift was now publishing.[125] Whatever the reason, *A Tale* was both an unmistakable triumph and something of a catastrophe for Swift.

Although political opponents sometimes identified Swift with his Tale-Teller after he changed parties, the two could not be more different. Swift shared the Tale-Teller's thirst for fame, of course, but he wanted to clamber above the crowd without becoming another prostitute modern scribbler. He was consistently scrupulous about the terms on which he served others. Having 'a scruple of entring the Church meerly for support', for example, he had sought ordination in Ireland only after he refused Temple's offer of a place in the office of the Master of the Rolls in Ireland.[126] Once his good Irish living gave him a leg up, he could write because he did not have to do so for pay. Unlike his Tale-Teller, he saw what he wrote not as a potentially profitable commodity but within the traditional paradigm of letters. With the exception of *Gulliver's Travels*, which benefited from Pope's assistance, Swift did not publish his works for gain: 'I never got a farthing by anything I writ', he claimed in 1735, 'except one about eight years ago, and that was by Mr. Pope's prudent management for me'.[127] He delighted in public acclaim, and he certainly wanted to impress. Above all, he hoped to impress a patron. Ehrenpreis has argued that Swift, a posthumous child, was looking for surrogate fathers in his relationships with powerful men: 'What Swift wanted was not a boss-worker connection but a familial tie'.[128] Probably he wanted neither. In a society characterized by elaborate networks of kinship and clientage, a patron uses his interest to benefit his protégé. Such support is quasi-familial but by no means necessarily paternal. After all, Somers was only sixteen years older than Swift, Harley only six. By freely serving a well-connected superior, Swift hoped be as freely rewarded in the ideal spirit of patronage.

Only in connection with someone else's writing, Michael Treadwell observes, does Swift identify himself as a professional rather than 'a gentleman volunteer in the literary wars'.[129] He did so when he was defending his editing of Temple's works, replying on 10 November 1709 to Temple's sister Lady Giffard's public repudiation of his edition of Temple's *Memoirs. Part III*:

Madam; I pretend not to have had the least share in Sr Wm Temples Confidence above his Relations, or his commonest Friends; (I have but too good Reasons to think otherwise) But this was a thing in my way; and it was no more than to prefer the Advice of a Lawyer or even of a Tradesman before that of his Friends, in Things that related to their Callings. Nobody else had conversed so much with his Manuscripts as I, and since I was not wholly illiterate, I cannot imagine whom else he could leave the Care of his Writings to.[130]

Socially inferior and dependent on the patron whose failure to prefer him obviously still galled, Swift sacrifices caste to assert the professional competence of someone who knows his trade. In less awkward circumstances, Swift did not present himself as a mere professional. When Harley offered him £50 in 1711, he was deeply offended. The offer violated what Swift took to be the spirit of their relationship, treating a willing gentleman ally like a mere employee. So when Hoppit calls Swift 'the most brilliant hack of his generation',[131] he acknowledges Swift's undoubted mastery of his craft in a way that slights the distinction, vital to Swift, between the service freely offered to an influential friend and a commodity offered for sale. No matter what enemies said, Swift was not the Tale-Teller.

He valued the voice of the marketplace, but he did not see books as commodities. He knew that his value to the great depended on his ability to catch the fashion of the moment. He knew that sales therefore mattered. 'The book was greedily bought', he boasted about *Discourse*. Knowing that purchasers are not always readers, however, he added something more important: 'and read'. He kept an eye on Prince Posterity. Later, in *Verses on the Death of Dr. Swift*, he sardonically imagined a posthumous discussion of his reputation! He would later praise Henry St John (eventually Viscount Bolingbroke) because his books were 'thumb'd and spoil'd with *Reading*' in contrast to 'a great Man of my Acquaintance', presumably Sunderland, 'who knew a *Book* by the *Back*, better than a *Friend* by the *Face*, though he had *never convers'd* with the former, and often with the latter'.[132] Books mattered to Swift, as did the conversation of men who read and wrote them: 'WHEN I am reading a Book, whether wise or silly, it seemeth to me to be alive and talking to me'.[133] Temple, Somers, Harley: Swift chose his potential patrons among highly literate writers and bibliophiles. He could never write just for pay.

The power Swift displayed in *A Tale of a Tub* was impressive, but his circumstances meant that it was no more timely a book than *Discourse*. Shortly after it was published in May 1704, he returned to Ireland. Church and domestic concerns would keep him in Ireland for the next three years, leaving him out of such lively political debates as that over the Act of Union with Scotland, which received royal assent in May 1707. He busied himself with his parish and his cathedral and with putting his finances in order. He was in no position to blush and confess his authorship in the appropriate circles. He had published *A*

Tale to a mixed reaction, and he had established an acquaintance with potential patrons who were currently out of office. Otherwise, his trip to England as the new and decidedly Anglican Queen Anne assumed the throne had not proved rewarding. He seemed to be as far as ever from the kind of recognition he was hoping for.

3 'AN ENTIRE FRIEND TO THE ESTABLISHED CHURCH': CHURCHMAN AMONG THE STATESMEN AND WITS

Living in Ireland after the publication of *A Tale of a Tub*, Swift busied himself with his parish and the chapter of the cathedral. A clergyman opposed to the very idea of parties, he also seems to have thought through, pragmatically as well as more reflectively, how he might further his acquaintance with the Whig statesmen who had responded so encouragingly to his *Discourse*. That he returned to London as what we would call a lobbyist on behalf of his Church shows how practically he was able to combine his political connections with his clerical office. The essays he produced so rapidly after his return to London place his Church at the centre of his political thought. Swift could engage in partisan politics only as a High-Churchman committed to the Revolution settlement and the Protestant succession, a position that limited but certainly did not eliminate political choice. To readers today, this High-Church stance reveals Swift at his most unappealing – jealous of the rights of the legally established church, protective of his own clerical privileges, and intolerant of any deviation from orthodoxy. What some might call his Anglo-Irish sectarian bigotry – English prejudices about the Irish too have a long history – deserves to be read in the context of contemporary European politics, where it seems less extreme than it does today. Swift also reveals compassion for the straitened conditions in which many clergyman struggled to fulfil their duties and a shrewd grasp of their origins in the very Reformation that created the national Church he served.

In London as an agent of that church, he renewed his acquaintance with the Whig lords and, much more gratifying, found himself part of a circle of wits, writers who like him scented opportunity in the strife of party. The most important of them were Joseph Addison and through Addison, his friend Richard Steele. Just as he was displaying his own ability to catch the taste of the town as Isaac Bickerstaff, Swift gratifyingly found himself intimate with, and valued by, the writers whose periodical essays in the *Tatler* and later the *Spectator* would give the definitive expression to that taste. Although modern scholars question his contribution, he prided himself on his early involvement in the *Tatler*, which placed him at the very centre of the literary scene. Unluckily, the agent of the Church failed in his mission, after which events would lead him from the Whigs to the Tories. Although Swift's shift betrayed no political principles – he made as good (or as ill) a fit with the one group as with the other – political parties are in part tribal. Personal networks commanding loyalty are as important as ideology to party identity. A loyal friend, Swift found painful the rupture of treasured friendships that followed on his defection. The defensiveness of his accounts of this period, like the vindictiveness of his later attacks on his former friend Steele, provides a measure of his pain. Even his treasured friendship with Addison failed to survive, a failure to which differences of personality were likely as crucial as differences over policy. Although the end of these friendships demonstrates the power of political differences to divide even kindred spirits, the friendships themselves demonstrate that Swift could indeed, under different circumstances, have functioned as a Whig. It is misleading to see his Whig dalliance as somehow less 'natural' or 'appropriate' than his later Tory affiliation.

Swift enjoyed a rewarding, often exhilarating visit to London. His mission conferred some dignity, and it gave him the authority to approach the statesmen whose support he sought. He participated in a community of Whig writers, joining what Ehrenpreis playfully calls 'the literary sinecure-hunters of London'. Although some penniless writers would no doubt have contented themselves with mere sinecures, positions granting secure incomes but unburdened by many duties,[1] this characterization obscures what was clearly professional ambition. In a hierarchical society dominated by patronage, a place rather than a professional salary rewarded talent and industry. Swift and his friends were competing not for easy indolence but for challenging positions that would provide scope for their considerable talents. Those in power valued writers who could appeal to public opinion, for closely matched political parties contested frequent elections that turned on attitudes to divisive issues, the conduct of a long war as well as threats to (for some, from) the established church. Writers were needed to rally partisan supporters, possibly even persuade the undecided. In this heady environment, those with talent could aspire to positions of real influence on affairs of state.

Easily the most important writer – and Swift's most important friend – in this circle was Joseph Addison, whose long service to the Whigs was abundantly rewarded. In the year Swift published his *Tale of a Tub* to catch eyes, Addison had published his most important poem, *The Campaign*. Commissioned by Halifax to celebrate Marlborough's great military victory at Blenheim, the poem succeeded so well that Addison was rewarded with the position of Undersecretary of State in 1705. The standard of literary accomplishment, like the rewards hoped for, was extremely high. In London in 1708, Swift seems to have sought Addison's acquaintance. By 1 March he dined with Addison and Addison's old school-fellow Steele. By July, Swift is referring to the three friends as a 'Triumvirate',[2] perhaps with a playful allusion to the triumvirate of Marlborough, Godolphin, and Harley who had dominated the previous ministry.[3] Undoubtedly Addison provided Swift's most valued literary friendship before he met the writers who formed the Scriblerus Club, and when Addison became a secretary to the Earl of Wharton, now Lord Lieutenant of Ireland, Swift wrote to Archbishop King:

> Mr. Addison who goes over first Secretary, is a most excellent Person, and being my most intimate Friend, I shall use all my Credit to set him right, in his Notions of Persons and Things. I spoke to him with great Plainness upon the Subject of the Test, and, he says, he is confident my Lord Wharton will not attempt it, if he finds the Bent of the Nation against it.[4]

Friendship and politics could clearly not be easily separated, and Swift's circle of influence appeared to be usefully expanding. But Addison was no mere connection, he was Swift's 'most intimate Friend'!

Swift prepared to assume a conspicuous place in this crowd of literary-political aspirants with a display of his almost unrivalled ability to catch the taste of the town, an elaborate April Fools' Day joke at the expense of the almanac-maker John Partridge.[5] He was, of course, already the author of two successful, remarkably learned works. His *Discourse*, had recently been included in the third volume of *A Collection of State Tracts, Publish'd on Occasion of the Late Revolution in 1688. And during the Reign of King William III*, joining (*inter alia*) another 1701 tract usually attributed to Somers himself, *Jura Populi Anglicani; or, The Subject's Right of Petitioning Set Forth*.[6] *A Tale of a Tub* had quickly gone through four editions, and Swift was already working with his publisher, Benjamin Tooke, to prepare a fifth.[7] In January 1708, Swift published his brilliant parody, *Predictions for the Year 1708. Wherein the Month and Day of the Month are Set Down, the Persons Named, and the Great Actions and Events of Next Year Particularly Related, as They Will Come to Pass. Written to Prevent the People of England from being Further Impos'd on by Vulgar Almanack-makers. By Isaac Bickerstaff Esq*. The full title is pertinent. Swift mimics almanac style but boldly challenges the vagueness of almanac predictions. A learned man rather than a mechanic, Swift's Bickerstaff takes offence at the imposition of foolishness by the vulgar, especially when it takes in members of the political nation: 'But I rather wonder, when I observe Gentlemen in the Country, rich enough to serve the Nation in Parliament, poring in *Partrige's* Almanack, to find out the Events of the Year at Home and Abroad; not daring to propose a Hunting-Match, until *Gadbury*, or he, hath fixed the Weather'.[8] Like Partridge's *Merlinus Liberatus*, Job Gadbury's *Ephemeris: or, A Diary Astronomical, Astrological, Meteorological* was a popular almanac. Targeting these works, Bickerstaff directs the first of his remarkably specific predictions to John Partridge, who will die, he predicts, on 29 March 1708. Partridge's own *Answer to Esquire Bickerstaff's Strange and Wonderful Predictions for the Year*

1708 kept Bickerstaff current, apparently allowing Swift to suppress the reply he had prepared.[9] At the end of the month, in time for April Fools' Day, Swift could publish a verse broadside, *An Elegy on Mr. Partrige, the Almanack-Maker, who Died on the 29th of this Instant March, 1708*,[10] and *The Accomplishment of the First of Mr. Bickerstaff's Predictions*, which describes the self-confessed fraud's death and apologizes that the predicted time of death was four hours off. Since Partridge's protests in his 1709 almanac kept his status as the butt of a joke in the air, Swift responded in verse and prose. *A Famous Prediction of Merlin, the British Wizard*, by 'T. N. Philomath', another of Swift's broadsides (verse plus commentary), took its title from Partridge's *Merlinus Liberatus*; his tract, *A Vindication of Isaac Bickerstaff Esq.*, resumed the voice of Bickerstaff himself.

Swift chose his target with care. Partridge was a lower-class and dissenting opponent of the Church whose almanacs had in the past fomented political unrest.[11] Like the broadsides Swift also produced during this playful campaign, almanacs were among the most popular items published in England, where they contributed to Protestant national consciousness.[12] Attacking something so popular with lower-class and rustic readers contributes, as did satire of clownish rural squires, to the development of the intellectually alert urbanity that distinguished eighteenth-century wit from its less discriminating (or more socially inclusive) predecessors.[13] It certainly distinguishes the author of Bickerstaff, who aspired to a wide readership, from the professional hacks and credulous readers common further down the social and literary scale. And since that wit was to be the project of the phenomenally successful collaborations by his new friends, the *Tatler* and the *Spectator*, it comes as no surprise that Swift and Addison became such thorough friends and, with Steele, formed a happy triumvirate.

For Swift's jest did catch the fancy of the town. When Steele was plotting the *Tatler*, he cashed in on Swift's success by borrowing the Bickerstaff persona, as he acknowledged in the dedication to the first volume of the collected *Tatlers*:

> But a Work of this Nature requiring Time to grow into the Notice of the World, it happened very luckily, that a little before I had resolved upon this Design, a Gentleman had written Predictions, and Two or Three other Pieces in my Name, which rendered it famous thro' all Parts of *Europe*; and by an inimitable Spirit and Humour, raised it to as high a Pitch of Reputation as it could possible arrive at.[14]

The exemplary success of the *Tatler*, in which Addison helped Steele, and then of the *Spectator*, by Addison with Steele's help, make them Swift's rivals, perhaps his superiors, at catching the taste of the town. Swift was delighted to find himself part of a triumvirate at the centre of literary life in the fashionable town. Supported by the Bickerstaff persona, Steele, whose first prose work had been *The Christian Hero* (1701), could in turn puff Swift's *Project for the Advancement of Religion* in *Tatler* no. 5 (21 April 1709). Swift contributed a few numbers and two of his best poems, *A Description of the Morning* (no. 9 (30 April 1709)) and

Description of a City Shower (no. 238 (17 October 1710)).[15] He prided himself on also contributing several hints.

Although some late *Tatler* papers were partisan, these works are commonly political only in the broadest sense. They shape manners and frame attitudes to cultural change while providing the idiom of urbane debate. The campaign against duelling that Steele inaugurated in *Tatler* no. 25 (7 June 1709) or his attempt to define the gentleman by manners as well as birth in no. 169 (9 May 1710) are examples, as is Swift's letter on corruptions in style in no. 230.[16] Addison's famous allegory of Public Credit in *Spectator* no. 3 (3 March 1711) genially inches such discussion onto terrain that was also contested by political partisans. Everything was potentially political, as Swift indicates when he denies his rumoured author-ship of Shaftesbury's *Letter concerning Enthusiasm* in a letter to Ambrose Philips: 'by the free Whiggish thinking I should rathr take it to be yours'.[17] The most neutral prose could raise the market value of a writer who successfully attracted enough readers, and all three members of this short-lived literary triumvirate would be engaged to write more polemical tracts. When the failure of his mis-sion called Swift back to Ireland in June, not long after the first *Tatler* appeared in April 1709, he left behind the final volume of Temple's *Memoirs*, published with a brief Whiggish preface. He was joining Addison, already in Ireland attending the Lord Lieutenant. But despite his cherished personal ties with the Whigs, political events would soon draw him to the Tories.

Nevertheless, Swift was not simply a wit who aspired to government employ-ment. It is impossible to grasp his political life without recognizing that ordination as minister of an episcopal national church was the decisive event in his adult life. It had always been an option. A career in the Church offered one of the few paths to advancement for talented men of modest means or humble backgrounds, a path perhaps even more important in Ireland than in England.[18] It meant that the appropriate reward for services to a ministry would be promotion to what Peterborough called 'a Lean Bishoprick, or a fatt Deanery' within the Anglican Church.[19] But Swift's commitment to the Church was profound, not merely self-serving; there is no convincing reason to regard Swift's decision to be ordained in Ireland as merely opportunistic. However much his timing reflected his exas-peration with Temple, the authority of a national church suited him. He had taken a long time to fix on a career, and he had certainly been willing to consider other options should they present themselves, but he acted on conviction and his decision was irrevocable. That may be why he was so eager to be able to reject another option, to display the fact that he was not driven to the church purely for an income. For what could be more characteristic of Swift than an assertion of independence that aligned him with an authoritative institution? Who was Jonathan Swift? From that moment, as his very dress would announce to every-one, he was a priest in the Church of Ireland. So he publicly identified himself on the title pages of Temple's works: as domestic chaplain to his Excellency the Earl of Berkeley, one of the Lords Justices of Ireland; as Vicar of Laracor, prebendary of St Patrick's, Dublin; as a Doctor of Divinity, his title awarded by the Anglican Trinity College, Dublin. Later in life, he would identify himself as Dean of St Patrick's, Dublin. His place in the Church fixed his public identity even when, to his chagrin, it also highlighted the flagrant indecorum of, most conspicuously, the author of *A Tale of a Tub*.

Between his return to Ireland after the publication of *A Tale of a Tub* and his return to London in 1707, Swift published no political tracts. It seems likely, though, that a spate of writing associated with 1708 reflects the ongoing intellectual engagement with partisan politics provoked by his acquaintance with Whigs. The most striking feature of these essays, taken together, is that they turn, without exception, on the political implications of Swift's identity as a Churchman. Even the apparent exceptions to this rule, the playful Bickerstaff papers (January–March 1708), target a dissenting opponent of the established church, the almanac maker John Partridge. So do his incomplete Remarks on Tindal's *Rights of the Christian Church Asserted*, published only posthumously, which disparage the integrity and the intelligence of a writer who attacked not only Roman Catholicism but also the authority of the ordained clergy and the validity of any church established by civil authority. The unlicensed press that permitted the publication of such unorthodox views fostered a widespread sense that the Church was under attack, and Swift's authoritarianism informs his consistently held conviction that freedom of conscience does not entail freedom of expression. Attempts to abolish the sacramental test, a valuable safeguard of the national church, which required civil, military, and naval office holders to take communion in the established church, fed the same fear. The Test had been extended to the Church of Ireland only in 1704, likely at the instigation of the High-Church Earl of Nottingham, and though its effects may have been largely symbolic, its protection became a rallying cry for Irish churchmen like Swift and Archbishop King.[20] To a beleaguered institution, any symbol of support was potent.

Swift, F. P. Lock shrewdly observes, 'joined a profession that was declining in respect, influence, and importance'; his views of clerical possibilities and privileges was, Lock adds, 'anachronistic'.[21] Nevertheless, they were no less sincere than his equally backward-looking admiration for the permanent models of virtue and society supplied by ancient Greece and Rome. On the title page of *A Project for the Advancement of Religion and the Reformation of Manners*, published in April 1709 and dedicated to the Countess of Berkeley, Swift identifies himself only as a person of Quality and supplies as epitaph a Horatian apostrophe to whoever might end civil rage and restrain unfettered licentiousness.[22] He addresses this pious tract to the devout noblewoman he had teased by parodying Boyle's *Meditations*, a favourite devotional book, in 'A Meditation upon a Broom-Stick'.[23] But his epitaph implicitly addresses the Queen, much as Horace presumably directed his apostrophe to Augustus. The *Project* expresses Swift's conviction that enforcing a moral order would stabilize civil society. It makes large claims for the social authority to be wielded by the Church and its clergy under a suitably Anglican monarch, Queen Anne, who would both set an example of pious living and demand it from those who would be her courtiers. In such a society, the clergyman could take their rightful place as gentlemen, chastening the licentious, as Swift exhorts them to do:

> If the Clergy were as forward to appear in all Companies, as other Gentlemen, and would a little study the Arts of Conversation, to make themselves agreeable, they might be welcome at every Party, where there was the least Regard for Politeness, or good Sense; and consequently prevent a Thousand vicious or prophane Discourses, as well as Actions.[24]

If the religious settlement underpins the social order, as Swift thought it did, then it is important for the clergy to take their place with other gentlemen in polite circles. His concern with clerical income is not so much self-serving as programmatic, an attempt to make this possible. When he jokes in *An Argument against Abolishing Christianity* that England contains over ten thousand parsons 'whose Revenues added to those of my Lords the Biships, would suffice to maintain, at least, two Hundred young Gentlemen of Wit and Pleasure, and Free-thinking; Enemies to Priest-craft, narrow Principles, Pedantry, and Prejudices', his joke turns on his indignation that the clergy are, as every fashionable gentleman knew, impoverished: 'it seems a wrong computation, that the Revenues of the Church throughout this Island, would be large enough to maintain ... even half that Number'.[25]

Political attempts to bolster or limit the Church's authority centred on the sacramental test. Assertions of the Church monopoly on office commonly took the form of Tory attacks on occasional conformity, the practice whereby Protestant dissenters took communion in the established church just often enough to qualify for office. Jack's triumph as Lord Mayor of London in *A Tale of a Tub* targets an office notorious for this abuse, as it seemed to Anglican observers. Attempts to weaken that monopoly usually took the form of Whig attacks on the sacramental test itself as an unfair limit on civic participation by otherwise loyal Protestant dissenters. As *A Tale of a Tub* demonstrates, Swift approached these conflicts with the hostility to sectarian difference still evident in Catholic-Protestant relations in the north of Ireland, where (to use Swift's terms in *A Tale*) Martin's voice now seems inaudible in the noisy contest between Jack and Peter. Supporters of the Church of Ireland could be just as intransigent. Swift's angry conviction that dissenters are treacherous subversives is the corollary of his devotion to a legally established national church. In the otherwise playful *Argument against Abolishing Christianity in England*, Swift treats any easing of the restrictions on dissenters as if it amounted to eliminating even nominal Christianity in England. There is no reason to doubt his seriousness about this. In *A Letter from a Member of the House of Commons in Ireland to a Member of the House of Commons in England concerning the Sacramental Test*, he impersonates an MP but everywhere reveals the clergyman.[26]

In the most wide-ranging of the political essays he wrote in 1707–8, *The Sentiments of a Church-of-England Man with Respect to Religion and Government*, Swift makes similarly strong claims for the authority of the Church while also addressing the claims of state and suggesting a cautious relationship with parties. He seems to have incorporated within this deliberately impersonal tract the substance of Swift's critique of Tindal.[27] Adopting what was to become his favourite partisan stance – the pose of studied impartiality – Swift defends the episcopacy of the established church as 'most agreeable to primitive Institution; fittest, of all others for preserving Order and Purity, and under its present Regulations, best calculated for our Civil State'. He tolerates dissent only grudgingly: 'it would not be agreeable with so mild a Government, or so pure a Religion as ours, to use violent Methods against great Numbers of *mistaken* People, while they do not manifestly endanger the Constitution of either'.[28] But he accuses dissenters who want access to civic office of being 'not so over nice to distinguish between an unlimited Liberty of Conscience, and an unlimited Freedom of Opinion'.[29] Swift never confuses freedom of conscience with freedom of expression. He opposes both an unlicensed press and the civic participation by dissenters defended in it:[30]

> So that, upon the whole, where *Sects* are tolerated in a State, it is fit they should enjoy a full Liberty of Conscience, and every other Privilege of free-born Subjects, *to which no Power is annexed*. And to preserve their Obedience upon all Emergencies, a Government cannot give them too much Ease, nor trust them with too little *Power*.

The failed bill against occasional conformity was opposed for pursuing too aggressively what Swift nevertheless sees 'an Evil in it self'.[31] Dissenters should not assume from its failure that the Test itself was inappropriate. Nothing in *Sentiments* is at odds with Swift's resolute defence of the sacramental test.

Growing up in Ireland, Swift had inhaled sectarian antagonisms with the very air he breathed. He knew from his first parish at Kilroot, in the north of Ireland, that the Church of Ireland was beleaguered in ways even an ill-paid English curate could scarcely imagine, not far from minority status even among Ireland's Protestants. So he greeted threats to the established church with a savage rhetoric that even then sounded to many English ears like an archaic echo of the Marian and Elizabethan religious persecutions. In England, where religious minorities were very small, a sense of security had already led to a degree of tolerance, and by 1828, less than a century after Swift's death, even Roman Catholics would win freedom of worship in England. After all, adherents of the Church of England had in 1698–9 had proved themselves strong enough to force James II from the throne for favouring Roman Catholics. When Swift expresses his determination to confine civic and corporate offices to members of the established Church, it is his experience in Ireland that leads him to sound so intransigent.

Sectarian intolerance gives the same immediacy to Swift's accounts of the seventeenth-century English civil wars. For Swift, their dominant theme was persecution of the established church: 'considering the cruel Persecutions of the Episcopal Church, during the Course of that horrid Rebellion and the Consequences of it, until the happy *Restoration*; is it not manifest, that the persecuting Spirit lyes so equally divided between the *Papists* and the Sectaries, that a Feather would turn the Balance on either Side?'[32] This late statement – from *Queries Relating to the Sacramental Test* (1732) – echoes the intransigence of his *Sermon upon the Martyrdom of K. Charles I*, preached at St Patrick's, Dublin, on 30 January 1726. Swift actually blames the rebellious Protestant Parliament for the Irish rebellion:

> First, the Irish rebellion was wholly owing to that wicked English parliament. For the leaders in the Irish Popish massacre would never have dared to stir a finger, if they had not been encouraged by that rebellious spirit in the English House of Commons, which they very well know must disable the King from sending any supplies to his Protestant subjects here; and, therefore, we may truly say that the English parliament held the King's hands, while the Irish Papists here were cutting our grandfathers throats.

On this rebellion Swift blames a rise of atheism, the corruption of the aristocracy, and as a consequence of the royal family's flight to the continent, the seduction of James II to Roman Catholicism. Were it not for wicked dissenters, conscientious Anglicans would not have had to rationalize their resistance to a Catholic monarch!

Centrally, though, rebellion exemplifies and fosters the unending disintegration into factions (sects in the church, parties in politics) that leaves the nation vulnerable to war and invasion:

> Secondly, That murderous Puritan-parliament, when they had all in their own power, could not agree upon any one method of settling a form either of religion or civil government, but changed every day from schism to schism, from heresy to heresy, and from one faction to another. From whence arose that wild confusion still continuing in our several ways of serving God, and those absurd notions of civil power, which have so often torn us with factions more than any other nation in Europe.[33]

To an unusual degree, then, Swift treats Roman Catholicism and dissenting Protestantism as interchangeable threats to the survival of his church. His religious intolerance is inescapable and distinctive.

Little masks Swift's disturbing refusal to discriminate degrees of infidelity to the national church he served. What the dissenters claim for themselves, he asserts, 'may be equally applied to admit *Papists, Atheists, Mahometans, Heathens,* and *Jews*'.[34] Modern liberal democracies have accepted that logic, but Swift would see only a collapse of order in the prospect. So would the Protestant dissenters he despised, who saw themselves not as infidels but as loyal fellow Protestants. In *An Argument against Abolishing Christianity in England*, also written in 1708, Swift argues playfully (but in deadly earnest) that to abolish the Test is to abolish Christianity; indeed, it is to abolish even the nominal Christianity imposed on dissenters by the requirement to qualify for civic office by sometimes taking communion in the Church of England. This is hardly a moderate position. Nevertheless, Swift with some justice distinguishes himself from the High-Church extremists who, at the height of the debate over occasional conformity, were mimicked by Defoe in *The Shortest Way with the Dissenters* (1702). He contrasts himself with the polemicist Charles Leslie: 'any Man who reads the Papers published by Mr. *Lesly*, and others of his Stamp, must needs conclude that if this Author could make the Nation see his Adversaries, under the Colours he paints them in; we had nothing else to do, but rise as one Man, and destroy such Wretches from the Face of the Earth'.[35] Swift does not, I think, misrepresent Leslie, whose characteristic aggression can be suggested by the title of one of his anti-Quaker tracts: *The Snake in the Grass; or, Satan Transform'd into an Angel of Light. Discovering the Deep and Unsuspected Subtilty which is Couched under the Pretended Simplicity of Many of the Principal Leaders of those People Call'd Quakers*.[36]

On the other hand, Swift asserts, the label *moderation* has been misappropriated by a different band of extremists:

> On the other Side, how shall we excuse the Advocates for *Moderation*; among whom, I could appeal to an Hundred Papers ... which lay such Principles to the whole Body of the *Tories*, as, if they were true, and believed; our next Business should, in Prudence, be to erect Gibbets in every Parish, and hang them out of the Way. But, I suppose it is presumed, the common People understand *Raillery*, or at least *Rhetorick*; and will not take *Hyperboles* in too literal a Sense; which, however, in some Junctures might prove a desperate Experiment. And this is *Moderation*, in the *modern* Sense of the Word; to which, speaking impartially, the Bigots of both Parties are *equally* entituled.[37]

Swift attacks the dissenters' misuse of *moderation* again in *Brotherly Love*, a 1717 sermon that revealingly refers to the dissenters as 'Fanaticks' throughout![38] By playing obviously dissenting extremists against the Jacobite extreme of the Tory clergy – and characteristically using 'modern' as a disparaging term – Swift represents himself as a genuine a moderate. Although he will not actively persecute dissenters, he will fiercely deny them any access to power.

For Swift takes a very Hobbesian view of political power and the laws that it creates. There is, he consistently argues, 'an absolute, unlimited, legislative Power, which is originally in the Body of the People' and (in England) 'is placed in the Three Estates (otherwise called the Two Houses of Parliament) in Conjunction with the King'. He believed that his Church came as close as was now possible to the primitive church, but he also knew that its legal standing, unlike its spiritual authority, was established by the legislative power which could at any point dis-establish what it had established:

> And whatever they please to enact or to repeal in the settled Forms, whether it be Ecclesiastical or Civil, immediately becometh Law or Nullity. Their Decrees may be against Equity, Truth, Reason and Religion, but they are not against Law; because Law is the Will of the supreme Legislature, and that is, themselves. And there is no Manner of Doubt, but the same Authority, whenever it pleaseth, may abolish Christianity, and set up the *Jewish*, *Mahometan*, or *Heathen* Religion. In short, they may do any Thing within the Compass of human Power. And, therefore, who will dispute that the same Law, which deprived the Church, not only of Lands, misapplied to superstitious Uses, but even the Tythes and Glebes, (the antient and necessary Support of Parish Priests) may take away all the rest, whenever the Lawgivers please, and make the Priesthood as primitive, as this Writer, or others of his Stamp, can desire.[39]

Swift is attacking Tindal ('this Writer'), whose *Rights of the Christian Church Asserted* treated the church established by law as if it were created by that law: 'here lies the Mistake of this superficial Man, who is not able to distinguish between what the Civil Power can hinder, and what it can do'. For Swift Henry VIII had pillaged the church as well as cropping Roman superstitions, providing evidence of the Church's vulnerability before legislative power. In politics, Swift often seems Hobbesian because of his bleak recognition that political power is absolute but not necessarily right.

This distrust of political power may explain why, when Swift presents what he feels is the genuinely moderate position, there is nothing soft about his version of the Anglican *via media*. He approaches sectarian difference with seventeenth-century ferocity. The Puritan role in the English civil wars partly explains his determination to keep any shred of power from dissenting hands. To what he calls the dissenters' 'Cant of *High-Church*, and *Persecution*, and being *Priest-rid-den*' and to the attacks on the universities 'for infecting the Youth of the Nation with arbitrary and *Jacobite* Principles', Swift retorts that dissenters themselves joined with '[*Their*] *Brethren the Roman Catholicks*', abandoning the reformed Church of England to support James II when he promised toleration; that is why Swift shows Jack frequently being mistaken for Peter in *A Tale of a Tub*.[40] He dismisses the sufferings of dissenters under Charles II as 'not, by any Means, a Plea of Merit, equal to the Constancy and Sufferings of the Bishops and Clergy; or of the Head and Fellows of *Magdalen* College; that furnished the Prince of *Orange's* Declaration with such powerful Arguments, to justify and promote the Revolution'.[41] The Tory Reaction whereby Charles rallied the Anglican elite and routed the Whigs had seemed real enough to the dissenters who found the penal laws against them now strictly enforced, but for Swift it pales before the sufferings of the churchmen who courageously resisted James II's attempts to place Roman Catholics in office.[42] To churchmen, Swift feels, England owes the Glorious Revolution itself. Dissent is an error with the potential to destabilize the state.

What we now find intolerable in Swift is this intolerance. He is genuinely and intensely intolerant of Protestant dissent. It is the aspect of his thought most at odds with his appealing commitment to liberty. As a humanist as well as an Anglican priest, Swift believed in the necessity of common forms. In faith, they were recorded in *The Book of Common Prayer*, a devotional guide that seems almost inevitable in a people who appeal to common law. For the humanist too, only common forms can discipline restless, unruly human nature. Swift's attitudes were not extreme.[43] His language is violent, but he concedes instead of opposing the right, which English dissenters did enjoy, to worship privately without persecution. By contemporary European standards, that looks like a significant concession. The word *refugee* had recently entered English to describe Protestant fugitives from religious persecution, specifically the thousands of Huguenots who had fled persecution in France following Louis XIV's revocation of the Edict of Nantes in 1685. In England too, memories of sectarian warfare were vivid and recent, as they were in Swift's native Ireland and in Scotland, where the displacement of episcopal clergy after the Glorious Revolution intensified Swift's distrust of Presbyterians. Discursive rather than physical aggression represents a genuine softening of historical animosities. Moreover, as Ruth Herman reminds us, Swift's hardening line towards dissent, usually linked to England's partisan electoral politics, was remarkably free from personal hostility toward individuals.[44] His later friendship with Pope is the most conspicuous, but not the only, evidence that his personal relationships could cross sectarian lines.

Important as it is to place Swift's stated resentments in historical and polemical context, and to recognize that even greater extremes framed his choices, scholars increasingly acknowledge that we should not blunt the edge of his intolerance. Partly in response to Herman, Hammond remarks that Swift's sectarian hostilities inform even apparently tolerant passages of *Gulliver's Travels*, leaving them uncomfortably at odds with liberal democratic conceptions of religious tolerance and civic inclusiveness.[45] S. J. Connolly persuasively interprets Swift's sermon on the martyrdom of Charles I as 'a nakedly party political document' by a man locked in the resentments of the past:

> Swift's argument is striking in its single-minded partisanship: the civil wars, in his view, happened because Puritan conspirators worked behind the scenes to inflame constitutional grievances that were in themselves susceptible to negotiation, in order to create the circumstances in which they could impose their religious dogmas on society as a whole. There is also the quite clear suggestion that the principles which had led them to do this remain alive in the dissenters of Swift's own day. On an issue of past politics that remained of considerable contemporary relevance,

Swift thus reveals himself to be either the prisoner or the unscrupulous purveyor of political and religious so strong as to distort his whole presentation of events. He also displays a disquieting facility for tendentious argument, tunnel vision and conspiracy.[46]

That Swift does not sacralize kingship puts him apart from English Tory extremism. An angry High-Church sectarianism forms as inseparable a part of his engagement in politics as his commitment to liberty and the Revolution.

In Swift's writings, as in the politics of Swift's day, the established Church and partisan politics were closely entwined. There is consequently no need to disparage his defection to the Tories as a self-serving abandonment of his earlier principles. Nor is it necessary to salvage his integrity by savaging his dalliance with the Whigs as misguided. *Sentiments of a Church-of-England Man* and *An Argument against Abolishing Christianity in England* were published only in his *Miscellanies in Prose and Verse* in 1711, where they appeared along with his *Project*, his *Letter from an Member of the House of Commons in Ireland*, the Bickerstaff papers, and some poems. Serving a Tory ministry by then, he obviously wanted these tracts to provide a retrospective display of political consistency. Nevertheless, we can probably credit what he says. Although a shift of party is not negligible, it overstates the evidence to claim, with Boyle, 'If Swift had religious principles during this period, they were either Whig or so inchoate and malleable that they cannot properly go under that term.'[47] Truculent and indecorous, Swift invariably spoke as a member of his Church. When he claims to have described himself to Somers as a High-Church Whig, he provides a reliable key to his politics. He had publicly demonstrated his hostility to dissent and his commitment to the primitive purity of the church by law established as early as *A Tale of a Tub*. He did not suddenly get religion – that is, become High Church – when he turned Tory. Although he wrote an unpublished tract to oppose the bill against occasional conformity, he sought assurances that the bill's opponents shared his commitment: 'I cannot but think (if mens highest assurances are to be believed) that several, who were against this bill, do love the Church, and do hate or despise Presbytery.'[48] The equivalence between loving the church and hating dissent is telling, as is the fact that he asked for this reassurance. It is harder to read his failure to publish. It might express discomfort with the task, but timing is everything in political debate. Swift had already published *A Discourse* too late to affect the turn of events. Another tract suggesting that the he followed events rather than shaping opinion would do little to raise his stock. His decision not to publish it later perhaps reflects his new allegiances and a desire not to complicate his picture of his obvious consistency, but he did publish his *Project* and his *Letter* on the Test while still hoping for Whig favour. His religious convictions form a consistent part of his political thought.

His political allegiance, unlike his clerical office, was not a matter of personal identity. But Church politics placed a partisan in the political landscape only in conjunction with his constitutional position. Rooted in the mid-seventeenth century civil wars, political affiliations were determined by positions on two major axes, the religious and the political.[49] '"We routed Jack Presbyter, horse and foot", wrote an exultant Tory' after the defeat of a Whiggish measure in William's first Parliament.[50] Just this partisan political idiom informs the caricatures of Jack and Peter in *A Tale of a Tub*. Since individuals struggled with the claims of both religious and constitutional issues, there was some diversity of opinion within each political camp. When Ehrenpreis suggests Swift's limited power 'to stretch his own opinions to fit those of the Junto', for example, his language reveals the inadequacy to this terrain of a simple binary division between Whig and Tory: *Sentiments* 'seems ultimately a disguised attack on policies normally attached to the Whigs, and an exposition of the doctrines which the anti-Jacobite "church party" shared with the "new country party"'.[51] Ehrenpreis's distinction struggles with what one historian calls 'the hybrid nature of Toryism in Anne's reign'.[52] The Tories were no less heterogeneous than the Whigs, who divided between country Whigs and court Whigs. Since a constitutional issue could divide non-Jacobite from Jacobite Tories (members of the 'church party'), defining Swift as 'really' Tory rather than Whig, say, distorts significant political complexities and forecloses options that seemed valid to him.

Suspicious of party, Swift recognized that he could not rely wholly on his conviction that, given unalterable human depravity, historical change would normally take the form of degeneration from a past ideal. Acquaintance with the powerful Whigs prompted Swift to think about party: 'It was then I first began to trouble myself with the difference between the principles of Whig and Tory; having formerly employed myself in other, and, I think, much better speculations.'[53] When Swift discussed party principles with Somers, he claimed, he positioned himself, as contemporaries did, on both political (constitutional) and religious axes. In highly evasive terms, he reflects that he was, 'in politics', a Whig:

> I talked often upon this subject with Lord Sommers; and told him, that, having been long conversant with the Greek and Roman authors, and therefore a lover of liberty, I found myself much inclined to be what they called a Whig in politics; and that, besides, I thought it impossible, upon any other principle, to defend or submit to the Revolution ...[54]

Swift stops well short of embracing a specifically partisan identity. In politics, he was 'much inclined to be', he concedes, 'what they called a Whig'. He affirms a constitutional position he held without wavering: the Glorious Revolution was necessary and therefore justified. On the basis of that position, he would throughout his life identify himself as an Old Whig, a label that expresses his commitment to the Revolution settlement while evading a statement of contemporary party allegiance. Writing this self-justifying account after the fall of the Tory ministry that replaced the Whigs, the ministry he disobliged Whig friends by serving,[55] Swift suggests that he has behaved consistently. At the time, he felt an inclination to ally himself with the group led by Lord Somers, the Court Whigs, but an inclination is not a commitment. He remained suspicious of faction and refused to identify himself explicitly with a particular party.

Swift claimed to have explained his religious as well as his political position to Lord Somers. The ordained minister who dedicated *A Tale of a Tub* to Somers in 1704 may well have done so. He may have felt inclined to identify himself as a Whig 'in politics',

> But, as to religion, I confessed myself to be an High-churchman, and that I did not conceive how any one, who wore the habit of a clergyman, could be otherwise ... That I would not enter into the mutual reproaches made by the violent men on either side; but, that the connivance, or encouragement, given by the Whigs to those writers of pamphlets, who reflected upon the whole body of the clergy, without exception, would unite the church, as one man, to oppose them: And, that I doubted his Lordship's friends did not consider the consequence of this.

In the originally disparaging phrase that Swift adopts, *high* means 'extreme' or 'strong'.[56] Swift is making strong claims for the authority of the established church as part of the legal framework established at the Restoration and, following James II's threat to it, the Revolution. Identifying himself as a High-Churchman, he is asserting that a gulf divides the episcopal Church of England from Protestant dissent. He is willing to defend the dignity of his office, and the political consequences of attacks on the clergy, even to Somers and Lord Halifax, 'to whom I have talked in the same manner'.[57] Swift enters partisan politics as what he remains, a High-Church supporter of the Revolution.

These positions, it worth noting, do not predict a particular party allegiance. People of similar background and convictions could find themselves in different political camps. High-Church influences led Tindal to Roman Catholicism, back to the Church of England, and then to deism. Ireland produced not only the Whiggish Swift but also, to name another clergyman, the non-juring Jacobite polemicist Leslie – not to mention the freethinker Toland. However, Swift's early writings do confirm what he says he told the Whigs. His position on the Revolution gave him a point of contact with Whig appeals to the law and the ancient constitution though not to extreme contract theory and the right of resistance; a threat to the church or an attack on its clergy would, as he warned, divide him from them. While it would hardly have been politic (or necessary) to say so to a Whig statesman as shrewd as Somers, the corollary also held. Although Swift's standing as a High-Church clergyman gave him a point of contact with the Tories, a threat to the Revolution settlement would divide him, as a member of what Ehrenpreis calls 'the anti-Jacobite "church party"', from other

Tories. On the death of Queen Anne, the Tories would split along just this fault line.

Whig reliance on dissenting support notwithstanding, the routine partisan accusation that they were enemies of the established church represents a lurid distortion of the facts. Since Protestant dissenters amounted to a mere six per cent of the population, a party could hardly confine its appeal to them.[58] The bill that Swift agreed to oppose after discussing it with Somers, Peterborough, and Burnet did not remove any constraints on the dissenters; it simply avoided tightening them further. In 1709, the Whig Sir James Montagu – brother of a Junto lord – actually moved that the House of Commons condemn a dissenting pamphlet that attacked the Test! In exchange for the High-Church Tory Earl of Nottingham's support for Whig foreign policy, the Whigs supported the bill against occasional conformity that passed in 1711![59] Even after the proscription of the Tories following the Hanoverian succession, the Whigs stopped short of eliminating the sacramental test. It is easy to overstate the extent to which even Low-Church Whigs saw themselves as champions of dissent. If we consider Swift as a potential Whig, it is certainly safe to say that he would be at daggers drawn with radical Whigs who sympathized with the dissenters' longing for unrestricted access to civic office. But it is equally safe to say that many Whigs wanted nothing of the sort.

If we consider Swift as a potential Tory, on the other hand, it is easy to see that his intransigent High-Churchmanship would find a more congenial home among the Tories. But it is also clear that he would find himself in difficult company 'in politics'. Although Tories like Swift supported the Revolution and felt that the subject owed obedience not to the Crown alone but to the Crown-in-Parliament, many Tories retained absolutist leanings, feeling that the subject owed passive obedience directly to the monarch personally. Even a compensating emphasis on High-Church measures could not always mask this division within the Tories. Late in 1702, for example, the Tory-dominated House of Commons that had attempted to pass an act against occasional conformity moved a one-year extension to the time within which office holders had to take an oath abjuring James Edward Stuart, the Old Pretender. Required by an Act of William III, the oath offended Jacobite Tories who felt, on religious grounds, that they must not resist the direct heir of James II. Continuing the parliamentary dissension that Swift had attacked in *Discourse*, the Whig-dominated House of Lords returned the bill to the Commons after adding anti-Jacobite amendments that thwarted the intention of the bill, notably a declaration making it treason to try to subvert the Protestant succession. The amended Act passed on 13 February 1703 – an outcome possible only if a significant number of Tories voted with the Whig minority.[60] Given the right circumstances, some Tories could join with Whigs to subvert a High-Church Tory bill that was inconsistent with their constitutional views. On this contested middle ground, it makes sense that Swift felt himself drawn first to the Whig jurist Lord Somers and later to the opposition-Whig-turned-Tory Robert Harley. Swift could come to terms with Tories who had travelled far enough from the royalism of the Exclusion Crisis, emphasizing other aspects of Tory thought. As Harris argues, 'rather than seeing the Tories as royal absolutists, it is better to see them as conservative legal-constitutionalists, deeply committed to the rule of law and the Anglican Church'.[61] Swift's reluctance to identify himself in partisan terms seems appropriate, because he would likely find himself in a minority within either party. Whigs and Tories could find themselves sharing, not always comfortably, the terrain on which pragmatic political decisions were made, and Swift could be comfortable there.

In the second portion of *Sentiments of a Church-of-England Man*, Swift's commitment 'as to religion' governs the way he presents his principles 'in politics'. His opposition to absolutism is as visceral and consistent as his resentment of dissent, an impulse rather than a reasoned position:

> Where any one *Person* or *Body* of Men, who do not represent the *Whole*, seize into their Hands the Power in the last Resort; there is properly no longer a Government, but what *Aristotle*, and his Followers, call the *Abuse* and *Corruption* of one. This distinction excludes arbitrary Power, in whatever Numbers; which, notwithstanding all that *Hobbes*, *Filmer*, and other have said to its Advantage, I look upon as a greater Evil than *Anarchy* it self; much as a *Savage* is in a happier State of Life, than a *Slave* at the Oar.[62]

This conviction that even anarchy is preferable to life under an absolute ruler distinguishes Swift from those extreme Tories for whom an absolute order is preferable to disorder. He consequently finds Filmer – the spokesman for the Tory absolutist tradition continued by Leslie – no more appealing than Hobbes. He approaches the question of political power with little of the veneration for the sacred person of the divinely sanctioned monarch that characterizes much Tory constitutional discussion.[63]

In fact, Swift's discussion is strikingly impatient with theoretical elaborations of divine right or constitutional theory. Like heated religious quarrels between rivals who 'agree in all Fundamentals, and only differ in some Ceremonies; or, at most, meer speculative Points', Swift asserts, partisan quarrels demonstrate the human impulse toward pointless dissension::

> For Instance; do not the Generality of *Whigs* and *Tories* among us, profess to agree in the same *Fundamentals*; their Loyalty to the Queen, their Abjuration of the *Pretender*, the Settlement of the Crown in the *Protestant* Line; and a *Revolution Principle*? Their Affection to the Church Established, with Toleration of *Dissenters*? Nay, sometimes they go farther, and pass over into each other's Principles; the *Whigs* become great Asserters of the Prerogative; and the *Tories*, of the People's Liberty ...[64]

Swift overestimates the breadth of Tory commitment to the Protestant succession. He underestimates the extent to which a struggle for the spoils of office animates partisan disagreements. But he is consistently impatient with political parties and with the elaborate political arguments that magnify their differences.

Nor does the Revolution compel complex analysis. To suggest that James had any reason to fear his father's fate is 'an improbable Scandal'. His flight therefore justifies acting to restore government: 'As to the *Abdication* of King *James*, which the Advocates on that Side look upon to have been forcible and unjust, and consequently void in it self; I think a Man may observe every Article of the *English* Church, without being in much Pain about it'.[65] It nevertheless did pain many in the English Church, including those non-jurors who doubted the legitimacy of the Convention Parliament, which was not lawfully called by a king. Swift treats gently but without special sympathy 'those, who, from a meer Scruple of Conscience, refuse to join with us upon the Revolution Principle; but for the rest, are, I believe, as far from loving arbitrary Government, as any others can be, who are born under a free Constitution, and are allowed to have the least Share of common good Sense'.[66] He ignores, as if they were insignificant, Anglican absolutists. If monarchy is not constrained by law, he feels, the most tyrannical actions cannot be resisted, leading to intolerable consequences: 'I desire no stronger Proof that an Opinion must be false, than to find very great Absurdities annexed to it; and there cannot be greater than in the present Case: For it is not a Speculation, that Kings may run into such Enormities as above-mentioned ...'.[67] Legitimate power, on the other hand, is always limited:

> Hence appears the Absurdity of that Distinction between a King *de facto,* and one *de jure,* with respect to us; For every *limited* Monarch is a King *de jure,* because he governs by the Consent of the *Whole*; which is Authority sufficient to abolish all precedent Right. If a King come in by *Conquest,* he is no longer a *limited* Monarch: If he afterwards consent to Limitations, he becomes immediately King *de jure,* for the same Reason.[68]

In brief, Swift dismisses distinctions over which some in his Church agonized. His comfort with an effective king in possession could align him with those who saved appearances by adopting a providential interpretation of the Revolution, but he seems primarily committed to a king who will rule effectively within constitutional limits.

Swift's origins are pertinent here. The bloody war against James II's tyranny had shaped Anglo-Irish attitudes, fostering gratitude for the support of a strong, effective monarch in possession of the crown and a disinclination to question the sources of effective authority. Connolly characterizes the dominant pattern as 'a marked concern with effective authority as opposed to legitimacy, and a notably greater willingness than their English counterparts to discuss the whole episode in terms of war and of the breakdown and reconstitution of the political order'.[69] Swift's pragmatic resistance to interpretation of the constitution no doubt reflects

Anglo-Irish experience. Nevertheless, he treats non-jurors and proponents of passive obedience with remarkable gentleness. He treats their error as a misreading, a literal-minded application to the monarch of a loyalty due to the legislature as a whole. Since the most savage satire of *A Tale of a Tub*, like that of Pope's *Dunciad* later, is directed at inept readers, Swift's gentleness is surprising. He respects, it seems, the sound impulse to work within the frame of the law. His motive is, in part, tactical: he is writing for an English audience, who regarded the Revolution as bloodless. But it also embodies Swift's position as a clergyman of the Church of England. The errors of the clergy and the Church they serve inevitably command his sympathy if not his assent.

Swift engaged with party, that is, as someone inclined to the Whigs, as his background encouraged, but in fact capable of positioning himself on a contested middle ground. Swift returned to London in 1707 with his first political mission, a task at once political and religious. His experience as an emissary for the Church of Ireland both tested his convictions and, at the practical level on which writing inevitably supports a party position, shaped his political commitments. He had been in England when the Queen had announced what came to be known as Queen Anne's Bounty, a fund for poor Church-of-England clergymen to be created by revenue previously paid to the Crown from clerical first fruits and tenths.[70] The advantage of a similar grant from the Church of Ireland's first fruits and twentieths naturally struck members of that Church, and Swift campaigned vigorously both for that goal and, as someone acquainted with powerful Whig statesmen, for his role in seeking it. By the end of December 1704, Swift, perhaps impertinently, is reminding Archbishop King 'to use some of your Credit towards bringing to a good Issue the Promise the Queen made, at my Lord Bishop of Cloyne's Intercession, to remit the First Fruits and Tenths of the Clergy' and encouraging him to also seek the remission of a second tax, the crown rent.[71] The annual cost to the crown, he estimated, would be under £1,000, far less than the English grant had cost, and the benefit to oppressed clergy significant.[72] Visiting bishops and the Lord Lieutenant of Ireland occasionally took up the topic, so it took time to marshal support for Swift's proposal: 'I confess I was always of opinion that it required a Sollicitor of my Level, after Your Grace had done Your Part,' he writes from Leicester in December 1707, but he is still awaiting instructions: 'I am in the dark how far my L^d L^t is pleased to approve my having any Share in solliciting that Business Your Grace spoke to me about'. He is also awaiting a letter of authorization signed by the archbishops and bishops available in Dublin, a letter that would reach him only in February.[73]

This ticklish task required boldness, deference, and scrupulous attention to forms. On a visit to London in 1705, King had deferred to the Lord Lieutenant, the Duke of Ormond, who had power to act independently.[74] After agreeing to Swift's role, he advised in December 1707 that it would be good if Swift could engage Lords Somers and Sunderland but unfortunate if appealing to another interest offended the Lord Lieutenant, now the Earl of Pembroke.[75] In April 1708, Somers asked Swift for his opinion about the Test clause, 'which I gave him truly, thô with all the Gentleness I could, Because I am inclined and oblidged to value the Friendship he professes for me; so he is a Person whose Favor I would manage in this Affair of the First-fruits'.[76] Unfortunately for Swift, the Jacobite danger put the Irish Test into play. Especially after the Pretender's attempt to invade Scotland in spring 1708, Irish dissenters could make the case to the English government that Protestant Ireland would be stronger if the Protestant interest were not divided; that is, if dissenters were not excluded from military office. As William King put it in a letter of 7 April 1708, 'great Art is used to advance the Dissenters Interest on this occasion'.[77] Swift vividly makes the opposite case, but many English ministers understandably feared Roman Catholic Jacobites backed by France more than Irish Presbyterians. Hence Swift's tact. He needed Somers and asked him, as a step toward securing an interview with Lord Godolphin, the Lord Treasurer, to ask Lord Sunderland to allow him to renew their acquaintance. Somers complied, and by June, much put off by busy statesmen, Swift has an appointment with Godolphin himself.

The result was bitterly disappointing to Swift, although it was some time before failure was certain. Swift had heard as early as January, 'whispered by some who are fonder of politicall Refinements than I', that what he sought could perhaps only be purchased by agreeing to support the elimination of the sacramental test in Ireland. According to Swift's masterful account to King of his interview with Godolphin in June, verbal indirection made the crude bargain obvious but never explicit:

> that as to those [first fruits] in Ireland, they were an inconsiderable Thing, not above 1000*l*. or 1200*l*. a Year, which was almost nothing for the Queen to grant upon two Conditions. First, That it should be well disposed of. And secondly, That it should be well received with due Acknowledgments; in which Cases he would give his Consent, otherwise to deal freely with me, he never would. I said as to the first, that I was confident the Bishops would leave the Methods of disposing it entirely to her Majesty's Breast; as to the second, her Majesty, and his Lordship might count upon all the acknowledgments, that the most grateful and dutiful Subjects could pay to a Prince. That I had the Misfortune to be altogether unknown to his Lordship, else I should presume to ask him whether he understood any particular Acknowledgments. He replied, by Acknowledgments, I do not mean any Thing under their Hands, but I will so far explain my self to tell you, I mean better Acknowledgments than those of the Clergy of England.

Requesting further clarification of what King in a letter of 12 August 1708 calls 'the oraculous saying of the great man', Swift hears only, 'I can only say again, such Acknowledgments as they ought'. Swift and Robert Southwell, Secretary of State for Ireland, later 'agreed in our interpretation of the Oraculous saying, which has perplexed you; and fixed it upon the Test'.[78] For King as for Swift, this was an impossible price to pay. Swift could not get what he wanted. King continued to hear rumours that Pembroke had independently achieved the grant, but this proved yet another false hope.

The appointment of the Earl of Wharton as Lord Lieutenant of Ireland in December 1708 increased Swift's difficulties. One of the Junto lords, Wharton was a career politician and skilful electioneer who came from an aristocratic dissenting background. A principled champion of the dissenters, he ably opposed High-Church initiatives like the bills against occasional conformity. Since he also had a reputation for dissoluteness, including the drunken desecration of a parish church, he presented a target hard for Swift to resist: 'He goeth constantly to Prayers in the Forms of his Place, and will talk Bawdy and Blasphemy at the Chapel Door. He is a Presbyterian in Politics, and an Atheist in Religion; but he chuseth at present to whore with a Papist'.[79] This comes from *A Short Character of His Excellency Thomas Earl of Wharton, Lord Lieutenant of Ireland*, a brilliant libel that Swift published only two years later in conjunction with an attack on Wharton in the *Examiner*. For Swift, Wharton clearly embodied the principles and vices that provoked his sectarian prejudices: religious dissent is political faction; any heterodoxy tends to irreligion and immorality.

Of course an emissary of the Church of Ireland cannot neglect the Lord Lieutenant [as chaplain] of Ireland, and King encouraged him to cultivate the new head of government in Ireland. This would further his own ends as well as his Church's: 'As to your own concern, you see hardly any thing valuable is obtained any otherwise than by the government; and therefore if you can attend the next Lord Lieutenant, you, in my opinion, ought not to decline it'; but Swift would not court the Earl's favour: 'I made no manner of application for the post', he said to Dean Stearne.[80] Wharton appointed Ralph Lambert. A fellow student of Swift's at Trinity College, Lambert had preached a sermon urging Protestant unity in Ireland. When the deanery of Down became available the next year, it went to Lambert, who was supported (Swift believed) by the Archbishop of Canterbury and other English bishops; he would eventually become a bishop. As King had advised his truculent emissary, 'hardly any thing valuable is obtained any otherwise than by the government'. In his memorials to Harley about the first fruits, Swift claimed that it was because of Lambert, censured by the lower house of Convocation for a tract he had written, that Wharton had prorogued Convocation, ending consideration of the first fruits.[81] Those preferred instead of him thwarted his legitimate goals. By December, he vented his frustration in *A Letter from a Member of the House of Commons in Ireland to a Member of the House of Commons in England concerning the Sacramental Test*. He did so anonymously, of course, but not unrecognizably in the circles that mattered.

Frustration strengthened Swift's Irish identity. It was not just that it seemed difficult to obtain a modest benefit for the Church of Ireland, a benefit Swift thought had already been promised. Rather, the people whose favour he was seeking seemed determined to undermine one of the few legal protections his church enjoyed. Archbishop King complained in September 1708 that it was futile to plead the good of Ireland: 'For I found the good of Ireland has no weight at all. And it is a great mistake in all the applications we make, to allege as we commonly do that such a thing will help or mischief us, for perhaps those considerations will have a quite different effect from what we intend'.[82] In his *Letter*, Swift forces Irish realities (as he saw them) on the attention of English readers. The distinction of parties is largely irrelevant in Ireland, he claimed, where almost everyone staunchly supports the Protestant succession, 'So that the Parties among us are made up, on one side, of *moderate Whigs*', clearly the camp in which he sees himself,[83] and the ever fissioning minority:

> on the other, of *Presbyterians* and their *Abettors*; by which last I mean, such who can equally go to a *Church* or a *Conventicle*; or such who are indifferent to all Religion in general; or, lastly, such who affect to bear a personal Rancor towards the Clergy.[84]

He asserted his belief in 'the National Church, and the only one established by Law', expressed willingness to grant to Dissenters the toleration they enjoyed in England, 'But if once we repeal our *Sacramental Test*, and grant a *Toleration*, or suspend the Execution of the Penal Laws,' he argued, 'I do not see how we can be said to have any Established Church remaining; or rather why there will not be as many Established Churches as there are Sects of Dissenters'.[85] This sense of a society disintegrating into atoms links *Letter* with *A Tale of a Tub*. His political principles inform his defence of the Irish Test as well as conversations with Somers.

Swift's sense of alienation from Ireland's English masters appears not just in these routine assertions but also in a famous bit of sarcasm that asserts Ireland's willingness to sacrifice its interests on the altar of English convenience:

> If your little Finger be sore, and you think a Poultice made of our *Vitals* will give it any Ease, speak the Word, and it shall be done; the Interest of our whole Kingdom is, at any Time, ready to strike to that of your poorest *Fishing Town*; it is hard you will not accept our Services, unless we believe, at the same Time, that you are only consulting our Profit, and giving us Marks of your Love.[86]

More gravely, Swift urges that the number of Dissenters in Ireland makes them more dangerous than the numerous and by now thoroughly subjugated Roman Catholics:

> It is agreed, among Naturalists, that a *Lyon* is a larger, a stronger, and more dangerous Enemy than a *Cat*; yet if a Man were to have his Choice, either a *Lyon* at his Foot, bound fast with three or four Chains, his Teeth drawn out, and his Claws pared to the Quick, or an angry *Cat* in full Liberty at his Throat; he would take no long Time to determine.[87]

Swift's fear of dissent here expresses itself as the startling verbal aggression that we associate with the colonial outrage in his later Irish tracts. The English reader may not agree, but he is likely to remember both message and messenger.

The writer of this last passage would obviously not see eye to eye with a Protestant like Wharton. Swift nevertheless approached the new Lord Lieutenant on the subject of the first fruits in March 1709, when Wharton not surprisingly put him off. Swift sees that there is at present little he can do: 'I observe such a Reluctance in some Friends, whose Credit I would employ, that I begin to think no further of it'.[88] He never had a kind word for this particular Whig nor, he claimed, a warm word from him:

> It was the first time I was ever in company with the Earl of Wharton; he received me with sufficient coldness, and answered the request I made in behalf of the clergy with very poor and lame excuses, which amounted to a refusal. I complained of this usage to Lord Sommers, who would needs bring us together to his house, and present me to him; where he received me as drily as before.[89]

Where there was more sympathy, Wharton could be a powerful patron. He made Addison one of his secretaries and then arranged for him to become an MP in Ireland as well as England. Attempting to direct Swift where his own interest lay, Somers had obliged him to deliver a letter to Wharton in Ireland. Despite some bluster to his friends, Swift behaved himself publicly even though he would not court Wharton, and Addison continued to have hopes for his friend. Since Wharton had a sharp eye for the prevailing winds, he provoked no confrontation over the Test. The session went smoothly despite a minor storm in Convocation, which met at the same time as Parliament. When the lower house of Convocation heated itself trying to forward censure of Lambert for a pamphlet he had written, Wharton ended the debate by ending the parliamentary session.

By September, he and Addison were back in London, and Swift was neither better nor worse off than before. Swift had not changed his personal situation for the better. Apart from the pleasure of Addison's company, nothing since his return to Ireland had sweetened the bitter pill of failure. Unwilling to abandon principle and bargain with Godolphin, Swift failed to win any preferment honourably or dishonourably. The bishopric of Waterford had gone to another despite Somers's support. While he pursued his failed mission in England, King had cautioned that his chances of preferment in Ireland suffered by his absence: 'Had you been here, I believe something might have been done for you before this'.[90] He was deservedly proud of his commitment to principle: 'I would beg your Grace,' he wrote to King, 'to have favourable Thoughts to me on such an Occasion, and to assure you that no Prospect of making my Fortune, shall ever prevail on me to go against what becomes a Man of Conscience and Truth, and an entire Friend to the established Church'.[91] So it proved. Swift's political ambitions contained a core of principle, and he would not sacrifice the Test.[92] Discouragement and self-pity colour his anticipation of Ireland: 'I shall go for Ireland some Time in Summer, being not able to make my Friends in the Ministry consider my Merits, or their Promises, enough to keep me here, so that all my Hopes now terminate in my Bishoprick of Virginia'.[93] Swift had early considered a position abroad. Here, this forlorn (and obscure) hope expresses his disillusionment with both London and Dublin.[94] The failure of his modest mission was galling.

This failure was not Swift's alone. Guided by Somers, the Whigs had proved themselves adept at recognizing and recruiting talented writers. Despite their victory in the 1708 general election, however, they failed to reward Swift, who had courted their favour for most of a decade. Although J. Kent Clark commends Wharton for his judicious appointments, he represents this oversight as a significant failure:

> His greatest mistake in distributing favours was his failure to select Jonathan Swift, then a Whig, as his chaplain. Instead he chose Dr Ralph Lambert, who was shortly appointed dean of Derry. Had Wharton fastened the great satirist to the Whig establishment he might have deprived Robert Harley's government of its finest propagandist and saved himself many lashes.[95]

A High-Churchman, Swift nevertheless expressed fervent Whig principles. He had demonstrated formidable talents ready to be called into service. He had met only fair words.

Grander events now shaped Swift's political development, eventually bringing new opportunities. Addison's return to Ireland in May 1710 brought friendship to a man who had just lost his mother.[96] Unfortunately, he came with Wharton, whose return renewed fears for the Test. Written in anticipation of this new Parliament but published only posthumously, Swift's *A Letter to a Member of Parliament in Ireland upon the Chusing a New Speaker there* is the first essay on Irish politics that Swift directed to Irish readers. Selecting a speaker committed to the Test, Swift argued, is a mark of the Irish House's independence of the English government. Anticipation of the choice allowed Swift to think through the tension between the sense of the house and the partisan obligations (or hopes of office) that swayed MPs to support minority measures backed by a ministry: 'A Majority with a good Cause are negligent and supine. They think it sufficient to declare themselves upon Occasion in Favor of their Party; but, sailing against the Tide of Favor and Preferment, they are easily scattred and driven back.' Swift accepts the importance of party to the workings of Parliament, but he is appealing to members' spirit of independence by presenting a Country analysis of the way in which the Court can use place to corrupt the independence of Parliament. In context, he is also appealing to a developing sense that the Irish Test is a bulwark of national independence. The 'High-flying Whigs' may speak for the dissenters against the Test; 'the Dissenters and their high-flying Advocates', he later says.[97] But 'the Moderate Men, both of High and Low Church' – the moderate Whigs of his *Letter concerning the Sacramental Test*, which was reprinted in Ireland in 1709 – 'profess to be wholly averse from this Design, as thinking it beneath the Policy of common Gardners to cutt down the onely Hedge that shelters from the North'.[98] The threat from the north is, of course, the Presbyterianism of Ulster; the hedge, the Test. Swift's stance here will become a staple of his propaganda. He speaks with common sense – here in the voice of a practical gardener – for and to the level-headed rural landowners who form the political nation. As so often, Swift would find that an Irish Parliament failed to make Irish sense: the Commons mildly approved the government's nominee for speaker. But the Irish spokesman was developing a skillful grasp of parliamentary behaviour and national politics that would serve him well.

More promising, war and the Church, the political concerns closest to Swift, were already bringing down the Junto by the time Wharton and Addison reached Dublin in 1710. Despite a brilliant series of allied military victories under the Duke of Marlborough, the War of the Spanish Succession had dragged on since 1702. Although France too was exhausted, the allies demanded more than Louis XIV would grant. In the spring of 1709, he broke off negotiations that had raised hopes of a peace. As had also been the case in 1706, the obstacle was the allied demand that Louis's grandson, the Duke of Anjou, now enthroned as Philip V of Spain, renounce the Spanish throne to prevent any possibility that a single monarch might unite the Spanish and French thrones. Adopted by the House of Lords in 1707, after disasters in Spain, the commitment made in 'Somers's millstone motion of "No peace without Spain"' figured in a Parliamentary address setting out acceptable peace conditions in March 1709, helping to scuttle negotiations. Marlborough's request to be made captain-general for life, denied by the Queen, doubtless reflected his sense that the inconclusiveness of the war could undermine commitment to the war. Unless the allies could conquer France itself, not just defeat its armies in the low countries and on the Danube, military victory led only to diplomatic failure and further war.[99] Back in London, Swift would find himself deeply engaged in these issues. What mattered immediately was that the Junto, committed to a vigorous land war, was increasingly out of touch with a war-weary nation, especially after Marlborough's pyrrhic victory at Malplaquet in September 1709.

The Junto compounded its problems by turning a nuisance into a *cause célèbre* that allowed the opposition to paint them – as Swift claimed to have warned – as enemies of the established church. A firebrand High-Churchman who had been educated with Addison at Magdalen College, Oxford, Sacheverell provided the nuisance. On 5 November 1709, he preached a sermon to the Lord Mayor and Aldermen of London at St Paul's. 5 November was celebrated as the anniversary of Protestant England's providential escape from menacing Catholicism in 1588 (destruction of the Spanish Armada), 1605 (failure of the Gunpowder plot), and 1688 (William's landing at Torbay to oppose James II). Yet Sacheverell provocatively took 'In perils amongst false brethren' as the text of a diatribe denouncing the danger to the Church posed by dissenting Protestants. Enormously popular once published and critical of the government, Sacheverell's sermon, needless to say, offended a ministry that had displayed its Low-Church solidarity with dissenting Protestants by passing an Act naturalizing foreign Protestants, something many Anglicans feared would invite foreign dissenters to flock to England. The nuisance became *cause célèbre*, however, only when the ministry tried to make its point by impeaching the preacher. Delayed and then dragged out, his trial (27 February to 20 March 1710) before the House of Lords attracted massive crowds and provoked widespread popular demonstrations for the Church and Sacheverell. His narrow conviction and mild sentence – suspension from preaching for three years – was popularly regarded as a vindication. Sacheverell was widely celebrated and well rewarded. A populace hungry after a poor harvest, weary of being taxed to support an apparently endless Protestant war against Catholic France, turned against a Whig ministry that threatened the Church. It wanted, and gradually got, a change of ministry.

In Swift's Dublin, that change created new opportunities for the Church of Ireland and its eager emissary. Swift returned to England in August on the royal yacht with the Lord Lieutenant, once again an emissary for the first fruits. He had a commission from the archbishops and bishops of Ireland urging the bishops of Ossory and Killaloe, then in England, to pursue the matter but to entrust it to Swift should they have to leave London. The time before the appointment of a new Lord Lieutenant of Ireland seemed especially opportune for a less exalted emissary like Swift. Astonishingly, he met rapid, gratifying success. More predictably, bureaucratic delays and the political rivalries among the Church's agents lessened what he gained and deprived him of the acknowledgment he felt was his due. As the drama of the First Fruits played itself out, Swift rapidly found himself enmeshed in new political circles that gratified his ambition by actively courting him for what he could contribute to the paper war between the new ministry and the opposition. Swift became a remarkably effective political writer during that propaganda campaign, developing the skills he later exploited as the Drapier. He enjoyed his first political success as an agent for his Church.

Swift returned to London in September 1710, eager to approach the new ministry. He had already assured King that 'all Affairs in the Treasury are governed by Mr. Harley', who was also the head of the new ministry. Although he had yet to meet Harley, he had been approached through an intermediary during his last London stay. 'I will apply to Mr. Harley, who formerly made some Advances towards me,' he wrote to King, 'and unless he be altered, will, I believe, think himself in the Right to use me well'.[100] Swift found progress toward assurance of success gratifyingly rapid. By the end of September, he had an appointment to meet Harley. After meetings in early October, Swift is hopeful. A man of evident piety, Harley listens attentively, presents his memorial to the Queen, and seems to be one who loves the Church.[101] By 15 October, he tells Swift that the queen has 'consented to give the First-Fruits and Twentieth Parts, and will, we hope, declare it to-morrow in the cabinet'; by 21 October the queen has 'granted' them but requires secrecy 'because the queen designs to signify it to the bishops in Ireland in form, and to take notice, That it was done upon a memorial from me'. By 3 November, he has 'leave to write the primate and archbishop of Dublin ... but they are to take no notice of it, till a letter is sent them by the queen's orders from lord Dartmouth, secretary of state, to signify it'.[102] Formalities must follow, but Swift has been courted by a great man who values him:

> I believe never any thing was compassed so soon, and purely done by my personal credit with Mr. Harley, who is so excessively obliging, that I know not what to make of it, unless to shew the rascals of the other party that they used a man unworthily, who had deserved better.[103]

After prolonged failure, this was gratifying. Swift has chalked up a genuine success. In a few months, he has accomplished more than was earlier managed in years. Even a man more bound than Swift was by vows elsewhere would find it difficult to resist seduction.

By the time he was comfortably in bed with the Tories, however, administrative procrastination and ecclesiastic politics combined to renew familiar exasperations and confirm Swift's conviction that reward would invariably elude his grasp. Swift wanted rapid progress but encountered delays. At the end of the year, he presses St John to intercede with Harley and learns early in the new year that a warrant has been passed to draw up a patent. Dated 7 February 1711 – well after the Duke of Ormond has become the new Lord Lieutenant of Ireland – the patent would be announced publicly only in Ormond's address to the Irish Parliament on 12 July 1711. By November, Swift had expressed alarm that the bishops of the Church of Ireland, kept in the dark, were asking Ormond to solicit had already been granted, and Swift has been asked to surrender his own authorization. Angry, Swift he would later blame the bishops' intervention for thwarting his scheme of a remission of the crown rents.[104] By the time the First Fruits were formally granted, Swift's role was largely invisible, especially to those who preferred to assume that their efforts in conjunction with Ormond's had been effective. Suggestively, the bishop of Kildare, who had asked for Swift's authorization to be reclaimed and who later quashed a motion by the Board of First Fruits to thank Swift, was engaged in a legal dispute with Archbishop King. As King sympathetically admonished Swift in a letter on 1 September 1711, such rivalries provide the stuff of human nature and, therefore, politics:

> You know there are some, that would assume to themselves to be the only churchmen and managers, and can't endure that any thing should be done but by themselves, and in their own way; and had rather that all good things proposed should miscarry,

than be thought to come from other hands than their own, whose business it is to lessen every body else, and obstruct whatever is attempted, tho' of the greatest advantage to Church and State, if it be not from their own party.[105]

Swift's ecclesiastical mission thus provided a remarkably thorough schooling in partisan politics, although Swift was slow to take the point. He would greet the rivalries that later tore apart the Tory ministry with the same pained surprise.[106]

The pain that fuelled Swift's baffled anger sprang from the assertive but vulnerable independence at the root of his political stance. After a lifetime of dependence, he craved recognition of his independent worth. To be slighted as an anonymous underling offended him. Others, including King, encouraged to claim the reward his efforts had earned, and he acknowledged a modest ambition to the Earl of Peterborough: 'My ambition is to live in England, and with a competency to support me with honour. The Ministry know by this time whether I am worth keeping; and it is easier to provide for ten men in the Church than one in a civil employment'.[107] A letter from King urged him to secure 'some preferment, that may be called a settlement' but adds a warning that a solemn exercise of his gifts on a worthy subject was called for to 'answer some objections against you'.[108]

By writing as he did, Swift no doubt marred his own chances of preferment. Many works were fuelled by hostility or personal pique, including those on the Test that were collected in his *Miscellanies in Prose and Verse*, published in February 1711 and immediately popular.[109] The recent fifth edition of *A Tale of a Tub* added an Apology to distance the mature emissary of the Church from the youthful author and chasten an occasional passage but incorporated footnotes to satirize his critic, William Wotton.[110] In response to a cool reception by his old acquaintance Godolphin, whom the Queen had commanded to break his staff of office as Lord Treasurer, he retaliated with a clever lampoon, *The Virtues of Sid Hamet the Magician's Rod*, that was 'cried up to the skies; but nobody suspects me for it'[111] he claimed in October 1710. And if the ideal propagandist needs to combine anger with craft, Swift's *Character of the Earl of Wharton* demonstrates his suitability for political writing. As King pointed out, however, deft malice is hardly a commendation in a candidate for Christian preferment:

> We have published here a Character of the Earl of Wharton, late Lord Lieutenant of Ireland. I have so much [X]a[n]ity and justice as to condemn all such proceedings. If a governor behave himself ill, let him be complained of and punished; but to wound any man thus in the dark, to appeal to the mob, that can neither inquire nor judge, is a proceeding that I think the common sense of mankind should condemn. Perhaps he may deserve this usage; but a good man may fall under the same.[112]

Swift must have winced – and hoped for continued anonymity. No great harm was done, for Wharton enjoyed great rank, wealth, and power, but the sense that

Swift's anger is sometimes barely under control must have troubled fellow church-men like King.[113] Although his authorship of many of these works remained unknown, he was widely known as the author of *A Tale of a Tub*. It is suggestive that plans to introduce him to the queen, even have him preach before her, came to nothing.[114] An unusual Whig or Tory, Swift was clearly also an unusual vicar. Although it alarmed even his allies, the passion that fired his campaign for remission of the first fruits and twentieths animated his writing before and after he turned his attention, to use his terms to Somers, from religion to politics.

4 THE ECHO OF THE COFFEE HOUSE AND THE VOICE OF THE KINGDOM: PROPAGANDIST FOR A PEACE

At the beginning of his career as a writer for an English ministry, Swift arrived from Ireland as a vicar with a mission for his church. Welcomed by Robert Harley, the new premier minister, he rejoined but soon distanced himself politically from a circle of Whig friends that included the writers he most esteemed. At its end, his old mission for the church and a new political mission both accomplished, he departed for Ireland as a dean, distancing himself physically but not socially or politically from a new circle of Tory friends that included the writers he now most esteemed. He had found the political adjustment relatively easy, the estrangement from former friends wrenching. In the ministry's policy of ending the War of the Spanish Succession, he found a worthy cause. Disdaining coffee house chatter and affecting to speak for the nation, he put his mastery of Grub Street at the service of rural squires. In a series of brilliant essays and pamphlets attacking the personalities and institutions typical of the fiscal-military state, he extended *A Tale of a Tub*'s analysis of venal modernity to discredit the former Whig ministry and, especially, the Duke of Marlborough. Despite painful divisions within the ministry and within the Tory ranks, he helped them achieve the Peace of Utrecht, offending Britain's allies but winning solid treaty benefits as well as ending the war. Thanks to his self-destructive habit of lashing out angrily in print when his ministry seemed threatened, he won only an Irish reward for his English service. Blinded by his confidence that his own High-Church, Old Whig politics was virtually universal, he failed to anticipate the disintegration of the ministry and the party during the succession crisis provoked by Queen Anne's physical decline and death in 1714. After three and a half years of unparalleled success, he returned to Ireland from a defeated ministry, closely associated with a party that was tainted by suspicion of the Jacobitism he had never taken seriously. A few months after forming the Scriblerus Club, the society of wits he had always yearned for, he was exiled (as it often felt) to the country of his birth.

A month after meeting Harley, Swift had permission to communicate the success of his mission to the Archbishop of Armagh, his primate, and to King.[1] The day before he confided this success to Stella, *Examiner* no. 14 (2 November 1710) had already been published.[2] He was already writing for the new ministry. By obtaining the Queen's remission of the first fruits and twentieths for the Church of Ireland, Harley had secured his man. He added to an already impressive propaganda team a formidable writer whose talents the Whigs had spurned. Swift found a new mission. He would support a political goal important to the Queen, to the Harley-led ministry she had gradually appointed, and, judging from the Tory electoral triumph of 1710, to most of the political nation. He was to defend the ministry's policy of negotiating an end to the war, directing that defence, in the first instance, to an audience that embodied not only the stability of land but also his own beleaguered sense of independence, 'the smaller English country squires and the clergymen, freeholders, and tenants who made up the social complex dominated by such squires'.[3] The consequences of his shift of loyalty were momentous, affecting his society, his public character, and (though this could not have been foretold) his future in opposition and in Ireland. The effect on his society is conspicuous. By late May 1711, he will observe to Stella, 'Prithee, don't you observe how strangely I have changed my company and manner of living? I never go to a Coffee-house; you hear no more of Addison, Steele, Henley, lady Lucy, Mrs. Finch, lord Somers, lord Hallifax, &c. I think I have altered for the better'.[4] 'In the first half of [Queen Anne's] reign', W. A. Speck confirms, 'nearly all his private correspondence was with Whigs ... After 1710 their names almost completely disappear, and new ones occur, most of them Tories such as Henry St. John and Francis Atterbury.' Swift found this shift more wrenching than he here admits, and it naturally led to suspicion that he was self-serving rather than principled.[5] Apart from a difficult personal adjustment, however, it is surprisingly hard to see what of significance changed when Swift finally began writing in service of a ministry. He remained a High-Church clergyman committed to the Revolution settlement. After a decade of courting favour from without, he could write from within. He suddenly had an exhilarating scope for his talents, and he was serving a ministry that was, he thought, pursuing the national good by bringing to an end a long and expensive war. The cause of peace tapped his deepest convictions while inviting him to fulminate against the forces of modernity that were, he was coming to see, inextricably entangled in the cause of war.

Harley's success in winning over Swift is not surprising. He had a sharp eye for what his public relations team still needed. A man in his forties with a mission to accomplish, Swift had returned to England ready to reach out to those now in power. The cold reception from Godolphin that he avenged in his poetic lampoon, *The Virtues of Sid Hamet the Magician's Rod*, freed him to do so:

'Tis good to see what lamentable confession the Whigs all make me of my ill usage: but I mind them not. I am already represented to Harley as a discontented person, that was used ill for not being Whig enough; and I hope for good usage from him. The Tories drily tell me, I may make my fortune, if I please; but I do not understand them, or rather, I do understand them.⁶

In a bit of arrant flattery, Harley, Peterborough, and Prior praised Swift's lampoon after dinner.⁷ Frustrated by a decade's failure to win support from the Whigs, Swift was ripe for the plucking. Harley speedily accomplished his mission for the Church of Ireland. Although £1,000 a year remitted to the Irish Church left him not a penny better off,⁸ he found himself courted as a man who could serve the ministry.

On the strength of his pen, Swift had earlier won the acquaintance of the Junto lords. Having spent formative years discussing public policy with William Temple and a circle that extended to the King, he seems to have expected as much. Remarkably, he now gained access to yet a third community of powerful statesman, this time one that flattered his feeling that the Whigs had slighted him. A moderate former Whig, Harley like Somers was a remarkably able states-man and a bibliophile. He genuinely impressed Swift. While it would be wrong to overstate Swift's intimacy with the inner circles of policy making, there can be no doubt that Swift and Harley became warm friends despite the social dis-parity between an Anglo-Irish vicar and the English prime minister. When the ministry eventually fell apart, Swift expressed his loyalty to Harley. More telling, he included Harley in the Scriblerus Club, his new circle of wits, even though in this setting it was Harley who was out of his depth. In London in 1710, Harley gratified the ambitious writer by praising him, by presenting his Church's request to the Queen, and by assuring him of his success. In response, Swift agreed to edit the *Examiner*, becoming government pamphleteer and eventually *chef de propa-gande* for a ministry that coordinated a stable of writers. In this role – the French phrase reveals how new, even alien, this nameless position was – he managed what we now call the media for the government.⁹ His primary task as Examiner and pamphleteer was to persuade staunch Tories inside and outside the House to have patience with the ministry's moderation and, often, indirection. *A Tale of a Tub* had listed only three machines available to an orator, the pulpit, the stage itinerant and the ladder. Swift might seem to have found a fourth, but he seems in practice to have combined the familiar three. The air of unshakeable authority that exasperated his opponents certainly bespeaks the pulpit, but entertaining the literate mob associates him with the stage. Ready to exaggerate the perils he faced, he may even have imagined himself mounting the ladder to the noose when he later found himself with a price on his head for what he had said in print.

Personality obviously played a part in these new relationships. Principle coop-erated with 'a common sense of injured merit', Ellis suggests, to cement Swift's

friendship with Harley.[10] To this might be added a shared conviction of personal
rectitude, although Harley's led him to justify political deviousness in his cause,
and Swift's fostered the stark black-and-white contrasts of political caricature.[11]
Swift blossomed under his new success. The vanity he occasionally paraded in
his new role reveals how much his belated recognition pleased him. Consider
Examiner no. 45 (7 June 1711), which slyly acknowledges his kinship with Grub
Street:

> For my own Particular, those little barking Pens which have so constantly pursu'd
> me, I take to be of no further Consequence to what I have writ, than the scoff-
> ing Slaves of old, placed behind the Chariot, to put the General in mind of his
> Mortality; which was but a Thing of Form, and made no Stop or Disturbance in the
> Shew. However, if those perpetual Snarlers against me, had the same Design, I must
> own they have effectually compass'd it; since nothing can well be more mortifying,
> than to reflect that I am of the same Species with Creatures capable of uttering so
> much Scurrillity, Dulness, Falshood and Impertinence, to the Scandal and Disgrace
> of Human Nature.[12]

Swift paraded his genuine if limited power. As Mainwaring complained in *Medley*
no. 37 (11 June 1711), 'having occasion to compare himself to some body, who
shou'd he pitch upon but a very Great Conqueror?'[13] Swift imagines his critics
as slaves given significance only by his exalted presence. Like *A Tale of a Tub*'s
embodiment of popular success, a '*Mountebank in* Leicester-Fields',[14] however,
Mr. Examiner and his critics take their places together in a 'Shew' for the crowd.
Swift acknowledges that he is, scandalously, 'of the same Species' as 'those perpetual Snarlers'.[15]

White Kennet's hostile 1713 character of Swift suggests that Swift retained a
degree of self-important bustle:

> Dr. Swift came into the coffeehouse, and had a bow from every body but me. When
> I came to the antechamber to wait before prayers, Dr. Swift was the principal man
> of talk and business, and acted as a master of requests. He was soliciting the earl of
> Arran to speak to his brother the Duke of Ormond, to get a chaplain's place estab-
> lished in the garrison of Hull for Mr. Fiddes, a clergyman in that neighbourhood,
> who had lately been in gaol, and published sermons to pay fees. He was promising
> Mr. Thorold to undertake with my lord treasurer, that, according to his petition,
> he should obtain a salary of 200 per annum, as minister of the English church at
> Rotterdam. He stopped F[rancis] Gwynne, esq., going in with his red bag to the
> Queen, and told him aloud that he had something to say to him from my lord
> treasurer. He talked with the son of Dr. Davenant to be sent abroad, and took out
> his pocket book and wrote down several things, as *memoranda*, to do for him. He
> turned to the fire, took out his gold watch, and, telling him the time of the day, com-
> plained it was very late. A gentleman said 'he was too fast'. How can I help it', says
> the doctor, 'if the courtiers give me a watch that won't go right?' Then he instructed
> a young nobleman, that the best poet in England was Mr. Pope (a papist), who had

begun a translation of Homer into English verse, for which he must have them all subscribe; 'for', says he, the author *shall not* begin to print till *I have* a thousand guineas for him'. Lord treasurer, after leaving the Queen, came through the room beckoning Dr. Swift to follow him: both went off just before prayers.[16]

In Speck's words, Swift looks like 'the complete hanger-on at court'.[17] If sharp observation rather than malicious invention lies at the heart of this account, he may have performed his hard-earned and late-won public importance with something of the drag queen's gleeful excess. He made high claims for his Church, after all, and a certain amount of clerical swagger suited the High-Church reaction sparked by the Sacheverell Trial. Kennet, by contrast, was a Low-Church Whig associated with the editors of the *Medley*, the *Examiner*'s principal critic. An aspirant to clerical preferment jealously observing a successful rival, he is obviously a hostile witness. Maliciously, he exploits the reputation for irreligion that dogged Swift, as Archbishop King had warned him, because of his literary indecorum.[18] When he sneers at Pope's religion, he seems far pettier man than the High-Church target of his malice. As a Catholic, Pope was debarred from public office; the subscription would help a talented writer win the independence Swift and Kennet could find in the Church.[19] Swift enjoyed, perhaps immodestly, a modest amount of public importance as an associate of the most powerful ministers of the crown. Pomposity is hardly evidence of unscrupulousness, however, and even this caricature shows him generously trying to confer patronage on a writer less fortunate. We know from other sources that he prided himself on recommending Whig wits to his Tory masters.[20]

Although Swift cherished a sense of community, small rival communities pettily conflate the personal with the political. Swift and his closest Whig friends commendably tried but failed to separate the personal from the political. Parties are not just ideological positions. A political party will command loyalty by the presence or promise of judiciously distributed rewards of office, and it may thereby achieve a formidable degree of parliamentary coherence.[21] Nevertheless, its presentation of itself or a rival as a group united by beliefs shared by everyone within it and nobody outside it is pure wish fulfilment. The Whigs and Tories of Swift's day were as rife with internal disagreements as most political parties, and Swift could find ideological companions in either group. But a party is also a community who agree to mediate serious ideological and tactical differences through discussion, sometimes heated, among themselves. Its coherence is as much tribal as ideological. Swift imagined a community of wits that could ignore the frontier between parties, and he tried especially hard to remain friends with Addison, but he had in fact defected to a rival tribe. 'Mr. Addison and I meet a little seldomer than formerly, although we are still at bottom as good friends as ever', he wrote optimistically in November 1710, 'but differ a little about party'. A month later it was becoming obvious that despite their mutual respect, they cannot maintain their former intimacy:

> Mr. Addison and I are different as black and white, and I believe our friendship will go off, by this damned business of party: he cannot bear seeing me fall in so with this ministry; but I love him still as well as ever, though we seldom meet.[22]

Characteristically, Swift blames Addison for the strain he has imposed on their relationship. Since Wharton was one of Addison's patrons and an important part of the former Whig ministry that Swift was now maligning in print, there is something more than a little clueless about his feeling that he should be able to denigrate him in *Examiner* no. 18 (30 November 1710) and his scurrilous *A Short Character of His Excellency Thomas Earl of Wharton* (December 1710) without ruffling the feathers of friendship. The best that can be said for Swift is that cluelessness is sometimes a symptom of love. In the same *Examiner*, Swift playfully called Addison, now retired from the *Whig-Examiner*, a 'younger Brother, who Deceas'd about two Months ago'.[23] The affection is genuine, the political tension profound. Where confrontation made it impossible not to face the pain of the rupture between friends, as later happened with Steele, Swift will defensively explode in savage denunciation.

To explain this triumph of party over friendship, it is sometimes convenient to represent Addison as definitively Whig, Swift as somehow essentially Tory. But Swift's political position is never typical. His close creative association with Addison, and with Steele, demonstrates that they are not poles apart ideologically. What separates them is temperamental and discursive. 'Mr. Addison and I are different as black and white', Swift admits, but both writers identify themselves with Cato. Part of the admired '*Sextumvirate*' of heroes admired in *Gulliver's Travels*,[24] the classical figure of incorruptible opposition is at the centre of *Cato*, Addison's 1713 play, and *Cato's Letters*, John Trenchard and Thomas Gordon's Country Whig attack on the corruption responsible for the South Sea Bubble in 1720.[25] But Cato was part of their shared cultural background, a character type especially appealing to Swift.[26] While Addison's *Cato* domesticates a classical ideal in widely accessible English, however, *A Discourse* and *A Tale of a Tub* brandish Swift's Latin learning like a weapon. While Addison seems to imagine a dynamic present and even an optimistic future, Swift clings to an idealized past from which we can only degenerate. While Addison, like William King, belonged to the sect of mankind that hoped for the best, Swift characteristically feared the worst. Addison imagines Mr. Spectator as part of a club, a diverse group that includes a Worcestershire baronet, a fashionable member of the Inner Temple, a prosperous merchant, an army officer, an aging gallant, and a learned clergyman obviously less High Church than Swift.[27] Whether the topic is as neutral as it commonly seems to be or as politically charged as Addison's vision of Lady Credit in *Spectator* no. 3 (3 March 1711), which Swift challenged in *Examiner* no. 38 (19 April 1711), Addison imagines the political nation in remarkably inclusive terms as a community engaged in a continuing dialogue. With Steele in *The Tatler* and

The Spectator, he develops a supple discursive instrument for articulating consensus, an instrument that sometimes serves as a model for the public sphere theorized by Jürgen Habermas. The presence of Swift's 'sectarian truculence' on the same terrain, however, reveals the limitations of the model without obscuring Addison's distinctive achievement.[28] Because he imagines the political nation as a single, homogeneous social group, Swift slides easily between Mr. Examiner's standing as a country squire and his characteristic voice of disembodied authority.[29] Speaking for those alarmed by the social changes Addison embraces, Swift adopts an aggressive discourse that hardens social and partisan differences.[30] His version of the public sphere seems closer to the potentially riotous street crowd than the coffee house.

It is revealing that Addison wrote the first *Spectator*, Steele the description of the club in the second. In keeping with their relatively inclusive vision of the political nation, Addison and Steele seem to have been genuinely collegial and collaborative writers. Addison contributed forty-seven papers to the *Tatler* and collaborated with Steele on another twenty-two. The *Spectator*, the essay periodical that replaced the *Tatler*, was dominated by Addison but again represents a genuine collaboration on a common project. Swift's undoubtedly genuine contribution to the early *Tatler*, on the other hand, is uncertain. Richmond P. Bond concludes that contributors other than Steele and Addison 'were few, and their part in the journal either indeterminate or negligible'.[31] For Swift was not collaborative in anything like this sense. Looking forward to Swift's next set of wits, the Scriblerus Club, it is safe to say that the best works produced by Swift, Pope, Gay, and Arbuthnot are not *Three Hours after Marriage* or *The Memoirs of Martinus Scriblerus*, interesting as those collaborations are. These writers took hints from one another, brilliantly making them their own in, say, *The John Bull Pamphlets*, *The Beggar's Opera*, or *The Dunciad*. But Swift's closest literary associates are as fiercely independent as he is, quick to pick up hints but reluctant to surrender their prickly autonomy, imagining themselves in their writing in different ways. 'Given their contentious and rivalrous personalities', Patricia Bruckmann conjectures, 'it is just possible that a continuation of real meetings [ended by Swift's departure for Ireland] might have split them apart'. Their autonomy suits Swift's identification of the political nation with crusty small gentry and clergy. In the days of the *Tatler*, Swift more often than not contributed not papers but hints. Among the Scriblerians later, every hint was both a gift and a challenge. It is sometimes suspected, for example, that Swift's hint 'for our friend Gay' in a 1716 letter to Pope provided the germ of Gay's phenomenally successful *The Beggar's Opera*: 'Or what think you of a Newgate pastoral, among the whores and thieves there?'.[32] If this is the distance between hint and fulfilment, it is no surprise that we have trouble attaching Swift to *Tatler* papers he felt he deserved some credit for. Engaged in one another's works with playful, incisive intelligence, Swift and his friends maintained distinct identities. Suggestively, Pope was no better than Addison at revising Swift's poetry.[33] Their intensely competitive mutual emulation suggests that temperament played a large role in Swift's drift from the society of the Whigs.

Swift's change of context was not unusual, for members of both parties faced ideological challenges. They had to adapt as their convictions collided with recalcitrant events. Hence the uneven Tory shift from Exclusion-Crisis royalism toward legal-constitutionalist support for a limited monarchy.[34] Contemporary political rhetoric, J. G. A. Pocock argues, reveals people who shared an inherited political idiom moving in unanticipated directions as they grappled with unprecedented political realities:

> The analysis of the Machiavellian economics of Davenant has left us in a position to construct a schema of the attitudes toward land, trade, and credit of the Court and Country, Whig and Tory writers of the reigns of William III, Anne, and George I. These men ... were not constant in their political allegiances. Swift, Davenant, Defoe – to go no further – were found in differing company at different times of their lives, and ... these changes of front are best explained not by attempting to assess questions of commitment and consistency, venality and ambition, but by recognizing that they were employing a highly ambivalent rhetoric, replete with alternatives, conflicts, and confusions, of which they were well aware and in which they were to some extent entrapped. An anatomy of the great debate as between the 'landed' and 'monied' interests, conducted by the journalists and publicists of Anne's reign, reveals that there were no pure dogmas or simple antitheses, and few assumptions that were not shared, and employed to differing purposes, by writers on either side.[35]

There were many versions of Cato. Even opponents shared so many assumptions that it is impossible to extricate the label from the political situation in which someone claimed or was tarred by it.

The drift of events carried statesmen, too, to unexpected destinations. A Tory loyal to Charles II and even James II, Godolphin eventually found himself associating with the Whigs whom Harley dislodged in 1710. Marlborough, too, began as a Tory but followed the logic of his war policy into a Whig ministry with Godolphin. Since the high cost of the war expanded opportunities for government patronage, compromising the independence of the House, Country opposition to William III's war policy in the 1690s gradually threw the opposition Whig Robert Harley into Tory company: 'the logic of the anti-executive position as it developed in William's reign was essentially Tory'.[36] Had elections not produced a Tory landslide in 1710, he might even have participated in a Tory dominated mixed administration, as he had before his fall in 1708. Political writers shared many of their confusions with their political masters.

A loyal friend given an opportunity to exercise his talents in a different arena from his friends, Swift also formed new friendships. He celebrates his new circle in *Examiner* no. 27, playfully teasing them for qualities he in fact admires. Several have claims to wit and learning. Of Harley and St John, he speaks especially warmly. The latter, for example, remains accessible. Swift implicitly contrasts him with Sunderland: 'Besides, he has clearly mistaken the true use of *Books*, which he has thumb'd and spoil'd with *Reading*, when he ought to have multiplied them on his Shelves: Not like a great Man of my Acquaintance, who knew a *Book* by the *Back*, better than a *Friend* by the *Face*, though he had *never convers'd* with the former, and often with the latter.' Swift was attracted to St John's brilliance but, usually, steadied by Harley's integrity. Praising Harley's frugality with government funds, he also teases him gratefully for his openness to the clergy: 'And surely there is one Thing never to be forgiven him, that he delights to have his Table fill'd with *Black Coats*, whom he uses as if they were *Gentlemen*'. The last comment comes from the author of the solemn and undoubtedly sincere *Project for the Advancement of Religion and Reformation of Manners*. The clergy were often too poor to insist on their rank, let alone their national importance, and public disrespect was not uncommon. An anti-High-Church fable in the 1710 election accused the clergy of being parasites by representing an indignant countryman about to crush the flea ('Sir Blackcoat') that had been sucking blood from his backside![37] Even in less hostile contexts, the clergy could find themselves treated as upper servants. Swift was delighted to find himself in a congenial circle of intelligent, conversable statesmen whose leader was also a man of piety.[38]

Through Harley, Swift found not just a congenial circle but also a worthwhile political cause, the attempt to extricate his nation from the War of the Spanish Succession. Principle as well as opportunity won him over to the new ministry:

> But, to say the truth, the present ministry have a difficult task, and want me, &c. Perhaps they may be just as grateful as others: but, according to the best judgment I have, they are pursuing the true interest of the public; and therefore I am glad to contribute what is in my power.[39]

Since the new ministers might be no more sure to reward him than 'others' had been, he seems to have committed himself to a cause rather than a prize. The horrors of war always evoked his most passionate responses:

> This kingdom is certainly ruined as much as ever any bankrupt merchant. We must have *Peace*, let it be a bad or a good one, though no-body dares talk of it. The nearer I look upon things, the worse I like them. I believe the confederacy will soon break to pieces, and our factions at home increase. The ministry is upon a very narrow bottom, and stand like an Isthmus between the Whigs on one side, and violent Tories on the other. They are all able seamen, but the tempest is too great, the ship too rotten, and the crew all against them.[40]

When he looks nearer upon things, Swift fears the worst.

Significantly, he is looking through Harley's spectacles without the politician's pragmatic alertness to what can be done. Support for a war on the continent was conventionally more Whig than Tory; hence Marlborough's presence in a

Whig administration. Tories on the other hand tended to be more isolationist, favouring a blue-water foreign policy. Naval engagements rather than land wars played to traditional strengths, leaving the nation (it was felt) free of dangerous and expensive military entanglements while providing lucrative opportunities to pillage overseas colonies. The French threat to the English succession and subsequent English victories had initially created support for the Whig war policy. As the war dragged on inconclusively, however, the landed proprietors who paid the taxes that funded it grew weary. This created an opportunity for Harley, a politician as suspicious of party as Swift. He tried to avoid committing the administration – and the Queen – to a single party, preserving his freedom to manoeuvre. Unlike the extreme Tories, he wanted peace but not any peace at any price. Unlike the Whigs, he was unwilling to insist on dislodging the Bourbon ruler from the Spanish throne now that that policy had become untenable. Since Swift invariably saw himself defending the narrow ground that Martin carved out from the rival threats of Peter and Jack, he vividly represents Harley's ministry standing like an isthmus between extremes. He found Harley's vision of his situation compelling.

Swift's first task was to take over the *Examiner*, a Tory weekly intended to explain administration policy to country gentry and clergy. The need for a skilled hand is suggested by the fact that collected editions omit Atterbury's paper on passive obedience and hereditary right. Harley did not want to voice the views of the Tory extreme. Rather than stirring up High-Church backbench intransigence, he wanted to rally the Tories behind the moderate administration: 'their great difficulty lay in the want of some good pen, to keep up the spirit raised in the people, to assert the principles, and justify the proceedings of the new ministers'. He needed support for a strong peace, neither a Tory peace at any price nor a Whig insistence on all the original war aims.[41] Harley's initial editors, a group including William King of St Mary Hall, Oxford, Henry St John, John Freind, Francis Atterbury, and Matthew Prior, had not been up to the task: 'some were too busy, and others too idle to pursue it'.[42] By taking over, Swift could impose consistency and, kept on message by frequent conversations with Harley, could remain in line with the ministers' direction.

The task was welcome, for Swift surely belongs among those Pocock characterizes as 'seeking to defend virtue against innovative forces symbolized as trading empire, standing armies, and credit'.[43] He denounced war and its monstrous offspring, the modern. The modernity he satirized in *A Tale* emerges in his analysis as a creature of the venality fostered by wartime debt and consequent subservience to the monied interest. Attacking it suited his flair for caricature. He could pit land, stability, classical learning, and traditional virtue against unstable forms of capital, unlettered self-promotion, and corruption. Trade subverted inherited ranks by creating wealth that was not grounded on the stability of land, unstable capital drawn to speculative instruments like stocks.[44] It fostered fierce international conflicts that necessitated standing armies and the elaborate financial mechanisms – a national bank, a funded national debt, and great stock companies – needed to pay for them.[45] It was the source of the corruption through which a nation and a people degenerated from the virtues of the past. Swift's very first *Examiner* (2 November 1710) displays him in full flight:

> But the War continuing, and growing more expensive, Taxes were encreased, and Funds multiplied every Year, till they have arrived at the monstrous height we now behold them. And that which was at first a Corruption, is at last grown necessary, and what every good Subject must now fall in with, tho' he may be allowed to wish it might soon have an End; because it is with a Kingdom, as with a private Fortune, where every new Incumbrance adds a double weight. By this means the Wealth of the Nation, that used to be reckoned by the Value of Land, is now computed by the Rise and Fall of Stocks: And altho' the Foundation of Credit be still the same, and upon a Bottom that can never be shaken; and though all Interest be duly paid by the Publick, yet through the Contrivance and Cunning of *Stock-jobbers*, there has been brought in such a Complication of Knavery and Couzenage, such a Mystery of Iniquity, and such an unintelligible Jargon of Terms to involve it in, as were never known in any other Age or Country of the World.[46]

Swift sees only degeneration springing from this expensive war: 'that which was at first a Corruption, is at last grown necessary'. The steadiness of landed wealth gives way to the dizzying roller-coaster ride of the stock market. Simple honesty gives way to complication and mystery. Plain language gives way to unintelligible jargon. The case for peace is clear.

Still, Harley had to proceed with caution. Partisan Tories – that is, most Tories – wanted him to replace all Whig office holders with Tories, an impulse Harley resisted on principle. He favoured retaining competent officers who would serve the ministry.[47] Replacing Treasury officers with Tory backbenchers baying for the blood of the money men would hardly help him put national finances on a sound footing. The dismissal of Godolphin, widely respected for his administrative skills, had proven especially alarming, and a collapse of financial credit or a rift with military allies would weaken the ministry. Addison's allegorical portrait of skittish Public Credit in *Spectator* no. 3 (3 March 1711), for example, pandered to these fears. It had to be countered in *Examiner* no. 38 (19 April 1711) with a portrait of Credit as a robust rather than sickly woman:

> But the *National Credit* is of another Complexion; of sound Health, and an even Temper, her Life and Existence being a Quintessence drawn from the Vitals of the whole Kingdom. And we find these *Mony-Politicians*, after all their Noise, to be of the same Opinion, by the Court they paid Her, when she lately appear'd to them in the form of a *Lottery*.[48]

Fortunately, Harley too was a skilled manager, and Whig fear-mongering failed. The first of his money-raising lottery schemes was, as Swift gloats, over-subscribed.[49] A politician who had made his name as a member of the Commission of Public Accounts, he was devoted to sound administration and financial restraint. Since Swift worked so closely with Harley the devious strategist for peace and rival of St John, it is easy to lose sight of Harley the sound public administrator. It is probably worth recalling his colleague the Earl of Dartmouth's opinion that he owed his eventual fall in part to 'the insatiable avarice and resentment of those that could not bear a four years cessation from plunder'.[50] Like Godolphin, Harley is remembered as an effective administrator: 'four years cessation from plunder' can be worn as a badge of honour.

Negotiating peace was clearly a task for politics, however encouraged by the administrator's grasp of public finances. Swift had to cast doubts on the policies and integrity of the former ministry. His predominant theme is the self-interested venality of those who opposed the ministry. Indicting Wharton for corruption, Swift represents him as Verres, the corrupt governor of Sicily condemned by Cicero: 'The Morning was spent in taking Bribes, and selling Employments, the rest of it in Drunkenness and Lust'.[51] Despite his own initial reservations, he also targeted the Duke of Marlborough, whose credit with the Queen and unprecedented success as a commander of British forces in the field made him a formidable opponent of the new ministry's goal of peace.[52] In two of his best papers, Swift accuses the Duke of Marlborough, lavishly rewarded by the Queen and the nation, of avarice. Responding to the Whig charge that the ministry was ungrateful to the great general, Swift in *Examiner* no. 17 (23 November 1710) tots up the sums paid by the ancient Romans for a general's triumph and by the British nation to reward Marlborough with various employments, Woodstock, and the construction of Blenheim palace (named for his greatest victory). By his computation, 'A Bill of *Roman* Gratitude' totals £994 11s. 10d., a significant but not an extravagant sum. By contrast, 'A Bill of *British* Ingratitude' – of what the Whigs allege is ingratitude, that is – totals a staggering £540,000![53] By talking directly about money, Swift left Marlborough and the Whigs on the defensive despite their accomplishments. He gave his readers a concrete basis for comparison. Discrediting Marlborough, he was also discrediting the Whigs, accusing them of profiting from a prolonged war that pandered to the moneyed interest they served.

Swift returned to the attack in no. 28 (8 February 1711), a brilliant paper devoted to the meanness of avarice. Swift ended with the letter he would have written to Crassus, the avaricious member, with Octavius and Mark Anthony, of the first triumvirate. (Since Godolphin and Marlborough had been duumvirs – triumvirs with Harley until he was forced out in 1708 – the application was not far to seek.) Praising before condemning, he speaks as if he were the voice of every soldier and every Englishman: 'send for ... all your Friends; conjure them to tell you ingenuously which is your great Fault, and which they would chiefly wish you to correct; if they do not all agree in their Verdict, *in the Name of all the Gods*, you are acquitted'.[54] The Examiner communicates only what every well-wisher already knows. Like their great general, the Whigs are devoted to gain and the emerging market in unstable speculative capital. This explains their self-interested desire to prolong an inconclusive and protracted war despite the national good. This is not Swift's only tactic. In no. 21 (21 December 1710), Swift turns to Marlborough's desire to be General for Life, rejected by Queen Anne, to emphasize the need to subordinate the military to civil authority. Swift reminds his readers that the army subdued Parliament during 'the Great Rebellion against King *Charles* the First'.[55] But the attack on venality and the subversion of landed stability is at the core of his *Examiner* essays.

Swift does not present himself as a partisan rival. Instead, he claims that he impartially examines the good of the nation: 'It is a Practice I have generally follow'd, to converse in equal Freedom with the deserving Men of both Parties; and it was never without some Contempt, that I have observ'd Persons wholly out of Employment, affect to do otherwise'. In no. 42 (17 May 1711), he again claims impartiality: 'I Never let slip an Opportunity of endeavouring to convince the World, that I am not Partial, and to confound the idle Reproach of my being hired or directed what to write in Defence of the present Ministry, or for Detecting the Practices of the former'. Since he goes on to announce that he has examined the current ministry's actions with equal rigour but cannot 'accuse them of one ill or mistaken Step', the stance is clearly disingenuous. The *Examiner* was a ministry journal. Published as part of St John's election platform, *A Letter to the Examiner* (1710) reads like his extreme Tory 'manifesto' for the journal.[56] Despite its rhetorical force, then, Swift's pretence lacked credibility. Yet Swift insisted on his independence. The ministry did not directly dictate to him, and he certainly did not think of himself as serving a party rather than, through her chosen ministry, the Queen. In no. 23, a parody of the *Examiner*'s critics, he claims that 'nothing is so inconsistent as this Writer [i.e., Mr. Examiner]; I know not whether to call him a Whig or a Tory, a Protestant or a Papist'. Unlike 'our *Faction* (for so with great Propriety of Speech they [the Whigs] call the Queen and Ministry, almost the whole Clergy, and nine parts in ten of the Kingdom)', Swift argues, the Whigs cannot claim to be a national party, 'being patched up of heterogeneous, inconsistent Parts, whom nothing served to unite but the common interest of sharing in the Spoil and Plunder of the People'. His party is no faction but the nation itself, while his opponents constitute not a party but a heap of scraps. Criticizing the Act naturalizing foreign (dissenting) Protestants, he refers to 'Some *Persons*, whom the Voice of the Nation authorizes me to call her *Enemies*'. 'I write this paper for the Sake of the *Dissenters*', he says in no. 37 (12 April 1711), 'whom I take to be the most spreading Branch of the *Whig-Party*, that *professeth Christianity*'. This High-Church jibe tickles his fancy enough to bear repeating in no. 39 (26 April 1711): 'Those among the *Whigs* who believe a GOD, will confess, that the Events of War lie in his Hands'.[57]

The servant of a church reformed to bring it as close as possible to the church's primitive simplicity and established by law, Swift believed that he served the living Word. This conviction rather than rhetorical convenience carries him to his position of detached authority, and the vanity that amused his critics was merely its outward and visible sign. In politics, he consequently believed that he spoke for the political nation itself. In the counter-claims of his opponents, he heard not voice but echo, the heterodox chatter of idolatrous sects. Such certainty is the sure mark of a partisan, but Swift never doubted that he was speaking against a faction, not for a faction. He shared the ministry's goal, a peace to end the war. His primary loyalty was to Harley, who was trying to steer the ship of state between partisan extremes. There could be no valid reason to oppose the ministry, he asserted in *Examiner* no. 34 (22 March 1711), because most Tories were, like himself, Old Whigs. Those who now called themselves Whigs were not only not proper Whigs (that is, Old Whigs), they were not a coherent group at all:

> I am not sensible of any material Difference there is between those who call themselves the *Old Whigs*, and a great majority of the present *Tories*; at least by all I could ever find, from Examining several Persons of each Denomination. But it must be confessed that the present Body of *Whigs*, as they now constitute that Party, is a very odd mixture of Mankind, being forced to enlarge their Bottom by taking in every Heterodox Professor either in Religion or Government, whose Opinions they were obliged to encourage for fear of lessening their Number; while the Bulk of the Landed Men and People were entirely of the old Sentiments.[58]

Swift consistently represented himself as an Old Whig. In his eyes, the Court has bribed modern Whigs to forsake their original principles. Their heterogeneity precludes unity, which can only be grounded on a common interest. *Examiner* no. 22 (28 December 1710) associates indiscriminate heterodoxy with petty mercantile republics, where men imagine that 'Trade can never flourish unless the Country becomes a common Receptacle for all Nations, Religions and Languages'.[59] This is unEnglish, inappropriate to 'the Dignity of an Imperial Crown; which with Us is best upheld by a Monarch in possession of his just Prerogative, a Senate of Nobles and Commons, and a Clergy establish'd in its due Rights with a suitable Maintenance by Law'. The *Examiner* is consistent with the sectarian intransigence of Swift's writings on the Church, as is evident in the way he treats dissenters and Whigs as if they were one and the same.[60]

In *The Conduct of the Allies* as in the *Examiner*, Swift speaks confidently for an idealized vision of English landed society:

> It is the Folly of too many, to mistake the Eccho of a *London* Coffee-house for the Voice of the Kingdom. The City Coffee-houses have been for some Years filled with People, whose Fortunes depend upon the *Bank, East-India*, or some other Stock: Every new Fund to these, is like a new Mortgage to an Usurer, whose Compassion for a young Heir is exactly the same with that of a Stockjobber to the Landed

Gentry. At the Court-End of the Town, the like Places of Resort are frequented either by Men out of Place, and consequently Enemies to the Present Ministry, or by Officers of the Army ...[61]

At the cultural centre, Swift places, as unobtrusively as Martin in *A Tale of a Tub*, the landed gentleman and his young heir. They embody the political stability of the kingdom – the health of the body politic. Absent from this scene but central to it is their proper place, the country estate that literally grounds the virtue without which there can be no independent House of Commons.

Around these pillars of the state swirl parasites who have the same relationship to the gentry that the critic has to the writer in *A Tale of a Tub*: 'The *True Criticks* are known by their Talent of swarming about the noblest Writers, to which they are carried meerly by Instinct, as a Rat to the best Cheese, or a Wasp to the fairest Fruit'.[62] Preying on the gentleman and his heir like rats and wasps are the bogies of Country ideology – place men and the moneyed interest. Place men become parasites because they forfeit their independence for places that leave them financially dependent on the administration. Stock jobbers and other money men appropriate to themselves wealth that really belongs to the nation. An expensive war being at issue, Swift includes soldiers with others who rely on government sinecures. To an MP in opposition, a place is a bribe. They bequeath a legacy of national debt that encumbers landowners through burdensome, even ruinous taxes. Hence the evil usurer who casts a speculative eye on the young heir. The characteristically venal modernity that Swift exposes in *A Tale of a Tub* is a natural consequence of the political corruption that flourishes in the soil of war.

Like others defending Country virtues, Swift struggles with the paradox that the moneyed and the landed were hardly distinct groups. The gentry were happy to invest their wealth. When he returned to the Commons after the Guiscard incident, for example, Harley addressed the national debt and won over disgruntled Tories with a bill creating the South Sea Company. The Company was to assume a large portion of the unfunded national debt in exchange for the revenue from some taxes and, especially, the profits expected once a peace treaty secured it a monopoly of the trade in slaves with Spanish America. Since Tories resented Whig-dominated funds, Harley not only addressed the national debt but was able 'to create a tory – or, at least, non-whig – rival to the whig-dominated Bank of England'.[63] The financial institutions that alarmed Swift were in fact changing his world by being absorbed into it. It was conventionally the opposition that attacked reckless government spending, jealously guarding the Commons' control over finances, but war weariness allowed Swift to speak for an administration that had adopted the Country rhetoric of opposition.[64] Similarly, Swift disparaged the coffee house, an institution that symbolizes what is sometimes called the public sphere, but he conducted his propaganda campaign within that sphere. In the coffee house, readers discussed the day's newspapers and pamphlets while

enjoying the fruits of international trade – coffee, tea, or chocolate and their pro-
miscuous partner sugar. Despite his authorship of the anti-Grub-Street satire, *A
Tale of a Tub*, Swift was a creature of the institutions he satirizes. His task was to
get MPs in the coffee houses to echo what he presented as the voice of the nation.
He condemned those who 'conceived the World to be no wider than *Exchange
Alley*',[65] conveniently overlooking the fact that the path from the rural estate to
the House of Commons led through the coffee house and Exchange Alley.

Given such contradictions, the impersonal authority that Swift so comfortably assumes best served the purposes of attack. Tories of all stripes could rally
behind a confident assertion that landed virtue was invariably Tory and demon-
strably superior to the venality, godlessness, and confusion that were invariably
Whig. Swift knew well the routine accusations that accompanied partisan labels.
Since it was Tory, he playfully announces in no. 26 (25 January 1711), 'the Design
of the Present P—t and M—y was to bring in *Popery*, *Arbitrary Power*, and the
Pretender'; since they were Whigs, 'some late Men had strong views towards a
Commonwealth, and the Alteration of the *Church*'.[66] Swift's audience would rec-
ognize the familiar insults and enjoy being told that only the second was true.
Precisely because of his assurance that no other position was reasonable, however,
his authority deserts him when he explicates Tory beliefs:

> let the Reader judge from which of these two Parties a Prince hath most to fear; and
> whether her M—y did not consider the Ease, the Safety and Dignity of Her Person,
> the Security of Her Crown, and the transmission of Monarchy to her Protestant
> Successors, when She put Her Affairs into the present Hands.[67]

In practice, even this modest assertion was potentially divisive. Gentry opinion
was far more heterogeneous than Swift concedes or even recognizes. There were
Tories not yet comfortable with a Protestant succession outside the Stuart line,
and they gave colour to the Whig charge that the Tories adhered to the doctrine of
passive obedience. Addressing this belief, Swift acknowledges 'Passive Obedience
as charg'd by the WHIGS' in *Examiner* no. 34 (22 March 1711): 'That a King,
even in a limited Monarchy, holding his Power only from God, is only answerable
to Him. That such a King is above all Law ...'. Since this conviction would make
the Tory who held it a Jacobite and therefore, given the Act of Succession, a traitor, the Whig accusation was potentially damaging.

As he had done in *Sentiments of a Church-of-England Man*, Swift insisted that the
monarch personally did not command absolute obedience: 'as every Body knows,
this Power is lodged in the King or Queen, together with the Lords and Commons
of the Kingdom'.[68] He is replying to a 'Libel', William Benson's anonymous pamphlet feeding Whig fears of Tory absolutism by blaming passive obedience for the
rise of absolutism in Sweden.[69] As Swift conceded to Peterborough in a letter,

the piece is shrewdly written: and, in my opinion, not to be answered otherwize than by disclaiming that sort of passive obedience which the Tories are charged with. This dispute would soon be ended, if the dunces who write on each side, would plainly tell us what the object of this passive obedience is in our country. For, I dare swear, nine in ten of the Whigs will allow it to the legislature, and as many of the Tories deny it to the Prince alone: And I hardly ever saw a Whig and a Tory together, whom I could not immediately reconcile on that article, when I made them explain themselves.[70]

Peterborough like Swift is a former Whig recruited by Harley. It is obvious in this letter that Swift is no more 'natural' a Tory than a Whig. He is too unsentimental about the person of the monarch for the former, too High Church for the latter.

Swift is very clear-sighted. If the old fashioned Tory doctrine of passive obedience to the monarch personally leaves the Tories vulnerable to charges of absolutism and Jacobitism, then they must discard it. So he dismisses it as pedantry. On this, the winds of change were actually blowing in Swift's direction, toward his kind of political centre. Tories were gradually coming to attach loyalty to a constitutionally limited monarch, much as post-Revolution Whigs were coming to identify the people of their radical appeals with the legislature of King, Lords, and Commons.[71] But even under pressure, attachments change slowly and, often, painfully. Swift's claim that his common sense is universal is bluster: 'as every Body knows', 'nine in ten of the Whigs', 'as many of the Tories'. 'Every Body' knew nothing of the sort. Events would demonstrate that the minority of Tories who were committed Jacobites were roughly matched in numbers by equally committed Hanoverians, and these Parliamentary Jacobites were less likely to present themselves as absolute monarchists than as staunch constitutionalists who owed allegiance to the King-in-Parliament.[72] Nevertheless, many English readers failed to share the Anglo-Irish pragmatism with which Swift dismissed their reservations about the Revolution. He underestimated, perhaps failed to see, profound divisions within Tory ranks.

Swift was equally blind to the personal division on which the ministry he served would eventually founder, the intense rivalry between Harley and St John, the ministers he most admired. When Antoine de Guiscard stabbed Harley while being interrogated for treason, Swift was grief stricken, as his letter to William King about the incident reveals.[73] Perhaps for that reason, he allowed himself to retail in *Examiner* no. 33 (15 March 1711) St John's fiction that he was the intended target:

The Murderer confessed in *Newgate*, that his chief Design was against Mr. *Secretary St. John*, who happened to change Seats with Mr. *Harley*, for more Convenience of examining the Criminal: And being asked what provoked him to Stab the *Chancellor*? he said, that not being able to come at the *Secretary*, as he intended, it was some satisfaction to Murder the Person whom he thought Mr. *St. John* loved best.[74]

Swift's naivety here is embarrassing. St John hoped to reap sympathy that would otherwise accrue to Harley, to succeed him as prime minister should he not recover or displace him if he should.

St John had some cause for resentment. Harley had slighted him on first form-ing his ministry, and although he was a Secretary of State, Harley began secret peace negotiations with the French in 1710 without involving or informing him. He recognized that the charismatic and independent St John would be far more willing than he was to negotiate a peace utterly independent of the allies. St John's power in a struggle with Harley, after all, rested on the October Club, a group of about 150 fervent Tories who resented Harley's moderation, especially his refusal to replace all Whigs in office. Harley, who had furthered Swift's mission to secure the first fruits, gratified his Church-Party House of Commons by passing bills to establish property qualifications for MPs (partly to resist a Place Bill that would weaken administration control of the House) and to fund the building of fifty new churches in London, a centre of dissent. Between the October Club and the Whigs, who hoped to pressure Harley into sharing power with them, Harley was losing control of the House when the attack by Guiscard created a groundswell of sympathy for him. It helped that the Tory passions St John inflamed in Harley's absence exposed the Secretary's inability to manage the passage of necessary financial bills through House. It also helped that Harley returned with his popu-lar measure creating the South Sea Company while ensuring supply for the war effort as a prerequisite for negotiating a good peace.[75] That the Queen ennobled him as the Earl of Oxford and Mortimer and made him Lord Treasurer seemed to express the wishes of the nation. The Guiscard incident thus exacerbated St John's and Harley's rivalry while making Harley's supremacy, and their mutual depend-ence, seem obvious and necessary.[76]

This would be true of later stages of their destructive rivalry as well. Fond of indirection, Harley was remarkably steady, while his rival was brilliant but slippery, both qualities captured in his nickname, 'man of mercury'. (Of the important early eighteenth-century writers, only the 'protean' Defoe is as persist-ently labelled for his shiftiness.) Harley was by far the more principled:

> St John was by nature frank, impulsive, volatile; Harley secretive, oblique and phlegmatic. Their political talents were sharply contrasted, with St John the more brilliant debater and more indefatigable administrator and Harley the subtler nego-tiator and more skilful parliamentary manager. Their concepts of public life and its obligations were likewise very different. Harley was not only incorruptible, but meticulous in his attitude to public money; whereas St John, as he showed over the Quebec contracts (1711) and the commercial negotiations with Spain (1713–14), believed that nests were meant to be feathered.[77]

Rushed through cabinet while Harley was incapacitated following the assassina-tion attempt, the Quebec expedition led by Abigail Masham's brother was, like many of St John's more swashbuckling efforts, unsuccessful. Like his later attempts to profit from the peace treaty, it was also tainted by venality. Tied by deep bonds to Harley but fascinated by St John's brilliance, Swift was also drawn to St John's extravagance and extremism. A loyal friend, he tolerated in St John some of the personal failings he excoriated in Wharton. Devoted to both St John and Harley, he had long remained oblivious to the rivalry revealed by St John's response to the Guiscard affair: 'Mr. St John was either mistaken, or misinformed: However, the matter was thus represented in the weekly paper called the Examiner, which Mr. St John perused before it was printed, but made no alteration in that passage'.[78]

A strength in a polemicist, Swift's blithe conviction that his landed constituency spoke with one voice, in effect with his voice, was a political weakness. His gift of brilliant partisan stylization seems to have precluded a nuanced grasp of the personalities and passions that make politics so much more complex than ideology. His career as an English polemicist, like his career as a Church-of-Ireland lobbyist, encountered disappointment and political wrangling in the arms of the victory itself. Pursuing their straightforward goal through the shady and devious ways available to them, the ministers he served achieved a good peace in the Treaty of Utrecht. Combined with the Tory differences of principle that Swift tried to deny, their rivalry tore apart his party. He may himself have been a casualty of the rivalry between the Lord Treasurer and the Secretary. He left the *Examiner* in June, after the end of the Parliamentary session, in part because his anonymity was wearing thin.[79] By August, he is engaged in further ministerial business, undoubtedly with an eye on *The Conduct of the Allies*, the most important of his English political pamphlets. Where Ellis sees a smooth transition from one task to the next, however, Downie argues that Harley disciplined Swift for drifting too far into St John's orbit. He argues in part from Defoe's parallel experience, and it seems likely that Swift was, at the very least, left hanging long enough to grasp that he owed his role and the importance it conferred to the prime minister, whose renewed attentions he (like Defoe) welcomed.[80]

Since Swift cherished (and paraded) his independence, this must have been a difficult lesson. 'I do not write for a Party', he proudly declares, boasting that '[t]he present M[inistr]y are under no Necessity of employing prostitute Pens'.[81] He is, to put it mildly, misleading his reader, but he repeats the same thing in *Some Remarks upon a Pamphlet, Entitl'd, A Letter to the Seven Lords*, the August 1711 tract that announced his continued place in Harley's camp:

> if I durst tell him my Name, which he is so desirous to know, he would be convinced that I am of a Temper to think no Man great enough to set me on Work ... [Their] Malice ... is not intended against *Me*, but the present Ministry, to make the World believe, that what I have published, is the utmost Effort of all they can say or think against the last: Whereas it is nothing more than the common Observations of a private Man, deducing Consequences and Effects from very natural and visible Causes.[82]

Swift is not lying. He evidently did not regard himself as a hireling, a point he made to Harley when he indignantly rejected a payment of £50. He supported not a party but a moderate ministry headed by Harley. Although he hoped to merit a suitable reward for the service freely offered, he had not sold his pen. After the initial offer of payment, Harley made concessions to his difficult protégé's independence, treating him as a friend, not as an employee. If Swift was not viewing the fray with the Olympian detachment he affected, neither was he quite the hack his critics denounced him as. In the debate over the war, and over the kind of society war was creating in England, Swift had declared a common cause with the Harleyite camp.

Swift's task was to disseminate and control information on behalf of a group founded on limited information if not actual mistrust. At its centre was Robert Harley, a remarkably skilled parliamentary manager and administrator whose subtlety earned him the nickname 'Robin the Trickster'; one modern historian calls him 'the most devious politician of the age'.[83] Swift seems not to have known that Harley managed Defoe directly, independently of Swift and the subordinate writers Swift regarded as his understrappers, coordinating Defoe's efforts to complement Swift's.[84] Swift eventually imagined himself sufficiently necessary to insist on staying after dinner even though Bolingbroke asked him to leave so that he and Oxford, as he had become, could discuss confidential business.[85] Although the anecdote can suggest Swift's self-importance, the existence of inner counsels beyond his reach should not obscure how far he had worked himself into ministerial confidence. He had become important but long remained, perhaps naively, unaware that his friends made up an innermost cabinet that was itself divided. Harley acted as independently of his headstrong rival as he could manage. Initiated in secret as early as 1710, the peace policy depended on Britain operating in secret from its allies until the ministry presented the results of its treachery as a *fait accompli*, and even St John was involved only when the Guiscard assassination attempt temporarily disabled Harley. The cabinet was not informed until Swift was nearing the end of his service as Examiner.

Fortunately, internal tensions did not matter while they shared a common commitment to negotiating a peace. Even in tactical trifles, Swift usually kept his eyes on this prize. Having exposed divisions in the ministry through his *Examiner* paper on the Guiscard incident, he diverted attention by counterattacking the Whigs through 'a little bit of mischief'.[86] *Some Remarks upon a Pamphlet, Entitl'd, A Letter to the Seven Lords of the Committee appointed to Examine Gregg* defends Swift's charge, in the *Examiner*, that the would-be assassin Guiscard shared a common purpose with the Whig lords who had interrogated William Gregg, a minor clerk in Harley's office. Gregg had been found guilty of treasonous correspondence with France. Under pressure from his interrogators Gregg had refused to implicate Harley, but the episode had helped Godolphin and Marlborough oust him from the administration in early 1708. By presenting Guiscard as, in effect, an agent of Whig hostility to Harley, Swift expressed his fear for Harley by treating all his opponents like the would-be assassin:

> This Writer wonders how I *should know their Lordship's Hearts, because he hardly knows his own*. I do not well see the Consequence of this: Perhaps he never examines into his own Heart, perhaps it keeps no correspondence with his Tongue or his Pen: I hope at least, it is a Stranger to those foul Terms he has strowed throughout his Letter; otherwise I fear I *know it too well*: For *out of the abundance of the Heart the Mouth speaketh*. But however, Actions are pretty good Discovereres of the Heart, though the Words are not ...[87]

A minute attack on an offensive pamphlet, *Remarks* also displays the angry edge of Swift's confident rectitude. Asked how he can know the Whig lords' hearts, he replies by quoting from Matthew 12:34: 'O generation of vipers, how can ye, being evil, speak good things? for out of the abundance of the heart the mouth speaketh.'[88] Like his *Short Character* of Wharton, the *Remarks* allow Swift to vent his anger. Provoked by Guiscard's assassination attempt, it readily comprehends all of Harley's enemies: they are, simply, evil.

Another side of Swift's mastery of publicity, first displayed as Bickerstaff, is the deadpan hoax. In September, Swift returned to it in a trifle, a slight but deft and revealing secret history: *A New Journey to Paris: together with some Secret Transactions Between the Fr—h K—g, and an Eng— Gentleman. By the Sieur du Baudrier. Translated from the French*. Prior's past diplomatic experience and contacts in France made him a useful emissary after initial contacts through the Earl of Jersey revealed French interest in a peace. His arrest as a possible spy while returning incognito from France, however, let the cat out of the bag prematurely. The ministry immediately drew Whig fire. Like a tub meant to distract a whale from the ship of state,[89] Swift tossed *A New Journey* into the debate to confuse or distract critics of the ministry. Although the intercourse at its centre is diplomatic rather than sexual, it is a secret history in the tradition of Delarivier Manley's *New Atalantis*, down to garden assignations promising access to the King's mistress, Madam Maintenon. Like other works in this tradition, it presents itself as a translation.[90] Since his point, from his title on, is the banality rather than the significance of his secret history, he adopts the voice of Prior's French servant. In *New Journey* as in *Gulliver's Travels*, that is, an unreliable and socially low narrator represents a journey through (his phrase to Stella) 'a formal grave lie, from the beginning to the end'.[91] Swift counts on his sure command of his readership: 'I will dictate to [my printer] a formal relation of Prior's journey, with several particulars, all pure inventions; and I doubt not but it will take'.[92] Since English readers will automatically discount a French valet's story as self-serving and unreliable, Swift's form subverts whatever confession it may also contain. He also circulates some useful lies. Through Prior, the minister is responding to a French initiative, not beginning to treat separately. He is unyielding on the ministry's demanding terms, which include removing Louis's grandson from the Spanish throne. Indeed, they provoke the French to echo the *Examiner's* view of the war:

> Were ever such Demands made to a great Monarch, unless you were at the Gates of his Metropolis? For the Love of God, Monsieur *Prior* relax something, if your Instructions will permit you, else I shall despair of any good Success in our Negotiation? ... As able as you are to continue the War, consider which is to be most preferred, the Good of your Country, or the particular Advantage of your *General*; for he will be the only Gainer among your Subjects?[93]

Finally, of course, Prior baffles the ostensibly French narrator by preferring England's widely distributed prosperity to a French court whose unrivalled magnificence reduces the rest of the nation to squalid poverty. Swift thus panders to English chauvinism while representing a truth (the fact of negotiation) through 'a pure Invention from Beginning to the End'.[94] Unluckily, some readers, apparently including Prior, found his lie uncomfortably close to the truth. But the pamphlet did take, running quickly through three editions.[95]

Bickerstaff soon applied this deft touch to a graver purpose. *The Conduct of the Allies*, the most important single pamphlet in the Tories' pro-peace propaganda campaign, was Swift's most brilliant success as an English propagandist. In it, Swift was preparing for parliamentary debate in support of negotiating a peace without Spain. Since the Spanish succession had provided the occasion for the war, argument was needed. To many, the Whig slogan 'No peace without Spain' had come to seem impractical and, thanks to recent events, quixotic. Louis XIV's grandson, Philip of Anjou, was too solidly ensconced on the throne of Spain to be readily unseated. Although a kingdom uniting France and Spain remained an alarming prospect, it was a contingent one. Philip became second in line in April 1712, but he was still not the heir to the French throne. By contrast, the allies' candidate for the Spanish throne had recently become Emperor of Austria. Insisting on his candidacy would therefore prolong a bloody, expensive war 'in direct Violation of a fundamental Maxim, *The Ballance of Power*',[96] as Swift would put it in the *Examiner* for 16 January 1712. Military successes to date had restored that balance by curbing French expansionism, the real provocation for the war. On these grounds, the Tories and much of the nation felt justified in negotiating a peace that left the Spanish throne in Philip's hands.[97] But the Whigs denounced any peace without Spain as betrayal of their allies and ingratitude to the general whose victories had enhanced Britain's international standing. Since the Whigs dominated the House of Lords, these objections created a significant political obstacle. Where St John would gladly ignore the allies, therefore, Harley was devoting some of his practised deviousness to coming up with terms acceptable to the Dutch, Britain's most important allies.

Swift's pamphlet had to state the ministry's position compellingly. An ill informed or otherwise readily answered pamphlet would allow the opposition to dictate the terms of the debate. A position not easily grasped could not rally popular opinion. Throughout the fall of 1711, Swift was closeted with St John and Harley as they supplied and checked facts that Swift was marshalling. Corrections continued even while Swift was, with his usual complete engagement, seeing the pamphlet through the press, and beyond in subsequent printings.[98] *The Conduct of the Allies* appeared on 27 November, timed to influence debate when the parliamentary session began on 7 December. As Swift gleefully reports in *Journal to Stella*, his ninety-six–page tract was a splendid success. The printer reported the need for a second edition two days later: it sold out in five hours, necessitating a third and then, by 5 December, a fourth, 'which is reckoned very extraordinary, considering 'tis a dear twelve-penny book, and not bought up in numbers by the party to give away, as the Whigs do, but purely upon it's own strength'.[99] A small-print fifth edition for wider distribution halved the length and the price, these being distributed in bulk to country supporters, and by 28 January Swift tells Stella that a seventh edition is planned and that eleven thousand copies of his tract have been sold, 'a most prodigious run'.[100] He especially prided himself on the tract's role in parliamentary debates, where motions often followed his wording.[101] He played a conspicuous role in a conspicuously successful publicity campaign.

Combining Bickerstaff's deft appeal to the public with *A Tale of a Tub*'s force, *The Conduct of the Allies* played brilliantly on a national sense of grievance. Swift presented the argument that England had been involved unfairly in a long, bloody continental war that served the interests of allies who were not shouldering their fair share of the burden. Extensively quoted treaties argue that the allies have expected a secondary participant to assume the role of a principal without meeting their own commitments fully. Victory in battle has failed to produce a satisfactory peace: 'Ten glorious Campaigns are passed, and now at last, like the sick Man, we are just expiring with all sorts of good Symptoms'.[102] Here Marlborough is vulnerable to attack:

> So that whether this War were prudently begun or not, it is plain, that the true Spring or Motive of it, was the aggrandizing a particular Family, and in short, a War of the *General* and the *Ministry*, and not of the *Prince* or the *People*; since those very Persons were against it when they knew the Power, and consequently the Profit, would be in other Hands.
>
> WITH these Measures fell in all that Sett of People, who are called the *Monied* Men; such as had raised vast Sums by Trading with Stocks and Funds, and Lending upon great Interest and Præmiums; whose perpetual Harvest is War, and whose beneficial way of Traffick must very much decline by a Peace.[103]

Much as external allies have abused England for their selfish gain, so have the self-interested at home, notably members of the former ministry. Elements of the *Examiner*'s campaign cohere: the burden of debt, the corrupting effect of place on parliamentary independence, the venality and self-interest of the General himself, the interdependence of warfare and an economy based on speculative capital. In Swift's symbolic map of the world around him, England's principal ally, Holland, embodies all those elements of corrupt modernity. The false ally mirrors the self-serving general. Swift touches on other elements, notably by appealing to a Tory sense that a naval war raiding wealthy West Indian colonies would be more lucrative and less costly, but his escalating attack on Marlborough and the former ministry – and on their allies abroad – is central. Identified with the war through his glorious victories, the once untouchable general became vulnerable when peace negotiations in 1706 and 1709 led nowhere. His desire to continue fighting until the allies conquered France came to seem self-interested. In 'Marlborough's final, pyrrhic, victory in battle at Malplaquet' in September 1709, the allies lost twice as many men as the French. Even when he succeeded in turning the French *ne plus ultra* defensive line in August, too many scented not imminent victory but continued bloodshed and expenditure.[104] He voted against the peace plan in the Lords on 7 December, rejecting government policy. Tarnished by a brilliant publicity campaign that fully exploited his weaknesses, he was now in opposition to the Queen and her ministers. He was relieved of his command on 31 December. Swift further exploited charges of corruption in a satiric poem, 'The Fable of Midas' (14 February 1712), but Marlborough had already been routed.

The pamphleteers of Swift's day gave no quarter. There was an ideological middle ground that could support Swift's dialogue with both some Whigs and some Tories, but in the bipartisan competition for office, there was certainly no *rhetorical* middle ground. As Swift had acknowledged in *Examiner* no. 26, party labels evoked the convenient stereotypes that provided the idiom of political disagreement. When he described a nation threatened by the twin evils of a venal, self-serving faction within and greedy, self-serving allies without, his antagonists drew the routine inferences.[105] A critic of the Whigs and the allies must be a supporter of their enemy, France; a supporter of France was evidently a royal absolutist who sympathized with the return of the Pretender. *Remarks on a False, Scandalous, and Seditious Libel Intituled* The Conduct of the Allies and of the Late Ministry, &c., for example, deftly rehearses these tropes:

> When I hear a Man is going to write against the late *Ministry*, I am always sure I shall find him upon these Topicks. He will ridicule the Revolution, and consequently the *Dutch*, who were the Occasion of it; and this he will pretend out of *unlimited Obedience* to her Majesty, who, without that Revolution cou'd never have been our Queen. He will rail at the Money'd Interest, because Trade goes along with it: And Trade and Credit are in a mortal Fright at the Name of *France* and Persecution.[106]

By the logic of partisan polemic, anyone holding one of these positions holds them all. Every member of any political party will be held accountable for the views of its extremists. That Swift does not 'pretend ... *unlimited Obedience*' to the Queen or ridicule the Revolution is irrelevant. He has attacked the former ministry and the allies. It is just as irrelevant to Swift's caricatures of the godless Whigs and their allies that, as the same tract puts it, 'most of 'em are as much for a Land-Interest and a Church-Interest as themselves'.[107] Expressions of respect for the Queen were interpreted as signs of passive-obedience Toryism; skepticism about the Barrier Treaty or the allies, support for the Pretender. The same objections had been raised, routinely but perhaps more aptly, against St John's *Letter to the Examiner* in 1710.[108]

Political debate took place within this strident rhetoric, which was intended to polarize response. It comes as no surprise therefore that a satirist should prove himself to be such an effective propagandist. Swift may have been no more (or less) inclined than other journalists and pamphleteers to caricature and demonize his opponents, but his unmatched satiric gifts made him particularly effective at it. Depictions of Swift as an entrenched Jacobite absolutist lack the bite of his attacks on the Whigs, the monied interest, or particular foes like Wharton and the Duchess of Somerset. Since he works with the same foul medium, it is important to sift the substance from the inflamed rhetoric within which it occurs. Swift's positions were not irrefutable. The Jacobite threat arguably did make England a principal in the war. Swift's numbers, more rhetorical than statistical, underrepresented potential Jacobite support, perhaps with a dark design.[109] Holland's security was arguably crucial to English security, a barrier against France: 'For tho' our Honour might be disengaged', Francis Hare claimed, 'our Interest is not, the Safety of *England* and *Holland* especially are inseparably interwoven, and neither can stand long without the other'.[110] As allies, the Dutch could be defended as bearing, proportionately, a heavier share of the burden of war than Britain. The strategy of extensive borrowing could be defended.[111] On the other hand, as Swift claimed, war was raising levels of debt, increasing the importance of speculative capital, and creating unprecedented scope for government patronage. So it is useful to recall just how extravagant this political rhetoric was. The disputed Anglo-Dutch Barrier Treaty was replaced by a more acceptable treaty that guaranteed both a protective barrier for the Dutch and support for the Hanoverian Succession in Britain. The Tories did not rally in force behind the Pretender, and in England, despite their fervent Jacobite rhetoric, the few who did reacted with timid indecision when the '15 invited them to act.[112] On the other political extreme, the Whigs, triumphant after the death of Queen Anne, eventually repealed the Schism Act that threatened dissenting schools but did not tamper with the Test Acts that guaranteed Anglican supremacy in civil and military office. Nor, of course, did they undermine the supremacy of the landed gentry. Lurid rhetoric preceded mundane outcomes.

The available political stereotypes did capture, with remarkable precision, the fears that haunted the politically divided nation that had emerged from the previous century's civil wars. Looking back on the mid-seventeenth-century civil wars, the Whigs feared a resurgence of the royal absolutism that had threatened Parliament under Charles I and then James II. Dissenters found this fear enriched by memories of the Tory reaction, as fiercely anti-Dissent as anti-Catholic, that followed the Exclusion Crisis.[113] When the Whiggish Defoe later exiles his Robinson Crusoe to another island between 1659 and 1687, between the Restoration and the Revolution, he reveals how vividly that portion of the Stuart nightmare lived in at least one dissenting imagination.[114] In the rhetoric of the day, the Pretender – Roman Catholic in religion and educated in absolutist France – personified everything such Englishmen feared. Other Englishmen, however, feared the resurgence of republicanism and attacks on the established episcopal church. In unorthodox religious pamphlets and proposals to abolish the Test, for example, they saw the return of Presbyterianism, the desecration of churches, and the elimination of monarchy. To many Englishmen too, as Swift had pointed out in *A Letter Concerning the Sacramental Test*, the angry cat of dissent seemed more dangerous than the bound lion of Roman Catholicism. Both groups were divided. Some Whigs could not reconcile themselves with royal authority enough to enter a ministry as the King's servants, while some Tories could not reconcile themselves to the necessary Tory-Anglican resistance to the King in the Glorious Revolution. An appeal to their fundamental fears, however, usually stifled these differences and polarized the electorate along party lines.

As a member of the sect of humanity that feared for the worst, Swift was well placed for political debate. The time was right for him, for he could appeal to a war-weary electorate impatient with a long period of high taxation. Although modern analysis Whiggishly suggests that the expenditure amounted to less than ten percent of national wealth and was therefore less crippling than the Tories feared, it was alarming. Fed by the military spending that consumed some two thirds of government expenditure, it more than doubled from 16.7 million pounds at the end of the Nine Years War to 36.2 million at the end of the War of the Spanish Succession. It was a recent phenomenon, developed only after the Revolution and following, Swift felt, an inappropriate Dutch model.[115] Like Swift, many landowners could imagine the debt only as a debilitating mortgage on a fixed estate. To resist the growth of an intrusive tax-collecting bureaucracy, the Commons had favoured direct taxes on land over indirect taxes like the excise. As a result, the squires to whom Swift appealed felt the financial burden directly.[116] Faith in capital rather than land and comfort with high levels of national debt took time to develop. Swift's antagonists could not make them attractive to his audience, and the more detailed replies lumbered into print too late to turn the tide of opinion. Although Swift oversimplified when he identified them with distinct groups of people, land and money did underwrite divergent visions of society, and there was genuine resentment of the growing number of people whose wealth and social standing were independent of land.[117] Swift appealed to profound English

anxieties over the cultural transformation now associated with the emerging fiscal-military state.

When another cause prayed on the rival fear, of course, Swift and his ministers
could quickly find themselves on the outside. But while an oppressive war created conditions ripe for peace, they reigned supreme. Swift could in fact remain
serenely above the fray. He did not have to skirmish with his critics, although in
February 1712 he added, as a kind of appendix, his attack on the Anglo-Dutch
Barrier Treaty of 1709, *Some Remarks on the Barrier Treaty, between Her Majesty
and the States-General. By the Author of the Conduct of the Allies*. The Dutch had
received the right to garrison a defensive barrier against France in the Spanish
Netherlands and had promised to support the Hanoverian Succession, possibly
(Swift controversially suggested) limiting the freedom to name the successor that
had served Parliament in such good stead in 1689 and afterward. The real point of
the protest, however, was primarily that the treaty, as an incentive to revive their
then-waning support for the war, granted generous and exclusive trading privileges in the Spanish Netherlands. As the war neared its end, the British decided
that they wanted a share of the benefits, and they feared that a peace might be
imperilled if Louis XIV, whose grandson was now King of Spain, objected. After
prolonged negotiations and much self-justification from the allies accused of bad
faith in *Conduct of the Allies*, Britain and Holland signed in March 1713 a second
Anglo-Dutch Barrier Treaty that gave Britain an equal share in trading privileges. Despite Whig fears, it retained a barrier and support for the Hanoverian
Succession.[118] Swift had made his case effectively, rallying opinion against the earlier treaty, but he says little in the *Journal to Stella* to suggest that this afterpiece
to his English political masterpiece engaged his best energies or his deepest convictions. The same can be said for *Some Advice Humbly Offer'd to the Members of
the October Club, in a Letter from a Person of Honour* (January 1712), an attempt
on his own initiative to insinuate to the extreme Tories that they should have
patience, because deep policy informs Harley's apparent inconsistencies and mistakes. It pleased him but did not sell: 'The little two-penny *Letter of Advice to the
October Club* does not sell; I know not the reason; for it is finely written, I assure
you; and, like a true author, I grow fond of it, because it does not sell'.[119]

Swift's playfulness probably reflects his relief at a crisis averted, for Oxford had
in truth mismanaged the opening of Parliament. The triumph in the Commons
that Swift celebrated was matched by defeat in the Lords, which passed a motion
opposing a peace without Spain. Swift's fears provoked splendid personal lam-
poons. One, like his satire of Marlborough, fell into the coordinated drive for
peace. The other, like his *Short Character of Wharton*, was politically pointless,
a self-destructive expression of personal animus. The Whigs carried the day in
the Lords by winning the defection of the High-Church Earl of Nottingham.
The price of his support against the peace was Whig support for his bill against
Occasional Conformity, passed later in the session. It says a lot about Swift's posi-

tion near the political centre that he responded indignantly to Nottingham's treachery and Whig perfidy – they were betraying their dissenting supporters to undermine the ministry – without expressing any sympathy for the Church issue for which a High-Church lord had abandoned the ministry's political goal. Responding to a hint from Harley, Swift prepared a ballad, 'two degrees above Grubstreet', to appear the day before Nottingham's speech against the peace: *An Excellent New Song. Being the Intended Speech of a Famous Orator against the Peace.*[120] Swift's ballad attributes Nottingham's defection to discontent at being left out of the ministry:

> But some will cry, 'Turncoat!', and rip up old stories,
> How I always pretended to be for the Tories:
> I answer; the Tories were in my good graces,
> Till all my relations were put into places,
> But still I'm in principle ever the same,
> And will quit my best friends, while I'm not in game.[121]

It is odd to see this High-Church former Whig calling Nottingham a turncoat for continuing the campaign against occasional conformity! But Nottingham's move allowed the Whigs to carry the vote against the peace, apparently imperilling the project that Swift and the ministers he supported thought was essential to the health, indeed the survival, of the nation.

For his tactical move in support of the Church against occasional conformity, Swift mocks Nottingham for associating with republicans. *Toland's Invitation to Dismal to Dine with the Calves' Head Club* (June 1712), a broadside imitation of part of Horace's Epistle 1.5, imagines the deist Toland inviting the High-Churchman Nottingham to a republican dinner celebrating the anniversary of the execution of Charles I![122] When it seemed that the French might sabotage the peace by refusing to allow English troops into Dunkirk, Swift returned to the theme in *A Hue and Cry after Dismal*, which imagines Nottingham travelling to Dunkirk disguised as a chimney sweep to persuade the inhabitants not to admit the English army. When the army was finally admitted, Swift celebrated with *Peace and Dunkirk, being An Excellent New Song* (July 1712). Such trifles, Ehrenpreis remarks, demonstrate Swift's 'quintessential playfulness'.[123] Impersonating an enemy to demonstrate his absurdity often brought out Swift's high-spirits and inventiveness. But the brilliance with which he caricatures his enemies perhaps also reveals that he found it almost impossible to engage thoughtfully with an opponent's position. Even when it is relatively harmless, his literary play can also feed a sneaking sympathy with his superiors' fear that he was a loose cannon likely to careen dangerously across the deck.

Swift was most effective, that is, when he was working towards a political goal shared with the ministry. He was less effective, though occasionally still brilliant, when left to his own devices or when he denied the ministry's divisions. Unguided and in despair at the Whig victory in the Lords, for example, Swift had vented his anger and frustration in *The Windsor Prophecy*, a lampoon at the expense of the Duchess of Somerset. He does so in response to a rumour that the Queen had secretly supported the vote, an apparent treachery that he rationalized by blaming one of her confidants, Somerset, and directing his anger at her. Adopting the device of editing an old prophecy, 'somewhat in the same manner with that of [*A Famous Prediction of*] *Merlin* in the *Miscellanies*',[124] the poem predicts dire consequences if Harley is relieved of the Lord Treasurer's white staff and attacks the Duchess of Somerset. Condemning the malign influence of royal favourites was a popular opposition tactic. Writers like Delarivier Manley had satirized Somerset's predecessor, Sarah Churchill, Duchess of Marlborough, in *The Secret History of Queen Zarah and the Zarazians* (1705) and other works. But Zarah arguably becomes an allegorical figure – for example, a figure of Faction – that permits analysis of some complexity.[125] Swift blames and demonizes a particular person, as if the policy long developed by the Queen and the ministry could be discarded because of a chat between the Queen and a confidant. At such a moment, Swift's grasp of the actual workings of politics seems embarrassingly weak. Suggestively, it was not Swift but a friend who shrewdly questions the source of the problem, the Lord Treasurer: 'Arbuthnott asked, How he came not to secure a majority?' Harley's answer looks weak even to Swift – 'A poor answer for a great minister' – but he does not draw the obvious inference that his master's carelessness created the problem.[126]

In *Windsor Prophecy* as in his earlier *Short Character of the Earl of Wharton*, Swift is venting his spleen and no more. He mocks the redheaded Duchess as Carrots and alludes to gossip that blamed her for the death of her previous husband in a duel.[127] This impolitic outburst is based it on an embarrassingly superficial analysis of the political problem facing the ministry, and it relies on a commoner's coarse insults to persuade the Queen to abandon a favourite. It has no viable political function. Moreover, whatever it did to ease his distress at the political dangers the ministry faced, this action was self-destructive, 'almost as though in a suicide pact with his supposedly doomed allies'.[128] For the *Prophecy* hardened the Queen's resolve not to prefer him in England, where all deaneries and bishoprics were in her gift.[129] Swift thought so. In a poem not published until 1735, Swift denounces the Duchess as 'an old red-pate, murdering hag', the Queen as 'a royal prude'.[130] Yet another royal favourite, Abigail Masham, had warned him not to publish his *Prophecy*. Swift claimed to have sent a letter to his printer that miscarried, but to Stella he expresses not chagrin at his tactlessness but pleasure in his cleverness: 'I like it mightily'.[131]

While Swift solaced himself with spiteful wit, Queen Anne and her ministry famously resolved the challenge posed by the Whig House of Lords through constitutional *force majeure*. She set a precedent by exercising her prerogative to create twelve new peers who would support the ministry, thus ensuring that the peace initiative would pass the upper house.[132] The ministry could proceed more or less as if it had not mismanaged the initial vote, and a peace congress opened in Utrecht at the end of January 1712. Swift had completed his principal task for the ministry when he published *Some Remarks on the Barrier Treaty* at the end of February. He now found time for a non-partisan work, the *Proposal for Correcting, Improving and Ascertaining the English Tongue in a Letter to the Most Honourable Robert, Earl of Oxford and Mortimer, Lord High Treasurer of Great Britain* (17 May 1712), one of the few works he published in his own name. This project had its origins in the essay on the corruptions of language that forms the bulk of *Tatler* no. 230 (28 September 1710), to which it alludes in a reference to 'an ingenious Gentleman, who for a long Time did thrice a Week divert or instruct the Kingdom by his Papers; and is supposed to pursue the same Design at present, under the Title of *Spectator*'.[133] It shares with Swift's political writing his conviction that change represents degeneration: 'The rude *Latin* of the *Monks* is still very intelligible; whereas, had their Records been delivered down only in the vulgar Tongue, so barren and so barbarous, so subject to continual succeeding Changes; they could not now be understood, unless by Antiquaries'. Appalled by this fluidity – 'continual succeeding Changes' – Swift sets as his goal '*Ascertaining* and *Fixing* our Language for ever'.[134] Like his political writing, it shares a conviction that myriad sources of corruption demand an authority modelled on the French Academy. As in his *Discourse*, the classical past supplies a stability must be vigorously preserved. English can emulate it only by determining and, in a characteristically Swiftian term, *fixing* its best state. Like an earlier earnest tract dedicated to an aristocratic patron, Swift's *Project for the Advancement of Religion*, it had no effect on the world Swift wanted to reform. Oxford had more pressing matters to consider. But the project was important to Swift, and in the farewell letter that ended his friendship with Steele a year later, he reminded Steele of his former esteem: 'You cannot but remember, that, in the only thing I ever published with my name, I took care to celebrate you as much as I could, and in as handsome a manner, though it was in a letter to the present Lord Treasurer'.[135] Swift's apolitical project links the Tory propagandist with the Whig associate of Addison and Steele.

Although Swift talked of perhaps returning to Ireland, he stayed on. Intimate with both the ministers and the printers – with the Court and with Grub Street – he assumed 'the role of unofficial *chef de propagande*'.[136] It is appropriate though not without irony that a principal accomplishment of the administration in 1712 was the passage, in May, of a Stamp Act, a tax of a penny a sheet on printed material. Swift could grumble about the press, and he undoubtedly resented the publication of religious opinions inimical to the Church, but he shamelessly exploited 'the liberty of the press' that he deplored.[137] It was Swift's own *Short Character* of Wharton that provoked Archbishop King to ask, in January 1711,

'Pray was there ever such licentiousness of the press as at this time?'[138] A master of the anonymous broadside, Swift can have felt only alarm at more extreme proposals to curb the press; for example, that every printed piece bear the name and address of author, printer, and publisher. He objected even to this tax, which led, he claimed, to the death of Grub Street. The broadsides he published to beat the tax include his satires of Dismal, *Peace and Dunkirk*, and *A Letter from the Pretender to a Whig Lord*, this last a feeble pamphlet in which the Pretender refutes a common prejudice by expressing his exclusive reliance on the Whigs.[139] As always, Swift denounced, celebrated, and above all participated in the public sphere not through the coffee house, which consumed its products, but through the scurrilous unruliness of Grub Street itself.

The peace conference notwithstanding, the ministry continued to need its press machine. The peace talks dragged on for over a year before the main treaties between Britain and France were finally signed in April 1713. There was plenty of room for second thoughts, and therefore room to reiterate ministry arguments. Swift was active in publishing the wittiest Tory propaganda other than his own, the five pamphlets by his Scottish friend John Arbuthnot that were printed between 4 March and 31 July 1712 and later collected as *The History of John Bull*.[140] Like Swift at his best, these three- and six-pence pamphlets domesticated the complex and the abstract in solidly English terms, treating the War of the Spanish Succession as a quarrel between John Bull (who is still the type Englishman) and his neighbours Nicholas Frog (the Dutch), Lord Strutt (Philip of Spain), and Lewis Baboon (Louis XIV, the Bourbon King of France). The title of the first captures popular feeling about the war: *Law is a Bottomless-Pit. Exemplify'd in the Case of The Lord Strutt, John Bull, Nicholas Frog, and Lewis Baboon. Who spent all they had in a Law Suit* (4 March 1712). The pretence that they were 'Printed from a Manuscript found in the Cabinet of the famous Sir Humphry Polesworth' anticipates the characteristic Scriblerian pedant, Martinus Scriblerus, but the tracts carefully represent the politics of peace. Arbuthnot associates the later ones with Manley as publisher, signalling his affinity with the domesticated politics of such works as *Queen Zarah* and *Memoirs of Europe*, which is also the tradition of Swift's *New Journey to Paris*.[141]

Arbuthnot's most substantial allusions, however, link his pamphlets with *A Tale of a Tub*, especially through the figure of Jack. The fourth pamphlet, *An Appendix to John Bull Still in His Senses: or, Law is a Bottomless-Pit* (10 May), represents the Whig betrayal of the dissenters to secure Nottingham. It depicts the arrest of Jack, who is apprehended, in an image of Low-Church accommodation with Dissent, 'smoking his Pipe very quietly, at his Brother *Martin's*'. Jack is eventually hanged, although not quite until dead. Arbuthnot's intertextual play reveals the alertness to hints that would characterize the Scriblerus Club when it began meeting in the spring of 1714. Indeed, his pamphlets were first collected in the joint *Miscellanies* (1727) by Pope, Swift, Arbuthnot, and Gay.[142] They display something of Swift's pointed play, but their frequent geniality is distinctively Arbuthnot's, as is the invention of Bull's sister Peg (Scotland) who regrettably succumbs to the dubious charms of Jack (Presbyterianism) in the third pamphlet. Luckily, Arbuthnot seems not to have seen the bitter fable in which Swift reacted to the Act of Union, *The Story of the an Injured Lady. Being a True Picture of Scotch Perfidy, Irish Poverty, and English Partiality*, written in early 1707 but not published until 1746.[143] Swift's friendships were fortunately more inclusive than his narrow ethnic and sectarian resentments would suggest.

While Swift grew closer to a circle of wits, his friends within the ministry and their party were falling apart. Peace achieved, the Queen's poor health would focus national attention on the succession, the issue that exposed the Tory divisions that the Old Whig propagandist so airily denied. In March, a discontented minority of the dissident October Club broke off to form a March Club of Hanoverian Tories whose Country opposition to Court corruption left them critical of the ministry. Primarily at the initiative of the headstrong Bolingbroke, who hoped to seize control of the peace process and force a separate peace, the government in May issued the infamous restraining orders to Ormond, Marlborough's successor as commander. Worse, they treacherously communicated this decision to the French but not to their allies, whom the French proceeded to challenge in the field.[144] The ministry was expecting an immediate decision by Philip to renounce France or give up Spain, but thanks to the restraining orders, it was awaiting rather than forcing military and diplomatic developments. The parliamentary initiative passed to the opposition Whigs, who inferred what had happened from Ormond's inactivity. A betrayal of the allies, the orders left the initiative with the French, who could act militarily without considering Ormond's forces. Swift's *Peace and Dunkirk* expresses ministerial relief that the French, no longer under severe pressure, had finally admitted an English force into Dunkirk.

To Swift's distress, relations between Oxford and Bolingbroke grew more and more strained. By 1712 they were, despite their common goal, rivals who differed in principle and approach. Oxford was committed to a peace that would prove acceptable if not welcome to Britain's allies, especially the Dutch. That diplomatic consideration was irrelevant to the backbenchers who provided most of the support for Bolingbroke, who personally shared Swift's dislike of the Dutch and longed for closer relationships with France. In Paris negotiating with the French in August, he exceeded his commission and left work to be redone by Oxford, who delayed his impetuous commitments with an eye on relations with the allies. Bolingbroke also committed the flagrant indiscretion of appearing at the opera when it was attended by the Pretender. A confrontation in cabinet on 28 September confirmed the breach between the ministers. Oxford remained in charge, and cabinet repudiated Bolingbroke's actions, but Oxford also had to recognize the increasing strength of Bolingbroke's support.[145] It added to Bolingbroke's resentment that he had been elevated to the peerage in the summer not as an earl (like Oxford) but as a viscount, 'a Title inferior by one degree' as Gulliver would phrase it in Lilliput.[146] He felt it as an insult. Offended by his immorality and free thinking, the Queen may well have been responsible for the slight, but he blamed Oxford.[147] Swift carefully avoided 'draw[ing] up the Preamble of his Patent ... a Work that might lose me a great deal of Reputation, and get me very little'.[148]

Knowledge of the administration's disintegration in 1714 should not obscure its genuine accomplishment. In 1713, the allies hammered out the details of the Peace of Utrecht, established through a series of treaties negotiated over the year. That peace is the crowning achievement of the ministry Swift served, one of the great accomplishments of Anne's reign. Attacked by the Whigs and resented by some allies, notably by Anne's eventual successor, the Elector of Hanover, the peace did end an expensive, destructive war. It curbed French expansionism for a generation. France kept Strasbourg and Lorraine but ceded conquests east of the Rhine and allowed the Dutch a protective barrier. Moreover, France acknowledged the Hanoverian succession and agreed not to harbour or support the exiled Stuarts. From Spain, Britain gained Gibraltar and Minorca as well as the coveted Asiento, the right to trade slaves to the Spanish Caribbean. In the Caribbean, it gained St Kitts. In North America, it gained Nova Scotia, Newfoundland, and trading posts captured by the French in Hudson Bay. There were many loose ends, and the remaining French territories in North America would figure in the next generation's major war, the Seven Years War of 1756–63. But there was no doubt who had won: 'Britain had gained much'.[149] Peace achieved, the party and the ministry had little to hold it together, as events would reveal, but the late-summer 1713 election resulted in a substantial Tory majority. Parliament had halved the land tax to its peacetime rate of two shillings in the pound, and the country squires knew who to thank.[150]

Swift too finally achieved a reward for his services to the government and to the peace, although his suspense was as agonizing as the contemporary anticipation of the ever-delayed (it seemed) peace. Archbishop King repeatedly urged him to make sure that he did something for himself, and he had hoped for English preferment. In February 1712, he had reminded Oxford of his interest when the dean of Wells died,[151] spending the next fourteen months in suspense about possible preferment to that deanery or one of two others that also became vacant (Ely and Lichfield). To his embarrassment, there were persistent rumours that he would receive Wells. In July 1712, Archbishop King actually congratulated him on the 'preferment [which] I hear her Majesty has bestowed on you';[152] in August, he was angry with Stella, 'because you talk as glibly of a Thing as if it were done, which for ought I know, is farther from being done than ever'.[153] Only on 13 April 1713 did Erasmus Lewis show him 'an Order for a Warrant for the 3 vacant Deanryes, but none of them to me'. Swift blamed Harley only for not giving him more timely notice 'if he found the Qu would do nothing for me'.[154] Sir David Hamilton's *Diary* records both pressure on the Queen to prefer Swift and her resolve not to do so.[155] Fortunately, by that time Swift was recommending John Stearne, the current Dean of St Patrick's, for a vacant bishopric. Stearne's elevation would leave the deanery open, and the Irish deanery was in the gift not of the Queen but of Ormond, the Lord Lieutenant. Oxford, Ormond, and the Queen, who had to approve the promotion to bishop, eventually agreed, but Swift was teased with counter-proposals. In what may have been in part a lesson in proper deference to his actual patron, Ormond expressed dislike of Stearne and urged Swift to name another deanery. Only when Swift resigned himself to his superior's will – 'I desired, he would put me out of the Case, & do as he pleased' – was he granted what he now wanted: 'then with great kindness he said he would consent, but woud do it for no man alive but me &c'. As Swift's confidence grows, his complaints increase: 'neither can I feel Joy at passing my days in Ireld: and I confess I thought the Ministry would not let me go; but perhaps they cant help it' (18 April). Nor could they. Swift's own indiscretions, not conspiratorial malice by the Archbishop of York or the Duchess of Somerset, created the obstacles he faced. Soon he is dreading the installation fees and related expenses: 'I shall not be the better for this Deanery these 3 years' (23 April).[156]

To English friends, Swift seldom wrote with joy about his life in Ireland. So Swift represented his preferment as an exile. Highly ambitious and extremely able, he had always felt disappointment keenly, as he admitted in a letter to Bolingbroke and Pope:

> I never wake without finding life a more insignificant thing than it was the day before: which is one great advantage I get by living in this country, where there is nothing I shall be sorry to lose; but my greatest misery is recollecting the scene of twenty years past, and then all on a sudden dropping into the present. I remember when I was a little boy, I felt a great fish at the end of my line which I drew up almost on the ground, but it dropt in, and the disappointment vexes me to this very day, and I believe it was the type of all my future disappointments.[157]

Swift seems to have viewed his life as a series of disappointments. When he wrote this in 1729, he no doubt felt a pang at the glories of his career two decades earlier. In the end, he had failed to establish himself in England. But he had in truth gained something significant, the most prominent deanery in what was, after all, his native land. A proud churchman, he would for the rest of his life identify himself as Jonathan Swift, D.D., Dean of St Patrick's, Dublin – on occasion simply as J.S.D.D.D.S.P.D. As Dean of Wells he might well have enjoyed a lively sustained literary interaction with his Scriblerian fellow wits. Living in England, he might also have contributed more fully to Bolingbroke's campaign against Walpole. But in hindsight it is hard to believe that he would have left the curiously modern political and literary legacy for which we remember the Dean of St Patrick's, Dublin.

Swift grasped the nettle of his Irish preferment firmly. In June, he returned to Ireland to be installed as Dean. Home for the first time since the summer of 1710, he showed no eagerness to return to England. His vertigo had returned, and spent much time in retreat at Laracor. In a letter to Vanessa (8 July 1713), he oddly blends discontent with pleasure at being home:

> At my first coming I thought I should have dyed with Discontent, and was horribly melancholy while they were installing me, but it begins to wear off, and change to Dullness. My River walk is extremely pretty, and my Canal in great Beauty, and I see Trouts playing in it ... I find you are likewise a good Politician and I will say so much to you; that I verily think, if the thing you know of had been published just upon the Peace, the Ministry might have avoided what hath since happened. But I am now fitter to look after Willows, and to cutt Hedges than meddle with Affairs of State. I must order one of the Workm[e]n to drive those Cows out of my Island, and make up the Ditch again; a Work much more proper for a Country Vicar than driving out Factions and fencing against them: And I must go and take my bitter Draught to cure my Head, which is spoilt by the bitter Draughts the Publick hath given me.

Swift shared with Pope and Gay a love of complexly ironic pastoral poses, and this is one of his richest before he acquired Naboth's Vineyard as Dean. He has reason for discontent. Ill, unappreciated, and (as he represents it) in exile, he did not enjoy his installation, the cost of which had oppressed him from the moment he was sure he would be dean. He misses the excitement of London. On the other hand, he is free from the factiousness of the ministers who, he laments, rejected a history of the peace that would, he vainly imagines, have fixed in public opinion a truth beyond partisan reproach. As he grumbles, he revels in his retreat. He celebrates the fact of possession: his cabin, his willows, his canal. Affecting the country vicar, he is adopting a Horatian pose, preferring his version of Horace's Sabine farm to the cares of the capital. Nevertheless, the new dean was not one to slight his greater consequence: in Dublin, '[I] returned not one Visit of a hundred that were made me but all to the Dean, and none to the Doctor'.[158] Had he been content simply to rusticate, he could have accepted Oxford's offer of a position as his personal chaplain,[159] a return to dependency he could not seriously contemplate.

The history on which he worked was published posthumously as *The History of the Last Four Years of the Queen*. Anticipating attacks on the peace, he had worked on it diligently once he was freed of heavy propaganda demands. Repeating his assessment to Vanessa, he wrote to Charles Ford, 'I am tempted to think, that if the Tract I left with M^r L— had been published at the time of the Peace, some ill Consequences might not have happened'.[160] He nevertheless seems to have thought of it as more than a timely polemic. He brought to it the ambition to write history that, fostered by Temple, had informed his *Abstract of the History of England* and his *Fragment of the History from William Rufus*, both published only posthumously.[161] In the summer of 1714, in fact, he would apply for the position of historiographer royal, a position once held by his 'near Relation' John Dryden.[162] In his memorial, he urged that 'it is necessary, for the honour of the Queen and in justice to her servants, that some able hand should be immediately employed to write the history of her Majesty's reign, that the truth of things may be transmitted to future ages, and bear down the falsehood of malicious pens'.[163] On these grounds, Ehrenpreis suggests that while Swift wanted to publish what he had, he may well have imagined it as a framework for a larger masterpiece.[164] He valued what he had completed. On the same scale as the slightly longer *Tale* volume, itself a collection of three works, and his collected *Examiner* papers, his *History of the Last Four Years* is his longest single work apart from *Gulliver's Travels*.[165] It pained him that the ministers did not welcome it, insisted on various revisions, and procrastinated until its time had past.[166] But how could the actors who disagreed on policies and competed for supremacy agree on a history? In places, the *History* retains the pungency of Swift's polemical satire, but it adds little in the way of perspective: 'He hath imbibed his Father's Principles in Government, but dropt his Religion, and took up no other in its stead: Excepting that Circumstance, He is a firm Presbyterian'.[167] This is recognizably the Earl of Wharton, similarly demonized elsewhere. Sadly but undoubtedly, modern historians second Swift's contemporaries' assessment. They quote the *Examiner* and his political pamphlets. Precisely because it is more personal, they prefer his self-justification in *Memoirs Relating to That Change Which Happened in the Queen's Ministry in the Year 1710*, written in 1714 and again published only posthumously. For similar reasons, they gleefully mine the *Journal to Stella*. But they largely neglect his attempt to have the last word on the events he was part of, the *History* on which he thought his fame could rest.

Swift obviously wrote more memorably as an engaged participant than as a historian. In 1713, he affected to be done with England and with politics, but neither had yet done with him. 'I heartily wish you were here', Erasmus Lewis wrote him on 9 July 1713, 'for you might certainly be of great use to Us by yr endeavours to reconcile, & by representing to 'em the infallible consequences of these Divisions'.[168] He repeated the plea on 30 July – 'my Lord Treasurer desires you will make all possible hast over, for we want you extreamly' – and 6 August: 'you and I have already laid it down for a Maxim that we must serve L^d T— without receiving orders, or particular Instructions, and I doe not yet see a reason for changing that rule, his mind has been communicated more freely to you than any other, but you won't understand it'.[169] Friendship as well as duty called him, and although he resisted the call, he was back in London on 9 September. (His warm poem to Oxford, *Horace, Epistle VII, Book I*, dates from October.) He returned to rivalry between the principal ministers, to a Tory party fragmenting as the Whigs accused its members of failing to support the Protestant succession, and to a former friendship that had curdled into enmity under the pressure of political rivalry. Recently elected MP of Stockbridge, Steele had been assuming the role of journalistic champion of the Whigs. He and Swift had already had a falling out in May over comments in the *Guardian*, which was quarrelling with the *Examiner*. By this point Swift was at an arm's length from the *Examiner*, of whose editor, William Oldisworth, he said, 'He is an ingenious fellow, but the most confounded vain Coxcomb in the World; so that I dare not let him see me, nor am acquainted with him'.[170] When Steele said, in a signed letter in *Guardian* no. 53 (12 May 1712), 'it is nothing to me, whether the *Examiner* writes against me in the Character of an estranged Friend, or *an exasperated Mistress*',[171] Swift felt the insult: a friend whose government place he had appealed to Harley to protect despite the difference of party was now publicly treating him as if he were responsible for an inferior coxcomb's insults.[172] The friendship was over.

Back in London, Swift found Steele his principal antagonist. He was rallying opposition around the cause of Dunkirk, whose fortifications the French, despite a commitment at Utrecht, had not yet demolished. Indeed, its people had recently petitioned Queen Anne to spare them. Writing as English Tory in *Guardian* no. 128 (7 August 1713), Steele had provoked a paper war on the subject of Dunkirk, for which Tories mauled him for disrespect to the Queen. Dunkirk provided the opposition with its perfect symbol. Treated as a typical French failure to honour treaty obligations, it allowed Whigs to call the Peace of Utrecht into question. A well guarded port, it posed a military threat to Britain. Better (from a Whig perspective), the Pretender had sailed from Dunkirk on his abortive 1708 attempt to invade Scotland. Since the Pretender was still harboured in Lorraine, Dunkirk allowed the opposition to raise fears that the Tories, who permitted these breaches of the treaty, represented a threat to the Protestant succession. Finally, it raised the question of trade in a way that exacerbated Tory divisions over the succession. A haven for French privateers, Dunkirk had been a threat to English shipping. Controlled by England, it promised commercial access to the formerly Spanish, now Austrian Netherlands. A ministry soft on Dunkirk, by contrast, seemed to prefer connections with France. In the April Parliament, Sir Thomas Hanmer and the March Club had led a principled Tory revolt against unfavourable articles in the treaty of commerce with France that was so dear to Bolingbroke. They voted with the opposition to defeat the bill. Closer relations with France seemed to symbolize sympathy for the Pretender, so these apparently commercial debates in fact raised the issue of the succession, on which Tories were divided. Since Bolingbroke blamed Oxford for his own failures of diplomacy and parliamentary management, the opposition was using Dunkirk to keep alive questions that had exacerbated divisions within the ministry.[173] No other issue could allow the opposition to play so effectively on ministry weakness.

Swift had already skirmished with Steele and other Whigs who raised alarm over the succession. In May 1712, William Fleetwood, Bishop of St Asaph, published *Four Sermons* with a preface that Steele promptly reprinted in *Spectator* no. 384, because it argued that resistance to James and support for the Hanoverian succession were entirely in accord with Christian doctrine.[174] Swift responded in *A Letter of Thanks from My Lord W[harto]n to the Lord B*^p *of S. Asaph in the Name of the Kit-Cat Club* (July 1712). Once again, he could impersonate a godless Whig, this time ironically thanking the bishop for rejecting Christian obedience to royal authority. Since his sympathy with clergymen rather than the bishops in the upper house of Convocation was of a piece with his sympathy for independent squires, he added a High-Church jab at the often Low-Church bishops: 'we have never been disappointed in any of our Whig Bishops, but they have always unalterably acted up, or, to speak properly, down to their Principles'.[175] In a shrewd paper contributed to the *Examiner* for 24 July 1712, Swift replied to Steele in kind by printing Fleetwood's original preface to one of the sermons, preached on the death of the Duke of Gloucester and originally published in 1700.[176] There Fleetwood carefully directed his concern at those who would exploit the tragic loss 'to turn a Kingdom into a Commonwealth';[177] that is, against the Whigs rather than the Tories who seem to be his current target:

> It was a great Masterpiece of Art in this admirable Author, to write such a Sermon, as, by help of a *Preface*, would pass for a *Tory* Discourse in one Reign, and by omitting that *Preface*, would denominate him a *Whig* in another: Thus by changing the Position, the Picture represents either the *Pope* or the *Devil*, the *Cardinal* or the *Fool*.[178]

Swift turns the bishop's opportunistic sermon into a clever but superficial trick to amaze the crowd, like double perspective pictures in which a shift of point of view transforms an image into its opposite.[179]

Partly in response to Steele's pamphlet, *The Importance of Dunkirk Consider'd: In defence of the Guardian of August the 7th. In a Letter to the Bailiff of Stockbridge. By Mr. Steele* (1713), Swift similarly attempted to discredit Steele by publishing *The Importance of the Guardian Considered, in a Seccond Letter to the Bailiff of Stockbridge. By a Friend of Mr. St—le* (1713). It is not that 'he never gave Steele the immense credit he deserved for daring to put his real name to his work'.[180] Rather, Swift saw only vanity in the new MP publishing his views over his name in a letter to the bailiff of his constituency. Steele seemed to be claiming an inordinate authority for private opinions addressed from himself to himself to be published in a journal he edited:

> to render this Matter clear to the very meanest Capacities, Mr. *English Tory*, the very same Person with Mr. *Steele*, writes a Letter to *Nestor Ironside*, Esq; who is the same Person with *English Tory*, who is the same Person with Mr. *Steele*: And Mr. *Ironside*, who is the same Person with *English Tory*, publishes the Letter written by *English Tory*, who is the same Person with Mr. *Steele*, who is the same Person with Mr. *Ironside*.[181]

Written a decade earlier, these layers of literary self-referentiality might have earned Steele a distinguished place in *A Tale of a Tub*. A former army officer, Steele represents naming himself as a courageous act that distinguishes him from the timidity of the Examiner, but the ploy backfires. If Steele's authority rests on his personal credibility, then to Swift it rests on a narrow foundation indeed. Swift adopts the obvious and necessary strategy of demonstrating that the MP for Stockbridge is, alas, a puppy:

> Mr. *Steele* is the Author of two tolerable Plays, (or at least of the greatest part of them) which, added to the Company he kept, and to the continual Conversation and Friendship of Mr. *Addison*, hath given him the Character of a Wit. To take the height of his Learning, you are to suppose a Lad just fit for the University, and sent early from thence into the wide World, where he followed every way of Life that might least improve or preserve the Rudiments he had got. He hath no Invention, nor is Master of a tolerable Style; his chief Talent is Humour, which he sometimes discovers in Writing and Discourse; for after the first Bottle he is no disagreeable Companion.[182]

For anyone who remembers the warmth and intellectual excitement of Swift's and Steele's early acquaintance, this passage essay makes painful reading.

In this exchange, Steele adopts a more modern position than Swift. He is closer to a political world in which any individual has a right to state his political opinions. But in Swift's day, anonymity was the impersonal choice, not the craven choice. Even writers with the professional authority of Baron Somers wrote anonymously. Swift's viability as the Examiner had been on the wane as soon as readers like Gay began guess his identity. Given Steele's opposite strategy, Swift's cruel insults are not gratuitous. It is unfair of Swift not to acknowledge the enormous success of the *Tatler*, but Steele's achieved public identity as a playwright and a journalist actually, Swift insists, subverts his political authority, denying it the impersonality of argument:

> You are to know then, that Mr. *Steele* publishes every Day a Peny-paper to be read in Coffee-houses, and get him a little Money. This by a Figure of Speech, he calls, *laying Things before the Ministry*, who seem at present a little too busy to regard such Memorials; and, I dare say, never saw his Paper, unless he sent it them by the Peny-Post.[183]

Writing in his own name, Steele stands convicted accused of self-interest and vanity. Perhaps only a fellow propagandist could write so scathingly of professional political argument.

After much advertisement and many delays, Steele produced, by subscription, *The Crisis: or, A Discourse Representing, From the Most Authentick Records, the Just Causes of the Late Happy Revolution*, dedicating it to the clergy of the established church in the hope that, thus instructed, they would recommend the Revolution

Settlement to their parishioners.[184] The Whigs hoped that their propagandist could shape debate as Swift had in *The Conduct of the Allies*. Swift promptly replied in his last substantial English political pamphlet, *The Publick Spirit of the Whigs: Set forth in their Generous Encouragement of the Author of The Crisis: With Some Observations on the Seasonableness, Candor, Erudition, and Style of that Treatise* (23 February 1714). He found answering Steele's miscellaneous pamphlet 'the most disgustful Task that ever I undertook'. He is personal enough: 'EVERY Whiffler in a laced Coat, who frequents the Chocolate House, and is able to spell the Title of a Pamphlet, shall talk of the Constitution with as much Plausibility as this very Solemn Writer, and with as good Grace blame the Clergy for medling with Politicks, which they do not understand'. What Steele presents as observation is in fact 'a miserable mangled Translation of six Verses out of that famous Poet' Virgil.[185] But Swift writes on behalf of the ministry and the clergy alike. That Steele presumed to instruct the clergy was offensive enough. The implication that the clergy were commonly Jacobite was, he thought, an outright lie:

> THIS honest, civil, ingenious Gentleman, knows in his Conscience, that there are not ten Clergymen in *England* (except Non-jurors) who do not abhor the Thoughts of the *Pretender* reigning over us, much more than himself. But this is the Spittle of the Bishop of *Sarum*, which our Author licks up, and swallows, and then coughs out again, with an Addition of his own Phlegm.[186]

Swift dismisses Steele as the lickspittle of an antagonist of more consequence. Bishop Burnet had like Fleetwood published an anomalous preface. The preface to the long anticipated third volume of his *History of the Reformation* appeared in advance of the work itself, expressing fear of popery (appropriately to his topic) and (illegitimately, Swift thought) the Pretender. That may be why his jaunty verse attack on Steele, *The First Ode of the Second Book of Horace Paraphrased and Addressed to Richard Steele, Esq.* (7 January 1714), also attributes *The Crisis* to 'Burnet's shrewd advice'.[187]

Swift had recently attacked Burnet in *A Preface to the B—p of S—r—m's Introduction to the Third Volume of the History of the Reformation of the Church of England. By Gregory Misosarum* (7 December 1713). In a parody designed to associate the Whigs with godlessness, *Mr. C[olli]ns's Discourse of Free-Thinking, Put into Plain English by Way of Abstract, for the Use of the Poor* (25 January 1713), he had (as Collins) gamely listed virtually everyone from Socrates and Hobbes to the Old Testament Prophets and Josephus as free thinkers. Clerical attacks on his party, however, provoked a special intensity. In the Bishop of Sarum's ability to 'smell *Popery* at five hundred Miles distance, better than *Fanaticism* just under his Nose', Swift again saw only the folly of those who would repeal the Irish test because they are more afraid of popery than dissent. Vehemently denying that Catholicism poses a greater threat than it had under Charles II, he asserts what he never doubted: 'those whom we usually understand by the Appellation of *Tory* or High-church Clergy, were the greatest Sticklers against the exorbitant Proceedings of King *James* the Second, the best Writers against Popery, and the most exemplary Sufferers for the Established Religion'.[188] Swift was a clergyman to whom this was a source of pride. He would have seen nothing revisionist in the notion that the Tory Anglican gentry and clergy were primarily responsible for the Glorious Revolution. In his view, his Old Whig politics were entirely consistent with his clerical office. One of his earliest odes had celebrated Archbishop Sancroft, who defied James but then became a non-juror, establishing himself as a Cato figure of principled withdrawal from public affairs.

In its defence of his Church and the Revolution, *The Publick Spirit of the Whigs* was consistent and assertive. The pamphlet rapidly went through several editions. Regrettably, Steele's rambling pamphlet contained a defence of the Act of Union that provoked Swift into a self-indulgent attack on the Scots in general and on the Scottish peers in the House of Lords in particular. Since the Tory majority in the House depended on the Scottish representative peers, their protest against an extension of the malt tax to Scotland – in violation (they thought) of the Act of Union – threatened the ministry. Their angry motion to dissolve the Union failed by only four votes.[189] More profoundly, Swift resented the Scots as Presbyterian regicides whose persecution of their episcopalian fellow Scots demonstrated what would follow any relaxation of the Test Act in Ireland. Just as profoundly, he resented the Act of Union as a betrayal of Ireland. England had embraced the Presbyterian Scots, slighting (and oppressing) the Anglican English of Ireland. This was the burden of Swift's first Irish tract, *The Story of the Injured Lady*, which represented Ireland as a credulous seduced maiden whose English seducer had abandoned her for an ill-bred and filthy scold.[190] Swift obviously found the Act of Union a source of pain. So his animus again outstripped prudence when his ministry was under attack. When the Scottish lords protested, five offensive paragraphs were cancelled in subsequent editions of *The Publick Spirit of the Whigs*, but the damage was done. Citing a condemnation of libellous pamphlets from a speech from the throne, Swift's old enemy Wharton argued that the Swift's fortunately anonymous pamphlet fit the bill. The House condemned it, and when John Barber revealed nothing useful under questioning, petitioned the Queen to post a reward for discovering the author of the seditious pamphlet. Oxford covertly sent his nervous propagandist a bill for £100 pounds to cover 'exigencys',[191] but a writer who helped to polish the speech from the throne found himself with a price of £300 on his head. Fortunately, the Lord Treasurer's protection held and Swift's authorship, widely suspected, was not revealed. His powerful friends had saved him. But the crisis was entirely the product of his own indiscretion.

Since the Act of Union is the most significant legislative accomplishment of Anne's reign, more significant even than the Peace of Utrecht, many found Swift's slurs offensive.[192] *The Publick Spirit of the Tories, Manifested in the Case of the Irish Dean, and His Man Timothy*, attributed to Steele, simply attacked Swift's own political apostasy, associating him with the Tale-Teller and quoting from 'a Late Poem written by a Reverend Divine' – ll. 35–8 of Swift's *Horace, Epistle VII, Book I* – to remind readers that Swift had once praised the Junto worthies he now attacked.[193] Evidence that Swift's authorship was an open secret despite his legal anonymity, this tract is otherwise negligible. However, Swift's protector, Harley, and Harley's most prolific propagandist, Defoe, had been instrumental in accomplishing the union that Swift disparaged. Informed by first-hand experience of Scotland and the negotiations, Defoe responded with 'his most direct attack on Swift'.[194] *The Scots Nation and Union Vindicated; from the Reflections Cast on Them, in an Infamous Libel, Entitl'd the Publick Spirit of the Whigs*, gave more thoughtful attention than Swift ever did – he had written from sectarian and ethnic prejudice – to what was, however, a side issue elevated to importance by Swift's heedless attack. The central issue was not the Union or Dunkirk but Tory support (or not) for the Hanoverian succession. Since a primary motive for England to seek the union was to ensure the Hanoverian succession in Scotland as well as England, the attack on the Union allowed Defoe to accuse Swift of Jacobite sympathies:

> But if any Thing provokes him more than usually against the UNION with *Scotland*, it seems to be the unalterableness of the Protestant Succession, which is establish'd by the said *Union*; and which for that Reason the Jacobites in both Parts of the Country are the only People that push at the Dissolving the said *Union*.[195]

This is a thoroughly Swiftian manoeuvre. Defoe condemns Swift by attributing to him a positive desire for what he takes to be the likely consequence and only sound reason for opposing the Union. Nothing else in Swift's tract supports this accusation. Indeed, the principal point of his attacks on Steele and Burnet is the opposite – to discredit as cynical and unfounded the Whig charge that the Tories did not support the Hanoverian succession. By venting his sectarian and ethnic prejudices in a gratuitous attack on the Scots, Swift undermines the primary thrust of his pamphlet.

Even Swift could not persuade the divided Tories, let alone the Whigs, that they shared the Dean's commitment to the Revolution Settlement and hence the Protestant succession. Nor, since the Queen's health was obviously failing, could he persuade readers that something else, anything other than the succession, was a more pressing concern. Anne had come close to dying in December. Swift published no more political pamphlets in England, and he rapidly wearied of the destructive struggle between Bolingbroke and Oxford to dominate the ministry. He seems to have had no awareness that Oxford and Bolingbroke both dallied with the Pretender, although the condition that he convert to Protestantism proved an insuperable obstacle. He did understand that the Elector of Hanover, one of the allies opposed to the Peace of Utrecht, did not look warmly on the Tories. If the divided leadership left the parliamentary Tories without direction, it is equally true that their unresolved disagreements created the conditions for the ministerial power struggle. For all Swift's sanguine and thoroughly sincere assertions of commitment to the Protestant succession, he could no longer speak as the one voice of the Tories. Some in the party were convinced Jacobites, others were staunchly Hanoverian, and many were ambivalent about what should happen on the death of Queen Anne. Worn out and deprived of a common cause around which to rally opinion, at the end of May Swift retired to visit a clerical friend, John Geree, at Letcombe Bassett in Berkshire. There he could escape the fray, avoid taking sides. There he wrote *Some Free Thoughts on the Present State of Affairs. Written in the Year 1714*, which the Queen's death in July kept him from publishing. Writing of himself in the third person, he says,

> during a very near and Constant Familiarity with the great Men at Court for four Years past, he never could observe even in those Hours of Conversation where there is usually least Restraint, that one Word ever passed among them to shew a Dislike of the present Settlement, although they would sometimes lament that the false Representations of their's and the Kingdom's Enemies had made some Impressions in the Mind of the Successor.[196]

What the party needed was unity, which a divided ministry could not provide. With the Pretender not an option, Bolingbroke hoped to seize firm control, appoint staunch Tories to every conceivable position to which an appointment could be made, and then greet the incoming monarch from a position of indispensable authority. Indecisive in moments of crisis, he would in the event have only a few days between Oxford's fall and the Queen's death, too little time to accomplish anything.

The story of Bolingbroke's rise and Oxford's fall is familiar.[197] Oxford lost the confidence of the Queen by asking for too great a title for his son, about to marry the heiress of the late Duke of Newcastle. He neglected the Court in grief for the death of his favourite daughter shortly after she gave birth to her first child. Accused of drunkenness as well as neglect, he capably fought a brilliant rearguard action that brought to light the corruption of Bolingbroke's associates, implicating him. His goal seems to have been to exclude Bolingbroke long enough to make it impossible for him to thwart, as he feared he would, the succession of the Elector of Hanover. To his opponents within the ministry, he looked like a dog in the manger, vindictively denying others what was no use to himself. Through charm, bribery, blackening his rival, a strategy to allure the Tory backbenchers, and a tactical rapprochement with Marlborough that appealed to Anne, Bolingbroke eventually won.[198] He rallied Tories by championing High-Church measures that Oxford could not oppose publicly without losing support. He worked to force Whigs out of the armed forces. His Schism Act confined education to members of the established church, threatening to eliminate dissenting academies like that at which, as Wharton charged in debate, Bolingbroke himself had been educated.[199]

Even Swift had reservations, and Nottingham, whose High-Church credentials are beyond dispute, voted against the Schism Act.[200] Yet Oxford had a much surer hold on those with religious conviction than his unprincipled rival for control of the church party: 'apart from Francis Atterbury, no leading Churchman seriously supported Bolingbroke'.[201] Bolingbroke won the last internecine battle, for Oxford fell on 27 July. But he lost the war. When the Queen died on 1 August, Oxford backed the Whigs in support of the Hanoverian succession, and the rest of Parliament fell in line. The Elector was allied with the Whigs, and the Tory ministry was at an end. As Erasmus Lewis shrewdly wrote to Swift on 3 August, 'all old schemes designs projects journey's &c: are broke by the great event'.[202]

Throughout these difficult days, Swift's letters express his loyalty to, and affection for, Oxford: 'in your publick Capacity you have often angred me to the Heart, but as a private man never once. So that if I onely lookt towards my self I could wish you a private Man to morrow'. 'I meddle not with his Faults as he was Minister of State', he wrote to Vanessa, 'but you know his personall Kindness to me was excessive; he distinguished and chose me above all other Men while he was great; and his Letter to me tother day was the most moving imaginable'.[203] Like Swift, Oxford was a man of the past committed to independence rather than party loyalty. He saw himself as a disinterested servant of an independent monarch. Who that monarch should be was also clear. As he said in a memorandum outlining 'arguments for Hanover', the obvious advantages were 'Security of our religion which cannot be under a Papist' and 'Securing our ancient rights which cannot be under one bred up in French maxims and who comes with the [intention?] to revive his father's quarrels'.[204] The Pretender, that is, posed both a religious threat and, as a French-reared absolutist, a constitutional threat. He was doubly unsuited to the British throne. No wonder even most Tories had doubts. Yet Oxford and his ministers had betrayed Britain's allies in pursuit of the peace, offending the heir to the throne who, as Elector of Hanover, was one of those allies. In 1715, the Whigs would impeach him. Confident of his own probity, he would wait out the accusations in the Tower, winning release two years later. Despite his failures of leadership, Bolingbroke, by contrast, grasped that parties and partisan patronage were central to parliamentary government, a principle the Whigs would apply with ruthless consistency during the long proscription of the Tories that followed George I's ascent to the throne. To that extent he belonged to the venal future that accepted the patronage opportunities created by the fiscal-military state. He could welcome it, for he had little probity to be confident of, but for the same reason he would flee to France at the suggestion of impeachment. Eventually he would bolt to the Pretender, involve himself in the failed uprising of 1715, and then offer to betray his Jacobite allies to the Whig ministry in exchange for a return to England.

At Letcombe Bassett Swift watched painful events from a distance but without detachment. He still hoped to influence events. Sent obliquely in disguised handwriting to Barber for printing, Swift's *Some Free Thoughts upon the Present State of Affairs* was shown to Bolingbroke by the nervous printer, delaying publication until too late: 'how comicall a Thing was it to shew th[a]t Pamphlet to Ld Bol— of all men living. Just as if *the Publick Spirit* had been sent to Argyle for his Approbation'.[205] Like his history of the treaty negotiations and his other essays in self-justification when he looked back on this period, it missed its time and was published only much later. Events moved too quickly for his pen. In retirement, he would find himself again an outsider, an associate of a dismissed ministry that Bolingbroke's actions made it easy to suspect of the Jacobitism he had so resolutely denied. Moreover, he ended his English political career as he had begun it, by distancing himself from his friends.

This time, happily, the distance was physical rather than political and social. His correspondence records the continuing warmth of the friendships it sustained. He remained friends with both Oxford and Bolingbroke, including Oxford in the close, informal literary society he had long craved. With Oxford, the group included Swift, Arbuthnot, Pope, Gay, and Swift's protégé from St Patrick's, the poet Thomas Parnell. (On becoming Dean, Swift unsuccessfully recommended Parnell to his own just-vacated prebend of Dunlavin.)[206] Pope's suggestion in October 1713 expressed Swift's wish, and the group rapidly took shape under his influence. Given his association with the fragmenting ministry, Swift's presence determined the group's Tory associations. The entire group of friends met only a few times in late winter and spring of 1714, usually in Arbuthnot's rooms at St James's. Pope and Parnell spent a few days with Swift at Letcombe Bassett, where political gloom precluded Scriblerian merriment. Pope's project of a mock-journal had developed into the parody unlearned works under the guise of a persona created by the group, Martinus Scriblerus. It provided a common focus for literary conviviality, concisely asserted shared standards, and provided a scope large enough to enable masterpieces as diverse as *The Dunciad*, *The Beggar's Opera*, and *Gulliver's Travels*.[207]

Swift set out for Ireland on 16 August, reaching Dublin on the 24th. He could look back on unprecedented success as press chief and pamphleteer for the Tory ministry. He could take pride in the accomplishment of a peace treaty that ended a long, ruinous war. If it galled him to contemplate a future in Ireland rather than England, he could look forward to improving his plot of Irish land at Laracor. He could also anticipate a future not as a country vicar but as the dean of an important cathedral. A letter to Ford written shortly after his arrival suggests that he did not anticipate a future writing on Irish politics: 'I cannot stop my Ears when People of the wisest sort I see (who are indeed no Conjurers) tell me a thousand foolish Things of the Publick: But I hope I shall keep my Resolution of never medling with Irish Politicks'.[208] Although he largely kept his resolution for a decade, it is hard to read these words without smiling, for in 1724 he would spectacularly return to political writing by addressing Irish causes. However, his record as a warrior of words notwithstanding, the case can be made that the legacy of friendship with a small group of wits who began meeting shortly before he left England was the most enduring gift of his days as an English political writer. The wit who had so hoped to impress Addison and Steele had formed the literary associations for which he is most remembered. Although Pope and Gay still had Whig associates – Pope contributed to the *Guardian* – their association with Swift, permanently tarred by his association with the Harley ministry, confirmed their bent for satire and ensured that they are all recalled as *Tory* satirists.

5 'DO I BECOME A *SLAVE* IN SIX HOURS, BY CROSSING THE CHANNEL?': THE DEAN, THE DRAPIER AND IRISH POLITICS

Swift returned to Ireland in August 1714 to take his oaths to the new monarch, resume his role as vicar of Laracor, and assume his duties as Dean of St Patrick's, Dublin. Now he was in exile, not simply enjoying a voluntary retreat. The disintegration of Harley's ministry had ended his career as an English propagandist. Worse, the incoming Whig ministry acted, and some of his friends then reacted, as if they wanted to confirm Swift's deep conviction of human fractiousness and factiousness. He returned under suspicion, tarred by the actual or apparent Jacobitism of some of his closest associates. Government spies now scrutinized his correspondence for evidence of his or his friends' treasonable involvement with the Pretender and his agents. St Patrick's Cathedral rather than the nation was now the centre of his responsibilities. In every sense, he lived at the margin of his old world, locked in opposition to the new order that had displaced it. He lived in Ireland, not England. He opposed the ministry in London rather than speaking for it. Even when he eventually adopted an Irish voice, he commonly found himself speaking from the margins of power to those who ruled Ireland. He could easily have settled into clerical inconsequence, busying himself with administration of the cathedral, skirmishing with his archbishop, dining out on tales of his glory days, and generally lamenting the unfulfilled promise of his youth. A decade of near silence suggested as much. But the author of *A Tale of a Tub* and *The Conduct of the Allies* found in his mid-fifties that he could not avoid meddling in Irish politics. If 'mad Ireland hurt [Yeats] into poetry', as W. H. Auden said,[1] it angered Swift into prose. About the time he began work on his deeply political masterpiece, *Gulliver's Travels*, he published his first political tract since 1714, *A Proposal for the Universal Use of Irish Manufacture* (1720), provoking a hostile administration to arrest his printer. Spurred by political developments, he interrupted work on *Gulliver's Travels* in 1724 to write his most brilliant and successful political tracts, later collected as *The Drapier's Letters* (1724–5). A few years later, however, he wrote *A Modest Proposal* (1729), a savage parody of futile pamphlets by well-intentioned projectors like himself. In these works, Swift again assumed the voice of his nation, this time not England but an increasingly assured Anglo-Irish nation.

Swift found, in short, that he could not escape the public identity created by his emotionally extreme rhetoric, which invited many to credit him with an extremist ideology, often Jacobite though occasionally radical Whig. Posing as someone above the conflict of party, he had nevertheless created a partisan public character open to counterattack, even to legal punishment. This lesson that he was in the thick of the battle, not an observer of it, informs his Irish tracts. He retained his distinctive and (to some) contradictory allegiances to liberty and to an authoritarian national church, but he remained an independent whose views would inevitably place him within a minority in any party. The Irish issues that engaged (and enraged) him were national, he thought, not simply partisan even to the limited extent that English party labels made sense in Ireland. Although he continued to play extremes against a middle that he often left implied, he came to speak to, and at his most compelling to speak as and for, a subject far more marginal than the notional English squire he had impersonated in the *Examiner*. He adopted not simply an Anglo-Irish perspective – what could be more marginal to the English? – but also the identity of a humble draper. This suggests how far behind Swift had left the Tale-Teller's (and the Examiner's) longing for a machine to elevate him above the crowd. Speaking from within the crowd, his only shelter from punishment now that his friends were no longer great, he articulated the aspirations and fears of an oppressed community. In Ireland, he found the voice that still speaks directly to readers who embrace a colonial identity that he rejected.

Supported by Whigs and Hanoverian Tories, including Oxford and Dartmouth, the accession of George I to throne took place remarkably smoothly. Supported by George, the Whigs ruthlessly secured their dominance. Bolingbroke was dismissed at the end of August, before George's arrival in England on 12 September 1714. Given clear signs of Court support for the Whigs, the election in January 1715 almost exactly reversed the party standings of the 1713 Parliament, reducing the Tories to a minority. When Parliament met in March, the Whig ministry exacerbated partisan animosity by preparing to impeach the ministers who had negotiated the Peace of Utrecht. Swift had as a Whig written his *Discourse* to oppose the Commons' drive, led by Harley, to impeach members of the Whig Junto over the partition treaties. He now endured the spectacle of a Whig ministry treating his Tory friends the same way over the peace treaties. The new Commons decided to impeach Oxford, Bolingbroke, Ormond, and the Earl of Strafford for negotiating the Peace of Utrecht. Oxford resolved to face down his accusers, but the reaction of his other friends can only have increased Swift's distress. To avoid arrest, Bolingbroke fled to France on 27 March. In June and July, articles of impeachment were brought to the bar of the House of Lords. On 16

July, Oxford was committed to the Tower to await trial. In late July, Ormond too fled to France, abandoning his effort to organize a Jacobite uprising in the West Country. There was enough popular unrest to encourage some that there was widespread Jacobite sympathy. It is as likely, though, that the discontent responded to the ministry's prosecution of the former ministers, for the reversal in the number of seats each party held did not express a shift in popular support. The parties divided the small electorate pretty equally in both 1713 and 1715, leaving many to resent any attempt to stigmatize the former ministry.[2] More than personal concern for his friends fed Swift's anger at the state of affairs under the new ministry.

The potentially serious Jacobite uprising of 1715 naturally provoked nervousness in Ireland, but apart from giving the dissenters an occasion to argue for a repeal of the Test in its aftermath, it had little effect there.[3] Since Jacobitism appealed to those Scots who were disaffected with the Union, it was a more serious matter in Scotland, where the Earl of Mar raised the Jacobite standard in September. Still, the Jacobite forces were defeated at Sherrifmuir in Scotland and Preston in northwestern England in November. By the time the Pretender himself landed in Scotland on 22 December, his desperate uprising was largely spent; he returned to the Continent on 4 February.[4] Bolingbroke had impulsively joined the Pretender in France, but even a former minister of War could not make up for Jacobite weaknesses in planning, resources, and military support. Jacobitism was isolated diplomatically. The duc d'Orléans, the regent during the minority of the new French king, had a claim on the French throne that depended on respecting the Peace of Utrecht, which excluded Philip V of Spain.[5] Since the French therefore offered only covert support, the Pretender could not, like William of Orange, invade at the head of a foreign army. Perhaps partly in consequence, English support for the Jacobite rising was weak. Tory criticism of the new regime could readily adopt a Jacobite colouring and support an anti-Hanoverian mob, but there was little readiness actively to resist the Protestant heir as determined in Parliament by the Act of Succession. 'In this context', writes Daniel Szechi,

> it is instructive to note that plebeian Tories-cum-Jacobites in England expressed themselves far more vociferously against the Hanoverian regime in rioting throughout the winter of 1714–15, reaching a crescendo in the spring and early summer, than their Scottish counterparts. Yet when the time for action came the social superiors of the mobs proclaiming 'King James III' or bawling 'No Cuckold! No Hanover' in streets and market-squares across the Midlands and south of England were paralysed with fear and indecision.[6]

Whatever disaffected Tories of rank were doing, they were not resolutely preparing for a Stuart restoration. Leaders were few, communication poor, the prospect of foreign support faint. Certainly the government soon felt confident that it could contain any unrest: George began a five-month visit to Hanover in July 1716.[7]

Nevertheless, it is important to give full credit to the emotional intensity contemporaries brought to the issues symbolized by the loaded terms Whigs and Tories flung at each other. A charge of 'godlessness' or 'Jacobitism' could be a calculating or cynical slur designed to discredit an opponent, but its effectiveness depended on its ability to trigger an intense response. In Swift's attacks on the Whigs in the *Examiner*, for example, the charge of godlessness functions as a shorthand for a passionate attachment to the established church and a concurrent fear that that church was threatened by, for example, the publication of unorthodox opinions or a legislative attack on the Test Act. Memories of the civil wars had yoked this fear with fear of a 'commonwealth' (republic). The Sacheverell trial that swept the Tories to office in 1710 demonstrates the strength of this association. Swift was no doubt calculating enough when he used the term in the *Examiner*, but there can be no doubt that he was deeply attached to the Church of Ireland nor that he was genuinely offended by Godolphin's attempt to barter support for a repeal of the Test in exchange for the first fruits. Although Swift did not acknowledge it, there was an equally genuine shorthand in the accusation of Jacobitism that even he could not avoid. Here the attachment was to the Revolution Settlement that had preserved the liberties of the subject, the concurrent fear that the Pretender would restore the dreaded royal absolutism (and Roman Catholicism) of James II and Charles I.

Both fears now seem grossly exaggerated.[8] They were the product of historical trauma, however, and they seemed real enough at the time. When Defoe accused the author of *The Publick Spirit of the Whigs* of Jacobitism, for example, he was mounting a complex political argument. It is far from obvious that he was attributing a particular political idea to Swift, a conviction that the Pretender rather than the Elector should succeed to the British throne on the death of Queen Anne. But he was deliberately polarizing debate, tarring Swift as one of Them, not one of Us. An English Presbyterian who had supported the Duke of Monmouth, Defoe had encouraged the Union under Harley's guidance. Viewing the Scots without Swift's ingrained ethnic and sectarian hostility, he genuinely thought that any attack on the Act of Union or on the Scots more generally weakened the united kingdom that had been created to ensure that different kings did not assume the thrones of England and Scotland. Intentionally or not, therefore, *The Publick Spirit of the Whigs* did, Defoe thought, serve the Jacobite cause. His argument was inevitably also personal. The author of *The Shortest Way with the Dissenters* could only view the High-Churchman Swift with the same hostility that Swift in turn directed at dissenters like Defoe. Whatever Swift's actual opinions on monarchy – and he never displayed anything like the intense personal attachment to a ruler that Defoe gave to William III – he looked like an agent of Jacobitism from Defoe's corner of the political landscape. By the same token, whatever his actual religious views, Defoe looked like the face of encroaching infidelity when Swift looked down from the political heights. The pictures partisans painted of their opponents were inaccurate, but they served their polemical aims very well.

Because his closest associates were suspected of Jacobitism, Swift found that he could not dizentangle himself from a strand of the Tory party that he had dismissed as negligible. He had remained loyal to Oxford in the conflict with Bolingbroke: 'I shall lose all favor with those now in power [Bolingbroke, Lady Masham, and their supporters] by following Ld Oxf^d in his Retreat', he wrote in July 1714.[9] But Oxford himself was under suspicion. Swift was also close to Bolingbroke. He enjoyed cordial relations with Ormond, to whom he owed his preferment, and his Duchess, who had generously given Swift portraits of herself and her husband.[10] The presumption that the prominent Tories were Jacobites seemed to be confirmed when Bolingbroke fled to France and then, just as impulsively and despite his protests to the contrary, joined the Pretender, becoming his Secretary of State. Other Tories bolted for cover. 'I send this to acquaint you', wrote Lewis in February 1715 – before Parliament had yet met – 'that if you have not already hid your papers in some private place in the hands of a trusty friend, I fear they will fall into the hands of your Enemy's';[11] he cited proceedings towards Strafford and Prior. Swift was not one of the negotiators of the peace, but the histories of the peace he was working on could have invited hostile scrutiny. After Ormond's impeachment, Swift wrote skeptically to Knightley Chetwode, 'I do not believe or see one word is offered to prove their old Slander of bringing in the Pretender. The Treason lyes wholly in making the Peace'.[12] Although Ormond was a weak peg on which to hang his fidelity to the Hanoverian succession, Swift is right that the peace was the actual target of Whig animosity and the source of the new King's resentment. The Whigs wanted to do to the Tories what Bolingbroke had hoped to do to them. They wanted to seize power and then discredit their opponents so thoroughly that they could no longer mount a serious bid for power. Although Swift saw the accusation of Jacobitism as a Whig lie to discredit loyal Tories, he had little doubt of seriousness of the attack. To Lord Harley, Oxford's son, Swift wrote in May 1715: 'there is nothing too bad to be apprehended in my opinion, from the present Face of Things'.[13]

Swift was slow to recognize that the smoke tainting him originated in an actual fire. In a letter to Chetwode, he brazens out the fact that his mail is being intercepted: 'I have been much entertained with news of my self since I came here, tis s[ai]d there was another Packet directed to me seised by the Government; but after opening several Seals it proved onely plum-cake'.[14] Archbishop King and the other Lords Justices of Ireland who were examining Swift's correspondence could in fact find more than cake. In a devoted but indiscreet letter to his 'best Friend and Patron', Barber said on 3 May 1715: 'Two Days before the *Captain* [i.e., Bolingbroke] went abroad, he sent for me, and amongst other things, asked me with great earnestness, If there was no possibility of sending a Letter safe to your hands? I answer'd, I knew but of one way and that was to direct to you under Cover to Mrs Van–. He reply'd, no way by Post wou'd do'.[15] Bolingbroke was right. Given the Jacobitism of several of his correspondents, letters to and from Swift commanded attention, and it would be hard to persuade anyone that Swift's own hands were clean. In December 1716, King ignited an epistolary quarrel by reporting to Swift 'a strong report that My Ld Bolingbroge will return here & be pardoned, certainly it must not be for nothing. I hope he can tell no ill story of you'.[16] In a letter to Archdeacon Walls, Swift complains that 'the Arch-Bp plainly lets me know that he believes all I have s^d of my self and the late Ministry with relation to the Pretender to be Court Lyes'.[17] His conviction of his own integrity made it hard for him to grasp how much circumstances told against him. The gossip that he guarded against in his personal relationships with Stella and Vanessa could be even more powerful in politics, where he was sometimes openly indiscreet.[18]

Swift's reply to King asserts, as he consistently did, that he was 'always a Whig in Politicks'. His self-justification reveals an odd mix of conscious rectitude with naivety and political principle:

And as to my self, if I were of any Importance I should be very easy under such an Accusation, much easyer than I am to think Your Grace imagines me in any danger, or that Ld Bolingbroke should have any ill Story to tell of Me; He knows, and loves, and thinks too well of me to be capable of such an Action. But I am surprised to think Your Grace could talk or act or correspond with me for some Years past, while you must needs believe me a most false and vile man, declaring to you on all Occasion[s] my Abhorrence of the Pretender, and yet privatly engaged with a Ministry to bring him in, and therefore warning me to look to my self and prepare my defence against a false Brother coming over to discover such Secrets as would hang me. Had there been ever the least Overture or Intent of bringing in the Pretend^r during my Acquaintance with the Ministry, I think I must have been very stupid not to have pickt out some discoveryes or Suspicions; and tho I am not sure I should have turned Informer, yet I am sure I should have dropt some generall Cautions, and immediatly have retired. When People say things were not ripe at the Queen's death, they say they know not what Things were rotten, and had the Ministers any such Thoughts they should have begun 3 years before, and they who say otherwise understand nothing of the State of the Kingdom at that time.[19]

Swift reveals himself as a loyal friend but a poor judge of character. Bolingbroke had already defected from the Jacobite court, and in hope of a pardon, he had agreed to betray information about English Jacobites to the ministry.[20] There was a basis for the rumour King had heard, and as he shrewdly surmised, any pardon would not be for nothing.

Bolingbroke cannot have had an honest story that would incriminate Swift. Such conversations were carefully kept out of his hearing, and he was not privy to Bolingbroke's devious correspondence with the Pretender – or with Oxford's.

Just as he was cheerfully oblivious to the significant minority of Jacobite parliamentarians, he everywhere betrays his naive certainty that he was too deeply in the ministry's confidence not to know everything. When he confesses that he 'must have been very stupid not to have pickt out some discoveryes or Suspicions', he seems to intend this as evidence that there was nothing to discover. But it is hard not to agree with him. A sophisticated propagandist, he seems at times to have been a political innocent. That Oxford botched his management of the House of Lords on the eve of the peace negotiations seems not to have crossed his mind. He subscribed instead to a bizarrely implausible conspiracy theory that grossly underestimated the queen while it overestimated the Duchess of Somerset's influence on policy. (In pursuit of her policy, the queen had gradually but resolutely changed her ministers; challenged, she would fight back by creating new peers.) That his brilliant but unsteady friend Bolingbroke was driven by a practically naked lust for power seems to have escaped only Swift, even though Bolingbroke fomented divisions within the Tories to serve his ends. Imagining that at some point cluelessness became a wilful refusal to see or even an active collusion adds an element of intrigue to this story. However, there is a lot of evidence that Swift's grasp of political behaviour lagged well behind his grasp of political principles. Even though he was trying to get Swift to take his situation more seriously, Archbishop King exonerated him, although he rebuked him at the same time: 'I never believed you for the P[re]tender, but remember that when the surmises of that matter run high, you retired, which agrees with what you say you ought to have done in that case'.[21] Swift's behaviour is sometimes more ambiguous than his assertion of integrity admits.

King had taken the measure of his able but headstrong subordinate. Had he not trusted that Swift was not 'for the Pretender', and had he not said so persuasively to the other Lords Justices, Swift would undoubtedly have found himself being interrogated, perhaps in London. More sympathetic to the Whig ministry than Swift, he like Swift staunchly upheld the privileges of the Church of Ireland and opposed relaxing the Test. He understood Swift's political principles. 'But pray by what artifice', he asked Swift in February 1709, 'did you contrive to pass for a Whig? As I am an honest man, I courted the greatest Whigs I knew, and could not gain the reputation of being counted one'.[22] This is an Irish comment, acknowledging their shared recognition of the imperfect fit between Irish experience and English parties. King had been imprisoned in Dublin Castle for resisting James II, and to the horror of those churchmen who felt that only passive resistance was acceptable, he was (and is) plausibly suspected of transmitting intelligence to William's forces. Moreover, he had written one of the most popular and important Irish defences of the Revolution, *The State of the Protestants of Ireland under the Late King James's Government* (1691).[23] No doubt aimed at churchmen, an abstract of his book circulated in London in 1713 under the title, *An Answer to All that Has Ever Been Said, or Insinuated, in Favour of a Popish Pretender*.[24]

King is usually celebrated as a Whig. Yet far from presenting a strongly Whig argument, he stopped short of advocating direct resistance, preferring to interpret the Revolution providentially.[25] Like Swift, then, he was a strong defender of the Revolution who resisted a strictly contractual view of royal authority. His position as a Lord Justice attests to the respect he commanded from the Whig ministry, even though he parted ways with it when the privileges of the Church were challenged or the independence of Irish institutions was questioned. He was less likely than Swift to treat views 'in politics' and views 'in the church' more or less independently, but like his famous subordinate, he was a High-Church Whig of a specifically Anglo-Irish sort. He seems to have enjoyed rubbing his cocky Dean's nose in the obvious Jacobitism of his associates, but he does not seem to have doubted his support for the Revolution settlement.

Then and now, the private lives of public individuals attracted speculation. Combined with his obvious eccentricity, Swift's habitual air of unimpeachable rectitude still provokes readers to look for evidence of his human fallibility, even culpability. Since 'Swift was, and remains, a man of secrets', as Michael DePorte writes,[26] he invited secret histories, a politically charged and increasingly important narrative form.[27] In one form, secret histories of Swift address his friendships with women. They look for signs that, as Swift himself said in *The Mechanical Operation of the Spirit*, 'however Spiritual Intrigues begin, they generally conclude like all others' (*Tale*, 288). In their most straightforward form, they adopt Horace Walpole's speculation, credited by Margaret Anne Doody, that 'coffee' in Swift's somewhat later letters to Vanessa is code for their sexual intimacy.[28] The Dean looks considerably less odd – more conventionally human – if Cadenus and Vanessa, as he called them in his famous poem, actually became lovers. A more elaborate secret history with even stronger eighteenth-century credentials addresses Swift's lasting relationship with Stella. According to this story, Swift and Stella were married in 1716, the service performed secretly and without witnesses by their friend St George Ashe, bishop of Clogher. It was a condition of the marriage that they continue to live apart, the marriage serving to safeguard Stella's reputation and perhaps also to allay her jealousy of Vanessa, the young woman who had followed Swift to Dublin. Even the extravagant romantic speculation that Swift and Stella were both illegitimate children of Sir William Temple dates back to the Earl of Orrery's 1752 life of Swift, the first but by no means the last to credit the secret marriage.

Gossip often follows an unconventional friendship between a man and a younger woman, of course, and in the eighteenth century it carries a faint odour of the misogynistic assumption that only one thing could compel a man to spend time with a woman. Although the evidence is circumstantial, however, this durable story originated among people who knew Swift. There can be no doubt that Swift's relationships with both Esther Johnson (Stella) and Hester Vanhomrigh (Vanessa) were extremely important to him. They began as mentor-pupil relationships, but from Eloisa and Abelard to the heroine and her mentor-lover in so many late eighteenth-century novels, the mentor-pupil relationship was regarded as erotic. Swift's relationships with Stella and Vanessa certainly developed into friendships with a strong sexual charge. Since eccentrics do sometimes behave conventionally, these stories satisfy some demanding scholars.[29] The skeptic can note that finding a key to Swift's secret history in an affair or a clandestine marriage accepts the explanatory power of romantic clichés that Swift invariably parodied. It has the further disadvantage that it humanizes Swift by making a hypocrite of Stella, too. As Downie reminds us, Stella represented herself in legal documents as a spinster.[30] What is certain is that Swift was a remarkably public figure whose unconventional private life provoked remark.

Speculation that Swift might actually be a Jacobite fulfils a similar narrative function in accounts of Swift's political life. It addresses a series of public eccentricities. It was easy for the Whigs to assume that Swift's blanket denial of Tory Jacobitism concealed his own criminal dalliance with the Pretender. They could then paint him as the most thorough of turncoats, not just a 'whimsical' Tory but a Jacobite. This story made sense of his friendships with the two most prominent Jacobites in the former ministry, Bolingbroke and Ormond. It simplified Swift, turning his odd mixture of brilliance and naivety into consistent work towards an insidious design, but it serviceably tidied up the messy political terrain. The tale tellers could represent everyone's struggle with complex uncertainties as a heroic conflict between good and evil; that is, between royal absolutism (alternatively, landed virtue) and the people's rights (alternatively, the monied interest). They could give the colour of romantic intrigue to Swift's determined opposition to the Whig regime or, alternatively, discredit the force of his critique by associating it with treasonable French absolutism.

The tale of Swift's Jacobitism is even older than accounts of Swift's marriage, perhaps because it told so well. Explicit counterclaims challenge the highly circumstantial evidence, but there is no need to invoke the incest taboo to make bizarre details seem less implausible. Given government supervision, no Jacobite in his senses would express his views openly. This story predicts lack of evidence, professions to the contrary: even evidence against this story can be construed as evidence for it. What else would a Jacobite do under the circumstances? Naturally enough given Swift's complexity, strong scholars position themselves on both sides of the debate.[31] A radical departure in some respects, the assertion of Jacobitism also returns to the traditional view, concisely developed by F. P. Lock, that Swift was essentially Tory. For Higgins, 'Swift may be recognized as, ontologically, a "naturalized" Tory of the Queen Anne and Hanoverian period'.[32] 'The consonance of Swift's political and ecclesiastical attitudes with identifiable Tory party-political positions' that Higgins observes is genuine but partial. Because political positions reflected a combination of religious with constitutional positions, even a tight yoking of Swift with Toryism leaves him at odds with some

Tories. Tory High-Church convictions overlapped significantly with Swift's. But so did Tory resistance to a Catholic Pretender. As a concise statement of his political position, Swift's description of himself to Somers as a Whig 'in politics' but a High-Churchman 'as to religion' has not been bettered. He represented himself not as a Tory, let alone a Jacobite, but as a Whig, typically as an Old Whig.

Although Swift did not idealize the Revolution, he invariably supported it. He attributed it in large part to the principled actions of 'those whom we usually understand by the Appellation of *Tory* or High-church Clergy.'[33] Free from some of the more familiar Tory attitudes, he dismissed Filmer not just as an absolutist like Hobbes but as an absolutist less important to his own political thinking than Hobbes. He almost never speaks of monarchical succession with the reverence that it inspired even among Tory legal-consitutionalists; that is, among Tories who accepted (as he did) a limited monarchy. Late in life, in the margins of the 1734 edition of William Howells's *Medulla Historiae Anglicanae*, he records a response to the Exclusion Bill that aligns him, as he always claimed, with the Old Whigs: 'Wd to God it had passed'.[34] In *The History of the Last Four Years of the Queen*, he brusquely dismisses French scruples about requiring Philip of Anjou to renounce his claim on the French throne:

> It must be confessed that this Project of Renunciation lay under a great Disrepute by the former Practices of this very King *Lewis* the Fourteenth, pursuant to an absurd Notion among many in that Kingdom, of a Divine Right annexed to the Proximity of Blood, not to be controuled by any humane Law.[35]

Even for many English Tories, however, attachment to hereditary succession was more than an outlandish scruple. For Swift, though, the Revolution and the Act of Succession has constitutional authority. Even in France, he adds, succession is not followed strictly.

Consistent with this position but at odds with both Tory and Whig orthodoxy, Swift denied any parallel between Charles I, the blessed martyr, and James II:

> Yet, this we may justly say in defence of the common people, in all civilized nations, that it must be a very bad government indeed, where the body of the subjects will not rather chuse to live in peace and obedience, than take up arms on pretence of faults in the administration, unless where the vulgar are deluded by false preachers .... This was exactly the case in the whole progress of that great rebellion, and the murder of King Charles I; but the late Revolution under the Prince of Orange was occasioned by a proceeding directly contrary, the oppression and injustice there beginning from the throne. For that unhappy Prince, King James II. did not only invade our laws and liberties, but would have forced a false religion on his subjects,

for which he was deservedly rejected, since there could be no other remedy found or at least agreed on.[36]

Swift blames the Puritan predecessors of contemporary dissenters for the death of Charles I. Many Tories would find a sermon on the martyrdom of Charles I an odd place for a defence of the Revolution, and many Whigs would find the sermon an odd subject for an avowed defender of the Revolution, but Swift was an odd Whig who became an odd Tory. Even his opposition to the war owes less to the conventional Tory preference for a blue-water foreign policy than to his distinctive vision of human combativeness. It is consistent with his attitudes that he was devoted to Robert Harley, another former Whig who 'loves the church'.[37] Harley had shepherded the Act of Succession, with all its limitations on royal prerogative, through the House of Commons.

That said, some of Swift's writings have invited other interpretations. His comment on the Exclusion Bill in the margin of Howells is anything but Tory or Jacobite. Examining his marginalia in Burnet's *History of His Own Time*, on the other hand, Brean S. Hammond concludes that 'Many of Swift's marginalia are Jacobite in sympathy, reverential towards Charles I and implacably hostile to William III'.[38] There is some slippage between this generalization ('Jacobite in sympathy') and the examples offered in support (reverence for Charles, hostility to William). In Swift, reverence for Charles I is not evidence of Jacobite sympathies. He shared it with many Anglo-Irishmen. An idealized vision of Ireland under James I and Charles I was an influential part of Sir John Temple's strategy of exaggerating the inexplicable horrors of the 1641 rising in his *History of the Rebellion*.[39] Far from revealing inherent Jacobitism, it went hand in hand with support for the reconquest of Ireland by Cromwell and then by William. Moreover, Swift felt little sympathy for particular monarchs, exiled or not. Even his 30 January sermon says little about Charles I's virtues, much about his wickedness of his murderers and their pernicious descendants, the dissenters. Swift was always ready to criticize monarchs, whether Charles II – 'certainly a very bad prince'[40] – or William III. He believed that both William III, whom he had met, and Anne, whom he had not, had unfairly denied him preferment. His sermon on mutual subjection, undatable in part because there is no reason to associate the sentiment more with one phase of Swift's life than another, observes that 'Princes are born with no more Advantages of Strength or Wisdom than other Men; and, by an unhappy Education, are usually more defective in both than thousands of their Subjects'.[41]

Hammond is a superb reader of Swift's reading, however, so his generalization may have more authority than the particulars he cites. So where does Swift's sympathy lie? He showed so little reverence for particular princes or the principle of hereditary succession that he clearly did not feel that the Pretender had been wrongly excluded from a throne that was his by divine right. The feeling that he

Swift shares with the Jacobites, then, is anger at those in power. In his annotations on Burnet, for example, he expresses a hostility toward William III that many Jacobites certainly shared, as they did his later antagonism toward George. Although he thought the Revolution was necessary, he regretted drastic changes. That is likely why he wished an Exclusion Bill had been passed by Charles II. He expressed his position on the Revolution to Pope:

> As to what is called a Revolution-principle, my opinion was this; That, whenever those evils which usually attend and follow a violent change of government, were not in probability so pernicious as the grievances we suffer under a present power, then the publick good will justify such a Revolution; and this I took to have been the Case in the Prince of Orange's expedition, although in the consequences it produced some very bad effects, which are likely to stick long enough by us.[42]

Swift supported monarchy but criticized many monarchs. In a similar spirit, he championed episcopacy but expressed fierce hostile to particular bishops, including Burnet. Bishops were often, after all, politically appointed broad-church Whigs. When he published anything, however, he entered an arena with little place for subtlety, a place in which he either risked misrepresentation or remained silent. He was not a man to nurse his anger in silence.

Consider the King of Brobdingnag's bafflement at the wars the British were involved in: 'He asked, what Business we had out of our own Islands, unless upon the Score of Trade or Treaty, or to defend the Coasts with our Fleet. Above all, he was amazed to hear me talk of a mercenary standing Army in the Midst of Peace, and among a free People'.[43] Although 'the King of Brobdingnag is primarily the paradigm of the good King', Higgins notes, 'the king and his views had seditious political resonance': 'In having a fictional king articulate what could be understood as a Jacobite political critique of the Hanoverian Whig regime, Swift gives his satire the atmosphere of a dynastic challenge'. More accurately given the existence of the dynastic challenge presented by a Pretender in exile, any critique of the regime could be given a Jacobite colouring. Equally, a supporter of the regime could mute the force of any criticism by associating it with a discreditable extreme. In this polemical context, moreover, a Jacobite would welcome the same (mis)reading. It could bolster the number who could be claimed for the cause, which would then seem more credible, more deserving of domestic and foreign support. As Higgins further notes, one response to *Travels*, *Gulliver Decypher'd*, said of the King of Brobdingnag's views that they 'were understood by contemporary readers as "a common *Jacobite* Insinuation"'.[44]

Yet *Gulliver Decypher'd* immediately qualifies that tactical misreading of the King's position by adding that opposition Whigs make the same criticism:

> EVERY Body knows, that all this has been a common *Jacobite* Insinuation, from King *William's Dutch Guards* to the last *Augmentation*; but, to our great Surprize, it

is of late, very frequently in the Mouths of a quite different Set of People, discarded Courtiers some call them, of whom we may truly say –

> *No King can govern, nor no God can please.*

For unless they are concern'd in the Administration, nothing goes right; and as to Religion, they are equally averse to all the different Modes of it. *Hobs, Harrington, Algernon Sidney*, and *Buchanan* are their only Prophets; tho' some of them admit *Julian Johnson*, Bishop *B – t*, &c. **** amongst the *Minores Prophetæ*.[45]

The real complaint here is that the opposition is discontented only because it lacks power. Power rather than principle determines politics. 'I never met with one honest and reasonable man out of power who was not heartily against all standing armies ...', 'Cato' had claimed in a critique of political parties, 'And I scarce ever met with a man in power, or even the meanest creature of power, who was not for defending and keeping them up'.[46] Requests to fund a standing army had rallied opposition against James II as well as William III,[47] and Swift had vivid memories of how effectively James had used a Catholic standing army to impose his rule on Ireland. *Gulliver Decypher'd* claims that the critique is now as common among disaffected Whigs, who also long for office, as it is among Jacobites, a term that in context is probably being applied to the Tories generally. Whig as he had been or Tory as he became, this tract asserts, Swift was disaffected solely because he was now in opposition.

The writer's surprise is disingenuous. Country concerns, including concern over the size of the peacetime standing army, crossed partisan and social lines. Country ideology provided a political idiom that the opposition shared with those in power. And it was remarkably successful in checking the excesses of the state.[48] Opposition to William too had included not just Tories but Country Whigs like Robert Harley, who were appalled by how easily Court Whigs had shed their 'traditional country sentiment of hostility to an overpowerful court'.[49] *Cato's Letters* had recently restated these opposition positions. Many in England opposed an expensive standing army not because they were Jacobites but because they remembered military rule after the civil wars. They were afraid that the army could allow the new Protestant king to become as absolute as the Roman Catholic king they had rejected. The decipherer's quotation from *Absalom and Achitophel* aligns the King of Brobdingnag with the Earl of Shaftesbury and the radical Whigs of the Exclusion Crisis.[50] He groups the pillars of Whig thought, Algernon Sidney and James Harrington, not only with Hobbes and George Buchanan, the eloquent sixteenth-century Scottish champion of the right to resist royal tyranny, but also with lesser modern Whigs like Burnet. Swift's overt expression of Country discontent places him on the same treacherous ground as both Jacobites and radical Whigs. Even Bolingbroke, it turned out, could not meld the diverse opposition into a unified political force. What is really radical about Swift's passage, it seems, is that Swift imagines a wise king who acts in power with the wisdom usually only encountered in opposition. His rejection of Gulliver's offer of gunpowder confirms his rejection of absolutism.[51]

Swift's *emotional* and *rhetorical* extremism can also encourage readers to assume that he belongs at an ideological extreme. Although he rejected extreme positions intellectually, he revelled in extreme statements. There was nothing placid about his *via media*. For all his affectation of Olympian detachment, he was a combative polemicist as comfortable in Grub Street as in a patrician friend's dining room. His habitual terrain was an embattled middle ground that had to be defended on two fronts, like Harley's position on the 'Isthmus between the Whigs on one side, and violent Tories on the other'.[52] In practice, it was almost impossible not to find oneself somewhere between the extremes defined by, say, radical Whig contractualism and the High-Church radicalism of the strident non-juring pamphleteer Charles Lesley. But a good polemic demonizes opponents, relegating them to an extreme, and Swift relished the task. He loved the thoroughly reductive arguments that provided the staple of the *Examiner*. A fierce exuberance animates his caricatures of Marlborough as a monster of self-serving avarice, Wharton as a depraved monster of unprincipled godlessness. The intense loyalty to his friends that led him to overlook similar failings in a friend like Bolingbroke was equally primitive, the obverse of his savage hostility toward his enemies. His thoroughly counter-productive attacks on the Duchess of Somerset – 'an old red-pate, murdering hag' – reveal the anger at the heart of his pamphleteering (and his satire) with special clarity. So does his *Sermon upon the Martyrdom of K. Charles I*, which draws its force from his uncompromising hatred of dissent. Swift greets political differences with aggression.

A Preface to the Right Reverend Dr. Burnet, Bishop of Sarum's Introduction captures, a little blandly but accessibly, Swift's habit of polarizing enemies in order to discredit them. A suggestive passage plays Bishop Burnet against his ideological opposite, Lesley:

> Without doubt, Mr. *Lesly* is most unhappily misled in his Politicks; but if he be the Author of the late Tract against Popery, he hath given the World such a Proof of his Soundness in Religion, as *many a Bishop* ought to be proud of. ... I detest Mr. *Lesly's* Political Principles as much as his Lordship can do for his Heart; but I verily believe he acts from a mistaken Conscience, and therefore I distinguish between the Principles and the Person. However, it is some Mortification to me, when I see an *avowed Nonjuror* contribute more to the confounding of *Popery*, than could ever be done by a hundred thousand such *Introductions* as this.[53]

Although Swift seldom writes this temperately, this is otherwise his habitual stance. Distinguishing as usual between religious and political principles, he condemns Leslie for the latter and Burnet for the former. Because Leslie was a Jacobite as well as a non-juror, that is, his politics were wrong. Since dissenters and broad-church Whigs condemned features of the established church as papist, however, it serves Swift's purpose to commend Leslie's strong statement of the church's antagonism toward Roman Catholicism, *The Case Stated, between the Church of Rome and the Church of England*.[54] The Pretender's Catholicism made him as unacceptable to most churchmen as he was to the Whigs. As in his Irish *Letter* on the sacramental test, however, Swift finds Roman Catholicism a less pressing danger than dissent. Since he underestimated this threat, the bishop of Sarum hoped to comprehend dissenters within the established church. To Swift, this did not just make him a less able champion of his church than Leslie. It made him a threat to it. So he denounces Burnet as the worse enemy but anathematizes both, forcing the reader to confront the way in which the flaws of each illuminate the other.

Applied with more passion, this tactic forced Peter and Jack, constantly colliding and constantly mistaken for each other, into the foreground of *A Tale of a Tub*. Even *A Letter to a Young Gentleman, Lately Enter'd into Holy Orders. By a Person of Quality* (January 1720) reveals Swift's characteristic strategies. This *Letter* expresses Swift's commitment to a straightforward, unadorned writing style – its principal interest for modern scholars – and to direct, pragmatic, conscientious preaching: 'As I take it, the two principal Branches of Preaching, are first to tell the People what is their Duty; and then to convince them that it is so'.[55] Like *A Project for the Advancement of Religion and the Reformation of Manners*, it reveals his commitment to an effective and gentlemanly clergy. Writing as a gentleman positions him as a member of the congregation and allows him some latitude to criticize the style of the church fathers.[56] Even here, though, Swift quickly turns from placid recitation of obvious truth (as he sees it) to enumeration of error:

> BUT I must remember, that my Design in this *Paper* was not so much to instruct you in your Business, either as a Clergyman, or a Preacher, as to warn you against some Mistakes, which are obvious to the Generality of Mankind, as well as to me; and we, who are Hearers, may be allowed to have some Opportunities in the Quality of being Standers-by.[57]

Swift does see most clearly what he opposes. Only a careless reader of *A Tale* would forget that Martin is the brother defending his beleaguered isthmus from attack on two sides. By neglecting him to impersonate Peter and Jack, however, Swift forces his reader to recall, by an effort, that Martin is the true hero. We know precisely because he is not at the centre of the satirist's attention. Unfortunately for Swift, careless readers of *A Tale* outnumbered the few who, like Somers, could relish the edgy ambiguities of his satire. Although *A Tale* garnered Swift a lasting reputation for unorthodoxy, even unbelief, it did not teach him caution. He clung to the emotionally charged rhetorical strategies that made him the writer he was.

Swift preferred a position of conscious independence. Rejecting party orthodoxy, he continued to describe himself as a Whig in politics and a High-

Churchman in religion. He was appalled when he encountered an English government that did the reverse: 'I am weary of being among Ministers whom I cannot govern', he wrote to Thomas Tickell on 7 July 1726, 'who are all Rank Toryes in government, and worse than Whigs in Church: whereas I was the first man who taught and practiced the direct contrary Principle'.[58] In *Verses on the Death of Dr. Swift*, he will playfully make the same claim of complete originality in his lines about Arbuthnot :

> Arbuthnot is no more my friend,
> Who dares to irony pretend;
> Which I was born to introduce,
> Refined it first, and showed its use.[59]

This is a compliment: Swift knows that he did not invent the irony he mastered. He knows that he shares his ironic gifts with the small but distinguished circle who will smile at the assertion. Similarly, Walpole's Whigs perversely supported the monarch too uncritically while sympathizing with dissent, at odds with the 'direct contrary Principle' that Swift shared with a small group of the discerning.

When perversity liberated his anger, Swift responded not with a positive alternative but with irony that was more likely to take the form of a devastating hostile impersonation. He had, S. J. Connolly accurately observes, 'a clearer idea of what he hated than of what he loved'.[60] At times, he could disappear, like Martin in *A Tale*, behind the spectacle of grotesque opposites who each travestied his most cherished commitments in religion and in politics. He could profitably show the corrupt Hanoverian regime its reflection in the mirror of despised Jacobitism. As an 'ideology of opposition', Jacobitism provided a convenient catch phrase for what was as likely to be a cluster of animosities – 'a political rhetoric of militant opposition' – as a considered political alternative.[61] However deliberate his political position, Swift shared many widespread animosities with those he would divide from in other contexts. The rhetoric of attack that sometimes associates him with Jacobitism can at other times associate him with its opposite, the ideology the Old Whigs whose Country opposition to the Junto had shaped his friend and chief minister, Harley. Drawing his inferences from Swift's sermon on the martyrdom of Charles I, for example, Connolly concludes that Swift was 'at best a prickly and unpredictable ally' of either the Whigs or the Tories. Swift's critique of Court Whig corruption aligns him with 'the so-called "real Whigs" or commonwealthmen, such as Molesworth, who retained the party label but were like him increasingly alienated from the power politics, opportunism and authoritarianism of the Junto and their successors. This affinity is acknowledged in the dedication of the fifth Drapier's letter' to Viscount Molesworth, whom Swift elsewhere associates with Burnet, Toland, Collins, and Tindal for his religious views.[62] If it served his polemical purpose, Swift could seem to occupy any extreme.

The strength of Ian Higgins's scholarly investigation of Swift's relationship with Jacobitism is that it situates Swift's writing in its polemical context.[63] To assert that Swift longed to see the Roman Catholic Pretender on the British throne – if that is what 'was a Jacobite' means – makes a mockery of the political beliefs he stated most consistently and defended most passionately. To acknowledge that we can to approach those texts only across the boggy terrain in which he situated them, however, confronts his refusal to silence himself despite his recognition that he could not extricate his public identity from the medium in which he created it. As his *Discourse* had shown, even an attempt to assert a nonpartisan position could be published only within a partisan context. As *Windsor Prophecy* shows, Swift was occasionally willing to risk everything to vent his anger in print. He could force his opponents to the discreditable political margins only by placing himself where he would be open to counterattack. In the accusations of Jacobitism that followed him to Ireland, Swift confronts the painful fact that he cannot both fight and position himself serenely above the fray. His anonymous tracts created a character for impiety and indiscretion that he could not shed. Friends with actual rather than discursive power shielded him from prosecution after he attacked the Scots lords, but Defoe's counterattack treated him as he treated others. It defined him as part of a group he opposed, thus marginalizing him as a traitor. Having found himself in the pillory for writing *The Shortest Way with the Dissenters*, Defoe must have relished the chance to teach Harley's High-Church ally a lesson about the hazards the writer faced. In the milieu characterized by Pocock for its inescapable ambivalences, any writer less strenuously impersonal than Addison was vulnerable, even the author of the *Examiner*.

Although his context had radically changed, however, Swift's Irish tracts continue to express his unrelenting independence and the lifelong commitment to liberty at the core of his opposition to absolutism. Both are apparent in the ringing assertion that stands as an epigraph to Downie's *Jonathan Swift, Political Writer*: 'I have lived, and by the grace of God will die, an enemy to servitude and slavery of all kinds'.[64] Swift makes this particular declaration, it should be noticed, in a letter written during a jurisdictional dispute with his archbishop (18 May 1727). King had insisted that the Dean be represented by a proxy during his visitation, and Swift was denying that any precedent justified this encroachment on the liberties of dean and chapter. People who, like Swift, see sacrosanct principles in the day-to-day frictions of bureaucratic interaction are often admirable. There can be no doubt, however, that they make difficult colleagues. Swift was clearly a champion of liberty from arbitrary exercises of power within the hierarchical structure of his society, and he was often prickly and difficult. His quarrel with Oxford over the offer of money for his writing and his reluctance to withdraw from a conversation between Bolingbroke and Oxford provide famous early examples of touchiness. In this instance, the archbishop allowed the matter of the proxy to drop.[65] But personal independence and political liberty went hand in hand for Swift, and the local nature of this skirmish does not diminish the significance of the commitment to liberty that he announced.

The frictions between Swift and King were usually structural rather than ideological, the routine consequence of overlapping jurisdictions. Each wanted to appoint his own supporters to the cathedral chapter. Where personal interest was not at stake, they often saw eye to eye on Church matters. Presenting themselves as Protestants who had rallied to resist a possible Jacobite invasion, the dissenters mounted a campaign for the repeal of the Test, a campaign that had the sympathy of the Whig administration in England. Swift, of course, was hostile to any relaxation of the privileges of the established Church, as were King and the bishops in the House of Lords – many of them appointments by Queen Anne's Tory, High-Church ministry. Their vigorous opposition preserved the Test, and in 1719 the Irish Parliament passed a lesser measure, a Toleration Act that offered Irish dissenters the freedom of worship that dissenting Protestants enjoyed in England.[66] King and Swift both likewise resented the appointment of English rather than Irish-raised candidates to positions within the Church of Ireland, feeling that Irish parishioners and the Irish Church were better served by their own. Agreement in religion laid a foundation for their agreement on issues in politics, issues that likewise raised national concerns.

On this larger front, too, a jurisdictional dispute sparked anger. A property dispute (Annesley *v* Sherlock) successfully appealed to the Irish House of Lords by one litigant had been reversed on appeal by the other to the English House of Lords. Liberty and property were watchwords of eighteenth-century politics, and this case affected both. Opposing execution of the British decision, the Irish House of Lords tried to uphold its jurisdiction as the final court of appeal for law cases originating in Ireland. As a last resort, it appealed directly to King George in November 1719. The address, probably drafted by King, made the case that the Irish, as subjects of as a distinct sister kingdom under his crown, should be governed only through laws to which they consented through participation in the Irish Parliament. This argument was not novel. King drew on a Lockian premise shared with William Molyneux, who had presented a similar argument in a book that influenced the development of Irish political thought, *The Case of Ireland's being Bound by Acts of Parliament in England Stated* (1698). Dedicated to William III, it had argued for Irish autonomy under the crown. It asserted the right of subjects to be subject only to laws to which they had given their assent, and it resisted the imperial claims of the English Parliament.[67] The Irish Lords' strong claim provoked strong counterclaims in Westminster. The January 1720 Declaratory Act asserted the British Parliament's right to pass legislation binding on Ireland and denied the Irish House of Lords standing as a court of appeal.

In practice, this declaration of Ireland's subordination did little to change legislative practice. Both parliaments continued the cumbersome procedure whereby the British Parliament approved heads of legislation for the subordinate institution.[68] But the explicit assertion of Irish subordination provoked widespread resentment toward England. Molyneux's tract was reprinted, and among the many signs of disaffection was *Hibernia's Passive Obedience*, a cheap tract printed by Edward Waters that anticipated (just) Swift's emergence as an Irish pamphleteer.[69] 'I also Concluded', wrote Waters, 'that tho' it might not be safe, for persons under Servile Tenures, to give vent to their own Sentiments; yet there could be no Risk, in quoting approved of Maxims, by the most Zealous Patriots of *Revolution Principles*'. These patriots are, it turns out, Swift. The most provocative passage in the *Letter concerning the Sacramental Test*, quoted from Swift's 1711 *Miscellanies*, serves as an epigraph. What follow are passages from *Sentiments of a Church of England Man* (on laws being determined only by representatives of the whole) and *Discourse* (on the breaking of the constitution).[70] The only other work that Waters calls attention to is a parody attributed to Sir Thomas Burnet, *Essays Divine, Moral, and Political by the Author of A Tale of a Tub*.[71] By the time Swift was ready to enter Irish political debate, Ireland had already, in the person of Waters, appealed to his writings for support.

Swift's first tract on Irish politics since his return exploits widespread anger at Britain's assertion of Irish subordination. During his first years back in Ireland, new and renewed friendships, professional duties, and concern for the friends he had left in England had preoccupied him. Saddened by Oxford's incarceration and looming trial – charges were dropped only in 1717 – he had focused on the past. He defended himself and his friends in *Memoirs Relating to That Change Which Happened in the Queen's Ministry in the Year 1710* and, more fully, *An Enquiry into the Behaviour of the Queen's Last Ministry*, both published only posthumously and now valued not as history but for insight into Swift.[72] When he re-entered political debate, he did so spectacularly with a pamphlet that appeared just after *Hibernia's Passive Resistance* in May 1720 and employed the same printer.[73] His very title reflects the passions that had roused the Irish in opposition to the English: *A Proposal for the Universal Use of Irish Manufacture, in Cloaths and Furniture of Houses, &c. Utterly Rejecting and Renouncing Every Thing Wearable that Comes from England* (April–May 1720). The argument itself, that the Irish should purchase Irish manufactured goods to reduce dependence on Britain and seize control of their destiny, was hardly original. Others had often said as much, as had Swift's unpublished *Answer to the Injured Lady*, which advised the lady (Ireland) and her tenants to maintain themselves independently of the gentleman (England) who had jilted her.[74] But Swift communicates passions as well as positions. Condemning oppressive landlords under an oppressive regime, he blames them for some of the poverty he sees everywhere:

I have heard *great* Divines affirm, that *nothing is so likely to call down an universal Judgment from Heaven upon a Nation, as universal Oppression*; and whether this be not already verified in part, *their Worships* the Landlords are *now* at full Leisure to consider. Whoever travels this Country, and observes the *Face* of Nature, or the *Faces*, and Habits, and Dwellings of the *Natives*, will hardly think himself in a Land where either *Law*, *Religion*, or *common Humanity* is professed.[75]

Anger is a thoroughly appropriate response to human misery that has a human cause, and Swift had no doubt that English laws had pernicious Irish effects.

At the root of Irish poverty, Swift saw English tyranny. Since the Irish were excluded from representation in the English Parliament, the administration did not represent the whole. The Irish were consequently slaves to an arbitrary government. Swift's analogies to the situation in Ireland are damning. Racking landlords, often absentees, 'have already reduced the miserable *People* to a *worse Condition* than the *Peasants* in *France*, or the *Vassals* in *Germany* and *Poland*; so that the whole *Species* of what we call *Substantial Farmers*, will, in a very few years, be utterly at an End'.[76] This is telling. In *A New Journey to Paris*, Swift had drawn the conventional contrast between a prosperous English people and the wretched the subjects of magnificent Continental monarchs.[77] This staple of English nationalism reappears in the proud contrast between the abject slaves of absolutism and, in Gulliver's words, '*English* Yeomen of the old stamp ... once so famous for the Simplicity of their Manners, Dyet and Dress; for Justice in their Dealings; for their true Spirit of Liberty; for their Valour and Love of their Country'.[78] Considering the current administration, Swift also recalls arrogant ministers from Lord Wharton's day, who 'were apt, from their *high* Elevation, to look *down* upon this Kingdom, as if it had been one of their *Colonies* of *Out-casts* in *America*'.[79] Swift would have no objection to Ned Ward's dismissive claim that 'Bishops, Bailiffs, and Bastards, were the three Terrible Persecutions which chiefly drove our unhappy brethren to seek their fortunes in our Forreign colonies'.[80] The comparison of the Irish with transported felons and dissenting fugitives from the Church is deliberately demeaning. Irish wretchedness reflects the imperial arrogance of its governors, whom Swift opposes by asserting traditional English liberties.

As a clergyman, it was Swift's daily responsibility to teach people their duty, notably the deference due to authority. In his sermon on brotherly love, Swift actually lamented 'that unhappy Disposition towards Politicks among the Trading People'. It is therefore startling that his *Proposal* publicly questions whether English laws can bind Christian subjects in Ireland:

> I WOULD be glad to learn among the Divines, whether a Law *to bind Men without their own Consent*, be obligatory *in foro Conscientiæ*; because, I find *Scripture*, *Sanderson* and *Suarez*, are wholly silent in the Matter. The Oracle of *Reason*, the great *Law of Nature*, and general opinion of *Civilians*, wherever they treat of *limitted Governments*, are, indeed, decisive enough.

Subjects as opposed to slaves have a right to assert independence and to seek it in their economic dealings. The force of Swift's argument is to encourage not rebellion, however, but an assertion of economic independence through the boycott of English goods in favour of Irish. He positions himself as an independent man who is asking the common shopkeepers of Dublin to appeal to their superiors: 'I COULD wish our Shopkeepers would immediately think on this *Proposal* [of 'a *Petition*' to Parliament], addressing it to all Persons of Quality, and others; but first be sure to get some Body who can write Sense, to put it into Order.'[81] This manoeuvre enacts deference while deftly encouraging active resistance. As significant consumers as well as legislators, only persons of quality can support local shopkeepers by making local good fashionable.

Although Swift's rhetoric is more alarming than the substance of his *Proposal*, his pamphlet is deliberately provocative. As the Kentish petitioners had learned when they were jailed by the House of Commons for supporting the Whigs and William III, eighteenth-century authorities did not welcome political assertion by commoners. Encouraging shopkeepers to suggest measures to their legislators was bound to smack of sedition. The administration found more than the tone of Swift's pamphlet alarming. A grand jury promptly indicted his pamphlet, and his printer was brought to trial. Swift tells the story in *A Letter from Dr. Swift to Mr. Pope*, dated 10 January 1721 but prudently not published until 1741:

> The Grand-Juries of the county and city were practised effectually with to present the said Pamphlet with all aggravating Epithets, for which they had thanks sent them from England, and their Presentments published for several weeks in all the news-papers. The Printer was seized, and forced to give great bail: After his trial the Jury brought him in Not Guilty, although they had been culled with the utmost industry; the Chief Justice sent them back nine times, and kept them eleven hours, until being perfectly tired out, they were forced to leave the matter to the mercy of the Judge, by what they call a special Verdict. During the trial, the Chief Justice, among other singularities, laid his hand on his breast, and protested solemnly that the Author's design was to bring in the Pretender; although there was not a single syllable of Party in the whole Treatise, and although it was known that the most eminent of those who professed his own principles, publickly disallowed his proceedings. But the cause being very so very odious and impopular, the trial of the Verdict was deferred from one Term to another, until upon the Duke of Grafton the Lord Lieutenant's arrival, his Grace after mature advice, and permission from England, was pleased to grant a *noli prosequi*.[82]

After the special verdict, a decision was delayed until late summer of 1721, perhaps to avoid the disaffection evident in the jury's intransigence. His printer had refused to name the author of the tract, although many suspected Swift, and Swift used all his influence to ensure a favourable verdict. In a letter to the leading Hanoverian Tory, Sir Thomas Hanmer, he asked for Hanmer's influence with the Duke of Grafton, the new Lord Lieutenant and Hanmer's stepson. Swift asserts that his 'weak hasty Scribble' is nonpartisan: 'There was nothing in the Pamphlet either of Whig or Tory, or reflecting upon any Person whatsoever'.[83] His appeal also involved the radical Whig Lord Molesworth, an ally in Irish politics though not the Church, the Duke of Wharton (son of his old enemy), and the Jacobite sympathizer, the Earl of Arran.[84] As Ehrenpreis wryly concludes, 'The whole spectrum of British politics, from Jacobite peer to Whig republican, had joined to rescue an Irish printer for the sake of an Anglican dean'.[85] Under the right circumstances, the division between Irish and English mattered more than the English distinction, only marginally relevant in Ireland, of Whig and Tory.

Nevertheless, Swift must have found it unsettling to become once more the object of government prosecution, especially as he now had to rely for protection not on his great friends but on the integrity of a Dublin printer. By writing, he had established a character vulnerable to legal challenge as well as libelous misrepresentation. The well-known letter to Pope that so cogently states Swift's political position also reflects on his situation as a writer. Because it is precisely his credit as a writer that concerns him, he addresses a fellow-writer: 'You are a much fitter Judge of what concerns the credit of a Writer, the injuries that are done him, and the reparations he ought to receive'.[86] That a dean of the established church shares his position of vulnerability with a Roman Catholic is one of the ironies that frames his self-defence. Swift naturally devotes much of his letter to asserting Old Whig positions, including his commitment to the Protestant succession, although he stops well short of admiration for the King whose ministers have tried to prosecute him: 'I neither know the names nor number of the Family which now reigns, further than the Prayer-book informs me'.[87] His distrust of standing armies and preference for annual parliaments align him with his usual Old Whig stance. These principles, he feels, are no longer fashionable among Whigs: 'intending to make my court to some people on the prevailing side, by advancing certain old whiggish principles, which it seems had been exploded about a month before, I have passed for a disaffected person'.[88] The conviction that modernity subverts permanent principles in the service of transient fashions is familiar from Swift's other writings, as are these principles and insults. But the letter to Pope is one of Swift's most engaging and thoughtful exercises in self-justification. He finds the attribution of weak writing to him as offensive as the accusation of treasonable opinions: 'All I can reasonably hope for by this letter, is to convince my friends and others who are pleased to wish me well, that I have neither been so ill a Subject nor so stupid an Author, as I have been represented by the virulence of Libellers, whose malice hath taken the same train in both, by fathering dangerous principles in government upon me, which I never maintained, and insipid productions which I am not capable of writing'.[89] In retrospect, it seems disingenuous of him to add that he is 'too much a politician to expose my own safety by offensive words' and that awareness of his declining powers prevents him from publishing the kind of feeble writing attributed to him. The Drapier's offensive words and *Gulliver's Travels* were still to come. But in 1721, Swift had reason to feel acutely aware that those who live by the pen are vulnerable to the pen.

The larger context of events confirmed Swift's pessimistic conviction that modern forces were corrupting the political and social order. In England, the South Sea Company had won a bidding war with the Bank to take over the national debt in exchange for a monopoly of what was presumed to be the enormously lucrative trade in slaves to Spanish America. The value of its stock had soared and then, in October and November, collapsed, ruining those who had invested late at inflated prices. 'Despair was general', Hoppit records laconically, 'suicides common'.[90] Company directors had colluded to keep stock prices high, and the name for this catastrophic market collapse, the South Sea Bubble, combines awareness that speculative gains are fragile – the bubble had burst – with a sense of the directors' culpability: 'to bubble' someone was to cheat him; a 'bubble' was a dupe. Opposition Whigs were as appalled as the Tories. In November 1720, John Trenchard and Thomas Gordon adopted the name of one of Swift's heroes as their pseudonym and began writing *Cato's Letters*, the most popular and influential critique of the corrupt alliance of the financiers with the Court that lay at the root of the South Sea Scandal.[91] Conventional Old Whig attacks on court Whig corruption, *Cato's Letters* parallel Swift's arguments in the *Examiner* at many points. Swift also vented his indignation in one of his most popular poems, 'The Bubble', printed in London in early January 1721. In it, he finds an astonishing array of analogies linked by the themes of delusion and greed.[92] Walpole had begun the task of restoring public credit in December 1720, but the crisis was profound. Ireland's fragile economy naturally felt the impact of the English storm. In a letter to Archbishop Wake (23 March 1721), King lamented the widespread misery:

> We were in a miserable condition in K. James's time; but we generally had meat & drink, tho' with insufferable slavery & oppression. But now we have nothing of those but what we bring on ourselves; yet the Poor are in danger of starving & many have Perish'd. The Jayles are full, not of State Prisoners as then, but of Debtors.[93]

Continued, such suffering would provoke Swift's most passionate Irish tracts. It certainly hardened his opposition to establishing a national bank for Ireland, a topic he briefly raised at the end of his *Proposal*.[94]

Yet Swift did not intervene decisively in the debate over setting up a national bank in Ireland. In the circumstances, the proposal looked like a step toward a destructive speculative bubble in Ireland. He may have thought the cause was hopeless, for he predicted its speedy passage through both houses to King.[95] In the most thorough study of pamphlets provoked by the bank proposal, Oliver W. Ferguson notes that no tract achieved much prominence. An anonymous tract, *The Present Miserable State of Ireland* (Dublin, 1721) anticipates some of Swift's themes and adopts the voice of a draper.[96] Swift seems largely to have confined himself to Grub-Street mockery of the hucksters promoting the scheme and the dubiousness of the subscribers, and his authorship of some material is uncertain. The two items that were included in editions of Swift's works in his lifetime are *The Wonderful Wonder of Wonders*, which has an arse at its centre, and *The Wonder of All the Wonders That Ever the World Wondered At*, which presents a carnival barker's pitch inviting gulls to witness performances that would obviously be fatal to everyone present. The examples, only slightly less gratuitously grotesque than the projects at the Academy of Lagado in Book III of *Gulliver's Travels*, include watching the 'Artist' plunge a red-hot bar of iron into a barrel of gunpowder.[97] Swift's view of the seriousness of the appeal is obvious. The most sophisticated of these possible contributions is *A Letter from a Lady in Town to Her Friend in the Country, Concerning the Bank. Or, The List of the Subscribers farther Explain'd* (December 1721). In the voice of a lady, Swift describes hearing bloated claims for the profits to be made and then receiving sager advice before the absurdity of the scheme becomes apparent. Swift avoids overt attack, Irvin Ehrenpreis shrewdly suggests, to avoid offending a friend, Lord Abercorn, who was proposed as governor of the bank.[98] In that case, Swift's art of impersonation serves (as it often did) his loyalty to friends as well as his commitment to a cause. The bank proposal was in fact voted down, and Swift did little to advance or hinder his credit in these slight *jeux d'esprit*.

The Whig government's discovery of the Atterbury Plot in May 1722 revived Swift's personal and political insecurities, increasing his contempt for informers and government spies.[99] Eager to renew confidence in the Whigs following the South Sea Bubble, the new Walpole administration ruthlessly pursued conspirators.[100] Yet another ally of the Tory ministry, this time Francis Atterbury, Bishop of Rochester, was implicated in a desperate Jacobite scheme. Although incriminating evidence did emerge much later, the serio-comic investigation at the time relied on low informers and artfully deciphered codes. Atterbury's identity in the correspondence turned grotesquely on the admitted fact that Harlequin, a dog lamed in transit, had been sent to Atterbury's wife from France, a detail that Swift mocked in a poem written (but not published) at the time, 'Upon the Horrid Plot Discovered by Harlequin the Bishop of Rochester's French Dog'. Since the administration did not have a case that would withstand scrutiny in court, it instead passed a Bill of Attainder that stripped Atterbury of his offices and exiled him. He sailed for the Continent on 18 June 1723, where he was carefully watched by government spies until he died in 1729.

Despite the flimsiness of the evidence and the apparent fecklessness of the plot, the case came at an opportune moment. It allowed Walpole's Whigs, who had been tainted by the South Sea scandal, to renew popular suspicion that Tories and High-Churchmen were Jacobite traitors. To an observer like Swift, it seemed obvious that foolish and harmless men were being punished by the powerful for self-interested motives. Walpole's Whigs did not see it that way, and the argument has recently been made that the Atterbury case reveals 'the precariousness of the Hanoverian state in the early 1720s'.[101] Such an explanation might justify the administration's ruthlessness as necessary policy, but most modern historians see what Swift and many of his contemporaries saw, a relatively secure regime exploiting an ineffective plot for gain. Even Walpole's modern biographer sees the suspension of Habeas Corpus and penalties against Roman Catholics as excessive because unnecessary. If the administration did not feel fairly secure, how is it that the alleg-edly dangerous conspiracy against the state led to a single state execution, that of the obscure lawyer Christopher Layer? The assassination plot against William III in 1696, by contrast, had led to the execution of nine highly placed Jacobites. Even then it had been apparent that the Jacobites were in a double bind: James's willingness to rely on a French invasion rallied English support for the Protestant regime, discrediting the cause, and Tory reluctance to sign a document support-ing William's legitimacy strengthened Whig support while weakening the Tories.[102] Precisely because the Jacobite threat had come to seem impotent, the Hanoverian government's much more moderate response seemed heavy handed.

The experience of living under suspicion and government scrutiny, revived by the spectacle of the Atterbury trial, affected Swift profoundly. He mocked the laboured deciphering of the conspirators' correspondence in a famous episode of *Gulliver's Travels*, that associates the government with readings as over-ingen-ious as those encouraged by Swift's Tale-Teller. According to Gulliver's account of political informers 'in the Kingdom of *Tribnia*, by the Natives called *Langden*',[103] 'Papers are delivered to a Set of Artists very dextrous in finding out the mysteri-ous Meanings of Words, Syllables, and Letters. For Instance, they can decypher a Close-stool to signify a Privy-Council; a Flock of Geese, a Senate; a lame Dog, an Invader ....'.[104] These dismissive jibes notwithstanding, the experience of living under government suspicion haunted Swift. It accounts for what Orwell calls his 'extraordinarily clear prevision of the spy-haunted "police State", with its endless heresy-hunts and treason trials, all really designed to neutralise popular discon-tent'.[105] It seems to have prompted Swift to reflect not just on dissension within the state but on the nature of community itself.

Possibly written as early as 1715, Swift's sermon *On False Witness* addresses the dangerous topic of political informers.[106] Swift enumerates types of false witness and suggests that an interested or malicious accusation constitutes false witness even if the statement is true. 'Even the Pulpit hath not been free from the Misrepresentation of these Informers', he protests, 'of whom the Clergy have not wanted Occasions to complain with Holy *David*. They daily mistake my Words, all they imagine is to do me Evil'.[107] Swift's shift to the first person signals the beginning of a quotation (Psalm 56: 5), but it carries a double weight, sounding as it does like a personal complaint by Swift himself. Swift's sense of his importance has not diminished from the time he imagined himself as a triumphant general. Here he aligns himself with King David, another righteous man of God who lived in exile, persecuted by an ungrateful monarch. Pragmatically, Swift wants to encourage his flock to be more guarded in conversation. But he also wants to mark the limits of the government's authority by explaining 'how far it is your Duty as good Subjects and good Neighbours, to bear faithful Witness, when you are lawfully called to it by those in Authority, or by the sincere Advice of your own Consciences':[108]

> EVERY good Subject is obliged to bear Witness against his Neighbour, for any Action or Words, the telling of which would be of Advantage to the Publick, and the Concealment dangerous, or of ill Example. Of this Nature are all Plots and Conspiracies against the Peace of a Nation, all disgraceful Words against a Prince, such as clearly discover a disloyal and rebellious Heart: But, where our Prince and Country can possibly receive no Damage or Disgrace; where no Scandal or ill Example is given; and our Neighbour, it may be, provoked by us, happeneth privately to drop a rash or indiscreet Word, which in Strictness of Law might bring him under Trouble, perhaps to his utter undoing; there we are obliged, we ought, to proceed no further than Warning and Reproof.[109]

In the interest of social harmony, of neighbourliness, Swift limits the obligation to bear witness against a neighbour. Testimony should rest on actions and on 'disgraceful Words ... such as clearly discover a *disloyal* and *rebellious* Heart'. The terms I emphasize describe the active subversion of the state, not someone's discontented grumbling or a man in his cups toasting the king over the water.[110] In the latter cases, a word of censure or warning is adequate. Swift finds divine as well as constitutional sanction for limits on the absolute authority of the administration. Individual liberty carries with it the Christian obligation to love one's neighbour.

In this sermon, Swift addresses his political situation as a clergyman charged with maintaining the social harmony of his community. Excessive zeal in pursuit of those who might disrupt the social order, he argues, in itself disrupts that order. In addition to the obvious social disruption, Jeanne Clegg acutely argues, this sermon addresses an epistemological challenge to traditional conceptions of social authority. The authority of the eyewitness, potentially a relative unknown or even an outsider, was displacing the authority of the man whose authority rested on his public character within the community.[111] The first-person claims to authority of Defoe's fictional narrators exemplify the new order, she argues, while Swift, who vouches for the narrator of *Memoirs of Captain John Creichton* in his independent Advertisement to the Reader, exemplifies the old.[112] In yet another area of his experience, this one intensely personal, Swift found himself enmeshed in a humanistic conception of human nature and society that was under attack by modernity. Hence his concern that not just his political views but his public identity as Dean of St Patrick's was being undermined. There is a personal and political dimension to Swift's emphasis, in *Gulliver's Travels*, on observation – on seeing, gazing, and scrutinizing, often with the aid of glasses.[113] For much of his life, Swift was himself, like Gulliver, the suspect object of careful scrutiny. To the uncomprehending political observer, he could even seem to be, like Gulliver in Brobdingnag, a *'Lusus Naturae'* – the diagnosis reflecting the 'Ignorance' of the observer.[114]

Through its high-handed disdain for the English community in Ireland, the British government provided an ideal occasion for Swift to speak on behalf of the Irish community to which he had come to belong. It had issued a patent to coin £100,800 worth of halfpence and farthings for Ireland. The patent had been issued in July 1722 to the Duchess of Kendal, the King's mistress, who had sold it for £10,000 to William Wood, an ambitious Wolverhampton ironmaster.[115] In the *Drapier's Letters*, Wood is immortalized as an obscure and contemptible mechanic. This is not fair. He was a man of some local importance who had become receiver-general of the land tax for Shropshire through the patronage of the Earl of Bradford. He was a successful, well-connected man of business who had also secured the patent to mint coins for the American colonies.[116] He is now known almost exclusively for his Irish coins and the controversy they provoked, because he was caught up in political events beyond his control. The problems with Wood's pence do not in fact originate with the man whose name they preserve, who became a counter in the struggle between the English administration, which had authorized his patent, and the Irish administration, which steadfastly resisted it.

Wood's tactless public statements did damage his cause and his public character. So did the arrogant assurance of the letters he wrote to his brother-in-law in Dublin, who allowed the contents to become public. It is more important that there were serious economic objections to the patent. The coins were to be worth less than their face value, Wood coining thirty pence to a pound of copper instead of the twenty-three customary in England. There were inadequate precautions to prevent counterfeiting. there was no check to prevent Wood from issuing even more coins than the already excessive limit specified in the patent. Because the coinage amounted to far too large a share of the Irish currency – some £400,000 in total – it threatened to drive out the already inadequate amount of silver coin in the kingdom.[117] There were equally grave political objections to the patent. At no point had the Irish been consulted. To the Irish, their political sensibilities recently bruised by the Declaratory Act, the proposed coinage looked like a tyrannical imposition on a subjected people. Combined with the perceived economic threat, these feelings united the Anglo-Irish community in opposition to the proposal. Even within England, the art of governing consisted largely in the management of local elites, yet the British administration had provoked the Anglo-Irish elite's resistance. Viewing decisions through an English lens and concentrating on local rivalries, it had neglected its Irish managers.[118]

Swift seems to have paid little attention to the coinage until local feeling was nearly unanimous against it. He was busy with *Gulliver's Travels*, and he had been working on *A Letter to a Young Lady on her Marriage*, not published until 1727. Shortly after Vanessa's death on 2 June 1723, he had embarked on a demanding four-month tour, on horseback, of the south and west of Ireland.[119] *Some Arguments against Enlarging the Power of Bishops, in Letting of Leases* (October 1723) expresses Swift's concern for the long-term stability and prosperity of the Church, which was threatened, he felt, by a bill that would allow bishops to lease church lands cheaply for long terms. Convinced that improvements to the land and inflation ('*the perpetual Decrease in the Value of Gold and Silver*') make it disadvantageous to the church to lease its lands at a fixed rate for long terms, Swift opposed the bill, which seemed attractive to the gentry who dominated the House of Commons.[120] This proposal roused Swift's intense commitment to the real value of land as the basis of political power and social authority:

> SEVERAL Colleges in *Oxford*, were aware of this growing Evil about an Hundred Years ago; and, instead of limiting their Rents to a certain Sum of Money, prevailed with their Tenants to pay the Price of so many Barrels of Corn, to be valued as the Market went, at two Seasons (as I remember) in the Year. For a Barrel of Corn is of real intrinsick Value, which Gold and Silver are not: And by this Invention, these Colleges have preserved a tolerable Subsistance, for their Fellows and Students, to this Day.[121]

Though it fed his commitment to the stability of land, however, this bill seems to have been part of his pragmatic service to the temporal as well as spiritual welfare of his church. It did not arouse the passion that he would devote to the cause of Wood's pence once it captured his attention.

A boycott requires sustained, persuasive publicity. It seems likely that Archbishop King, his ally Lord Abercorn, and Lord Midleton were leading the campaign to boycott the resented currency and that they asked Swift to participate in February 1724.[122] As in his glory days with Harley, Swift was to rally existing popular feeling behind a practical policy. Once again, he would be co-operating with leaders who, despite other differences, were united in pursuit of a goal. Because he was no longer a dependent aspirant to promotion, he could participate as an independent, collaborating with allies rather than working under a superior's direction. For Swift, this represents a significant increase in personal independence and an equally significant commitment to his community. When he published *A Proposal for the Universal Use of Irish Manufacture*, he had become a spokesman for Dublin's weavers, who were concentrated in the vicinity of St Patrick's Cathedral, and had developed this role through day-to-day contact with tradesmen, advising them, lending them money and, in hard times, directly witnessing their sufferings.[123] By adopting the identity of a Dublin woollen-draper who identified himself only by the initials M. B., Swift built on his standing as a champion of Dublin's weavers, who were concentrated in the vicinity of St Patrick's Cathedral. He spoke as part of a community that had symbolic value in Ireland as a conspicuous victim of English trade restrictions.[124] The character of the drapier is not merely a literary device.[125]

Once he committed himself, Swift found himself entangled in the events that led to the withdrawal of the patent in 1725. In the fall of 1723, the Irish Parliament had struck a committee to look into the coinage. Both houses had presented addresses to the King that produced only a bland royal assurance of concern for his people. In March 1724, Walpole ordered the English Privy Council to investigate the source of Irish unrest, but the Irish leaders did not do so. Since the Irish Parliament had been prorogued and original papers could not be removed, there were practical reasons not to comply.[126] It also seems likely that the Irish officials wanted not to legitimate, by participating, a process that would inevitably support the administration. This act of defiance ensured that the eventual decision represented only Wood's side of the dispute but that it lacked (in Irish eyes) any shred of legitimacy. The first of Swift's *Drapier's Letters* also appeared in March. *A Letter to the Tradesmen, Shop-keepers, Farmers and Common-People in General of the Kingdom of Ireland* spoke in the voice of a common tradesman, raising alarm at the disaster that would follow being forced to accept Wood's pence: 'my Friends, stand to it One and All: Refuse this *Filthy Trash*'.[127]

The Drapier speaks vividly about the destitution that would follow from the coinage scheme: 'I SHOULD never have done, if I were to tell you all the Miseries that we shall undergo, if we be so *Foolish* and *Wicked* as to take this *Cursed Coin*'.[128] His examples speak to ordinary experience: 'The Author of this Paper is informed by Persons who have made it their Business to be exact in their Observations on the true Value of these *Half-pence*; that any Person may get a Quart of Two-penny Ale for Thirty Six of them'.[129] (From Swift, this represents a significant degree of empathy with the poor. 'Wine is th[e] Liquor of the Gods, and Ale of the Goths', he had breezily pronounced in defence of his own, more gentlemanly consolation, later defended in an unpublished pamphlet.)[130] The half penny that, given to a beggar, 'will quench his Thirst, or go a good Way to fill his Belly' will in the new coinage 'do him no more Service than if I should give him three Pins out of my Sleeve'.[131] The Drapier combines humble examples with reassurance that his fellows, inevitably schooled in deference to their betters, have no legal obligation to accept the coinage. The King, he asserts, can compel subjects to accept only stamped gold and silver, not base metal. Adding divine to secular incentives, he denounces the coins not simply as base but as abominable: 'these *Half-pence* are like the *accursed Thing*, which, as the *Scripture* tells us, the *Children of Israel* were forbidden to touch'.[132] Here the Drapier speaks for resistance to oppression by the English community in Ireland, for popular Protestantism was inseparable from English and British patriotic feeling, which often imagined the nation as biblical Israel.[133] Humbly but firmly, the Drapier was asserting the rights – and the patriotic conviction that free-born Protestant subjects had such rights – of the English subjects resident in Ireland.

The Drapier re-entered the skirmish twice in August. On 6 August (in a letter dated 4 August), he replied to John Harding's 1 August newspaper account of Wood's proposals to the Privy Council, which included limiting the coinage to £40,000 and obliging nobody to accept more than five and a half pence at a time. Addressing Harding but hoping to reach 'all my Countryman', *A Letter to Mr. Harding the Printer, upon Occasion of a Paragraph in His News-Paper of Aug. 1st Relating to Mr. Woods's Half-Pence* (6 August 1724) maintains a consensus against compromise, rebutting Wood's points and condemning the arrogance of 'this little impudent *Hard-ware-Man*' who was defying the expressed opinion of not just the Irish Privy Council but 'the House of Commons in *Ireland*, which represents the whole People of the Kingdom'.[134] To the Drapier, the inferior coin amounts to an illegitimate tax, against which he explicitly appeals to Anglo-Irish patriotism:

> If the famous Mr. *Hambden* rather chose to go to Prison, than pay a few Shillings to King *Charles* I. without Authority of Parliament; I will rather chuse to be *Hanged* than have all my Substance Taxed at Seventeen Shillings in the Pound, at the Arbitrary Will and Pleasure of the venerable Mr. *Wood*.[135]

By taking his inspiration from John Hampden's opposition to Charles I's ship money, the Drapier implicitly compares Walpole's Whig administration or even George I with the King who in Whig ideology embodied tyrannical rejection of Parliament. Made directly, such an assertion would be intolerable, which is why Swift treats Wood as if he were the source of the politically unacceptable policy, not merely its agent. The impudent ironmaster Wood is as necessary a fiction as the Dublin draper, M. B.

Once the Privy Council in London confirmed the legitimacy of Wood's patent but accepted some alterations, notably Wood's agreement to limit the coinage to (a still excessive) £40,000, an order in council commanded the commissioners of the revenue to withdraw their orders against receiving the coin. The Drapier's success depended on united opposition by the lords justices and the Irish privy council.[136] Midleton, the Lord Chancellor, defied the ministry; his son, St John Brodrick, was an important voice of opposition in the commons. Even William Conolly, speaker of the Irish House of Commons and one of Walpole's staunchest Irish supporters, simply denied that such orders had been issued and argued that he had to comply with the rest of the lords justices and the feelings of the nation.[137] Meanwhile, Lord Carteret, who had replaced the feckless Lord Grafton as Lord Lieutenant and was determined to assert the ministry's authority, arrived in Dublin on 22 October, the day the Drapier's fourth letter appeared. *A Letter to the Whole People of Ireland* offered Swift's most ringing assertion of Ireland's standing as an independent kingdom, and at a meeting of the Irish privy council on 27 October, Carteret secured a resolution to prosecute the author, publisher, and printer of the pamphlet and the proclamation of a reward of £300 for the discovery of its author within the next six months.[138] But he did not achieve a blanket condemnation of the pamphlet itself, as opposed to 'several Seditious and Scandalous Paragraphs' in it. Several councillors wanted it made clear that the Drapier was not being prosecuted for what he wrote against Wood's pence.[139] In his vigorous (and Whiggish) assertion of Irish liberty and independence, Swift took leave of the more moderate consensus espoused by his allies among the Irish leadership. When A. Goodwin concludes that 'the advanced political ideas canvassed by Swift were totally unrepresentative of Irish feeling at the time', he overstates his case. Such views were in fact represented among the Irish establishment even though they were strong enough to divide the broad coalition united against Wood's pence. King came closer to Swift's views than Midleton, and he could safely voice them, as Ferguson observes, under parliamentary privilege. Even he may yet again have been appalled by his defiant dean's willingness to publish them.[140] Despite strong support for the champion of Irish resistance to the coinage, Swift once again found himself with a price on his head for what he wrote.

Harding was promptly arrested, but he was too seasoned a printer to admit knowledge of the author or awareness that anything in the pamphlet could be found objectionable.[141] Before the grand jury could consider a bill against Harding, Swift had a broadside distributed to influence the jurors. *Seasonable Advice. Since a Bill is Preparing for the Grand Jury, to Find against the Printer of the Drapier's Last Letter* appeared anonymously without a place of publication or the name of a printer.[142] In it, Swift emphasized the Drapier's impeccable standing with the Irish public, defended the fourth letter from the charge of sedition, raised the spectre that finding a true bill would in effect defend Wood's pence, and asked the jury to pity for 'a poor Man, perfectly innocent; I mean the Printer'.[143] On 21 November, Carteret chose to present this pamphlet rather than the bill against Harding to the grand jury, which refused to condemn it despite urging by Chief Justice Whitshed. When Whitshed discharged the jury and called another one, Swift had published, and saw that the new jurors received copies of, *An Extract of a Book, Entituled, An Exact Collection of the Debates of the House of Commons, Held at Westminster, Oct. 21, 1680.* The substance of the extract was the House's resolution 'That the Discharging of a Grand-Jury, by any Judge, before the End of the Term, Assizes, or Sessions, while Matters are under their Consideration, and not presented, is arbitrary, illegal, destructive to publick Justice, a manifest Violation of his Oath, and is a Means to subvert the Fundamental Laws of this Kingdom'.[144] When Whitshed presented the paper to his second jury on 28 November – the last day of Michaelmas term and so the last day of the jury's life – it defiantly replied in the terms of Swift's mock presentment against the purveyors of Wood's pence, distributed to the jurors in manuscript and promptly published as *The Presentment of the Grand-Jury of the County of the City of Dublin*.[145] Whitshed refused to accept the presentment, but the jury dissolved and Harding was released.[146]

Issues rather than personalities dominate Swift's writings as the Drapier, but his loyalty to Archbishop King and his anger at Wood and Whitshed naturally also expressed itself in verse, although the poems did not influence events.[147] The titles of *A Serious Poem upon William Wood, Brazier, Tinker, Hardware-Man, Coiner, Counterfeiter, Founder and Esquire* or *Wood, an Insect* capture the spirit of Swift's satire, as do the verses exploiting the fact that Whitshed's maternal grandfather had cut his throat.[148] A more revealing glimpse of how Swift conceived his public role forms the concluding paragraph of *Seasonable Advice*:

> I WILL conclude all with a Fable, ascribed to *Demosthenes*: He had served the People of *Athens* with great Fidelity, in the Station of an *Orator*; when, upon a certain Occasion, apprehending to be delivered over to his Enemies, he told the *Athenians*, his Countrymen, the following Story: Once, upon a Time, the *Wolves* desired a League with the *Sheep*, upon this Condition: That the Cause of Strife might be taken away, which was the *Shepherds* and *Mastiffs*: This being granted, the *Wolves*, without all Fear, made Havock of the *Sheep*.[149]

Harding is the person immediately threatened with prosecution, but he is a surrogate for the writer whose views he published; that is, for Swift, whose betrayer stands to gain £300.

With typical immodesty, Swift finds a classical analogy to his plight in Demosthenes, the greatest of the Athenian orators, the point of whose cautionary fable is that the people should not surrender the orator who has defended them. There is no reason to doubt the seriousness of Swift's analogy between ancient orator and modern political writer. His *Discourse* everywhere displays his reverence for classical models. Even when he slyly imagined the writer as an orator selecting one of three elevated machines in *A Tale of a Tub*, he was satirizing the vulgar egotism of the unprincipled modern hack who could only parody a genuinely dignified role. Since Demosthenes patriotically but unsuccessfully rallied the Athenians to resist conquest by the Macedonians, the comparison also flatters the Irish draper's fellow-patriots while condemning the brutal power of the English administration. In Demosthenes's fable itself, of course, the Irish people appear less flatteringly as sheep who need defenders to prevent them from being not just fleeced but (anticipating *A Modest Proposal*) actually devoured by English wolves. The Dean of St Patrick's appears in this fable as a pastor, one of the shepherds Swift has added to the fable.[150] Swift views the local Irish struggle as a version of the eternal struggle between liberty and tyranny, and he sees the writer's role, in ancient times the orator's, as a heroic one. Given the power ranged against him, he had every reason to do so.

Heroically though unwisely, Swift contemplated revealing his identity to test the Drapier's popular support against the ministry's legal resources. In *A Letter to the Lord Chancellor Middleton*, the first of two withdrawn pamphlets he published only later, he addressed the Lord Chancellor in his own voice; that is, he signs the letter J.S. and dates it 'Deanry House, Oct 26, 1724'. Despite this misleading date, his letter defends the Drapier from the charges in the 27 October proclamation. The tactic is deliberately provocative. Without quite identifying himself as the Drapier, he denies the imputation that the tract could be seen as seditious. In effect, he challenges Midleton, a vigorous opponent of the coinage, to side with the Drapier despite the Drapier's more extreme constitutional position, or to oppose the Drapier and thereby discredit himself with the Anglo-Irish people by seeming to accept the coinage. But when King sounded out Carteret on the possible consequences of the Drapier revealing himself, he learned that arrest would be certain. Swift prudently withheld his pamphlet, which was published only in Faulkner's 1735 collection of his works.[151] The arrest of Harding, an understrapper less likely to feel the full weight of the state's displeasure than a defiant dean, confirmed the wisdom of Swift's choice while allowing the anonymous author to instruct the grand jury surreptitiously.

But Swift had reason to feel defiant. While the government was pursuing him, citizens in Dublin were trying 'to get Dr. Swift the freedom of the City in a Goldbox', as Carteret's secretary, Thomas Tickell, observed in an amusing letter on the affair.[152] The full honour of having the freedom of the city presented in a gold box containing the diploma and a suitable inscription had to wait until May 1730, but in April 1725 Swift was, on a second vote in the absence of the Attorney-General of Ireland, awarded the freedom of the City of Dublin even though there was a price on his head.[153] Swift was confident that local opinion would back him completely, but the Atterbury case shows that a treason trial outside the ordinary courts was a distinct possibility. Swift was wise not to disclose his identity. His other withdrawn tract, *An Humble Address to Both Houses of Parliament*, was finished in June 1725. Swift left it with friends so that it could be printed for the opening of Parliament, as *Conduct of the Allies* had been. But Parliament had been prorogued to 6 August and then to 7 September so that the Lord Lieutenant could sound the ministry's intentions. By the end of August, he had learned that Wood had surrendered his patent. Swift's *Humble Address* was no longer needed. The speech from the throne would feature not a defence of the coinage but the King's generous compliance with the wishes of his Irish subjects. The Irish patriots and the Drapier who had spoken for them had won an important victory.

Even this cursory summary of events indicates that the *Drapier's Letters* were themselves events in the campaign against the pence, not just comments on it. Exceptionally, that campaign succeeded. When else has a writer so successfully rallied resistance to a government attempt to impose monetary policy? But Swift owes his success to his alliance with the Anglo-Irish leadership. Although he was opposing British government policy, not supporting it as he had done in *Conduct of the Allies*, he was again backing a united administration, this time Irish. The sharpest dart in his arsenal was no doubt his vivid portrait of the deprivation that would follow acceptance of the debased coinage. What united people was fear of the impact on a fragile economy in which hunger was common, famine frequent. But resistance expressed more than the conviction that government policy was bad. It gathered force from the belief that it was also illegitimate. Committed to continental wars, Englishmen tolerated relatively high levels of taxation because they believed in the legitimacy of the Crown-in-Parliament. The House of Commons approved taxes and kept close eye on spending. Irish opposition to Wood's pence in fact anticipates opposition to taxation by the North American colonists in the 1760s, another overseas population of Englishmen not represented in the institution that proposed to tax them.[154] Since the Church was not threatened, Swift found himself articulating the Old Whig convictions of his earliest political writing, in which savagery was preferable to slavery. He and his allies thought of themselves as Englishmen: 'And I ever thought it the most uncontrolled and universally agreed maxim, that *Freedom consists in a People being governed by laws made with their own Consent; and Slavery in the Contrary*'. He probably did believe that his words were uncontroversial, or would seem so in England: 'This I will venture to say; that the boldest and most obnoxious Words I ever delivered, would in *England* have only exposed me as a stupid Fool, who went to prove that *the Sun shone in a clear Summer's Day*'.[155]

Writing in Ireland with characteristic rhetorical extravagance, Swift finds that the conventional becomes radical in context:

> Were not the People of *Ireland* born as *free* as those of *England*? How have they forfeited their Freedom? Is not their *Parliament* as fair a *Representative* of the *People*, as that of *England*? And hath not their Privy Council as great, or a greater Share in the Administration of publick Affairs? Are they not Subjects of the same King? Does not the same *Sun* shine over them? And have they not the same *God* for a Protector? Am I a *Free-man* in *England*, and do I become a *Slave* in six Hours, by crossing the Channel?[156]

Challenging as it does the Declaratory Act that had so offended Irish feeling a few years earlier, such an argument becomes radical in Ireland.

Swift's extravagant rejection of Irish dependency roused official ire:

> LET whoever think otherwise, I *M. B.Drapier*, desire to be excepted. For I declare, next under God, I *depend* only on the King my Sovereign, and on the Laws of my own Country, And I am so far from *depending* upon the People of *England*, that, if they should ever *rebel* against my Sovereign, (which GOD forbid) I would be ready at the first Command from his Majesty to take Arms against them; as some of *my* Countrymen did against *theirs* at Preston. And, if such a Rebellion should prove so successful as to fix the *Pretender* on the Throne of *England*, I would venture to transgress that *Statute* so far, as to lose every Drop of my Blood, to hinder him from being *King* of *Ireland*.[157]

This is more complex than most of Swift's aggressive denials of Jacobitism. Swift expresses his devotion to his Protestant king by reminding him that Ireland, unlike England and Scotland, remained loyal in 1715: 'Nor was there ever among US the least Attempt towards an *Insurrection* in Favour of the PRETENDER. Therefore whatever Justice a FREE PEOPLE can claim, we have at least an *Equal* Title to it with our Brethren in *England*'.[158] Anglo-Irish soldiers actually fought against English and Scottish rebels at Preston.

Playing on the theme of superior Irish loyalty to the King has practical value for a draper justifying a modest act of resistance by pleading loyalty to his king. But how could a writer state his unflinching loyalty more offensively? Loyalty frees him, the Drapier argues, from dependence on the King's British ministers and the British Parliament. After all, he as an Irishman, like Swift, is not represented there. To press his point, he imagines a Jacobite rebellion succeeding in England despite the loyal protestations of a (by implication) craven British Parliament. This troubling assertion of the Drapier's (and Ireland's) unwavering devotion to Anne's Protestant successor allows Swift to reverse the glib accusation of Jacobitism commonly directed at the Irish by Englishmen like Wood. Swift through the Drapier imagines his own martyrdom in defence of the Protestant succession while simultaneously indulging the fantasy of a Jacobite humiliation of George I – the King who had approved Wood's patent. Defying one English community to defend the English liberty of another, the angry Anglo-Irish community clearly felt conflicting loyalties.

The form of the *Drapier's Letters* is as ideologically revealing as its sometimes inflammatory content. However divided the Anglo-Irish community's loyalties, Swift's rebelliousness is remarkably confident. There is little in the *Letters* of the self-division that underlies the hostile impersonations sometimes regarded as distinctively Swift's. Gulliver at the end of *Travels* perhaps provides the definitive example as he madly praises the superiority of the Houyhnhnm culture that has rejected him as a dangerous inferior. The disturbing energy of such passages is familiar: 'Swift takes on the guise of the enemy in order to do a wrecking job from the inside', writes Robert C. Elliott, adding that '[h]is brilliant counterfeiting is dangerously convincing': 'To what degree Swift's method indicates a secret "sympathy with the enemy" … one cannot know; but the fact is certain: when Swift fantasizes himself into the skin of one he hates, extraordinary energies are liberated.'[159] In a similar vein, Said goes so far as to claim, 'Swift is invariably attacking what he impersonates'.[160] But the impersonation in the *Drapier's Letters* enables his hostility without bearing the brunt of it.

To that extent the *Drapier's Letters* return to the strategy of the Bickerstaff papers. Although Swift attacks an astrologer in the guise of a rival astrologer, the learned and orthodox Isaac Bickerstaff is a more playful invention than Jack. Far from being a butt himself, Bickerstaff expresses a gentleman's easy superiority to the amusing the ignorance of his social inferior, the dissenting mechanic whose hold on the attention of gentleman readers offended Swift. That may explain why this product of a deft *jeu d'esprit* proved robust enough to support the *Tatler* as well, the urbane, gentlemanly periodical that Steele collected as *Lucubrations of Bickerstaff*. Even when they are not hostile, Swift's impersonations have an engaging authority that amounts to a life of their own. M. B. Drapier is an impersonation of this type. In him, though, Swift has left behind his social superiority and his longing for a place above the mob. Oddly, his most compelling Irish voice represents, the Dublin setting and Defoe's Presbyterianism significantly excepted, a brilliant impersonation of the urban tradesman more familiar to us from Defoe. The Drapier is a remarkably vivid character.

This marks an impressive shift of Swift's usual strategy. Formed by his association with Sir William Temple and the access Temple provided to the conversation of the great, Swift directed his *Discourse* and *A Tale of a Tub* to the most intellectually able members of the political elite, notably Baron Somers and then Robert Harley. He addressed the *Examiner* papers and his Tory pamphlets primarily to the rural gentry and clergy, but nothing about Swift's *Examiner* is more typical of him than his air of righteous superiority. By contrast, nothing is as remarkable about the *Drapier's Letters* as Swift decision to speak from within the crowd. Although it is plausible, as Jack B. Gilbert has argued, that the initials M. B. constitute a Swiftian allusion to Marcus Brutus, the Roman patriot praised in *Gulliver's Travels*,[161] the allusion remains a private association.[162] Swift refuses to cloak himself in the mantle of an ancient famous for manly integrity, like the authors of *Cato's Letters* and, half a century later, the *Letters of Junius*. He does the opposite. He asserts the writer's contemporary obscurity. Momentously, he thereby represents the drapers and weavers of Dublin – the ordinary Protestant shopkeepers who suffered in times of dearth – as a constituent interest of the Irish nation.

Although he credits his Drapier with 'some little Knowledge in the *Latin Tongue*', he is a humble draper formed by an apprenticeship in London.[163] He is liable to rebuke for meddling in politics, as Swift admits in his *Letter to the Lord Chancellor Middleton*:

> I know it will readily be objected; what have private Men to do with the Publick? What Call had a *Drapier* to turn Politician, to meddle in Matters of State? Would not his Time have been better employed in looking to his Shop; or his Pen in writing Proverbs, Elegies, Ballads, Garlands, and Wonders? He would then have been out of all Danger of Proclamations, and Prosecutions. Have we not able Magistrates and Counsellors, hourly watching over the Publick-Weal?

To this Swift responds that parliamentary addresses have failed, and that few might have been able to resist the infamous pence 'if some Pen had not been employed, to inform the People how far they might legally proceed, in refusing that Coin, to detect the Fraud, the Artifice, and Insolence of the Coiner'.[164] Swift is implicitly defending himself, the writer who actually deployed the pen to alert the people. He is also understating how subversive it was to imagine a humble shopkeeper on his own initiative making up for the deficiencies of his betters.

Swift's choice of voice is not just a rhetorical convenience. Since the Drapier supports a policy adopted by the Irish leadership in Church and state, he is no rebel. His presence is subversive only because his voice is not subsumed in that of his leaders. It has an authority of its own. His advice that it will take thirty-six of the new half pence to buy a quart of two-penny ale speaks to common needs and the consolations of the poor. Swift also speaks prophetically to collective fears of currency devaluation:

> IF a *Squire* has a mind to come to Town to buy Cloaths and Wine and Spices for himself and Family, or perhaps to pass the Winter here; he must bring with him five or six Horses loaden with *Sacks* as the *Farmers* bring their Corn; and when his Lady comes in her Coach to our Shops, it must be followed by a Car loaded with Mr. WOOD's Money. And I hope we shall have the Grace to take it for no more than it is worth.[165]

It is customary to emphasize Swift's comic exaggeration as well as his appeal to the common people who will suffer most: 'These examples are like elongated shadows, which are distortions but are nevertheless produced by tangible substance. Wood's halfpence threatened the common man's meat and drink.'[166] But the frightened voice of Swift's Irish shopkeepers is also oddly prophetic. In the developing capital-based economy against which he had long fulminated, economic and monetary threats to the welfare of whole populations would become more common. The squire with his 'loaden' horses and the bankers who would need twelve hundred horses to carry their deposits prefigure later historical crises. Only reliance on paper currency distinguishes Swift's fantasy from the hyper-inflation that afflicted Weimar Germany in the 1920s. As the Drapier, Swift voices the genuine fears of populations who feel vulnerable not just to natural catastrophes but, increasingly, to the consequences of government economic policies.

As these premonitions of the catastrophic devaluation of a suspect currency suggest, Swift can be both retrograde and prophetic. Clinging to the values of an agrarian past, he anticipates the destabilising triumph of a capital-based economy. He idealized the classical past, but he is implicated in and so remarkably alert to the process Michael McKeon calls the devolution of absolutism. 'Once postulated', McKeon observes, '... the conception of absolute, self-justified authority could be detached from the "body natural" of the absolute monarch and embodied elsewhere: in the courtier, in Parliament, even in the common people'.[167] Swift's loyalty to the Crown-in-Parliament marks a point at which many up-to-date Englishmen stabilized this devolution, preserving a degree of monarchical authority by constraining it within a parliamentary structure. More accurately, perhaps, they created a forum within which those with royalist loyalties or populist longings could spar under the watchful eye of a landed aristocracy eager to control but reluctant to eliminate patrilineal succession. Similarly, Swift is, as a propagandist, deeply involved in the public discussion of state affairs, an activity so subversive that it had once seemed to justify suppressing the coffee houses. Extending his imagination downward, Swift steps outside the charmed circle of the gentry to speak as the Drapier, embracing the proliferation of interests, each with its own claims, that together constitute the national community.[168] He imagines a society that resembles the colliding egos and quarrelsome siblings of *A Tale of a Tub* in new terms. He imagines it as if it were, in fact, a family; that is, as if the ties binding it were more powerful than the forces of division.

As the English in Ireland found themselves compelled to imagine an Anglo-Irish nation, Swift provided the focus for their widespread participation in a common act of self-preservation, a participation that gave coherence to a usually factious community:

> THERE is one comfortable Circumstance in this universal Opposition to Mr. *Wood*, that the People sent over hither from *England*, to *fill up our Vacancies, Ecclesiastical, Civil and Military*, are all on our Side: *Money*, the great *Divider* of the World, hath, by a strange Revolution, been the great *Uniter* of a most *divided* People.[169]

Swift like Archbishop King had long resented the tendency to fill deaneries and bishoprics as well as civil and administrative offices with English appointees; that is, with Englishmen from England as opposed to Englishmen raised and educated in Ireland – Englishmen like Swift and King. That Hugh Boulter, the newly appointed English Archbishop of Armagh, recommended withdrawing Wood's patent soon after his arrival in Ireland in November 1724 suggests that rival interests did pull together at a moment of crisis. That Boulter would later work to weaken the 'Irish' interest by encouraging English appointments suggests that only a strong external stimulus could consolidate this nascent Anglo-Irish political community. The ambivalence of Swift's accomplishment appears in his Anglo-Irish insistence that he too is English. His indignation at English stereotypes of the Anglo-Irish animates not just Swift's letter to Lord Midleton but also his *Letter to the Whole People of Ireland*. Those across the Irish Sea, he complains, 'look upon us as a Sort of *Savage Irish*, whom our Ancestors conquered several Hundred Years ago'.[170] This is false:

> As to the People of this Kingdom, they consist either of *Irish Papists*; who are as inconsiderable, in Point of Power, as the Women and Children; or of *English Protestants*, who love their Brethren of that Kingdom; although they may possibly sometimes complain, when they think they are hardly used.[171]

That Swift ignores Ireland's substantial population of Scottish Protestants, most of them Ulster-based dissenters from the Church of Ireland, further emphasizes Swift's thoroughly English vision of the Irish nation.

These profound limitations notwithstanding, Swift does momentously imagine the fragmented Anglo-Irish as a people.[172] Just as important, he articulates the aspirations of that imagined community as part of a sustained, successful political campaign motivated by fear of an external threat. Furthermore, he does so in the voice of a humble urban tradesman, a draper. This strategy is doubly decentring. Although the community imagined itself as English, it shifts its centre of political consciousness from England to Ireland by locating legitimacy in the Irish rather than the English Parliament. It places the voice of the political nation among the ordinary craftsmen and shopkeepers of Ireland, a shift down the social scale from the gentry who largely monopolized political discussion. It is true that Swift excluded from the political nation everybody outside the Church of Ireland and many within it. It is also true that conceived liberty more narrowly than we do and valued authority more.[173] But he expressed his views imaginatively, adopting a voice in which others could hear themselves. Despite Swift's hostility to dissent, for example, a dissenter could wholeheartedly echo M. B.'s eloquent rejection of the Catholic Pretender. Jonathan Swift – the Anglican Dean whose authorship of the *Drapier's Letters* was widely suspected – matters less than M. B. Drapier. The performer is less important than the performance through which a national audience participated in a public expression of its newly imagined community. Readers who listen not to the evident sectarian limitations of Swift's pamphlets but to a voice expressing the aspirations of a colonized people – of all colonized peoples – are reading Swift according to the spirit if not the letter of his own imaginative act of political sympathy.

The *Drapier's Letters* are the greatest triumph of Swift's political career. If Swift had not also written *Gulliver's Travels*, they might be remembered as his greatest literary triumph as well.[174] Rallied by the Drapier, the Irish patriots had defeated the British administration. Swift's weapon of choice had been, yet again, his mastery of voice. 'O Thou! whatever Title please thine ear', Pope addresses Swift in the *Dunciad*, 'Dean, Drapier, Bickerstaff, or Gulliver!' This sets up a series of teasing correspondences. The public character that Swift supports in his office as Dean – it is literally his official character – is a creation no more or less compelling than the character he created to narrate a fictitious travel narrative, *Travels into Several Remote Nations of the World*. Both share their existence with Isaac Bickerstaff and the Drapier, who are themselves equivalent. A character in an early April Fool's joke is comparable to M. B. Drapier, in whose voice Swift addressed a grave crisis and, as Pope adds, helped '[his] griev'd Country's copper chains unbind'.[175] But Swift's impersonations are never entirely independent creations. Bickerstaff established an Irish vicar's character as a wit worthy to associate with London's best, and M. B. Drapier was widely known to be the Dean of St Patrick's.[176] Clearly the 'mercurial' Bolingbroke and the 'protean' Daniel Defoe were not the only writers of the day conspicuous for their versatility, but it is hard to shake the conviction of something unyielding and constant at the centre of Swift's identities. Those less adulatory than Pope also recalled another persona that took on a life of its own, the Teller of *A Tale of a Tub*. He too was identified with the Dean, whom Swift's critics thereby painted as an infidel whose prostitute pen had served many factions. But it is a tribute to the mad vitality of Swift's invention that his enemies could caricature him effectively only by exploiting it. For the rest of his life, the Dean was also the Drapier. In those guises, he enjoyed a popular authority that few clerical writers have ever managed.

It is appropriate that the Dean came to sport his accomplishments as the Drapier, who embodied Swift's commitment to the weavers near St Patrick's. In *Verses on the Death of Dr. Swift*, a poem likely written in 1731, Swift imagines himself condemned and praised:

> Now Grub Street wits are all employed;
> With elegies the town is cloyed:
> Some paragraph in every paper,
> To curse the Dean, or bless the Drapier.[177]

The note to this passage in Faulkner's 1735 edition, closely supervised by Swift, suggests Swift's desire to fix meanings: 'The author imagines, that the scribblers of the prevailing party, which he always opposed, will libel him after his death; but that others will remember him with gratitude, who consider the service he had done to Ireland, under the name of M. B. Drapier, by utterly defeating the destructive project of Wood's half-pence, in five letters to the people of Ireland, at that time read universally, and convincing every reader'.[178] Here Swift defines the Dean as the responsible officer of the Church who bears the brunt of the Walpole regime's hostility, the High-Churchman who embodies (perhaps) Swift's political principles 'as to religion'. The Drapier, the heroic focus of popular affection for his services as one of the common people, then embodies Swift's Old Whig devotion to liberty, his principles 'in politics'.

Although he never again intervened so decisively in public affairs, the Dean and the Drapier fixed Swift's hold on the popular affections. He continued to write pamphlets on the Church and on Irish affairs, some published and some preserved in manuscript, but *The Drapier's Letters* are the crowning achievement of his life as a political writer. They outshine even *The Conduct of the Allies*, which benefited from the writer's direct involvement in the ministry, not to mention the elaborately coordinated press campaign managed by Harley. They represent a more independent collaboration his nation's political leaders, and they express a more daring as well as a more mature vision of his place within politics. They mark the place in which a remarkably intolerant Dean committed to the Anglican monopoly on civil and military office nevertheless also became a spokesman against oppression whose voice today commands the attention of readers grappling with the legacy of colonialism. That they do so while asserting Ireland's standing as a kingdom, not a colony, suggests how thoroughly Swift grasped the contradictions of his historical moment and teased out their implications. Nobody fashioned selves more brilliantly than Swift, but even he never again created a political voice as commanding as the Drapier's.

CONCLUSION: 'UPON THIS GREAT FOUNDATION OF MISANTHROPY'

Apart from two long visits to England in 1726 and 1727, Swift spent the rest of his life in Ireland, where he was publicly celebrated as the patriotic Drapier. He went to England in 1726 to publish *Travels into Several Remote Nations of the World*, the work on which his English fame primarily rests, and to renew his friendships with his fellow Scriblerians, the community of wits he had left behind him a dozen years earlier. His long work on his 'Travells', his excited friends' eager anticipation as news of his project gradually spread among them, and his elaborate plans to publish in England, not Ireland – everything reveals a confident writer expecting once more to capture the taste of the town. Swift had almost finished *Travels* when he turned his attention to the *Drapier's Letters*. In January 1724, shortly before he joined the campaign against Wood's pence, he told Ford that he had finished Book IV of *Travels* and started working on Book III, the last written: 'I have left the Country of Horses, and am in the flying Island, where I shall not stay long, and my two last Journyes will be soon over'.[1] After the Drapier's success, he returned to the task, completing it in August 1725: 'I have finished my Travells, and I am now transcribing them; they are admirable Things, and will wonderfully mend the World'.[2] He had invented a character more memorable even than the Drapier, although it was one less likely to be directly identified with the Dean than Bickerstaff or the Drapier. To the extent that *Travels* presents itself flatly as a travel narrative by one Lemuel Gulliver, 'First a Surgeon, and then a Captain of several Ships', it is a hoax that recalls his most playful early work, the Bickerstaff papers. Relishing this aspect of the book, Arbuthnot would pass on accounts of readers duped by it.[3] Swift had also written an intensely political book. *Travels* grows out of the intense re-engagement with politics that produced the works in which Swift most directly confronted those in power, *A Proposal for the Universal Use of Irish Manufacture* and the *Drapier's Letters*. Nevertheless, it is fiction, not tract. Since the Septennial Act (1716) had reduced the effectiveness of opposition writing by strengthening the court's hold over Parliament, Swift like Defoe was writing at a remove from political events. Ehrenpreis convincingly speculates that *Travels* grows out of Swift's thwarted desire to write a definitive history of the Tory ministry, a desire that the ministers themselves frustrated:

> I believe, therefore, that when Swift embarked on *Gulliver's Travels*, it was to convert these repressed impulses into the shape of a fantasy. He would thus generalize his response to the public events he had known and deliver his confirmed views on human nature as it was exhibited by English society, especially in the conduct of government.[4]

No wonder *Travels* both reflects and reflects upon Swift's lifelong engagement in politics.

Swift was the first to play up the contentiousness of his *Travels*. 'I have employd my time (besides ditching) in finishing correcting, amending, and Transcribing my Travells, in four Parts Compleat newly Augmented,' he bragged to Pope, 'and intended for the press when the world shall deserve them, or rather when a Printer shall be found brave enough to venture his Eares'.[5] This was not just play. While he was planning and writing his book, the government had arrested two of his printers, and the Atterbury affair had showed its willingness to punish a contentious clergyman outside the courts. Still, there was also a large element of conventional swagger, the boast of the heroic satirist who alone has the courage to denounce the vices of the mighty. Although some episodes did aptly send up contemporary politics, *Travels* usually paints a broad portrait of the venality that for Swift, and some modern historians, characterizes eighteenth-century English society – the trait that for Swift best explained contemporary degeneration from classical models.[6] The aspect of *Travels* that grows most directly from Swift's experience as a political partisan who distrusted political parties may in fact be its distrust of classification and its related satire of the first-person plural. Gulliver's efforts to identify himself with particular groups are usually as absurd as others' efforts to categorize him. On this topic, Swift had ample experience on which to base his strong views. To the annoyance of contemporaries and modern scholars alike, he answered as evasively as possible when he was pressed on where he fit into the political landscape. Yet questions from those who wanted to categorize him were inescapable, various, occasionally unfair.

When Swift returned to the Ireland that now regarded him as a hero, he continued to write, usually critically, about Irish affairs. He enjoyed the honours heaped on him, and he remained confident of his importance. Although he had the freedom of the City already, therefore, he campaigned for the distinction of having it awarded with a suitable testimonial in a gold box; through his friend Patrick Delany, he even sent a suitable inscription. But he was no less prone to literary indiscretions. In response to Delany's *Epistle to Lord Carteret* (December 1729), Swift provided a swinging denunciation of the servility modern patrons expected of poets. Now most famous for its celebration of Pope (ll. 71–88), *A Libel on the Reverend Dr Delany and His Excellency John, Lord Carteret* (February 1730) provoked Viscount Allen to denounce Swift publicly.[7] Swift protested in a letter to Pope that Allen's outbreak was 'an odd instance of his Madness': 'at the Privy Council, the Lord Mayor being sent for, accused me for the Author [of the *Libel*], and reproached the City for their resolution of giving me my freedom in a Gold-box, calling me a Jacobite Libeller &c. and hath now brought the same affair into the H. of Lords that the Printer &c may be prosecuted'.[8] It is typical of Swift that he would be denounced and honoured at the same time; he had received the freedom of the City while there was a price on his head. Voted his honour, Swift received it only on 27 May 1730, the day after the same honour, much more *pro forma*, went to John Hoadly, recently appointed Archbishop of Dublin. Such politics did not please him. He greeted the delegation by presenting the speech in praise of himself that he thought the occasion deserved.[9] *The Substance of What was said by the Dean of St. Patrick's to the Lord Mayor and some of the Aldermen, when his Lordship came to present the said Dean with his Freedom in a Gold Box*, first published in 1765, outlines the Dean's deserts without the ironies of *Verses on the Death of Dr Swift*.[10] As for Allen, Swift retaliated in verse – a poem in two parts called *Traulus* – after Parliament rose.[11] Swift was no easier a figure after his Irish success than he had been as the English ministry's propagandist.

Swift continued to comment, sometimes abrasively, on Irish affairs. In the absence of the circumstances that had allowed him to speak for a united community, however, he more often than not wrote as a lone projector rather than as the voice of a community. He and his friend Sheridan tried their hands at a varied and engaging weekly paper, the *Intelligencer*, that ran for twenty numbers; collected and published in London, it went through two editions in 1729–30, partly through its association with Swift's name.[12] But it was not profitable enough to support the talented younger collaborator they had hoped for. Swift continued to defend his Church and the sacramental test that guarded its privileges. He continued to comment harshly on the administration of Irish affairs, and he remained equally willing to disparage the beggarly population who suffered from its ineptitude. He sometimes wrote eloquently. He remained prolific. But of the twenty-four items collected in *Prose Works*, vol. 12: *Irish Tracts 1728–1733*, for example, eleven were published only posthumously. Apart from his collaboration with Sheridan, he spoke more as a lone projector than as the voice of a substantial community. Certainly by the high standards he had set in *Conduct of the Allies* and the *Drapier's Letters*, his essays had relatively little impact. It is suggestive that his most important prose tract after his final return to Ireland from England is not a tract but rather a parody of a tract, *A Modest Proposal*. In it, Swift again gave unforgettable expression to the feelings central to his political writing: his compassion for all victims of oppression, not just some categories of it, and his searing anger at the obtuseness and ineptitude that caused it.

Swift did not leave politics behind him when he visited England. Many of his English friends had been political allies. Arbuthnot had contributed to the pamphlet wars, for example, and Bolingbroke still had political ambitions. By collaborating with William Pulteney and the opposition Whigs, he hoped to forge a cohesive opposition to Walpole.[13] The *Craftsman*, the opposition journal that would print most of his essays on history and political party, began its run only on 5 December 1726, but the threat of this 'Patriot' opposition would provoke *Gulliver Decypher'd* to associate the King of Brobdingnag with dissident Whigs as well as with the Jacobites. Swift had also brought Irish concerns with him, carefully coordinating his message with Archbishop King. Since he had not lost his gift for gaining the attention of the powerful, he managed in April both to dine with Walpole and to secure a further interview with him. For this he was represented as someone looking for preferment in England, perhaps at the price of distancing himself from the opposition: such claims could help to discredit him if he did join the opposition propagandists. The day following his interview, he described the meeting in a letter to Peterborough, claiming that he 'had no other design in desiring to see Sir Robert Walpole, than to represent the affairs of Ireland to him in a true light'.[14] The letter reiterated his usual concerns: the English in Ireland, whose ancestors had been 'conquerors of Ireland', were denied equal footing with other Englishmen; 'they are denyed the natural liberty of exporting their manufactures'; preferments educational, ecclesiastical, and civil go to those from England, often without regard to qualifications.[15] Hoping to influence policy under the next king, he also courted the favour of Princess (later Queen) Caroline, relying in part – but excessively, it turned out – on the influence of Pope's friend and neighbour, Henrietta Howard, mistress of the bed chamber to Caroline.[16] Although he can hardly have been completely surprised to encounter views of Ireland 'alien from what I conceived to be rights and privileges of a subject of England',[17] Swift could not complain that he was denied a hearing. Although he was eventually disappointed in his hopes of the princess, too, he had managed to achieve extraordinarily direct contact with those at the top of the social hierarchy.[18] He was a politically significant public figure.

Just before his return to Ireland in August 1726, Swift arranged publication of the manuscript he had been sharing with his friends.[19] He acted with comic elaboration to maintain his anonymity. Ford, Pope, Gay, and Erasmus Lewis variously acted as intermediaries. Enclosed with a portion of the manuscript, a letter to the bookseller Benjamin Motte from Gulliver's cousin 'Richard Sympson' set conditions for publication, including payment of £200. All went smoothly, and on 13 August 'Sympson' agreed: 'I would have both Volumes come out together and published by Christmas at furthest'.[20] Even Swift's hopes cannot have exceeded his book's performance. By Christmas, *Travels into Several Remote Nations of the World* was in its third edition, after appearing in octavo on 28 October 1726 and requiring a second edition in November. Another followed in May 1727, and a further edition in smaller format was published in early 1728 (dated 1727, reissued in 1731). Newspapers promptly serialized it, and three Dublin editions also appeared in 1726–7.[21] Letters from his English friends kept Swift abreast of his success: 'I will make over all my profits to yow, for the property of Gullivers Travells', Arbuthnot wrote a week after *Travels* first appeared, 'which I believe will have as great a Run as John Bunian. Gulliver is a happy man that at his age can write such a merry book'.[22] His comment is quintessentially Scriblerian. Addressing a fellow wit in a circle animated by emulation, he expresses affectionate envy. Since Arbuthnot had invented John Bull, who is still the archetypal Englishman, his admiration was well worth having. Shrewdly, he associated *Travels* with the most enduring popular success of Swift's lifetime, *Pilgrim's Progress* (1678). More playfully, he developed one of Swift's jokes, the surprisingly advanced age (thirty-seven and a half years) at which the naive protagonist begins his travels.[23] Gulliver is undoubtedly not fortunate (Arbuthnot's 'happy'), but for all its pessimism about human nature, Swift's book is indeed 'merry'.

Two days later Gay reported:

> About ten days ago a Book was publish'd here of the Travels on one Gulliver, which hath been the conversation of the whole town ever since: The whole impression sold in a week; and nothing is more diverting than to hear the different opinions people give of it, though all agree in liking it extreamly. 'Tis generally said that you are the Author, but I am told, the Bookseller declares he knows not from what hand it came. From the highest to the lowest it is universally read, from the Cabinet-council to the Nursery. The Politicians to a man agree, that it is free from particular reflections, but that the Satire on general societies of men is too severe. Not but we now and then meet with people of greater perspicuity, who are in search for particular applications in every leaf; and 'tis highly probable we shall have keys publish'd to give light into Gulliver's design.[24]

Gay's comment, also flattering, has the advantage of addressing a degree of genuine apprehension that *Travels* might be accused of the particular political satire that could provoke official retaliation. Gay is trying to reassure the friend who had recently been a house guest: 'You may see by this, that you are not much injur'd by being suppos'd the Author of this piece'. Gay's caginess – 'If you are' the author, he continues – reveals unease that Swift's correspondence was still being read by a hostile administration. *Travels* is playful, but players in this game can suffer serious penalties.

Well aware of those penalties, Motte had nervously bowdlerized Swift's text where the topical political references seemed too pointed. Swift complained from Ireland to little effect, taking special offence at passages not just omitted but rewritten to soften them. When he supervised preparation of Faulkner's 1735 edition of his *Works*, Swift saw that most passages were restored, but even Faulkner sometimes flinched.[25] In Motte's editions, the satire of the Atterbury investigation had been cast as a hypothetical speculation rather than the practice 'in the Kingdom of *Tribnia*, by the Natives called *Langden*'.[26] The rebellion against Laputa by Lindalino, preserved in Charles Ford's manuscript of Swift's corrections, has been read as a somewhat elusive allegory of the campaign against Wood's pence.[27] Like Motte, Faulkner left it out of his edition. General satire of political parties was not censored, however, even though the passage describing Lilliputian factions – 'two struggling Parties in the Empire, under the Names of *Tramecksan*, and *Slamecksan*, from the high and low Heels on their Shoes' – alludes the Prince of Wales's rumoured sympathy with the Tories: 'We apprehend his Imperial Highness, the Heir to the Crown, to have some Tendency towards the High-Heels [Tories]; at least we can plainly discover one of his Heels higher than the other; which gives him a Hobble in his Gait'.[28] Gay's absent friend needed the reassurance he provided, for *Gulliver's Travels* was sometimes dangerously topical.

Most modern readers agree with Gay, though, that despite local allusions Swift's satire is general. Despite a scholarly tradition of allegorical reading, largely a product of the twentieth-century and now defunct, few now think that the many contemporary allusions are embedded in a sustained allegory of Swift's involvement with the Tory ministry.[29] Swift's political themes survive intact. The Lilliputians face what Swift, like Temple, regarded as the greatest of dangers: 'we labour under two mighty Evils; a violent Faction at home, and the Danger of an Invasion by a most potent Enemy from abroad'.[30] Scrutinized and denounced for his own political allegiances, Swift imagines the wise King of Brobdingnag laughing at Gulliver's earnest computation of English numbers by sect and by faction: 'the Prejudices of his Education prevailed so far, that he could not forbear taking me up in his right Hand, and stroaking me gently with the other; after an hearty Fit of laughing, asked me whether I were a *Whig* or a *Tory*'.[31] The King also condemns peacetime standing armies, topically enough as we have seen, rejecting with contempt Gulliver's offer of gunpowder so that he can 'destroy the whole Metropolis, if ever it should pretend to dispute his absolute Commands'.[32] Gulliver himself had rejected absolutism in Lilliput, where he embodied that controversial institution, the standing army.[33] Despite the emperor of Lilliput's request, he refused to reduce Blefuscu to absolute subjection.[34] In such episodes, Swift exploits a widely shared political idiom that locates him among the opposition writers but does little to categorize him more narrowly.

Some episodes invite association with features of Swift's political life. The Empress of Lilliput's implacable anger after Gulliver douses the palace fire surely somehow recalls Queen Anne's resentment of the satirist and pamphleteer whose radical indecorum had convinced her never to prefer him in the English Church. The human folly that reduces the fertile land of Balnibarbi to desolate sterility reflects the foolishness of the governors whose policies, Swift believed, had unnaturally impoverished Ireland. But such passages are neither narrowly partisan nor strictly allegorical. *Travels* is an elusive book. That its politically engaged readers can disagree even on Swift's party position is the point with which this study began. Orwell differs from Said; Gandhi approaches *Travels* with unexpected relish. Meticulous scholarship by Lock, Downie, and Higgins leaves key issues subject to debate.[35] Much of the abundant scholarship on the politics of *Gulliver's Travels* is embedded in the notes to teaching editions, informing a debate in progress. Higgins's informative annotations in the recent World's Classics edition of *Travels*, for example, provide an excellent introduction to the subject while suggesting – through their heightened sensitivity to potential Jacobite parallels – that the task is inescapably tendentious.[36] *Travels* everywhere betrays Swift's political involvement without defining a party-political position. It thereby provokes Swift scholars to positions only slightly less combative than his own.

Given Swift's assertive independence, the aspect of *Gulliver's Travels* that most thoroughly reflects his long engagement in partisan politics may be its satire of categorization. Swift was as watched and as questioned as Gulliver. Was he a Whig? a Tory? Was he an infidel? a Christian? Was he a Hanoverian? a Jacobite? Was he English? Irish? Swift's answers were usually evasive, but he could be savage when Englishmen categorized him as Irish. So it is hardly surprising that in *Travels*, categorical questions and the attempt to evade them crop up time and time again. To resist categories completely is to become an anomaly, a spectacle – a monster, a freak. Although the King of Brobdingnag wonders whether Gulliver might be a toy, 'a piece of Clock-work ... contrived by some ingenious Artist', for example, his 'three great Scholars' ponderously decide that Gulliver 'was only *Replum Scalcath*, which is interpreted literally *Lusus Naturæ*'.[37] All too often Gulliver himself insists on his own freakishness, his (the word seems inescapable) peculiarity. He repeatedly presents himself as a spectacle or a source of spectacle.[38] He allows Lilliputian troops to march between his legs, arranges for them to conduct cavalry exercises on his handkerchief. Purely for attention, he plays a Brobdingnagian spinet by banging a stick on one key at a time. It seems appropriate that the Lilliputians imagine starving him to death, 'leaving the Skeleton as a Monument of Admiration to Posterity'.[39] His remains will continue to provide the pleasures of spectacle without draining the treasury.

Gulliver's chosen vehicle for addressing the crowd is the stage itinerant. Like Swift's Tale-Teller, that is, he yearns to be the centre of attention, and he seems unable to imagine a subtler, suppler connection to community. Even the souvenirs of his travels – diminutive sheep, a gigantic tooth, a corn cut from a maid of honour's toe – amount to a cabinet of curiosities. The monkey that kidnaps Gulliver seconds the king's assessment, repeating the king of Brobdingnag's gesture while proving himself more adept than the scholars at categorizing his find appropriately: 'I have good Reason to believe that he took me for a young one of his own Species, by his often stroking my Face very gently with his other Paw'.[40] A similar recognition of kinship with Yahoos will unsettle Gulliver's categorical certainty in Book IV: 'My Horror and Astonishment are not to be described, when I observed, in this abominable Animal, a perfect human Figure'.[41] The

Yahoos recognize kinship too, but unlike the monkey, they despise Gulliver as an unnatural pet, 'as a tame *Jack Daw* with Cap and Stockings, is always persecuted by the wild ones, when he happens to be got among them'.[42] To distinguish one-self too thoroughly from one's kind is problematic, and Gulliver is far odder even than his eccentric author.

Although there can be no doubt that Swift admired Cato, *Travels* looks askance at even principled aloofness from society. In Balnibarbi, Gulliver meets a modern equivalent, Lord Munodi, an ideal country squire who resists the destructive intellectual fashions of Laputa. Like Swift, Munodi relies on the traditional: 'he was content to go on in the old Forms; to live in the Houses his Ancestors had built, and act as they did in every Part of Life without Innovation',[43] despite the contempt it earns him among the fashionable. This passage expresses Swift's humanist identification of human achievement with a past from which decline was the only possible change. But even Munodi acknowledges the difficulty of ignoring the society around him:

> he [Munodi] told me with a very melancholy Air, that he doubted he must throw down his Houses in Town and Country, to rebuild them after the present Mode; destroy all his Plantations, and cast others into such a Form as modern Usage required; and give the same Directions to all his Tenants, unless he would submit to incur the Censure of Pride, Singularity, Affectation, Ignorance, Caprice; and perhaps encrease his Majesty's Displeasure.[44]

Although this gloomy resignation may be intended to illuminate Swift's sturdier singularity, *Travels* rejects the possibility of ignoring society. When Gulliver obtains a vision of a '*Sextumvirate* to which all the Ages of the World cannot add a Seventh',[45] five of these models of independent virtue are ancients; the sixth, the only modern, is Sir Thomas More, martyred almost two centuries earlier. Even in such relatively conventional moments – there was nothing controversial about the Cato figure or the members of the sextumvirate – Swift treats extreme independence of society skeptically. His self-centred protagonist repeatedly raises perplexing questions about the limits of independence and the power of community.

When Gulliver clumsily includes himself in various categories, for example, he remains just as much a figure of fun. His attempts speak not just as an *I* but as part of a *we* lead him into absurdity. In Lilliput, for example, Gulliver is in fact a great man valued for his service to the state. He has been ennobled as 'a *Nardac*, of the highest Rank in that Empire',[46] like England's great victor in arms, the Duke of Marlborough. Like Marlborough, he participates in affairs of state: 'And when the Matter was debated in Council, the wisest Part of the Ministry were of my Opinion'.[47] Yet he can save the palace only because he has been drinking 'plentifully of a most delicious Wine, called *Glimigrim*, (the *Blefuscudians* call it *Flunec*, but ours is esteemed the better Sort)'.[48] Gulliver's 'ours', the oddest feature of this passage, identifies him as one of the Lilliputians despite the discrepancy of scale that permits his display of hydraulic might. The assertion that 'our' wine is superior to theirs is irrelevant to his urinary vigour as it is to his narrative purpose: his English readers will never taste glimigrim or flunec. This joke blossoms when Gulliver absurdly defends the Treasurer's wife from 'the Court-Scandal ... that she once came privately to my Lodging':

> But I defy the Treasurer or his two Informers. (I will name them, and let them make their best of it) *Clustril* and *Drunlo*, to prove that any Person ever came to me *incognito*, except the Secretary *Reldresal*, who was sent by express Command of his Imperial Majesty, as I have before related. I should not have dwelt so long upon this Particular, if it had not been a Point wherein the Reputation of a great Lady is so nearly concerned; to say nothing of my own ...⁴⁹

Gulliver has lost his sense of proportion. The intrigue is impossible; his English defence useless, for it will never reach Lilliputian readers. Otherwise pointless, this episode resembles the sexual boasting that Gulliver manages a little more suavely in Book III: 'The Women of the island have Abundance of Vivacity; they contemn their Husbands, and are exceedingly fond of Strangers'.⁵⁰

Such episodes create a space within which Swift can playfully reflect on his own relationship with partisan gossip. When his politics and his relations with Vanessa and Stella invited gossip, he resented what he regarded as baseless accusations. On the evidence of *Travels*, he felt that rumours of his political relations with the Pretender were no more plausible than rumours of Gulliver's sexual relations with a lady of the Lilliputian court. Gulliver's futile denunciation of his accusers allows Swift to express his genuine feeling in similar circumstances while distancing himself from it. But petty, self-interested, and implausible accusations figure routinely in court life, and Swift had in fact contributed his share through works like the *Windsor Prophecy*. Even Gulliver's exaggerated self-importance perhaps grows from Swift's wry reflections on his interactions with the great when he was a Tory propagandist less important in the inmost circle than he had imagined at the time. In Lilliput, Gulliver was physically 'great' but socially insignificant; his royal 'highness', socially great but diminutive. As a great writer otherwise of little consequence, Swift had associated with the politically great. Swift's satire of Gulliver often stings because it springs from self-reflection.

In Brobdingnag, Gulliver appropriately identifies himself with the English, but he does so in such an exalted strain that the King concludes that he and his kind are vermin. His protestations of valour after kidnapping by a giant ape produce 'nothing else besides a loud Laughter' that he moralizes:

> This made me reflect, how vain an Attempt it is for a Man to endeavour doing himself Honour among those who are out of all Degree of Equality or Comparison with him. And yet I have seen the Moral of my own Behaviour very frequent in *England*

since my Return; where a little contemptible Varlet, without the least Title to Birth, Person, Wit, or common Sense, shall presume to look with Importance, and put himself upon a Foot with the greatest persons of the Kingdom.[51]

Gulliver in no more pretentiousness after his kidnapping than he is when he tries to impress the king by identifying himself with 'our noble Country, the Mistress of Arts and Arms, the Scourge of *France*, the Arbitress of *Europe*, the Seat of Virtue, Piety, Honour and Truth, the Pride and Envy of the World'.[52] In Swift, egregious claims of distinction and uncritical identification with a category are invariably objects of satire. Even when the category is otherwise appropriate, an undiscriminating *we* illuminates the speaker's grave limitations. A writer who thought like this could not possibly identify himself whole heartedly with a political party.

Swift's interrogation of categories is obviously most searching in Book IV. That Swift sees Gulliver as a Yahoo is obvious enough. He looks like one, especially without the clothes that temporarily allow him to conceal the resemblance from the Houyhnhnm household that adopts him. While bathing in the river, he learns to his horror that a young female Yahoo finds him sexually attractive. This is decisive: 'For now I could no longer deny, that I was a real *Yahoo* in every Limb and Feature, since the Females had a natural Propensity to me as one of their own Species'.[53] In each book of *Travels*, the scatological emphasizes humanity's animal nature by exposing and thus undermining the elaborate decorum that denies any link between the socially high and the bodily low. Hence the impossible law that Gulliver's palace fire heroism puts him 'in open Breach of': 'That whoever shall make water within the Precincts of the Royal Palace, shall be liable to the Pains and Penalties of High Treason'.[54] The physical need is simply animal; the foolish (because impossible) denial of it, fully human. Lilliputian pretentiousness stands as exposed as Gulliver. The sexual, also present in each book, is also levelling, but its function is to identify kinds. However implausible, sexual speculation about Gulliver and the Treasurer's wife accepts his kindred humanity with the Lilliputians. When the Brobdingnagian maids of honour 'often strip me naked from Top to Toe, and lay me at full length in their bosoms' and when the 'hand-somest among these Maids of Honour ... would sometimes set me astride upon one of her Nipples', as Gulliver complains, they are indeed using him 'without any manner of Ceremony, like a Creature who had no Sort of Consequence'.[55] Insulting as they are, they are also acknowledging his masculinity and hence his humanity, as Gulliver recognizes. Why else insist that he has received the attentions of 'handsomest' maid of honour? Likewise, the Laputan women who prefer strangers to their speculation-obsessed husbands are affirming their (and by implication Gulliver's) common-sense humanity. Swift situates Gulliver within a remarkably expansive vision of humanity, asserting a basic but undeniable connection even (perhaps especially) when the usual sexual expressions of it are impossible. Through her desire for Gulliver, the female Yahoo includes her kind too within humanity. The partisan passion of modern readers shows how well Swift made the point.

Although we sometimes resist it, Swift makes a comparable case for the Houyhnhnms, the rational horses whose name and classical antecedents align them, too, with the human.[56] Even the brutal subjugation of the Yahoos on which their rational society is based, discussed in Chapter 1, marks them as all too human. This is the recognition that allows readers to associate Houyhnhnmland with totalitarianism (sometimes specified as Nazism), racism and imperialism. Orwell raised all these possibilities in 1946. A journalist committed to freedom of speech where Swift was a propagandist who distrusted it, Orwell was particularly sensitive to the totalitarian overtones of Houyhnhnmland, where public opinion has the coercive force to make Gulliver's master exile his odd pet. Nevertheless, Orwell also conceded that 'of the two, the Houyhnhnms are much liker human beings than are the Yahoos'.[57] Gulliver finds himself caught between rival versions of the human, not between two nonhuman species, only one of them human-oid. Hence Rawson's sharply worded observation, quoted above, that 'the tension created by Swift rests on opposite and contending perceptions of difference of species and racial difference within the same species'.[58] Swift gives weight to the latter by giving moral authority to the Houyhnhnms' recognition of kind:

> FRIENDSHIP and *Benevolence* are the two principal Virtues among the *Houyhnhnms*; and these not confined to particular Objects, but universal to the whole Race. For, a Stranger from the remotest Part, is equally treated with the nearest Neighbour, and where-ever he goes, looks upon himself as at home.[59]

This imperative is recognizably human. Swift makes Gulliver's challenge, and the reader's, greater than the Houyhnhnms' because he makes it impossible to define the human kind as narrowly as they do. Gulliver could impress us simply by extending these virtues to his fellow Englishmen, astound us by including the Portuguese captain whose acts of kindness mark him as a friend despite the difference of nationality and religion. He would still fall short of Swift's comprehensive vision.

But far from acknowledging European or even English humanity, Gulliver ignores Houyhnhnm virtues. He imitates instead their most superficial features, their gait and speech:

> By conversing with the *Houyhnhnms*, and looking upon them with Delight, I fell to imitate their Gait and Gesture, which is by now grown into a Habit; and my Friends often tell me in a blunt Way, that *I trot like a Horse*; which, however, I take for a great Compliment: neither shall I disown, that in speaking I am apt to fall into the voice and manner of the *Houyhnhnms*, and hear my self ridiculed on that Account without the least Mortification.[60]

Parading his eccentricity, Gulliver flaunts crashingly trivial signs of pretended membership in a superior kind. Precisely this kind of display, based on a jingoistic assertion of English superiority, had subverted his attempt to win the King of Brobdingnag's approval.

One of Swift's subject in *Travels*, then, is what we now call identity politics. Whether Gulliver denies his membership in a group or unthinkingly flaunts it, Swift makes it impossible not to ask, 'Who is *we*?' And by Book IV if not sooner, that question has become recognizably a version of the question, 'Who am I?' Swift himself had long grappled with such questions. An obscure dependent hoping to become independent, he had first established a public character as a clergyman within the Church of Ireland, thus aligning his restless ambition with the stability and authority of a public institution. As domestic chaplain to the Lord Lieutenant of Ireland he had a modest public role, one that expanded when he became vicar of Laracor and prebend of St Patrick's Cathedral. He was finally able to add the role of Dean of St Patrick's, which gave him a position of some local prominence. He had been ambitious for even more, but this was significant. He had a confident place within the only category he accepted without question. For Swift, membership in the Church *was* membership in the nation. Although he refused to identify himself with a party, he had managed to become an effective polemicist by aligning himself with particular groups – an English ministry with a goal he shared and the English community in Ireland.

Simultaneously, however, Swift invented a series of *I*'s free of his institutional identity. They provided an outlet for his ambition, in the process liberating his more subversive impulses. In his earliest and most revealing, as Teller of a *Tale of a Tub*, he attacked the enemies of the Church at the same time that he indulged while disciplining his ambition to distinguish himself in print, an ambition he associated with Grub Street. He was startled to discover that by adopting his exuberantly parodic *I*, he had parted company from many within 'our Church'. Identifying him with his egregious spokesman, they denounced him as their enemy. In his Apology, Swift defended himself without salvaging his reputation:

> Why should any Clergyman of our Church be angry to see the Follies of Fanaticism and Superstition exposed, tho' in the most ridiculous Manner? since that is perhaps the most probable way to cure them, or at least to hinder them from farther spreading. ... If the Clergy's Resentments lay upon their Hands, in my humble Opinion, they might have found more proper Objects to employ them on: *Nondum tibi defuit Hostis.*[61]

Perhaps because his church did not lack enemies, it included him among them. Swift complained, but he learned from this experience. In Isaac Bickerstaff, he adopted an identity that displayed his prowess less extravagantly, an *I* that, it turned out, his friend Steele wanted to share. Supporting the Tories, he found an acceptable way to indulge the orator's wish for a place above the crowd. As

Examiner and then as a Tory pamphleteer, he reconciled personal display with institutional authority by speaking in the voice of impersonal authority. With the Scriblerian wits, he created Martinus Scriblerus, an *I* more thoroughly collaborative than Bickerstaff. As the Drapier he found his most impressive political voice, accepting that the pamphleteer spoke most persuasively not from an altitude but for and from within the crowd.

It would be far too limiting to read *Travels* simply as an allegory of Swift's political experiences. It is useful to recognize, however, that during Swift's lifetime politics came to be dominated by political categories, the parties that we now regard as an essential organizing device of parliamentary politics. Like Harley, Swift resisted this development, holding to an older vision of service to the crown. But he grappled daily with the need to align the personal with some portion of a fragmented public. In most of the voices he invented, Swift tried to speak independently to and for a small group of powerful individuals. Gulliver's eagerness to talk to the leader of any society he visits has more than a touch of Swift's own experience of seeking out the great. He conceived of power in terms of a few great men working together, not as the result of party. He avoided identifying himself with any group larger than a circle of friends but smaller than the political nation. As his failed but serious effort to remain friends with Addison reveals, he definitely resisted categorizing himself in partisan terms. *We* apparently sounded less problematic if he could present himself as a participant in an inner circle, like the Junto lords or his friends in the Harley ministry. He saw the Scriblerians this way too, and this circle of remarkably distinct individuals shared enough of their literary program to be categorized together. (It might appal him, though, that the partisan term 'tory satirist' is roughly synonymous with 'Scriblerian writer'.) Even in the *Examiner*, where Swift adopted the voice of the rural gentry and clergy, Swift's first-person assurance is more remarkable than his ability to incorporate, or even recognize, the range of opinion his group actually included. When he eventually categorized himself with the ordinary shopkeepers of Dublin in the *Drapier's Letters*, he reached a political and literary position that the author of *A Tale of a Tub* could hardly have considered as a serious possibility. In its interrogation of what it means to identify oneself with a group, *Gulliver's Travels* represents, among many other things, a logical and suitably enigmatic culmination of Swift's reflections on his political life.

It does not follow that we should sentimentalize Swift as a writer who moved from patrician superiority to demotic engagement, from aristocracy to democracy. He makes a very poor fit with modern political categories. For one thing, he was remarkably comfortable with categories of difference and the patterns of exclusion from political life that created them. He could probably not imagine society without them. Even the Houyhnhnms have servants. That masters and servants differ in colour and ability, although each group is varied, probably reveals Swift's utopian hope for a world within which social distinctions would be both visible and natural. In the actual world, few writers worked harder than Swift to keep stark and unambiguous the boundaries between categories. The sacramental test, he felt, established a necessary boundary between those who could properly hold civic and military office and those who wilfully held aloofness from the national community. The latter, he felt, could claim to nothing more than the privilege of worshipping in private without persecution. Hence perhaps his suspicion of dissent from community norms even by an idealized dissident figure like Munodi. The thorough subjugation of the Roman Catholics troubled Swift not in the least: it was the essential precondition for his community's safety. Even his standing as an Anglo-Irish patriot turns on his categorical insistence that he was English and therefore entitled not to be taxed by a Parliament in which he was not represented. As we have seen, attempts to draw a boundary between Ireland and England, associating his community with the 'savage Irish', provoked his indignant rage. His comment on Walpole is revealing: 'Sir Robert Walpole was pleased to enlarge much upon the subject of Ireland, in a manner so alien from what I conceived to be rights and privileges of a subject of England, that I did not think proper to debate the matter with him'.[62] Swift does not do something that must be harder than it looks, because it is not common. He does not place the members of various subordinate categories beyond the pale of humanity. As his Irish tracts reveal, he feels that not even the most thoroughly subjugated deserve their wretchedness in times of famine and government neglect.

This is the burden of Swift's famous declaration of the impulse behind *Gulliver's Travels*:

> I have ever hated all Nations professions and Communityes and all my love is towards individualls for instance I hate the tribe of Lawyers, but I love Councellor such a one, Judge such a one for so with Physicians (I will not Speak of my own Trade) Soldiers, English, Scotch, French; and the rest but principally I hate and detest that animal called man, although I hartily love John, Peter, Thomas, and so forth. this is the system upon which I have governed my self many years (but do not tell) and so I shall go on till I have done with them I have got Materials Towards a Treatis proving the falsity of that Definition animal rationale, and to show it should be only *rationis capax*. Upon this great foundation of Misanthropy (though not in Timons manner) the whole building of my Travells is erected ...[63]

No wonder the tribalism of partisan politics offended Swift. He categorically hates mankind, he announces, excepting only worthy individuals. For many this passage confirms Swift's misanthropy. Despite his ethnic resentment of the Scots and his sectarian intolerance of Roman Catholic and Protestant dissenters, however, the individuals closest to him included Arbuthnot (a Scot) and Pope, the Catholic to whom he writes this letter. White Kennet's partisan caricature of him soliciting subscriptions for the same papist poet betrays a view of the world less generous – less humane – than Swift's.[64] Swift's suspicion of categories narrower than 'human' has much to recommend it.

Where Swift's profound horror of war necessitates his rejection of the parties or factions or sects that lead to conflict, Gulliver's partisanship leads him to celebrate war. Used to observing war's destruction from a safe distance,[65] he actually represents war to his Houyhnhnm master as a spectator sport: 'to set forth the Valour of my own dear Countrymen, I assured him, that I had seen them blow up a Hundred Enemies at once in a Siege, and as many in a Ship; and beheld the dead Bodies drop down in Pieces from the Clouds, to the great Diversion of all the Spectators'.[66] His partisan attachment to his countrymen permits his emotional detachment from the sufferings of war's victims. This is what appals the King of Brobdingnag:

> He was amazed how so impotent and groveling an Insect as I (these were his Expressions) could entertain such inhuman Ideas, and in so familiar a Manner as to appear wholly unmoved at all the Scenes of Blood and Desolation, which I had painted as the common Effects of those destructive Machines; whereof he said, some evil Genius, Enemy to Mankind, must have been the first Contriver.[67]

Gulliver's ability to relegate war's casualties to a category he is not part of is morally crippling; hence the king's suggestion that gunpowder has a satanic origin ('Some evil Genius, Enemy to Mankind'). Hence too Swift's resonant denunciation of the process by which 'A Crew of Pyrates' fleeing from a storm murder their innocent hosts to proclaim their 'title by *Divine Right*' to a colony.[68] It is possible to argue that the generalized savage humanity to which Swift assimilates the Yahoos reveals the impression of specific colonial encounters and, especially, the slave trade. But Rawson's argument that Swift assimilates the colonized, including the Yahoos, to a generalized image of 'the savage' has the advantage of giving full weight to the human as a primary category to which all victims of oppression belong.[69]

The celebrated Dean's home was now Ireland. A return to Dublin after a significant absence could be met by a hero's welcome.[70] Pretending to be the Drapier, he had found an assured identity as a patriot. He did not simply bask in his hard won fame, however. Irish realities did little to soften him, and he remained a truculent participant ready to offer caustic analyses of Irish affairs. Since he no longer spoke on behalf of a united elite, he found that he was sometimes just one projector among others. His last tract, for example, *A Proposal for Giving Badges to the Beggars in All the Parishes of Dublin. By the Dean of St. Patrick's* (1737), tries yet again to impose stability on social flux. The flux was typically Irish, the movement of beggars to the towns from their own parishes, which alone were legally required to maintain them. The proposed badges would address the problem by identifying particular beggars with particular parishes. Here as elsewhere, Swift displayed his flair for pungent disdain: 'To say the Truth, there is not a more undeserving vicious Race of human Kind than the Bulk of those who are reduced to Beggary, even in this beggarly Country'.[71] He also continued to have moments of acerbic insight. But he wrote within an established political identity as the Dean and the Drapier.

A Short View of the State of Ireland (1729) and his *Maxims Controlled in Ireland*, also written in 1729 though published only in 1765,[72] express Swift's continuing indignation at the misgovernment he held responsible for the perverse and unnatural misery of Ireland: 'THERE is not one Argument used to prove the Riches of *Ireland*,' he complains, 'which is not a logical Demonstration of its Poverty'.[73] That the people who should be the wealth of a nation are in Ireland a burden to it provokes fierce exasperation:

> It is another undisputed Maxim in government, that people are the riches of a nation; which is so universally granted, that it will be hardly pardonable to bring it in doubt. And I will grant it to be so far true, even in this island, that, if we had the African custom or privilege, of selling our useless bodies for slaves to foreigners, it would be the most useful branch of our trade, by ridding us of a most insupportable burthen, and bringing us money in the stead. But, in our present situation, at least five children in six who are born lie a dead weight upon us for the want of employment. And a very skilful computer assured me, that above one half of the souls in this kingdom supported themselves by begging and thievery, whereof two thirds would be able to get their bread in any other country upon earth.[74]

In the depressed state of the Irish economy, someone who could feed himself by his labour anywhere else can have value only as a commodity for export. This indictment of the unnatural economy produced by English misrule represents the ordinary Irish, a group that includes without being confined to the wild Irish papists, as savages disadvantaged by their inability to sell their fellows into slavery.

Widespread human misery accounts for Swift's bitter reflections in 1729. Although he would live through the even worse famine of 1741, recollected in popular memory as '*bliadhain an áir* (year of the slaughter)', several years of poor harvest at the end of the 1720s produced a famine so prolonged and severe that the population of Ireland actually declined between the mid-1720s and the early 1730s.[75] *A Modest Proposal*, the most powerful prose work Swift wrote after *Travels*, springs like his *Short View* from this misery. Like many modern economists, Swift did not assume a simple connection between famine and a shortage of food; he assumed that economic and political failings converted shortage into catastrophe for the famine's victims. Hence his indignant analysis in *A Proposal that All the Ladies and Women of Ireland Should Appear Constantly in Irish Manufactures*, another tract written in 1729 but published only posthumously:

> But since I am determined to take care, that the author of this paper shall not be discovered, (following herein the most prudent practice of the Drapier) I will ven-

ture to affirm, that the three seasons wherein our corn hath miscarried, did no more contribute to our present misery, than one spoonful of water thrown upon a rat already drowned would contribute to his death; and that the present plentiful harvest, although it should be followed by a dozen ensuing, would no more restore us, than it would the rat aforesaid to put him near the fire, which might indeed warm his fur-coat, but never bring him back to life.[76]

Modern economists prefer to present the link between shortage and dearth mathematically, calculating as accurately as possible the impact of limitations on trade, the sums annually transferred to absentee landlords or spent on imported fashions. Swift represents Ireland compellingly as a rat already drowned. Recognizing that public policy has distorted the Irish economy, he expresses a vivid moral outrage that refuses to sink the misery in the model that pretends to explain it. In fact, hostility toward 'skilful computers' who do the opposite provides a central strategy for *A Modest Proposal*.

For all its political edge, *A Modest Proposal* is not a tract at all. The last great work of the brilliant decade that also produced *A Proposal for the Universal Use of Irish Manufacture*, the *Drapier's Letters*, and *Gulliver's Travels*, *A Modest Proposal* is parody, an anti-tract that scorns the kind of well-meaning but feckless proposer Swift himself had been on many occasions. That conceded, it also epitomizes Swift's Irish pamphleteering. Like all of Swift's best work, it takes its energy from his searing anger at human folly. The people who govern Ireland have made it perverse, unnatural. Since *Proposal* includes an element of indignant self-reflection, it satirizes his own writings on Ireland: 'I desire the Reader will observe, that I calculate my Remedy *for this one individual Kingdom of* IRELAND, *and for no other that ever was, is, or I think ever can be upon Earth*. Therefore, let no man talk to me of other Expedients ...'.[77] What follows, at considerable length, 'is a catalogue of Swift's earlier and unambiguous proposals'.[78] Swift's best late tract concedes the futility of his tracts.

Such sensible proposals are foolish in a senseless country, the assumption is, so only a proposer who has taken leave of his senses can hope to succeed. The Modest Proposer therefore goes *Maxims* one better by proposing not slavery but cannibalism. In Ireland, the primitive and savage mesh seamlessly with the modern. The proposer exceeds even Gulliver, who did not consider eating Yahoos even though he unreflectingly used their skins:

> I finished a Sort of *Indian* Canoo, but much larger, covering it with the Skins of *Yahoos*, well stitched together, with hempen Threads of my own making. My Sail was likewise composed of Skins of the same Animal; but I made use of the Youngest I could get, the older being too tough and thick ...[79]

From prizing the skins of the 'Youngest I could get', it is but a short step to eating 'a young healthy Child, well nursed ... at a Year old',[80] as the proposer modestly suggests. Cannibalism may be an Anglo-Irish theme,[81] but Swift attributes it not to the wild Irish savages but to their governors, whom he credits with something like Gulliver's willingness to categorize himself apart from other human beings, and to England itself. He claims that the flesh of children is too delicate to be salted for export, ensuring that it will not threaten English interests, '*although, perhaps, I could name a Country, which would be glad to eat up our whole Nation without it*'.[82] In *A Modest Proposal* as in *Gulliver's Travels*, Swift represents all humanity as savages, remarking a difference only between the savage oppressed and their savage oppressors. When he wrote to Pope, 'principally I hate and detest that animal called man ... this is the system upon which I have governed my self many years,' he seems to have meant what he said. A warm friend, Swift excepted only particular individuals from his blanket condemnation of his kind.

Everything comes back to war. War is, he knew, inevitable and inevitably horrible. Everywhere in his political writing, Swift views the human lot as by nature a war of all against all. The only refuge from this grim fate, Swift was sure, required not innovation but inherited political structures that balanced competing powers against one another to preserve a degree of liberty. The Yahoos were not the worst he could imagine. Nor was *A Modest Proposal*'s cannibalism, which draws on memories of the famines that attend war. Worse than savagery was slavery, the subject's subservience to absolute power. As Swift had said in *The Sentiments of a Church-of-England Man*, 'arbitrary Power ... I look upon as a greater Evil than *Anarchy* itself; much as a *Savage* is in a happier State of Life, than a *Slave* at the Oar'.[83] So when Swift imagines in *Maxims Controlled in Ireland* that the ability to sell one another as slaves would improve the condition of Ireland, he probably cannot imagine a more damning assessment of the state of Ireland. Liberty is as consistent a commitment in Swift's thought as his commitment to the sacramental test that safeguarded the rights of the Church without which a wretched society would lack both moral order and a measure of solace.

Swift brings together savage features of eighteenth-century life that leave him a difficult figure for modern readers. For on one level, the slave was a figure in eighteenth-century political discourse, the subject of a legislature in which he was not represented. The Anglo-Irish patriot forced to accept an illegitimate currency would be, for Swift, a slave. But the slave was also a fact of eighteenth-century economic life, the African (usually) purchased for sale in the New World, where his labour produced sugar and tobacco for European consumers. For a slave of the second sort, the first kind of slavery must have looked like a figure of speech. Britons, including Swift, accepted the presence of the slave trade. In earlier writings, Swift had unabashedly defended England's right to the Asiento, the right granted in the Treaty of Utrecht to trade slaves to Spanish America;[84] this trade was intended to produce the handsome profits anticipated by investors in the South Sea Company. Only when they themselves felt oppressed did writers in the British isles invoke the slave trade critically, suggesting a damning analogy between the gentry at home and slave-owning planters overseas. Otherwise, the political discourse remained disappointingly independent of the discourse of actual plantation slavery and the African slave trade.

Yet Swift obviously made the connection and exploited it. The commodification of human beings links the cannibalism of *A Modest Proposal* with the slavery he considers briefly in *Maxims Controlled in Ireland*. It is hard to know in detail how he thought of the connection, but thinking of selling the Irish as slaves likely provided the germ of the more thoroughgoing sale of Irish flesh at the core of *A Modest Proposal*. In the end, cannibalism probably serves Swift's rhetorical purpose better than slavery. It was a form of savagery that remained outlandish, appalling, impossible, not one that had become, like slavery, the mainstay of the economy in a country that represented itself as a land of liberty.[85] It has in fact been argued that *A Modest Proposal*, as *Maxims* suggests, reflects attitudes common in a slave-trading society, the England of Swift's day.[86] It could, of course, be argued that the burden of Swift's analogy between cannibalism and the slave trade is merely, 'They have reduced us to the condition of savages'. But Swift was a champion of liberty. He did connect Irish oppression with chattel slavery and then made the imaginative leap to the cannibalism widely associated with savages. An extravagant analogy like the poultice made of Irish vitals in his *Letter concerning the Sacramental Test* implies as much locally, but Swift came to sustain the savagery of his analysis and elaborate it with disturbing detachment as a plausible solution to an economic crisis. During a protracted famine that highlighted the uselessness of those in power, he made a subterranean association not just conscious but vivid. His passions were again perhaps more extravagant than his positions, but his anger and the intensity of his horror at human oppression somehow allowed an intolerant sectarian cleric born in the seventeenth century to find voices in which readers today can address their own problems. Perhaps because it seems so remote from us in certain ways, Swift's political life illuminates our own in others. He continues to vex us.

NOTES

Introduction

1. *Verses on the Death of Dr Swift*, l. 297, ironically describing the freethinker Thomas Woolston. See *Poems*, pp. 493, 853, n.
2. *OED sv misprision n.*¹ 3.
3. *CW*, vol. 1. p. 342.
4. *Verses on the Death of Dr. Swift*, l. 351; *Poems*, p. 494.
5. J. Brewer, *The Sinews of Power: War, Money and the English State, 1688–1783*, 1st American edn (New York: Alfred A. Knopf, 1989), p. 141. The totals suggest that Protestant dissenters accounted for about 7 per cent of the population, Roman Catholics a little over 1 per cent; see C. Haydon, 'Religious Minorities in England', in H. T. Dickinson (ed.), *A Companion to Eighteenth-Century Britain* (Oxford: Blackwell Publishing, 2002), pp. 241–51; p. 242 and table 1.
6. For an informed introduction based on extensive scholarship, see S. J. Connolly, 'Religion in Ireland', in Dickinson (ed.), *Companion to Eighteenth-Century Britain*, pp. 271–80; pp. 271–2.
7. G. Orwell, 'Politics Vs. Literature: An Examination of *Gulliver's Travels*', in *The Collected Essays, Journalism and Letters of George Orwell*, ed. S. Orwell and I. Angus, 4 vols (New York: Harcourt, Brace and World, 1968), vol. 4, pp. 205–23; p. 209; L. I. Bredvold, 'The Gloom of the Tory Satirists', in J. L. Clifford and L. A. Landa (eds), *Pope and His Contemporaries: Essays Presented to George Sherburn* (Oxford: Clarendon Press, 1949), pp. 1–19; E. Said, 'Swift's Tory Anarchy', in *The World, the Text, and the Critic* (Cambridge, MA: Harvard University Press, 1983), pp. 54–71.
8. F. P. Lock, *Swift's Tory Politics* (Newark: University of Delaware Press, 1983), pp. vii, 137, 138, 142.
9. I. Higgins, *Swift's Politics: A Study in Disaffection* (Cambridge: Cambridge University Press, 1994), p. 8; my emphasis.
10. J. A. Downie, *Jonathan Swift: Political Writer* (London and Boston, MA: Routledge, 1984), pp. 83–4.
11. E. W. Said, *Culture and Imperialism* (New York: Vintage-Random House, 1993), p. 220.

12. W. B. Yeats, *The Variorum Edition of the Plays of W. B. Yeats*, ed. R. K. Alspach, assisted by C. C. Alspach (London: Macmillan, 1966), p. 958.

13. In 'Jonathan Swift, an Imaginary Interview by George Orwell', in *Orwell: The War Broadcasts*, ed. W. J. West (London: Duckworth and the British Broadcasting Corporation, [1942] 1985), pp. 112–16; pp. 112, 116, Orwell says that 'I believe *Gulliver's Travels* has meant more to me than any other book ever written', but he rejects Swift's pessimism: 'I see now where it is that we part company, Dr. Swift. I believe that human society, and therefore human nature, can change. You don't.'

14. Orwell, 'Politics Vs. Literature', pp. 209, 207, 223, 220, 213.

15. 'Letter to Maganlal Gandhi, *Vaisakh Vad 5 [May 8, 1911]*', in *Collected Works of Mahatma Gandhi*, 90 vols (Delhi: Publications Division, Ministry of Information and Broadcasting, Government of India, 1958–84), vol. 11, pp. 77–8; p. 77. I am grateful to Anthony Parel, Professor Emeritus of political science, University of Calgary, for first calling my attention to Gandhi's admiration for *Gulliver's Travels*.

16. E. W. Said, 'Swift as Intellectual', in *The World, the Text, and the Critic* (Cambridge, MA: Harvard University Press, 1983), pp. 72–89; p. 81.

17. Said, 'Swift's Tory Anarchy', p. 54.

18. L. Colley, *Captives* (New York: Pantheon-Random House, 2002), pp. 7–9.

19. Ibid., pp. 1–2.

20. Ibid., pp. 63–4.

21. See, for example, J. Hoppit, *A Land of Liberty? England 1689–1727*, The New Oxford History of England (Oxford: Clarendon Press, 2000), pp. 120–3.

22. A prescient reader, Orwell started some of the hares pursued by later scholarship. He notes that 'the Houyhnhnms are organised upon a sort of caste system which is racial in character, the horses which do the menial work being of different colours from their masters and not interbreeding with them' (Orwell, 'Politics Vs. Literature', p. 215); he even suggests that 'the Yahoos ... occupy rather the same place in their [the Houyhnhnms'] community as the Jews in Nazi Germany' (ibid., p. 218). He picks up the creepy hint of cannibalism: Gulliver 'sails away upon the ocean in his frail coracle made from the skins of Yahoos' (ibid., p. 206).

23. C. Rawson, *God, Gulliver, and Genocide: Barbarism and the European Imagination, 1492–1945* (Oxford: Oxford University Press, 2001), p. 16.

24. The fiscal-military state is the theme of Brewer, *Sinews of Power*.

1 Swift, War and Ireland

1. Orwell, 'Politics Vs. Literature', p. 207.

2. N. Gordimer, 'Lust and Death [Review of *Everyman*, by Philip Roth (Boston, MA: Houghton, 2006)]', *New York Times Book Review*, 7 May 2006, p. 10; the matching passion is sex and – a Swiftian preoccupation given a distinctively Rothian twist – the opposition of body and intellect.

3. See J. A. Downie, 'The Political Significance of *Gulliver's Travels*', in J. I. Fischer, H. J. Real and J. Woolley (eds), *Swift and His Contexts* (New York: AMS Press, 1989), pp. 1–19.

4. Said, 'Swift as Intellectual', p. 84.

5. T. Hobbes, *Leviathan*, ed. C. B. Macpherson (Harmondsworth: Penguin, [1651] 1968), p. 185 (part I. ch. xiii).
6. *PW*, vol. 2. p. 15.
7. *CW*, vol. 1, p. 226.
8. *PW*, vol. 2, p. 16.
9. A. Pope, *The Dunciad* (1742), IV.188, in *The Poems of Alexander Pope: A One-Volume Edition of the Twickenham Text with Selected Annotations*, ed. J. Butt (London: Methuen, 1963), p. 776. Pope ascribes this sentiment to the goddess Dulness, who longs for some 'pedant Reign' to bring 'Arbitrary Sway.'
10. See *PW*, vol. 4, p. 47; vol. 5, p. 231.
11. Hobbes, *Leviathan*. p. 186 (part I, ch. xiii).
12. *PW*, vol. 4, p. 247.
13. On the role of armies in the 'peaceful' revolutions of 1660 and 1688 – and the force of these examples on Jacobite hopes – see E. Cruickshanks and H. Erskine-Hill, *The Atterbury Plot* (Houndmills: Palgrave Macmillan, 2004), pp. 2–3.
14. Brewer, *Sinews of Power*, explores the development of the fiscal-military state; W. Prest, *Albion Ascendant: English History, 1660–1815* (Oxford: Oxford University Press, 1998) finds an organizing theme in Britain's rise in power.
15. L. Colley, *Britons: Forging the Nation 1707–1837* (New Haven, CT, and London: Yale University Press, 1992), p. 53.
16. Sir W. Temple, *An Introduction to the History of England* (London: Richard Simpson and Ralph Simpson, 1695), p. 18.
17. Quoted in S. J. Connolly, 'The Glorious Revolution in Irish Protestant Political Thinking', in S. J. Connolly (ed.), *Political Ideas in Eighteenth-Century Ireland* (Dublin: Four Courts Press, 2000), pp. 27–63; p. 49.
18. On appeal to the ancient constitution, see H. T. Dickinson, *Liberty and Property: Political Ideology in Eighteenth-Century Britain* (London: Weidenfeld and Nicolson, 1977), pp. 62–4.
19. See A. C. Elias, Jr, *Swift at Moor Park: Problems in Biography and Criticism* (Philadelphia, PA: University of Pennsylvania Press, 1982), pp. 73, 241, n. 13.
20. D. Szechi, *The Jacobites: Britain and Europe 1688–1788* (Manchester and New York: Manchester University Press, 1994), esp. pp. 54–9, 73–8, 92–4, 97–102.
21. Brewer, *Sinews of Power*, p. 141 The transformation from past behaviour is striking, as Brewer observes (pp. xiii–xiv).
22. *PW*, vol. 11, p. 129.
23. *PW*, vol. 2, p. 17.
24. *PW*, vol. 11, p. 132.
25. *PW*, vol. 11, p. 133.
26. *PW*, vol. 11, pp. 132–3.
27. Said, 'Swift as Intellectual', p. 56.
28. *PW*, vol. 10, p. 103. Alan Brodrick of Midleton in county Cork later became first Viscount Midleton; originally from Surrey, the family had an estate at Peper Harow, Godalming. Sir William Temple's estate at Moor Park was also in Surrey.
29. Said ends his quotation with 'out of your Hands'.
30. On the complexities of Anglo-Irish naming, see D. W. Hayton, 'Anglo-Irish Attitudes: Changing Perceptions of National Identity Among the Protestant Ascendancy in

Ireland *c.* 1690–1750', *Studies in Eighteenth-Century Culture*, 17 (1987), pp. 145–57.

31. Good recent accounts of the rebellion include N. Canny, *From Reformation to Restoration: Ireland, 1534–1660*, Helicon History of Ireland (Dublin: Helicon, 1987), pp. 38–49, and S. G. Ellis, *Ireland in the Age of the Tudors 1447–1603: English Expansion and the End of Gaelic Rule*, Longman History of Ireland (London and New York: Longman, 1998), pp. 334–51. See also G. A. Hayes-McCoy, 'The Completion of the Tudor Conquest and the Advance of the Counter-Reformation, 1571–1603', in T. W. Moody, F. X. Martin, and F. J. Byrne (eds), *A New History of Ireland III: Early Modern Ireland 1534–1691* (Oxford: Clarendon, 1976), pp. 119–36.

32. Although most of the family escaped, an infant perished. Written 1596 and commemorating suffering in the Desmond rebellion (1579–13), Spenser's *A Present View of the State of Ireland*, ed. W. L. Renwick (Oxford: Clarendon, 1970), circulated in manuscript to strengthen government policy; it was published only in 1633.

33. Hayes-McCoy, 'Completion of the Tudor Conquest', p. 131.

34. For Swift, 'this Kingdom was entirely reduced, by the submission of *Tyrone*, in the last Year of Queen *Elizabeth*'s Reign' (*PW*, vol. 10, p. 40).

35. See J. Shapiro, *A Year in the Life of William Shakespeare: 1599* (New York: Harper-Perennial, [2005] 2006). In *Culture and Imperialism*, Said famously begins his study of the impact of empire with Jane Austen's *Mansfield Park*; he does not, however, claim that one could not start earlier.

36. On the continuity between these two events, see the exemplary account – cogent and often tellingly sardonic – in T. Barnard, *The Kingdom of Ireland, 1641–1760* (Houndsmills: Palgrave Macmillan, 2004).

37. R. Doherty, *The Williamite War in Ireland 1688–1691* (Dublin: Four Courts Press, 1998), pp. 11–22. The armies of the competing nations, too, were international: 'During the campaign in Ireland in 1690, two British monarchs, James II and William III, fought each other with troops from France (both Huguenot and Catholic), the United Provinces, Denmark, Sweden, and Prussia' (Brewer, *Sinews of Power*, p. 41).

38. D. Dickson, *New Foundations: Ireland 1660–1800*, Helicon History of Ireland (Dublin: Helicon, 1987), pp. 22–8; J. G. Simms, 'The War of the Two Kings, 1685–91', in Moody, Martin and Byrne (eds), *A New History of Ireland III*, pp. 478–87.

39. *IE*, vol. 1, pp. 87–8. Barnard, *Kingdom of Ireland*, p. 34, notes the intrusion of two Catholic fellows at Trinity, which was less able to resist than Magdalen College, Oxford, had been under the same threat, and the atmosphere of hostility to Church of Ireland institutions.

40. See the accounts of the war in D. Dickson, *New Foundations*, pp. 29–40, and Simms, 'War of the Two Kings'.

41. On the Glorious Revolution as an event that simply re-established the Protestant order, see S. J. Connolly, *Religion, Law, and Power: The Making of Protestant Ireland 1660–1760* (Oxford: Clarendon Press, 1992), pp. 39–40, and Barnard, *Kingdom of Ireland*, pp. 38–9.

42. P. J. Corish repeats W. E. H. Lecky's estimate of 4,000 murdered and 8,000 refugees dead of other causes; see 'The Rising of 1641 and the Catholic Confederacy, 1641–5', in Moody, Martin and Byrne (eds), *A New History of Ireland III*, pp. 289–316; pp. 291–2. Shrewdly reading symbolic acts of desecration, N. Canny emphasizes deaths

from hunger and exposure in *From Reformation to Restoration*, pp. 208–10. S. J. Connolly trenchantly insists that 'tales of massacre, however exaggerated, were not invented'; see Connolly, *Religion, Law, and Power*, p. 16. Estimating actual deaths at 3–4,000, Toby Barnard notes a contemporary report that extravagantly put them at 154,000; see *Kingdom of Ireland*, pp. 15–18. I take the phrase 'black legend' from Barnard, p. 28, but all accounts acknowledge the mythologizing of events to appeal to popular feeling and shape policy.

43. *PW*, vol. 5, p. 193.
44. Sir John Temple, *The Irish Rebellion; or, An History of the Beginnings and First Progresse of the General Rebellion Raised Within the Kingdom of Ireland, Upon the Three and Twentieth Day of October, in the Year, 1641. Together with the Barbarous Cruelties and Bloody Massacres Which Ensued Thereupon* (London: Samuel Gellibrand, 1646); there were many subsequent editions. On its place in contemporary writing, see D. Rankin, *Between Spenser and Swift: English Writing in Seventeenth-Century Ireland* (Cambridge: Cambridge University Press, 2005), pp. 39–43. D. F. Passman and H. J. Vienken, *The Library and Reading of Jonathan Swift: A Bio-Bibliographical Handbook. Part I*, 4 Vols. (Frankfurt am Main: Peter Lang, 2003), vol. 3, p. 1801, erroneously assigns Sir John the dates of his younger son, also John.
45. Barnard, *Kingdom of Ireland*, p. 29.
46. See ibid., p. 4; see also Canny, *From Reformation to Restoration*, pp. 222–3.
47. Barnard, *Kingdom of Ireland*, p. 29; see also Canny, *From Reformation to Restoration*, pp. 216–18.
48. On the crucial role of the land settlement in Irish reactions to the struggle between William and James, see K. S. Bottigheimer, 'The Glorious Revolution and Ireland', in L. G. Schwoerer (ed.), *The Revolution of 1688–1689: Changing Perspectives* (Cambridge: Cambridge University Press, 1992), pp. 234–43.
49. Nicholas French, quoted in Rankin, *Between Spenser and Swift*, p. 238.
50. Bottigheimer, 'Glorious Revolution and Ireland', p. 239. On ethnic differences within each sectarian group, see pp. 240–1; the Catholics included both Gaels and English, the Protestants both English and Scottish.
51. Brewer, *Sinews of Power*, pp. 32, 44; Barnard, *Kingdom of Ireland*, p. 56. On the interplay of Irish concerns with English, see Connolly, *Religion, Law, and Power*, pp. 199–200.
52. D. Defoe, *The True-Born Englishman* (1700–1), in G. de F. Lord (gen. ed.), *Poems on Affairs of State: Augustan Satirical Verse, 1660–1715: Vol. 6: 1697–1704*, ed. F. H. Ellis (New Haven, CT: Yale University Press, 1970), pp. 259–309; pp. 270, 272 (ll. 171, 236). Defoe skilfully attacks both opponents of the 'foreign' King William III and the principle of descent whereby pure blood distinguishes nobles and gentry.
53. J. G. A. Pocock, 'Protestant Ireland: The View from a Distance', in S. J. Connolly (ed.), *Political Ideas in Eighteenth-Century Ireland* (Dublin: Four Courts Press, 2000), pp. 221–30; p. 224. 'The inability of communities of origin to understand or comprehend their communities of settlement', he wryly observes, 'is a theme more important than explored'.
54. On its seventeenth-century origins, see Rankin, *Between Spenser and Swift*, pp. 4–5 and notes; alternatively, the issue is to define the point at which it makes sense to regard Ireland in colonial terms.

55. D. G. Boyce, quoted by Hayton, 'Anglo-Irish Attitudes', p. 146.
56. J. Dryden, *Mac Flecknoe*, in *The Works of John Dryden II: Poems 1681–1684*, ed. H. T. Swedenberg, Jr and V. A. Dearing (Berkeley and Los Angeles, CA: University of California Press, 1972), pp. 54–60; p. 58 (ll. 139–40).
57. W.P., *The Jamaica Lady: Or, The Life of Bavia. Containing An Account of Her Intrigues, Cheats, Amours in England, Jamaica, and the Royal Navy. A Pleasant Relation of the Amours of the Officers of a Fourth Rate Man of War with Their Female Passengers, in a Voyage from Jamaica to England. With The Diverting Humours of Capt. Fustian, Commander of the Said Ship. And the Character of His Irish Surgeon; the Reason of His Preferment, and Manner of Obtaining His Warrant* (London: Tho. Bickerton, 1720), p. 35.
58. Connolly, *Religion, Law and Power*, p. 143, suggests that 'the real flaw in the structure of eighteenth-century Irish society' was that confessional differences 'debarred them from taking on as fully as they might otherwise have done the role of deferential subordinates'. The Catholic Irish remained a community apart.
59. Ibid., pp. 103–14, esp. pp. 110, 113–14.
60. Rawson, *God, Gulliver, and Genocide*; on a common stereotype of the savage, see esp. ch. 1.
61. On the development of the term, see N. Hudson, 'From "Nation" to "Race": The Origin of Racial Classification in Eighteenth-Century Thought', *Eighteenth-Century Studies*, 29:3 (1996), pp. 247–64. In her study of late nineteenth-century imperial stereotypes, A. McClintock suggests 'that English racism also drew deeply on the notion of the *domestic* barbarism of the Irish as a marker of racial difference'; see *Imperial Leather: Race, Gender and Sexuality in the Colonial Contest* (New York and London: Routledge, 1995), pp. 52–3.
62. Connolly, *Religion, Law, and Power*, p. 66.
63. *IE*, vol. 2, p. 93.
64. See Connolly, 'Glorious Revolution'.
65. Connolly, *Religion, Law, and Power*, p. 70.
66. J. C. Beckett, 'Literature in English 1691–1800', in T. W. Moody and W. E. Vaughan (eds), *A New History of Ireland IV: Eighteenth-Century Ireland 1691–1800* (Oxford: Clarendon Press, 1986), pp. 424–70; pp. 432–3.
67. Hobbes, *Leviathan*, p. 183 (part I, ch. xiii).
68. Connolly, *Religion, Law, and Power*, pp. 68–9.
69. Ibid., p. 69.
70. J. Swift, *A Tale of a Tub; To Which is Added The Battle of the Books and the Mechanical Operation of the Spirit*, 1710, ed. A. C. Guthkelch and D. Nichol Smith, 2nd edn (Oxford: Clarendon Press, 1958), p. 173.
71. C. Fabricant, 'Swift as Irish Historian', in C. Fox and B. Tooley (eds), *Walking Naboth's Vineyard: New Studies of Swift* (Notre Dame, IN: University of Notre Dame Press, 1995), pp. 40–72; p. 53.
72. Bottigheimer, 'Glorious Revolution and Ireland', p. 240.
73. B. Anderson, *Imagined Communities: Reflections on the Origin and Spread of Nationalism*, rev. edn (London: Verso, 1991).

74. See Connolly, 'Glorious Revolution', pp. 50–1; hence Swift's and Berkeley's dismissal of the '*de facto-de jure* distinction' (p. 49). Cf. Barnard, *Kingdom of Ireland*, pp. 63–4.

75. *PW*, vol. 2, p. 19.

76. *PW*, vol. 2, p. 22.

77. The '*Leader*' is 'always more *deformed* in Body, and *mischievous in Disposition*, than any of the rest'; he has a favourite 'whose Employment was to *lick his Master's Feet and Posteriors, and drive the Female* Yahoos *to his Kennel*' (*PW*, vol. 11, p. 262). The form of Gulliver's devotion to the Houyhnhnms – elevating the importance of his Houyhnhnm master and kissing his foot on leaving – thus expresses his Yahoo nature.

78. *PW*, vol. 11, p. 270.

79. *PW*, vol. 11, p. 271.

80. *PW*, vol. 11, p. 271.

81. Orwell, 'Politics Vs. Literature', p. 219.

82. See, for example, *The History of Timur-Bec, Known by the Name of Tamerlain the Great. Being an Historical Journal. Written in Persian by Cherefeddin Ali*, trans. F. P. de la Croix, 2 vols (London: J. Darby and others, 1723), vol. 1, pp. 425, 448, and P. Aubin's translation of F. P. de la Croix, *The History of Genghizcan the Great, First Emperor of the Antient Moguls and Tartars; in Four Books.. And Now Faithfully Translated Into English* (London: J. Darby and others, 1722), p. 353.

83. See G. Roberts, *The Four Years Voyages of Capt. George Roberts. Written by Himself* (London: A. Bettesworth and J. Osborn, 1726), pp. 285–6.

84. T. Boccalini, *Advices from Parnassus, in Two Centuries. With the Political Touchstone, and an Appendix Translated by Several Hands* (London: L. Stokoe, 1705), p. 181 (Advice 97); tortoises and ants model, respectively, the miser's self-containment and a joyless industry inimical to the arts.

85. But see [Anon.], *The Fatal Effects of Arbitrary Power and the Dangerous Condition of Court Favourites Demonstrated by the Wicked Intrigues of the Court of Philip II. King of Spain* (London: Jonas Brown and J. Richardson, 1715), p. 226, in which Antony Perez descends nervously to a crowd: 'For it is certainly known, that had not this been done, they were resolv'd to secure the Streets from End to End, like a general Hunting, and to destroy all Principals and Abettors, from the Highest to the Lowest, that had any Hand in this Affair, which would have been an unparallell'd Slaughter, and most dreadful Example'.

86. R. Porter, *English Society in the Eighteenth Century*, rev. edn (London: Penguin, 1991), p.17.

87. *PW*, vol. 11, p. 293.

88. J. Swift, *Gulliver's Travels*, ed. P. Turner (Oxford: Oxford University Press, 1986), p. 369, n.

89. *PW*, vol. 11, p. 271.

90. *PW*, vol. 11, p. 284.

91. *PW*, vol. 11, p. 279.

92. See *OED*, s.v. *tory*, n. and a. 1a.

93. A. C. Kelly thoughtfully explores parallels between Irish and Yahoo slavery in 'Swift's Explorations of Slavery in Houynhnmland and Ireland', *PMLA*, 91 (1976), pp.

846–55. Cf. M. Wilding, 'The Politics of *Gulliver's Travels*', in R. F. Brissenden (ed.), *Studies in the Eighteenth Century II: Papers Presented at the Second David Nichol Smith Memorial Seminar Canberra 1970*. (Toronto and Buffalo, ON: University of Toronto Press, 1973), pp. 303–22, for whom 'the Augustan rationality of the Houyhnhnm is founded on a system of slavery, just as Britain's attempts at those Augustan values had an economic foundation in the slavery of the West Indian plantations' (p. 318). In his view, the Houyhnhnms fear a breakdown of segregation that could lead to a slave revolt. In 'Three Times Round the Globe: Gulliver and Colonial Discourse', *Cultural Critique*, 18 (Spring 1991), pp. 187–214, C. Hawes reads *Travels* as an uncompromisingly anti-colonialist book in a way that overlooks Swift's ambiguous position as a colonist himself.

94. Rawson, *God, Gulliver, and Genocide*, pp. 366, n. 10, 259.

95. Kelly's 'Swift's Explorations' challenges this Houyhnhnm assumption, arguing that the 'natural Awe' the Houyhnhms inspire is simply a learned response, fear (p. 852).

96. R. Ballaster, *Seductive Forms: Women's Amatory Fiction from 1684 to 1740* (Oxford: Clarendon Press, 1992), pp. 155–6.

97. On the emergence of professional imaginative writing, see B. S. Hammond, *Professional Imaginative Writing in England, 1670–1740: 'Hackney for Bread'* (Oxford: Clarendon Press, 1997). The ties binding political debates over absolutism, secret histories, and domestic writing form the subject of M. McKeon, *The Secret History of Domesticity: Public, Private, and the Division of Knowledge* (Baltimore, MD: Johns Hopkins University Press, 2005).

2 Courting the Favour of the Great

1. *PW*, vol. 5, p. 192.

2. *PW*, vol. 1, p. 244.

3. *CW*, vol. 1, p. 125.

4. *CW*, vol. 1, p. 131.

5. *Tale*, p. 56.

6. *PW*, vol. 5, p. 194; *CW*, vol. 1, p. 139.

7. *PW*, vol. 5, p. 195.

8. *PW*, vol. 5, p. 193.

9. I follow the accounts in *IE*, vol. 2, pp. 9–15, and in L. A. Landa, *Swift and the Church of Ireland* (Oxford: Clarendon Press, 1954), pp. 25–34.

10. Quoted in T. Barnard, *A New Anatomy of Ireland: The Irish Protestants, 1649–1770* (New Haven, CT, and London: Yale University Press, 2003), p. 82. Swift hoped for English preferment, but was ordained in the Church of Ireland, found a patron in an Irish family connection, and found preferment in Ireland: the situation of other Anglo-Irish is pertinent. On the world of the protestant Irish clergy, see ibid., pp. 81–114.

11. Landa, *Swift and the Church of Ireland*, p. 34.

12. *IE*, vol. 2, pp. 13–14 values Swift's parishes at 'about £230 a year', his prebend at £15–£20; he adds that 'only six or seven clergyman' in the rural parishes of the diocese of

Dublin had 'incomes over a hundred pounds a year'. On the aspirations of the poorer Church-of-Ireland clergy, see Barnard, *New Anatomy*, p. 84.

13. The interpretation of the dedication in *IE*, vol. 2, pp. 34–5, has been challenged by Elias (*Swift at Moor Park*, pp. 72–3); on the popularity of Temple's works, see *Swift at Moor Park*, p. 239, n. 1.

14. Temple had published earlier volumes of *Miscellanea* in 1681 and 1690.

15. *PW*, vol. 1, p. 258.

16. *IE*, vol. 2, p. 48.

17. 'Some Thoughts upon Reviewing the Essay of Ancient and Modern Learning', included in *Five Miscellaneous Essays by Sir William Temple*, ed. S. H. Monk (Ann Arbor, MI: University of Michigan Press, 1963), pp. 72–97, is the only essay in the collection available in a modern scholarly edition. Swift's decision to lead with this political essay was not inevitable; the parallel with Swift's contemporary work on his own first pamphlet is significant (see *IE*, vol. 2, p. 49).

18. *PW*, vol. 1, p. 262.

19. Similarly, the Exclusion Crisis provoked the 1679 republication of Sir Robert Filmer's defences of absolute monarchy and the first publication of *Patriarcha* (1680), now his most famous work; see *Patriarcha and Other Political Works of Sir Robert Filmer*, ed. P. Laslett (Oxford: Blackwell, 1949), pp. 33–48. It also provoked John Locke to mount the counterargument to Filmer that he first published only in 1689; see *Two Treatises of Government: A Critical Edition with an Introduction and Apparatus Criticus*, ed. P. Laslett, rev. edn (New York: Mentor-New American Library, 1963), pp. 58–79.

20. *PW*, vol. 1, p. 266.

21. Sir W. Temple, *Letters to the King, the Prince of Orange, the Chief Ministers of State, and Other Persons*, ed. J. Swift (London: Tim. Goodwin and Benj. Tooke, 1703), p. 355; for the text of the note, see *IE*, vol. 1, pp. 98–9. According to Ehrenpries, Swift's four other notes are 'trifling' (*IE*, vol. 2, p. 79).

22. B. W. Hill, *Robert Harley: Speaker, Secretary of State and Premier Minister* (New Haven, CT, and London: Yale University Press, 1988), p. 65.

23. J. A. Downie, 'The Commission of Public Accounts and the Formation of the Country Party', *English Historical Review*, 91 (January 1976), pp. 33–51.

24. With *IE*, vol. 2, p. 46, cf. W. A. Speck, *The Birth of Britain: A New Nation 1700–1710* (London: Blackwell, 1994), p. 26, and H. T. Dickinson, *Bolingbroke* (London: Constable, 1970), p. 27.

25. Hill, *Robert Harley*, pp. 65–6.

26. Speck, *Birth*, pp. 30–3.

27. *PW*, vol. 1, p. 195.

28. *PW*, vol. 1, p. 219.

29. *PW*, vol. 1, p. 197.

30. *PW*, vol. 1, p. 200. On Davenant, see Ellis's note to this passage in *Discourse*, p. 131, n.

31. *PW*, vol. 1, p. 196.

32. *PW*, vol. 1, p. 229.

33. *Discourse*, pp. 161–2.

34. *IE*, vol. 2, pp. 48–9.

35. Sir W. Temple, *Miscellanea. The Third Part*. Published by Jonathan Swift, A.M. Prebendary of St Patrick's, Dublin (London: Benjamin Tooke, 1701), pp. 7–8; I silently correct a couple of obvious typographical errors.

36. *PW*, vol. 1, p. 224.

37. *PW*, vol. 1, p. 221.

38. *PW*, vol. 1, p. 234.

39. *IE*, vol. 2, pp. 57–8.

40. *PW*, vol. 1, p. 232.

41. *PW*, vol. 1, p. 230.

42. *PW*, vol. 9, p. 223.

43. *PW*, vol. 9, p. 223.

44. *IE*, vol. 2, p. 57.

45. On the language of Court-Country conflicts over the standing army, see J. G. A. Pocock, *The Machiavellian Moment: Florentine Political Thought and the Atlantic Republican Tradition* (Princeton, NJ: Princeton University Press, 1975), pp. 401–22.

46. *PW*, vol. 1, p. 199. See also *Discourse*, pp. 87, 130, n.

47. *PW*, vol. 1, p. 209.

48. Pocock, *Machiavellian Moment*, p. 458.

49. I take the word from Frank Ellis, who explores 'Swift's real mastery of his classical sources' in *Discourse*, pp. 156–62.

50. *Discourse*, pp. 160, 161.

51. For a description, see W. L. Sachse, *Lord Somers: A Political Portrait* (Manchester: Manchester University Press, 1975), pp. 183–4.

52. *IE*, vol. 2, pp. 47–8.

53. Ellis discusses publication and reception in *Discourse*, pp. 174–81; I quote from pp. 177–8.

54. *PW*, vol. 8, p. 119.

55. On the relationship between Swift and Burnet, see *IE*, vol. 2, pp. 84–90.

56. A copy of which Swift indignantly annotated (*PW*, vol. 5, pp. 266–94).

57. For a brisk, knowledgeable outline of the reputation and activities of Somers as a relatively young participant in the Convention Parliament, see Lois G. Schwoerer, *The Declaration of Rights, 1689* (Baltimore and London: Johns Hopkins University Press, 1981), pp. 47–50.

58. M. Goldie, 'The Roots of True Whiggism 1688–94', *History of Political Thought*, 1:2 (Summer 1980), pp. 195–236; pp. 209, 220. The tension exists between aspects of Whig thought, not kinds of Whigs, but Somers's gifts made him especially valuable at the former kind of argument. On the manoeuvrings of the Convention Parliament, see Schwoerer, *Declaration*.

59. T. Harris, *Politics under the Later Stuarts: Party Conflict in a Divided Society 1660–1715* (London and New York: Longman, 1993), pp. 168–9.

60. Ibid., pp. 169–70.

61. Hoppit, *Land of Liberty?*, pp. 175–6.

62. On Somers as patron of letters, see Sachse, *Lord Somers*, pp. 198–210.

63. *Correspondence*, vol. 1, p. 275.

64. See J. A. Downie, *Robert Harley and the Press: Propaganda and Public Opinion in the Age of Swift and Defoe* (Cambridge: Cambridge University Press, 1979), pp. 3–4.

65. *PW*, vol. 8, p. 112.

66. *PW*, vol. 7, p. 9.

67. *PW*, vol. 7, p. 5.

68. *Swift Vs. Mainwaring*, p. 390.

69. *PW*, vol. 10, p. 109.

70. *PW*, vol. 7, pp. 5–6.

71. F. R. Leavis, 'The Irony of Swift', in E. Tuveson (ed.), *Swift: A Collection of Critical Essays* (Englewood Cliffs, NJ: Prentice-Hall, 1964), pp. 15–29; pp. 16–17; it is presumably chief of the 'negative emotions he specializes in' (p. 17).

72. *PW*, vol. 7, p. 6.

73. Leavis, 'Irony of Swift', p. 22.

74. M. DePorte, 'Swift, God, and Power', in Fox and Tooley (eds), *Walking Naboth's Vineyard*, pp. 73–97; p. 78.

75. He visited England from April to October 1702, and again from November 1703 to May 1704.

76. On his place in establishing a Whig canon connected to republican principles, see Goldie, 'Roots', p. 196; J. G. A. Pocock, 'The Varieties of Whiggism from Exclusion to Reform: A History of Ideology and Discourse', in *Virtue, Commerce, and History: Essays on Political Thought and History, Chiefly in the Eighteenth Century* (Cambridge: Cambridge University Press, 1985), pp. 213–310; pp. 232–33.

77. G. Holmes, 'Religion and Party in Late Stuart England', in *Politics, Religion and Society in England 1679–1742* (London and Ronceverte, WV: Hambledon Press, [1975] 1986), pp. 181–215; 189–90.

78. *CW*, vol. 1, p. 147.

79. *CW*, vol. 1, pp. 147, 151.

80. *CW*, vol. 1, p. 161.

81. Leavis, 'Irony of Swift', p. 27.

82. Hill, *Robert Harley*, pp. 34–5.

83. *PW*, vol. 8, p. 120.

84. *PW*, vol. 8, p. 120.

85. The central argument of Harris, *Politics*; see especially p. 8.

86. In their edition of *Tale*, Guthkelch and Smith reprint the pertinent portion of Wotton's *Defense of the Reflections upon Ancient and Modern Learning* (1705) and Curll's *Complete Key to the Tale of a Tub* (1710); see *Tale*, pp. 319, 346.

87. Downie, *Jonathan Swift*, p. 95. For Teller-centred approaches, see especially R. Paulson, *Theme and Structure in Swift's Tale of a Tub*, Yale Studies in English no. 143 (New Haven, CT: Yale University Press, 1960) and *The Fictions of Satire* (Baltimore, MD: Johns Hopkins University Press, 1967); J. R. Clark, *Form and Frenzy in Swift's Tale of a Tub* (Ithaca, NY: Cornell University Press, 1970). On the counterattack mounted by Ehrenpreis and others, see R. C. Elliott, 'Swift's "I"', *Yale Review*, 62:3 (March 1973), pp. 372–91.

88. Hammond, *Professional Imaginative Writing*, p. 275; on *Tale* – his prime example is *Gulliver's Travels* – see pp. 270–1.

89. M. McKeon, *The Origins of the English Novel 1600–1740* (Baltimore, MD: Johns Hopkins University Press, 1987), pp. 217–18. This aligns it with conservative novels that also take a plague-on-both-your-houses view of these dominant narrative forms.

90. J. P. Hunter, *Before Novels: The Cultural Contexts of Eighteenth-Century English Fiction* (New York: Norton, 1990), pp. 106–9, esp. p. 108; Hammond, *Professional Imaginative Writing*, pp. 270–5.

91. *Tale*, p. 73.

92. On *A Tale* as a reaction to the world of self-promoting authors like John Dunton, see Hunter, *Before Novels*, pp. 106–9.

93. *Tale*, pp. 43–4.

94. *Tale*, p. 84.

95. *Tale*, p. 44.

96. *Tale*, p. 35.

97. 'And some there be, which have no memorial; who are perished, as though they had never been; and are become as though they had never been born; and their children after them.'

98. The passage is the first lesson of morning prayer for 16 November in the *Book of Common Prayer*.

99. In addition to the title page, see Wotton's notes (*Tale*, pp. 1, 30, n., 187, n., 323, 348), which were incorporated into the 1710 edition of *A Tale*.

100. Swift quotes from *De rerum natura* I.928ff, a passage repeated at IV.1ff.

101. *Mr. C—ns's Discourse of Free-Thinking. Put into Plain English, by Way of Abstract, for the Use of the Poor* (1713), in *PW*, vol. 4, p. 37.

102. *PW*, vol. 2, p. 70.

103. *Tale*, p. 75.

104. *Tale*, pp. 69–71.

105. *Tale*, p. 180.

106. E. Ward, *A Trip to Jamaica. With a True Character of the People and Island. By the Author of Sot's Paradise* (London: n.p., 1698), p. 3; italic and roman reversed.

107. *Tale*, p. 174.

108. Pocock, *Machiavellian Moment*, pp. 458–9, which relies on the analysis of patriot rhetoric in I. Kramnick, *Bolingbroke and His Circle: The Politics of Nostalgia in the Age of Walpole* (Cambridge, MA: Harvard University Press, 1968).

109. *Tale*, pp. 171–2.

110. Added to the poem in 1714 and 1723, prose remarks elaborately defend the paradoxes; see B. Mandeville, *The Fable of the Bees; or, Private Vices, Publick Benefits*, ed. F. B. Kaye, 2 vols (Oxford: Clarendon Press, 1924; fac. repr. Indianapolis, IN: Liberty Fund, 1988), vol. 2, pp. 386–400, for a full description of the editions.

111. Pocock, *Machiavellian Moment*, p. 459.

112. Influenced by Kramnick, *Bolingbroke and His Circle*, Pocock draws on later literary works like the *Dunciad*; he cites only specifically political works by Swift – the *Discourse*, the *Sentiments of a Church of England Man*, and the *Examiner*.

113. Pocock, *Machiavellian Moment*, p. 459.

114. See J. G. A. Pocock, 'The Mobility of Property and the Rise of Eighteenth-Century Sociology', in *Virtue, Commerce, and History*, pp. 103–23; p. 108, citing *PW*, vol. 7, pp. 68–78.

115. See C. Ingrassia, *Authorship, Commerce, and Gender in Early Eighteenth-Century England: A Culture of Paper Credit* (Cambridge: Cambridge University Press, 1998); like Pocock, Ingrassia concentrates on responses to the bursting of the South Sea Bubble; her paradigmatic examples include Alexander Pope as well as the more obviously commercial Eliza Haywood.

116. M. Treadwell, 'Swift's Relations with the London Book Trade to 1714', in R. Myers and M. Harris (eds), *Author/Publisher Relations During the Eighteenth and Nineteenth Centuries* (Oxford: Oxford Polytechnic Press, 1983), pp. 1–36.

117. Kathy MacDermott argues that satire of Grub Street defensively masks as an inferior form of traditional, classically inspired letters what is in fact a threatening new and commercial phenomenon; see K. MacDermott, 'Literature and the Grub Street Myth', in P. Humm, P. Stigant and P. Widdowson (eds), *Popular Fictions: Essays in Literature and History* (New York: Methuen, 1986), pp. 16–28. In such features of *A Tale* as the struggle between aristocratic patronage and the literary marketplace, Michael McKeon sees 'in effect, the laborious and contradictory birth of the author'; see *Secret History*, p. 62.

118. *Tale*, p. 55.

119. *Tale*, pp. lxv–lxvi.

120. See *IE*, vol. 2, pp. 326–31; DePorte, 'Swift, God, and Power', pp. 81–4.

121. K. Williams (ed.), *Swift: The Critical Heritage* (New York: Barnes and Noble, 1970), p. 36; ellipsis in original.

122. *Tale*, p. 322.

123. *Tale*, p. 4; roman for italic.

124. *Tale*, p. 5; italic and roman reversed.

125. Connolly, *Religion, Law, and Power*, pp. 71–2.

126. *PW*, vol. 5, p. 194; *IE*, vol. 1, p. 147.

127. *CW*, vol. 4, p. 107–8; *IE*, vol. 3, pp. 493–4.

128. *IE*, vol. 2, p. 461.

129. Treadwell, 'Book Trade', p. 5.

130. *CW*, vol. 1, pp. 270–1.

131. Hoppit, *Land of Liberty?*, p. 304.

132. *Swift Vs. Mainwaring*, p. 218; Ellis identifies the acquaintance as Sunderland.

133. *PW*, vol. 4, p. 253.

3 'An Entire Friend to the Established Church'

1. Ehrenpreis's phrase introduces a thoughtful appraisal of Swift's relationship with the more famous writers in this situation, including William Congreve, Matthew Prior, Joseph Addison and Richard Steele (*IE*, vol. 2, pp. 230–9).

2. *CW*, vol. 1, p. 198.

3. Godolphin and Marlborough were known as the duumvirs, but insiders recognized a triumvirate created because the peers relied on Harley to manage the Commons; see Hoppit, *Land of Liberty?*, p. 288.

4. *CW*, vol. 1, p. 227.

5. By returning to the fray, Partridge obscured the timing of the joke against him for some readers; see G. P. Mayhew, 'Swift's Bickerstaff Hoax as an April Fools' Joke', *Modern Philology*, 61:2 (May 1964), pp. 270–80.

6. For *A Discourse*, see *A Collection of State Tracts, Publish'd on Occasion of the Late Revolution in 1688. And During the Reign of King William III*, 3 vols (London: n.p., 1705–7), vol. 3, pp. 210–29. According to *Discourse*, p. 185, this is the third edition. On Somers's likely authorship of *Jura Populi Anglicani*, see Sachse, *Lord Somers*, p. 180, and Locke, *Two Treatises*, p. 406, n.

7. See *Tale*, pp. xix–xxi.

8. *PW*, vol. 2, p. 142.

9. Mayhew, 'Swift's Bickerstaff Hoax', pp. 273–4; *An Answer to Bickerstaff: Some Reflections upon Mr. Bickerstaff's Predictions for the Year MDCCVIII. By a Person of Quality* was first published published in 1765 in Swift's *Works* (see H. Teerink, *A Bibliography of the Writings of Jonathan Swift*, 2nd edn, ed. A. H. Scouten (Philadelphia, PA: University of Pennsylvania Press, 1963), p. 494).

10. Title later modified; see *Poems*, pp. 93–6, 627–9, nn.

11. N. F. Lowe, 'Why Swift Killed Partridge', *Swift Studies*, 6 (1991), pp. 71–82.

12. In 'Popular Entertainment and Instruction, Literary and Dramatic: Chapbooks, Advice Books, Almanacs, Ballads, Farces, Pantomimes, Prints and Shows', in J. Richetti (ed.), *The Cambridge History of English Literature, 1660–1780* (Cambridge: Cambridge University Press, 2005), pp. 61–86, Lance Bertelsen suggests some 400,000 circulating in the late seventeenth century, an extraordinary total (pp. 70–1). Since they contained calendars of important historical events, Linda Colley argues that they fostered national consciousness; see *Britons*, pp. 20–3.

13. Steele's *Tatler*, 169 (9 May 1710), for example, elaborately distinguishes the true landlord from a mere boorish incumbent.

14. R. Steele et al., *The Tatler*, ed. D. F. Bond, 3 vols (Oxford: Clarendon Press, 1987), vol. 1, pp. 7–8. When Steele collected the papers in 1720 as *Lucubrations of Isaac Bickerstaff Esq.*, he added Swift's published Bickerstaff works 'to render the Work Compleat'.

15. Ibid., vol. 1, pp. 47–8, 80–1; vol. 3, pp. 225–7.

16. See ibid., vol. 1, p. 192, n. 1 (for a brief account of the duelling series) and vol. 2, pp. 431–4. For Swift's letter, see vol. 3, pp. 190–6 or *PW*, vol. 2, pp. 173–7.

17. See *CW*, vol. 1, pp. 207, 208, n. 5. Shaftesbury's *Letter*, like Swift's *Tale*, was dedicated to Somers. Swift repeated his denial in the *Apology* added to the fifth edition of *A Tale* (*Tale*, p. 6 and n. 2).

18. Connolly, *Religion, Law, and Power*, p. 61, cites Swift's superior, William King, as a conspicuous example: the son of a tenant farmer, he became Archbishop of Dublin.

19. The phrase is Lord Peterborough's (*CW*, vol. 1, p. 342). The anachronistic term 'Anglican' acknowledges that Swift could seek a place in England or in Ireland, where the Church may have provided an even more important route to influence than in England.

20. On its effects, see Connolly, *Religion, Law, and Power*, pp. 162–3, and Barnard, *Kingdom of Ireland*, pp. 104–5. In England, the Corporation Act of 1661 had made taking Anglican communion a condition of participation in borough corporations,

and the first Test Act (1673) had made it a requirement for civil, military, or naval office.

21. Lock, *Swift's Tory Politics*, pp. 12–14.
22. See Horace, *Odes*, III.24.25–9.
23. For Thomas Sheridan's anecdote, see *PW*, vol. 1, pp. xxxiii–xxxiv.
24. *PW*, vol. 2, p. 53.
25. *PW*, vol. 2, p. 36.
26. A later tract, *A Letter to a Member of Parliament in Ireland upon the Chusing a New Speaker There*, makes support for the Test the crucial criterion for selecting a Speaker.
27. In 'Ehrenpreis's "Swift and the Date of *Sentiments of a Church-of-England Man*"', *Swift Studies*, 6 (1991), pp. 3–37, F. T. Boyle convincingly challenges the earlier date suggested by Ehrenpreis in 'The Date of Swift's "Sentiments"', *Review of English Studies*, 3 (1952), pp. 272–4, and *IE*, vol. 2, p. 124–31; on *Sentiments* and Swift's *Remarks on Tindal*, see pp. 32–4.
28. *PW*, vol. 2, p. 5.
29. *PW*, vol. 2, p. 3.
30. 'He thinks it a Scandal to Government, that such an unlimited Liberty should be allowed of publishing Books against those Doctrines in Religion, wherein all Christians have agreed' (*PW*, vol. 2, p. 10). See also *CW*, vol. 1, p. 191.
31. *PW*, vol. 2, pp. 12, 6.
32. *PW*, vol. 12, p. 258. Carole Fabricant suggests that Swift struggles with some success to free himself from the mythologies of the Rebellion; see Fabricant, 'Swift as Irish Historian', pp. 60–4.
33. *PW*, vol. 9, p. 223.
34. *PW*, vol. 2, pp. 6–7.
35. *PW*, vol. 2, p. 13.
36. C. Leslie, *The Snake in the Grass; or, Satan Transform'd Into an Angel of Light. Discovering the Deep and Unsuspected Subtilty which is Couched under the Pretended Simplicity of Many of the Principal Leaders of Those People Call'd Quakers* (London: Charles Brome, 1696). That a 342–page Preface precedes a 271–page argument suggests Leslie's stridency (and perhaps recalls *A Tale of a Tub*), but Leslie was a prolific and important writer whose theological tracts were reprinted and collected throughout the following century.
37. *PW*, vol. 2, p. 13.
38. *PW*, vol. 9, pp. 177–8.
39. *PW*, vol. 2, pp. 74–5.
40. See *Tale*, p. 204 and note.
41. *PW*, vol. 2, p. 9.
42. On the Tory reaction and Tory-Anglican resistance to James's absolutism, see Harris, *Politics*, pp. 119–32.
43. See DePorte, 'Swift, God, and Power'.
44. R. A. Herman, 'The Dean and the Dissenters', Dean Swift: The Satirist and His Faith. A Symposium on Jonathan Swift and Christianity, St Patrick's Cathedral, Dublin, October 19 2002, http://www.iol.ie/~rjtechne/swift/2002/herman.htm (accessed 28 February 2008).

45. B. S. Hammond, 'The Satirist and His Faith: An Overview', *Dean Swift: The Satirist and His Faith. A Symposium on Jonathan Swift and Christianity*, St Patrick's Cathedral, Dublin, October 19 2002, http://www.iol.ie/~rjtechne/swift/2002/hammond.htm (accessed 28 February 2008).

46. S. J. Connolly, 'Swift and Protestant Ireland: Images and Reality', in A. Douglas, P. Kelly, and I. C. Ross (eds), *Locating Swift: Essays from Dublin on the 250th Anniversary of the Death of Jonathan Swift 1667–1745* (Dublin: Four Courts Press, 1998), pp. 28–46; pp. 31, 35.

47. Boyle, 'Date of Swift's *Sentiments*', p. 37.

48. *CW*, vol. 1, pp. 151, 147.

49. Harris, *Politics*, pp. 8–9.

50. Sachse, *Lord Somers*, p. 49.

51. *IE*, vol. 2, pp. 124–5.

52. Hoppit, *Land of Liberty?*, p. 302.

53. *PW*, vol. 8, p. 120.

54. *PW*, vol. 8, p. 120.

55. Written in 1714, *Memoirs Relating to That Change which Happened in the Queen's Ministry in the Year 1710* was published only in 1765; see *PW*, vol. 8, pp. 210–11, *IE*, vol. 3, pp. 108–9.

56. *OED svv* 'high' 15 a and b, 'High-Churchman'. In *Land of Liberty?*, pp. 231–6, Hoppit suggests 'strong', surveying doctrine and, emphasizing the Sacheverell trial, politics.

57. *PW*, vol. 8, p. 120.

58. Hoppit, *Land of Liberty?*, pp. 219–20 and Table 4.

59. On the limits of whig support for dissenters, including these examples, see Harris, *Politics*, p. 155.

60. I follow Speck's account, according to which 'some 33 tories had voted against their colleagues'; see *Birth*, p. 49.

61. Harris, *Politics*, pp. 118–19. Although *IE*, vol. 2, pp. 127–8 treats shared sovereignty as unconvincing, the position was familiar enough to appeal to Sacheverell's defence counsel in 1710; see Harris, *Politics*, pp. 166–7.

62. *PW*, vol. 2, p. 15.

63. In 'Swift and Protestant Ireland', p. 32, Connolly notes this distinction from 'the pattern of extremist Tory rhetoric' in Swift's sermon on the martyrdom of Charles I.

64. *PW*, vol. 2, pp. 13–14.

65. *PW*, vol. 2, p. 20.

66. *PW*, vol. 2, pp. 21–2.

67. *PW*, vol. 2, p. 22.

68. *PW*, vol. 2, pp. 18–19.

69. Connolly, 'Glorious Revolution', p. 50.

70. Speck, *Birth*, pp. 57–8.

71. *CW*, vol. 1, p. 155; King later spoke directly to the Queen about the issue only to have her question the timing, thus expressing reluctance to act while Wharton was Lord Lieutenant (*CW*, vol. 1, pp. 308, 309, n. 3).

72. *CW*, vol. 1, pp. 155–6.

73. *CW*, vol. 1, pp. 163–4, 177.

74. *CW*, vol. 1, p. 157.
75. *CW*, vol. 1, p. 167.
76. *CW*, vol. 1, p. 187.
77. *CW*, vol. 1, p. 183.
78. *CW*, vol. 1, pp. 163, 193–4, 201, 203.
79. *PW*, vol. 3, p. 179.
80. *CW*, vol. 1, pp. 220, 222.
81. *CW*, vol. 1, p. 299.
82. *CW*, vol. 1, p. 205.
83. 'The Whigs carry all before them', Swift wrote to Robert Hunter in January 1709, 'and how far they wil pursue their Victoryes, we moderate Whigs can hardly tell' (*CW*, vol. 1, 229).
84. *PW*, vol. 2, p. 118.
85. *PW*, vol. 2, p. 115.
86. *PW*, vol. 2, p. 114. Swift had already written *The Story of an Injured Lady*, a reaction to the Act of Union between England and Scotland that presents Ireland as a jilted lover; suggestively, he begins this passage by quoting the extravagant devotion of a lover in Cowley. See *PW*, vol. 5, pp. 3–12; vol. 2, p. 114; *IE*, vol. 2, pp. 169–75.
87. *PW*, vol. 2, p. 122.
88. *CW*, vol. 1, p. 249.
89. *PW*, vol. 8, p. 120.
90. *CW*, vol. 1, pp. 275, 234.
91. *CW*, vol. 1, p. 213.
92. An important point cogently stated by W. A. Speck, 'From Principles to Practice: Swift and Party Politics', in B. Vickers (ed.), *The World of Jonathan Swift: Essays for the Tercentenary* (Oxford: Blackwell, 1968), pp. 69–86; p. 71.
93. *CW*, vol. 1, p. 245.
94. In November 1708, he hoped for a position as Queen's Secretary in Vienna, and about the time of his ordination he considered the position of chaplain to the English factory in Portugal (*CW*, vol. 1, pp. 215–16, 121).
95. J. K. Clark, 'Wharton, Thomas, First Marquess of Wharton, First Marquess of Malmesbury, and First Marquess of Catherlough (1648–1715)', in *ODNB*, article 29175.
96. According to Swift's moving account, his mother died on 24 April 1710, and he learned of her death at Laracor on 10 May 1710 (*PW*, vol. 5, p. 196), shortly after Addison reached Dublin. 'Pray dear Doctour continue your friendship', Addison asks in a letter announcing his imminent return, 'towards one who Loves and esteems You, if possible, as much as You deserve' (*CW*, vol. 1, p. 278).
97. *PW*, vol. 2, pp. 129, 132.
98. *PW*, vol. 2, p. 131.
99. Hoppit, *Land of Liberty?*, pp. 295–6, 298; on the role of the 1703 treaty with Portugal in locking the allies into this Spanish policy, see p. 113.
100. *CW*, vol. 1, p. 290.
101. Harley had been a dissenter but broke with dissent when the dissenters preferred lucrative contact with the Court to his principled Country opposition; see Hill, *Robert Harley*, p. 35.

102. *JS*, pp. 41, 45–6, 50, 59, 66, 80.
103. *JS*, p. 66.
104. *PW*, vol. 8, pp. 122–3.
105. *CW*, vol. 1, pp. 375–6. King is a shrewd judge of political behaviour; 'some are better at making their court than serving the Church', he observes elsewhere, 'and can flatter much better than vote on the right side' (*CW*, vol. 1, p. 319).
106. Ehrenpreis provides a judicious narrative (*IE* vol. 2, 399–405). It can be traced in its agonising convolutions in the *Journal to Stella* or the letters Swift exchanged with King from September 1710 to September 1711.
107. *CW*, vol. 1, p. 350.
108. *CW*, vol. 1, pp. 377–8.
109. Swift feigned innocence to Stella but bragged that 'they sell mightily' (*JS*, p. 203); there was a second edition two years later.
110. *IE*, vol. 2, pp. 326–38. On *A Tale*'s indecorum, consider William King of Christ Church, Oxford: charged with writing it, he exonerated himself in a pamphlet against the work (*IE*, vol. 2, pp. 327–8).
111. *JS*, p. 59.
112. *CW*, vol. 1, p. 329. King writes a little later, 'I hear an answer is printing to the Earl of Wharton's Character. Pray was there ever such licentiousness of the press as at this time?' (*CW*, vol. 1, p. 331). His view is typical of clerical mistrust of the press.
113. See *CW*, vol. 1, pp. 315–18; *IE*, vol. 2, p. 402 and n. 1.
114. *JS*, pp. 126, 327. In addition to publishing *A Tale*, Swift had already offended Lady Giffard, who was a friend of the Queen's friend, the Duchess of Somerset; he would later insult the Duchess directly by publishing *The Windsor Prophecy* in 1711.

4 The Echo of the Coffee House

1. *JS*, p. 80; *CW*, vol. 1, pp. 311–12.
2. No. 13 in collected editions, which omitted the original no. 13, Francis Atterbury's extreme assertion of hereditary right. See *Swift Vs. Mainwaring*, p. lxx.
3. See R. I. Cook, *Jonathan Swift as a Tory Pamphleteer* (Seattle, WA, and London: University of Washington Press, 1967), pp. 19–30; I quote from p. 20.
4. *JS*, p. 282.
5. Speck, 'From Principles to Practice', p. 69; Speck considers but rejects the notion that Swift was simply self-serving.
6. *JS*, pp. 35–6.
7. *JS*, pp. 59–60.
8. See *Swift Vs. Mainwaring*, p. xxv.
9. The term is now standard: see J. Arbuthnot, *The History of John Bull*, ed. A. W. Bower and R. A. Erickson (Oxford: Clarendon Press, 1976), p. liv; Downie, *Robert Harley and the Press*, p. 162, and *Jonathan Swift*, p. 174.
10. *Swift Vs. Mainwaring*, p. xxvii.
11. For this reading of Harley's character, see Hill, *Robert Harley*, pp. 106–7.
12. *Swift Vs. Mainwaring*, p. 470.
13. *Swift Vs. Mainwaring*, p. 471.

14. *Tale*, p. 46.
15. Ellis sharply compares this with Gulliver's recognition that he too is a Yahoo; see *Swift Vs. Mainwaring*, p. 470, n. Other pertinent associations include the writer snarled over by critics in *A Tale*.
16. *Correspondence*, vol. 5, pp. 228–9.
17. Speck, 'From Principles to Practice', p. 70; also quoted Downie, *Robert Harley and the Press*, p. 132.
18. A book on 'some serious and useful subject in your profession ... will answer some objections against you' (*CW*, vol. 1, pp. 377–8).
19. A. Pope et al., *Memoirs of the Extraordinary Life, Works, and Discoveries of Martinus Scriblerus: Written in Collaboration by the Members of the Scriblerus Club* (1741), ed. C. Kerby-Miller (New York: Russell and Russell, [1950] 1966), pp. 21–2.
20. See *JS*, p. 589.
21. On the consistency of most members' voting patterns, see Harris, *Politics*, pp. 149–52.
22. *JS*, pp. 97, 127. A year later, enjoying supper with Addison and Philips, he says 'we were very good company; and yet know no man half so agreeable to me as he is' (*JS*, p. 360).
23. *Swift Vs. Mainwaring*, pp. 68 and nn. 68–9.
24. *PW*, vol. 11, p. 196.
25. Written by a Whig then in opposition, Addison's play won Tory applause, too. See also J. Trenchard and T. Gordon, *Cato's Letters; or, Essays on Liberty, Civil and Religious, and Other Important Subjects*, 6th edn, 2 vols (1755), ed. R. Hamowy (Indianapolis, IN: Liberty Fund, 1995).
26. On Cato in the period, see J. W. Johnson, *The Formation of English Neo-Classical Thought* (Princeton, NJ: Princeton University Press, 1967), pp. 95–103. On Swift's fondness for the type, see also F. P. Lock, *The Politics of Gulliver's Travels* (Oxford: Clarendon Press, 1980), p. 15.
27. See *Spectator*, 2 (2 March 1711), in J. Addison et al., *The Spectator*, 5 vols, ed. D. F. Bond (Oxford: Clarendon Press, 1965), vol. 1, pp. 7–13.
28. For an accessible survey that acknowledges the ill fit of the 'Tory satirists' with Addison and Steele's Whiggish public sphere, see T. Eagleton, *The Function of Criticism: From The Spectator to Post-Structuralism* (London: Verso, 1984), pp. 10–11, 25–6. See also Hammond, *Professional Imaginative Writing*, pp. 145–91. I rehearse this contrast of Addison with Swift in 'Politics and History', in C. Fox (ed.), *The Cambridge Companion to Jonathan Swift* (Cambridge: Cambridge University Press, 2003), pp. 31–47; pp. 42–3.
29. *Swift Vs. Mainwaring*, pp. 66–7 (*Examiner*, 18 (30 November 1710), pp. xxxiv–xxxv).
30. W. A. Speck, 'Social Status in Late Stuart England', *Past and Present*, 34 (July 1966), pp. 127–9.
31. R. P. Bond, *The Tatler: The Making of a Literary Journal* (Cambridge, MA: Harvard University Press, 1971), p. 18; cf. Steele and others, *The Tatler*, vol. 1, pp. xiii–xvi.
32. P. C. Brückmann, *A Manner of Correspondence: A Study of the Scriblerus Club* (Montreal and Kingston, ON: McGill-Queen's University Press, 1997); *CW*, vol. 2, p. 178.

33. See B. Hammond, 'Scriblerian Self-Fashioning', *Yearbook of English Studies*, 18 (1988), pp. 108–24 (esp. pp. 121–22 on Pope and Swift's *Verses on the Death*); see also *IE*, vol. 2, pp. 143–48 (on Addison and Swift's *Baucis and Philemon*).

34. See, for example, Harris, *Politics*, pp. 166–8.

35. Pocock, *Machiavellian Moment*, p. 446. The text in question *The True Picture of a Modern Whig* (1701), by Charles Davenant, in whom Pocock detects 'an intellectual scaffolding ... a language of assumptions and problems more consistent than his behavior and shared to a considerable degree by writers on both sides of the political divide' (p. 437).

36. Harris, *Politics*, p. 165.

37. 'The Flea and Countryman', in [Anon.], *The Perils of False Brethren: Set Forth in the Fable of the Boy and the Wolf* (London: n.p., 1710), pp. 7–8.

38. *Swift Vs. Mainwaring*, pp. 217–18.

39. *JS*, p. 108.

40. *JS*, p. 206.

41. See W. A. Speck, '*The Examiner* Examined: Swift's Tory Pamphleteering', in C. J. Rawson (ed.), *Focus: Swift* (London: Sphere Books, 1971), pp. 138–54; pp. 145–6, 142.

42. *PW*, vol. 8, p. 123.On the origins of the *Examiner*, see Downie, *Robert Harley and the Press*, p. 127, and *Swift Vs. Mainwaring*, p. xxv, which includes Delarivier Manley in the group.

43. Pocock, *Machiavellian Moment*, p. 458.

44. See Pocock, 'Mobility of Property', and for a narrative-centred view of Swift's role in these developments, McKeon, *Origins of the English Novel*, pp. 169–72.

45. The classic studies are P. G. M. Dickson, *The Financial Revolution in England: A Study in the Development of Public Credit 1688–1756* (London: Macmillan, 1967), and Brewer, *Sinews of Power*.

46. *Swift Vs. Mainwaring*, pp. 7–8.

47. Hill, *Robert Harley*, p. 147.

48. *Swift Vs. Mainwaring*, p. 377.

49. P. G. M. Dickson, *Financial Revolution*, pp. 71–4.

50. G. Burnet, *Bishop Burnet's History of His Own Time: With Notes by the Earls of Dartmouth and Hardwicke, Speaker Onslow, and Dean Swift*, 2nd edn enlarged, 6 vols (Oxford: Oxford University Press, 1833), vol. 6, p. 50, n; Brewer, *Sinews of Power*, p. 119. Cf., with an eye to Defoe's *Secret History of the White Staff*, P. R. Backscheider, *Daniel Defoe: His Life* (Baltimore, MD, and London: Johns Hopkins University Press, 1989), pp. 353–4.

51. *Swift Vs. Mainwaring*, p. 71.

52. 'I really think they will not do well in too much mortifying that man' Swift wrote in December 1710 (*JS*, p. 145).

53. For Swift, four or five years' income. *Swift Vs. Mainwaring*, pp. 55–6.

54. *Swift Vs. Mainwaring*, p. 231; italic and roman reversed.

55. *Swift Vs. Mainwaring*, p. 115.

56. Dickinson, *Bolingbroke*, pp. 73, 9. Swift addresses the *Letter* in *Examiner*, 29 (15 February 1711).

57. *Swift Vs. Mainwaring*, pp. 1, 427–8, 144, 68, 344, 466, 356, 390.

58. *Swift Vs. Mainwaring*, p. 314.
59. *Swift Vs. Mainwaring*, pp. 129–30. In his *True-Born Englishman*, Defoe, another of Harley's agents, the thoroughly mercantile Defoe subverts landed pretensions to family by arguing that history proves England just such a common shore.
60. See *Examiner*, 31 (1 March 1711) for the possibilities for civil dissension in Whig support of dissent.
61. *PW*, vol. 6, p. 53.
62. *Tale*, p. 103.
63. Brewer, *Sinews of Power*, p. 120. Cf. Hoppit, *Land of Liberty?*, p. 303.
64. On this political language, see Brewer, *Sinews of Power*, pp. 159–61. Harley's drift to the tories began with ties forged on commissions of public accounts; see Downie, 'Commission of Public Accounts'.
65. *Examiner*, 38 (19 April 1711), *Swift Vs. Mainwaring*, p. 377.
66. *Swift Vs. Mainwaring*, pp. 192–3.
67. *Swift Vs. Mainwaring*, pp. 344–5.
68. *Swift Vs. Mainwaring*, pp. 315, 317; italic and roman reversed.
69. *Swift Vs. Mainwaring*, p. 276 and n.; W. Benson, *A Letter to Sir J— B—, by Birth a Swede, but Naturaliz'd, and a M—r of the Present P—t: Concerning the Late Minehead Doctrine, Which Was Establish'd by a Certain Free Parliament of Sweden, to the Utter Enslaving of That Kingdom* (London: A. Baldwin, 1711).
70. *CW*, vol. 1, p.335.
71. W. A. Speck, *Reluctant Revolutionaries: Englishmen and the Revolution of 1688* (Oxford: Oxford University Press, 1988), p. 247.
72. Hoppit, *Land of Liberty?*, p. 308; D. Szechi, *Jacobitism and Tory Politics 1710–14* (Edinburgh: John Donald Publishers, 1984), pp. 52–4.
73. 8 March 1711; *CW*, vol. 1, pp. 336–8.
74. *Swift Vs. Mainwaring*, p. 303.
75. Hill, *Robert Harley*, pp. 148–9, 152–3.
76. Dickinson, *Bolingbroke*, pp. 81–3; Dickinson identifies St John's 'flaw' as 'temperamental instability' (p. 9).
77. G. Holmes, 'Harley, St. John and the Death of the Tory Party', in *Politics, Religion and Society in England 1679–1742* (London and Ronceverte, WV: Hambledon Press, 1986), pp. 139–60; p. 141.
78. *PW*, vol. 8, p. 128.
79. *Swift Vs. Mainwaring*, pp. xxi–xxii, cites John Gay's *The Present State of Wit*: "'The reputed Author is Dr. *S—t*".
80. With *Swift Vs. Mainwaring*, p. xxxiii, cf. Downie, *Robert Harley and the Press*, pp. 137–8, and *Jonathan Swift*, pp. 151–4. In Downie's earlier account, Swift's cryptic record of another offer of £50 marked renewed contact with Harley; cf. *JS*, p. 322 and n. 13.
81. *Swift Vs. Mainwaring*, p. 404.
82. *PW*, vol. 3, pp. 194–5.
83. Speck, *Birth*, p. 65; cf. Hoppit, *Land of Liberty?*, pp. 303–4.
84. Downie, *Robert Harley and the Press*, pp. 129–30, 147–8.
85. *JS*, p. 589.
86. *JS*, p. 333.

87. *PW*, vol. 3, p. 195. Cf. *PW* vol. 3, p. 249 for the passage to which Swift is responding.

88. Evident religious conviction provided one of Swift's ties with Harley; Downie notes common use of a biblical passage in *Conduct of the Allies* and Harley's 'Plaine English to all who are Honest, or would be so if they knew how': see J. A. Downie, '*The Conduct of the Allies*: The Question of Influence', in C. T. Probyn (ed.), *The Art of Jonathan Swift* (London: Vision Press, 1978), pp. 108–28; pp. 123–4.

89. *Tale*, p. 40.

90. On Manley and the trope of translation, see Ballaster, *Seductive Forms*, p. 129.

91. *JS*, p. 457; see also *IE*, vol. 2, p. 479.

92. *JS*, p. 349.

93. *PW*, vol. 3, p. 215.

94. *CW*, vol. 1, p. 384; Swift's letter to King (1 October 1711) accounts for his 'Account of Mr. Prior's Journey to France' and confesses the advanced state of peace negotiations.

95. *JS*, pp. 357–8 and 357, n. 5.

96. *PW*, vol. 6, p. 167.

97. For a table of the Spanish succession and an account of the timely deaths, see Hoppit, *Land of Liberty?*, p. 108 fig. 2, pp. 121, 305. Philip eased fears by renouncing his claim to the French throne.

98. See Davis's account (*PW*, vol. 6, pp. vii–ix).

99. *JS*, pp. 422–30.

100. *JS*, pp. 431, 474.

101. *JS*, pp. 480, 482, but cf. 488.

102. *PW*, vol. 6, p. 20.

103. *PW*, vol. 6, p. 41.

104. Hoppit, *Land of Liberty?*, p. 120.

105. Replies are listed in Teerink, *Bibliography of the Writings of Jonathan Swift*, pp. 287–9.

106. [Anon.], *Remarks on a False, Scandalous, and Seditious Libel Intituled The Conduct of the Allies and of the Late Ministry, andc.* (1711), in *Swiftiana III: On Swift's Remarks on the Barrier Treaty and His Conduct of the Allies 1711–1712* (New York: Garland, 1974), pp. 9 and 7 (on Jacobitism). Cf. [Anon.], *Remarks Upon Remarks; or, The Barrier-Treaty and the Protestant Succession Vindicated. In Answer to the False and Treasonable Reflections of the Author of The Conduct of the Allies*, in *Swiftiana III*, p. 3.

107. *Remarks on a False, Scandalous, and Seditious Libel*, p. 3.

108. See [Anon.], *A Letter to Isaac Bickerstaff, Esq; Occasion'd by the Letter to the Examiner* (1710), in *Swiftiana II: Bickerstaffiana and Other Early Materials on Swift 1708–1715* (New York: Garland, 1975), pp. 6, 11–12.

109. *Remarks on a False, Scandalous, and Seditious Libel*, p. 6.

110. F. Hare, *The Allies and the Late Ministry Defended Against France and the Present Friends of France* (1711), in *Swiftiana III*, pp. 33–4.

111. F. Hare, *The Allies and the Late Ministry Defended Against France, and the Present Friends of France, Part II* (London: A. Baldwin, 1711), pp. 60–1; F. Hare, *The Allies*

and the Late Ministry Defended Against France, and the Present Friends of France, Part IV (London: E. Sanger, 1712), pp. 4–7.

112. Szechi, *Jacobites*, p. 75.

113. Harris, *Politics*, pp. 121–3.

114. R. Braverman, *Plots and Counterplots: Sexual Politics and the Body Politic in English Literature, 1660–1730* (Cambridge: Cambridge University Press, 1993), p. 250.

115. *PW*, vol. 7, pp. 68–9.

116. Brewer, *Sinews of Power*, p. 30, table 2.1, pp. 38–41 and tables 2.2–3, pp. 99–100.

117. Speck, 'Social Status'.

118. Hill, *Robert Harley*, pp. 123–4, 179–80, 192.

119. *JS*, pp. 474–5. Harley suspects the author only when some of it is read to him, and sales later pick up a little 'but I believe it's fame will hardly reach Ireland' (*JS*, pp. 470, 478).

120. See Swift, *JS*, pp. 430, 431.

121. *Poems*, p. 118 (ll. 21–6).

122. See the excellent notes in *Poems*, pp. 125–6, 654–5. On the free-thinking Toland's role in the republican tradition of Whig thought, see Goldie, 'Roots', p. 196.

123. *IE*, vol. 2, p. 569.

124. *JS*, p. 445.

125. R. Herman, *The Business of a Woman: The Political Writings of Delarivier Manley* (Newark, DE: University of Delaware Press; London: Associated University Presses, 2003), pp. 51–2. Downie questions the traditional attribution to Manley in 'What if Manley Did Not Write *The Secret History of Queen Zarah?*', *Library*, 5:3 (2004), pp. 247–64.

126. *JS*, p. 434.

127. See *JS*, pp. 435, 436, and *Poems*, pp. 119, 648–50; see also Rogers's biographical sketch, pp. 933–4.

128. *IE*, vol. 2, p. 521.

129. D. Hamilton, *The Diary of Sir David Hamilton*, ed. P. Roberts (Oxford: Clarendon Press, 1975), pp. 40, 57; Downie, *Jonathan Swift*, pp. 180–1.

130. *The Author upon Himself*, ll. 1–2; see Swift, *Poems*, pp. 163–5, 670–1; 'murdering' repeats *Windsor Prophecy*'s accusation that she was responsible for the murder of her husband, allegedly killed by a sexual rival.

131. *JS*, pp. 444, 446–7, 454.

132. In fact, she called up the eldest sons of two peers and created ten new ones (*CW*, vol. 1, pp. 408, 409, n. 9).

133. *PW*, vol. 4, p. 16.

134. *PW*, vol. 4, pp. 18, 14.

135. *CW*, vol. 1, p. 497. Perhaps because of the quarrel, when the essay appeared in Faulkner's 1735 *Works*, a footnote identified the gentleman as Addison. According to *Correspondence*, vol. 1, p. 360, n. 1, 'In the context the allusion to Steele would be unmistakable'. Arguing with reference to Addison's treatment of English in *Spectator*, 135 (4 August 1711), Woolley claims that 'one may recognize that *Addison* was clearly indicated from the very first' (*CW*, vol. 1, p. 497 and n. 5, pp. 362, 363, n. 6).

136. Downie, *Jonathan Swift*, p. 174.

137. *CW*, vol. 1, p.191.

138. *CW*, vol. 1, p.331.
139. For Swift's solidarity with Grub Street, see *JS*, pp. 177–8, 553,–4 and 553, n. 10. On the Stamp Act, see Downie, *Robert Harley and the Press*, pp. 150–1, but cf. J. Black, *The English Press in the Eighteenth Century* (Philadelphia, PA: University of Pennsylvania Press, 1987), p. 11.
140. For publication information, see the excellent Arbuthnot, *History*, pp. 278–86.
141. Arbuthnot, *History*, pp. lxxviii, lxxx; Herman, *Business*, pp. 214–20, makes a case for Manley's direct involvement, but a nod to her political histories seems more likely.
142. Arbuthnot, *History*, pp. 78, 221, n., xxiii–xxiv.
143. *IE*, vol. 2, pp. 169–70.
144. On this and on the rivalry of the ministers, see Dickinson, *Bolingbroke*, pp. 97–110, and Hill, *Robert Harley*, pp. 181–9.
145. On the conflict between Oxford and Bolingbroke, see Holmes, 'Harley, St. John', pp. 138–52; on the cabinet confrontation, see pp. 147–8.
146. *PW*, vol. 11, p. 66.
147. Dickinson, *Bolingbroke*, pp. 99–100.
148. *JS*, p. 545.
149. Hoppit, *Land of Liberty?*, p. 123; Hoppit's discussion, pp. 120–3, judiciously balances British self-interest with allied gains.
150. *CW*, vol. 1, pp. 471 and 473, n. 2 (Swift to Archbishop King, 28 March 1713).
151. *CW*, vol. 1, p. 414.
152. *CW*, vol. 1, p. 431.
153. *JS*, p. 552.
154. *JS*, p. 660.
155. Hamilton, *Diary*, pp. 40, 43, 47.
156. *JS*, p. 655 and nn. 660–7, esp. 663 (20 April 1713).
157. *CW*, vol. 3, p. 230 (5 April 1729).
158. *CW*, vol. 1, pp. 513–14.
159. *JS*, p. 280.
160. *CW*, vol. 1, p.516.
161. *PW*, vol. 5, pp. 1–78; on Swift's ambition be become a historian, see *IE*, vol. 2, pp. 60–5.
162. *CW*, vol. 4, p. 88; Swift was Dryden's second cousin once removed (*IE* vol. 1, pp. 4–5).
163. *PW*, vol. 8, p. 200.
164. *IE*, vol. 2, pp. 744–8.
165. Not intended for publication, his longest continuous project is the *Journal to Stella*.
166. Harold Williams outlines the history of the *History* in *PW*, vol. 7, pp. ix–xxviii.
167. *PW*, vol. 7, p. 10.
168. *CW*, vol. 1, p. 515.
169. *CW*, vol. 1, 519, 525.
170. *JS*, p. 637.
171. *The Guardian*, ed. J. C. Stephens (Lexington, KY: University Press of Kentucky, 1982), p. 210. The former mistress was Swift's successor at the *Examiner*, Delarivier Manley; now living with Swift's printer, John Barber, she was often his hostess for dinner. See also no. 41, which Swift thought accused him of infidelity, and no. 63, which

compared the *Examiner's* applause to 'the Adulation of a Prostitute' (p. 241). They exchanged wounded letters, each trying for dignity in a painful situation (*CW*, vol. 1, pp. 491–7).

172. See also Stephens's outline of the quarrel, *Guardian*, pp. 650–1.

173. Dickinson, *Bolingbroke*, pp. 107–9. With his estimate that 'some 72 Tories' opposed the ministry, cf. Hoppit, *Land of Liberty?*, p. 308, who estimates that 'nearly eighty moderate, 'whimsical' (i.e. Hanoverian) Tories' did so.

174. On Fleetwood's previous brush with the pro-peace ministry, see *Spectator*, vol. 3, p. 440, n. 1; his preface is also reprinted in *PW*, vol. 6, pp. 192–5.

175. *PW*, vol. 6, pp. 152–3

176. *PW*, vol. 6, pp. 160–1; cf. W. Fleetwood, *A Sermon Preach'd August the 4th 1700* (London: C. Harper, 1700), pp. 5–6.

177. *PW*, vol. 6, p. 161.

178. *PW*, vol. 6, p. 159.

179. On such shifts in perspective elsewhere in Swift, see D. Oakleaf, '*Trompe l'Oeil*: Gulliver and the Distortions of the Observing Eye', *University of Toronto Quarterly*, 53 (1983–4), pp. 166–80.

180. *IE*, vol. 2, p. 708.

181. *PW*, vol. 8, p. 8.

182. *PW*, vol. 8, p. 6.

183. *PW*, vol. 8, p. 12.

184. R. Steele, *The Crisis; or, A Discourse Representing, from the Most Authentick Records, the Just Causes of the Late Happy Revolution* (London: n.p., 1714), p. i.

185. *PW*, vol. 8, pp. 66, 41, 43–4.

186. *PW*, vol. 8, p. 38.

187. *Poems*, p. 157 (l. 5).

188. *PW*, vol. 4, pp. 74, 63.

189. See the succinct account of the event and collateral exasperations in A. Murdoch, 'Scotland and the Union', in Dickinson (ed.), *Companion to Eighteenth-Century Britain*, pp. 381–91; pp. 383–4.

190. Published posthumously but written at the time of the Union; see especially the caricature of the lady's Scottish rival (*PW*, vol. 9, pp. 3–4).

191. *PW*, vol. 8, pp. 198–9; *CW*, vol. 1, p. 589.

192. The centrality of the Union accounts for W. A. Speck's emphasis, in *Birth*, on the first decade of the century.

193. R. Steele, *The Publick Spirit of the Tories, Manifested in the Case of the Irish Dean, and His Man Timothy* (London: J. Roberts, 1714), pp. 5–6; cf. *Tale*, p. 70. Timothy is William Oldisworth, alluding to his reply to Tindal.

194. Backscheider, *Defoe*, p. 298; on Harley, Defoe and the Union, see pp. 203–52 and A. McInnes, *Robert Harley, Puritan Politician* (London: Victor Gollancz, 1970), pp. 78–82.

195. D. Defoe, *The Scots Nation and Union Vindicated, from the Reflections Cast on Them in an Infamous Libel Entitl'd, The Publick Spirit of the Whigs* (London: A. Bell, 1714), p. 19.

196. *PW*, vol. 8, pp. 90–1.

197. Valuable accounts centred on the rivals are Hill, *Robert Harley*, pp. 193–222, and Dickinson, *Bolingbroke*, pp. 111–33.
198. Hoppit, *Land of Liberty?*, p. 310.
199. Dickinson, *Bolingbroke*, pp. 3–4.
200. *CW*, vol. 2, p. 28, *IE*, vol. 2, pp. 734–5.
201. Dickinson, *Bolingbroke*, p. 120.
202. *CW*, vol. 2, p. 44.
203. *CW*, vol. 1, p. 628, vol. 2, p. 42.
204. Hill, *Robert Harley*, p. 215; conjectural reading in Hill.
205. *CW*, vol. 2, p. 14.
206. *CW*, vol. 1, pp. 479–80; King had promised it to another (*CW*, vol. 1, p. 493). Refuted by C. J. Rawson ('Addison and the Parnell Brothers', *Notes and Queries*, 6:10 (1959), p. 396), the tale that Swift's recommendation was successful survives in B. Coleborne, 'Parnell, Thomas (1679–1718)', in *ODNB*, article 21390.
207. See both the admirably concise statement in Brückmann, *A Manner of Correspondence*, pp. 3–4, and the fuller account in Kerby-Miller, *Memoirs of Martinus Scriblerus*, pp. 23–41.
208. *CW*, vol. 2, p. 76. On Letcombe Bassett as a retreat from Irish partisanship as well as English in 1713, see *IE*, vol. 2, pp. 713–22; King kept him informed without quite piquing his interest.

5 'Do I become a *Slave* in Six Hours, by Crossing the Channel?'

1. W. H. Auden, 'In Memory of W. B. Yeats', l. 34, in *W. H. Auden: A Selection*, ed. R. Hoggart (London: Hutchinson Educational, 1961).
2. On the fate of the ministers, see Dickinson, *Bolingbroke*, pp. 134–5, and Hill, *Robert Harley*, pp. 228–9. On popular unrest and electoral support, see Hoppit, *Land of Liberty?*, pp. 392–3, and Linda Colley, *In Defiance of Oligarchy: The Tory Party 1714–1760* (Cambridge and New York: Cambridge University Press, 1982), 120.
3. See Swift to Knightley Chetwode, 17 December 1715 (*CW*, vol. 2, pp. 149–150); J. L. McCracken, 'Protestant Ascendancy and the Rise of Colonial Nationalism, 1714–1716', in Moody and Vaughan (eds), *A New History of Ireland IV*, pp. 105–22; pp. 109–10; D. Dickson, *New Foundations*, p. 63.
4. Szechi, *Jacobites*, pp. 76–8, and (more fully), *1715: The Great Jacobite Rebellion* (New Haven, CT, and London: Yale University Press, 2006), pp. 138–81.
5. Szechi, *1715*, pp. 90–1.
6. Szechi, *Jacobites*, p. 75.
7. Hoppit, *Land of Liberty?*, p. 397.
8. The debate remains lively, but the balance of recent argument favours sceptics about the number and influence of the Tory Jacobites, and the significance of the Jacobite challenge itself. For an introduction, see Szechi, *Jacobites*. With R. Sedgwick, *The House of Commons 1715–1754*, The History of Parliament, 2 vols (New York: Oxford University Press for the History of Parliament Trust, 1970), cf. Colley, *In Defiance*, and Szechi, *Jacobitism and Tory Politics*. Evidence of later Jacobite influ-

ence on the parliamentary Tories receives searching scrutiny in A. Hanham, '"So Few Facts": Jacobites, Tories, and the Pretender', *Parliamentary History*, 19:2 (2000), pp. 233–57. Recent studies examine specific events; see Cruickshanks and Erskine-Hill, *Atterbury Plot*, and Szechi, *1715*.

9. *CW*, vol. 2, p. 35.
10. *CW*, vol. 1, pp. 458–9.
11. *CW*, vol. 2, p. 112.
12. *CW*, vol. 2, p. 131.
13. *CW*, vol. 2, p. 114.
14. *CW*, vol. 2, p. 129.
15. *CW*, vol. 2, p. 123.
16. *CW*, vol. 2, p. 193.
17. *CW*, vol. 2, p. 202.
18. 'I ever feared the Tattle of this nasty Town; and I told you so', he wrote Vanessa in December 1714 (*CW*, vol. 2, p. 102).
19. *CW*, vol. 2, pp. 204, 205.
20. Dickinson, *Bolingbroke*, pp. 143–4.
21. *CW*, vol. 2, p. 215.
22. *CW*, vol. 1, p. 233.
23. More fully, W. King, *The State of the Protestants of Ireland Under the Late King James's Government, in Which Their Carriage Towards Him is Justified, and the Absolute Necessity of Their Endeavouring to be Freed from His Government, and of Submitting to Their Present Majesties is Demonstrated* (London: Robert Clavell, 1691).
24. W. King, *An Answer to All that Has Ever Been Said, or Insinuated in Favour of a Popish Pretender. Exhibited in an Abstract of The State of the Protestants in Ireland Under King James the 2d's Government. Written by Dr. King, Now Lord Archbishop of Dublin* (London: A. Baldwin, 1713).
25. Connolly, 'Glorious Revolution', pp. 34–6.
26. M. DePorte, 'Riddles, Mysteries, and Lies: Swift and Secrecy', in *Reading Swift: Papers from the Fourth Munster Symposium on Jonathan Swift*, ed. H. Real and H. Stover-Leidig (Munich: Fink, 2003), 115.
27. McKeon, *Secret History*, pp. 469–73.
28. See M. A. Doody, 'Swift and Women', in Fox (ed.), *Cambridge Companion to Jonathan Swift*, pp. 87–111; pp. 104–5.
29. See ibid., pp. 99–100 (Doody thinks the relationship with Stella partly sexual but unconsummated), and D. Nokes, *Jonathan Swift, A Hypocrite Reversed: A Critical Biography* (Oxford: Oxford University Press, 1985), pp. 216–18 and note.
30. Downie, *Jonathan Swift*, pp. 341–3.
31. The principal combatants are Ian Higgins (for) and J. A. Downie (against). With Higgins, *Swift's Politics*, esp. pp. 38–95 (on Swift's Tory Jacobite contexts), see Downie, *Jonathan Swift*, esp. pp. 344–5, and J. A. Downie, 'Swift and Jacobitism', *English Literary History*, 64:4 (1997), pp. 887–901.
32. Lock, *Swift's Tory Politics*; Higgins, *Swift's Politics*, p. 8, from which I take the phrases quoted just below.
33. *PW*, vol. 4, p. 63.
34. *PW*, vol. 5, p. 264.

35. *PW*, vol. 7, p. 150.
36. *PW*, vol. 9, pp. 229–30.
37. *JS*, p. 50.
38. B. Hammond, 'Swift's Reading', in Fox (ed.), *Cambridge Companion to Jonathan Swift*, pp. 73–86; p. 78.
39. Rankin, *Between Spenser and Swift*, p. 73, discussing Temple's influence on Richard Lawrence, a republican soldier turned settler (pp. 63–74).
40. *PW*, vol. 5, p. 283.
41. *PW*, vol. 9, pp. 142–3. Of this sermon and the two published with it in 1744, Louis Landa says, 'It cannot be said with any assurance that they were composed or preached when Swift was Dean of St. Patrick's (*PW*, vol. 9, p. 137).
42. *PW*, vol. 9, p. 31.
43. *PW*, vol. 11, p. 131.
44. J. Swift, *Gulliver's Travels*, ed. C. Rawson, annot. I. Higgins, Oxford World's Classics (Oxford: Oxford University Press, 2005), p. 306, n.
45. [Anon.], *Gulliver Decypher'd; or, Remarks on a Late Book Intitled, Travels Into Several Remote Nations of the World. By Capt. Lemuel Gulliver. Vindicating the Reverend Dean on Whom It is Maliciously Father'd. With Some Probable Conjectures on the Real Author* (London: J. Roberts, 1726), p. 38, a response to *PW*, vol. 11, p. 131.
46. Trenchard and Gordon, *Cato's Letters*, p. 690.
47. Ibid., p. 710 and nn.
48. I follow the argument of Brewer, *Sinews of Power*, pp. 156–61.
49. Goldie, 'Roots', p. 195.
50. J. Dryden, *Absalom and Achitophel*, in *Works of John Dryden II*, pp. 2–36; p. 7 (l. 48).
51. *PW*, vol. 11, pp. 134–5.
52. *JS*, p. 206.
53. *PW*, vol. 4, pp. 79–80.
54. C. Leslie, *The Case Stated, Between the Church of Rome and the Church of England. Wherein is Shewed, That the Doubt and the Danger is in the Former, and the Certainty and Safety in the Latter Communion* (London: G. Strahan, 1713).
55. *PW*, vol. 9, p. 70.
56. The argument of *IE*, vol. 3, pp. 84–5.
57. *PW*, vol. 9, p. 71.
58. *CW*, vol. 2, pp. 649–50.
59. *Poems*, p. 487 (ll. 55–9).
60. Connolly, 'Swift and Protestant Ireland', p. 34.
61. On the uncertainties of the label, see Harris, pp. 209–10; on Jacobitism as a rhetoric of opposition, see Higgins, *Swift's Politics*, pp. 166–7. Jacobitism too appropriated a Country rhetoric of opposition.
62. Connolly, 'Swift and Protestant Ireland', pp. 32–4, *PW*, vol, 4, p. 70. On the dedication to Molesworth, see *The Drapier's Letters to the People of Ireland Against Receiving Wood's Halfpence*, ed. H. Davis (Oxford: Clarendon Press, 1935), pp. 287–9.
63. In addition to Higgins, *Swift's Politics*, see Higgins's extensive annotations in *Travels*, ed. Rawson.
64. *CW*, vol. 3, p. 88.

65. L. A. Landa, *Swift and the Church of Ireland* (Oxford: Clarendon Press, 1954), pp. 92–3.

66. I closely follow McCracken, 'Protestant Ascendancy', pp. 109–10.

67. *IE*, vol. 3, pp. 123–4; William Molyneux, *The Case of Ireland's Being Bound by Acts of Parliament in England Stated* (Dublin: Printed by Joseph Ray, 1698), was frequently reprinted. On a Lockian strand in the argument and on its influence, see Dickson, *New Foundations*, 47–48.

68. McCracken, 'Protestant Ascendancy', pp. 110–11, and 'The Political Structure, 1714–60', in Moody and Vaughan (eds), *A New History of Ireland IV*, pp. 57–83; pp. 77–8.

69. O. W. Ferguson, *Jonathan Swift and Ireland* (Urbana, IL: University of Illinois Press, 1962), pp. 53–4.

70. [Anon.], *Hibernia's Passive Obedience Strain to Britannia* (Dublin: n.p., 1720), pp. 3, 6–8; cf. *PW*, vol. 2, pp. 114, 15; vol. 1, pp. 228–9.

71. T. Burnet, *Essays Divine, Moral, and Political. By the Author of the Tale of a Tub, Sometime the Writer of the Examiner, and the Original Inventor of the Band-Box-Plot* (London: n.p., 1714); see *Hibernia's Passive Obedience*, p. 5.

72. *IE*, vol. 3, pp. 108–13; cf. J. Swift, *An Enquiry Into the Queen's Last Ministry*, ed. I. Ehrenpreis (Bloomington: Indiana University Press, 1956), pp. xxiv–xxviii.

73. Ferguson, *Jonathan Swift and Ireland*, p. 54, nn. 81 and 82.

74. *PW*, vol. 9, pp. 11–12.

75. *PW*, vol. 9, p. 21.

76. *PW*, vol. 9, p. 21.

77. *PW*, vol. 3, pp. 213–14.

78. *PW*, vol. 11, p. 201.

79. *PW*, vol. 9, p. 21.

80. E. Ward, *A Trip to New-England with a Character of the Country and People, Both English and Indians* (London: n.p., 1699), p. 3.

81. *PW*, vol. 9, pp. 26–7.

82. *PW*, vol. 9, pp. 173, 19, 17.

83. *CW*, vol. 2, p. 345.

84. With *CW*, vol. 2, pp. 345–6, cf. Hanmer's reply of 22 October 1720 (*CW*, vol. 2, pp. 349–50).

85. *IE*, vol. 3, p. 130.

86. *PW*, vol. 9, p. 25.

87. *PW*, vol. 9, p. 26.

88. *PW*, vol. 9, p. 33.

89. *PW*, vol. 9, pp. 33–4.

90. Hoppit, *Land of Liberty?*, p. 335. See the brief account of the financial issues in Brewer, *Sinews of Power*, pp. 125–6.

91. On the thrust of the attack, and the popularity of the letters, see Trenchard and Gordon, *Cato's Letters*, vol. 1, pp. xxxi, xxxv.

92. *Poems*, pp. 207–14, 695, which adopts a later title; Teerink, *Bibliography*, pp. 307–9.

93. *CW*, vol. 2, pp. 369–70.

94. Ferguson, *Jonathan Swift and Ireland*, pp. 61–4; italic and roman reversed.

95. *CW*, vol. 2, p. 398.

96. Ferguson, *Jonathan Swift and Ireland*, pp. 61–2. I draw on Chapter 3, 'The Bank Tracts and Other Pieces', all of it valuable.

97. *PW*, vol. 9, p. 285.

98. *IE*, vol. 3, p. 164.

99. For its impact on Swift, see E. Rosenhiem, Jr, 'Swift and the Atterbury Case', in H. K. Miller, E. Rothstein and G. S. Rousseau (eds), *The Augustan Milieu: Essays Presented to Louis A. Landa* (Oxford: Clarendon Press, 1970), pp. 174–204.

100. See the brisk accounts in J. H. Plumb, *Sir Robert Walpole*, 2 vols (London: Allen Lane-Penguin, [1956–60] 1972), vol. 2, pp. 43–9; Hoppit, *Land of Liberty?*, pp. 411–12.

101. Cruickshanks and Erskine-Hill, *Atterbury Plot*, p. xi.

102. Plumb, *Sir Robert Walpole*, vol. 2, pp. 46, 49; C. Rose, *England in the 1690s: Revolution, Religion and War*, A History of Early Modern England (Oxford: Blackwell Publishers, 1999), pp. 52–3. Cf. Hoppit, *Land of Liberty?*, p. 412.

103. *PW*, vol. 11, p. 191.

104. *PW*, vol. 11, p. 191. Harlequin inspires the lame dog; for an interpretation of the full list in terms of Atterbury, see Rosenhiem, 'Swift', pp. 192–9.

105. Orwell, 'Politics Vs. Literature', p. 213.

106. Ehrenpreis dates the sermon to 1715, citing parallels with a letter to Chetwode of 17 December 1715 (*CW*, vol. 2, pp. 149–51). Swift is, he argues, deliberately defying a formal prohibition against preaching on political topics (*IE*, vol. 3, p. 18, n. 1, pp. 16–18).

107. *PW*, vol. 9, p. 183.

108. *PW*, vol. 9, p. 181.

109. *PW*, vol. 9, pp. 187–8.

110. The definitive study of popular expressions of Jacobitism is P. K. Monod, *Jacobitism and the English People 1688–1788* (Cambridge: Cambridge University Press, 1989).

111. J. Clegg, 'Swift on False Witness', *Studies in English Literature, 1500–1900*, 44:3 (Summer 2004), pp. 461–85.

112. Ibid., p. 479; on *Gulliver's Travels*, see pp. 478–80.

113. P. Rogers, 'Gulliver's Glasses', in Probyn (ed.), *Art of Jonathan Swift*, pp. 179–88; on empirical observation as an inherently distorting strategy, cf. Oakleaf, '*Trompe l'Oeil*', pp. 166–80.

114. *PW*, vol. 11, p. 104.

115. Swift, *Drapier's Letters*, pp. 191–2.

116. With the brief, neutral account of Wood's career by M. B. Rowlands, 'Wood, William (1671–1730), Ironmaster', in *ODNB*, article 29898, see J. M. Treadwell, 'Swift, William Wood, and the Factual Basis of Satire', *Journal of British Studies*, 15:2 (Spring 1976), pp. 76–91, who concludes that Swift was 'absolutely right' about Wood's rapacity.

117. Ferguson, *Jonathan Swift and Ireland*, pp. 86–8, 94–5; cf. D. Dickson, *New Foundations*, pp. 66–7.

118. The best general account of the controversy remains A. Goodwin, 'Wood's Halfpence', *English Historical Review*, 51 (October 1936), pp. 647–74, but McCracken, 'Protestant Ascendancy', pp. 111–14, contains a useful brief summary of events. The

best account centred on Swift is Ferguson, *Jonathan Swift and Ireland*, pp. 83–138, but see also *Drapier's Letters*, pp. ix–lxvii, and *IE*, vol. 3, pp. 187–318. On Walpole and his rivals, see Plumb, *Sir Robert Walpole*, vol. 2, pp. 66–77.

119. On Swift's preoccupations in 1723, see *IE*, vol. 3, pp. 205–6. The account of his journey in J. McMinn, *Jonathan's Travels: Swift and Ireland*, foreword by M. Foot (Belfast: Appletree Press, 1994), pp. 74–88, includes a map (p. 75).

120. *PW*, vol. 9, p. 47; on this topic, see Landa, *Swift and the Church of Ireland*, pp. 97–111.

121. *PW*, vol. 9, p. 51.

122. Ferguson, *Jonathan Swift and Ireland*, p. 96; *IE*, vol. 3, p. 207.

123. Ferguson, *Jonathan Swift and Ireland*, pp. 58–9.

124. L. Bertelsen, 'Ireland, Temple, and the Origins of the Drapier', *Papers on Language and Literature*, 13:4 (Autumn 1977), pp. 413–19; pp. 414–16.

125. On Swift's use of *drapier*, the older French spelling of English *draper*, and its possible connection to Temple's gallicisms, see ibid., p. 419. Except where it identifies quotations from Swift's *Drapier's Letters*, *drapier* appears in the *OED* only in the etymology of *draper* and *drapery*.

126. Goodwin, 'Wood's Halfpence', pp. 660–1.

127. *PW*, vol. 10, p. 11.

128. *PW*, vol. 10, p. 8.

129. *PW*, vol. 10, p. 12.

130. *CW*, vol. 1, p. 199 (to Ambrose Philips, 10 July 1708); *PW*, vol. 12, pp. 124–6.

131. *PW*, vol. 10, p. 12.

132. *PW*, vol. 10, p. 12.

133. Colley, *Britons*, pp. 11–54.

134. *PW*, vol. 10, pp. 22, 18, 20.

135. *PW*, vol. 10, p. 20.

136. Goodwin, 'Wood's Halfpence', p. 661.

137. McCracken, 'Protestant Ascendancy', pp. 111–12.

138. 'The 6 months are over, so the Discoverer of the Draper, will not get the 300ll as I am told' (Swift to Knightley Chetwode, 27 May 1725; *CW*, vol. 2, p. 555).

139. Goodwin, 'Wood's Halfpence', pp. 671–2.

140. In resisting Goodwin's claim – 'Wood's Halfpence', p. 670 – I follow Ferguson, *Jonathan Swift and Ireland*, pp. 120–2.

141. Ferguson, *Jonathan Swift and Ireland*, p. 125.

142. J. Swift, *Seasonable Advice. Since a Bill is Preparing for the Grand Jury, to Find Against the Printer of the Drapier's Last Letter* ([Dublin]: n.p., 1724); the title differs slightly in *PW*, vol. 10, pp. 69–71.

143. *PW*, vol. 10, p. 71.

144. *PW*, vol. 10, p. 73.

145. *PW*, vol. 10, pp. 75–6.

146. I follow Ferguson, *Jonathan Swift and Ireland*, pp. 126–28, and *IE*, vol. 3, pp. 281–3.

147. See the chronological list of Swift's known contributions, prose and verse, in Teerink, *Bibliography of the Writings of Jonathan Swift*, p. 313; Swift, *Drapier's Letters*, pp. 374–83, lists all verse provoked by the pence or the Drapier.

148. See *Poems*, pp. 273–90 and 738–51.

149. *PW*, vol. 10, p. 71.
150. The fable usually features only dogs, sheep, and wolves; see North's translation, quoted *Drapier's Letters*, p. 271, n.
151. Swift, *Drapier's Letters*, pp. xlv–xlviii; Ferguson, *Jonathan Swift and Ireland*, pp. 124–5; *IE*, vol. 3, pp. 271–7 and p. 271, n. 2.
152. Swift, *Drapier's Letters*, pp. xliv–xlv.
153. *IE*, vol. 3, p. 298.
154. Brewer, *Sinews of Power*, p. 176.
155. *PW*, vol. 10, pp. 86–7.
156. *PW*, vol. 10, p. 31.
157. *PW*, vol. 10, p. 62.
158. *PW*, vol. 10, p. 35.
159. Elliott, 'Swift's 'I'', p. 383; cf. F. Brady, 'Vexations and Diversions: Three Problems in *Gulliver's Travels*', *Modern Philology*, 75:4 (May 1978), pp. 346–67; p. 346.
160. Said, 'Swift as Intellectual', p. 87.
161. *PW*, vol. 11, p. 196. J. G. Gilbert, 'The Drapier's Initials', *Notes and Queries*, 10 (June 1963), pp. 217–18, a suggestion accepted by Ehrenpreis (*IE*, vol. 3, p. 208 and n. 4).
162. 'If there is any special significance in the letters M. B., or the spelling 'Drapier', no one appears yet to have discovered it' (Swift, *Drapier's Letters*, p. 186).
163. *PW*, vol. 10, p. 82.
164. *PW*, vol. 10, p. 110.
165. *PW*, vol. 10, p. 6.
166. Ferguson, *Jonathan Swift and Ireland*, p. 101.
167. McKeon, *Secret History*, p. 5.
168. Ibid., pp. 75–6, 18–19.
169. *PW*, vol. 10, p. 61.
170. *PW*, vol. 10, p. 64.
171. *PW*, vol. 10, p. 104.
172. I draw (obviously) on Benedict Anderson's influential analysis of nationalism, *Imagined Communities: Reflections on the Origin and Spread of Nationalism*, revised ed. (London: Verso, 1991).
173. Lock, *Swift's Tory Politics*, p. 3.
174. A brilliant success, *A Tale of a Tub* served Swift's denigrators too often to count as an unqualified triumph.
175. Pope, *The Dunciad*, I.17–18, 22, in *Poems of Alexander Pope*, p. 351.
176. A. C. Kelly makes the case for Swift's conscious management of his image in *Jonathan Swift and Popular Culture: Myth, Media, and the Man* (New York: Palgrave, 2002).
177. Swift, *Verses on the Death of Dr Swift*, ll. 165–8; *Poems*, p. 489.
178. *Poems*, p. 850.

Conclusion: 'Upon this Great Foundation of Misanthropy'

1. *CW*, vol. 2, p. 487.
2. *CW*, vol. 2, pp. 586; cf. vol. 2, p. 588 (also to Ford). On the composition of *Travels*, see *IE*, vol. 3, pp. 442–6.

3. *CW*, vol. 3, p. 45.
4. *IE*, vol. 3, pp. 445–6.
5. *CW*, vol. 2, p. 606.
6. Swift's theme also organizes Porter, *English Society in the Eighteenth Century*.
7. *IE* vol. 3, 646–50. Swift's replies to Delany also included *An Epistle upon an Epistle from a Certain Doctor to a Certain Great Lord: Being a Christmas Box for Dr Delany* (1729); see *Poems*, pp. 400–9, 805–10.
8. *CW*, vol. 3, p. 284; cf. vol. 3, p. 309.
9. I follow the detailed account in *IE*, vol. 3, p. 655.
10. *PW*, vol. 12, pp. 145–8.
11. *Poems*, pp. 422–27, 816–17; *IE*, vol. 3, pp. 656–60.
12. *Intelligencer*, pp. 3–6, 288–97.
13. For a brief account of the emerging 'Patriot' opposition and its 'country' antecedents, see Hoppit, *Land of Liberty?*, pp. 414–16. Bolingbroke's role receives full treatment in Kramnick, *Bolingbroke and His Circle*, and B. S. Hammond, *Pope and Bolingbroke: A Study in Friendship and Influence* (Columbia, MO: University of Missouri Press, 1984).
14. *CW*, vol. 2, p. 642.
15. *CW*, vol. 2, p. 643.
16. On Swift's relationship with Howard, see *IE*, vol. 3, pp. 587–93.
17. *CW*, vol. 2, p. 642.
18. Ferguson, *Jonathan Swift and Ireland*, pp. 140–3 and, on collaboration with King, pp. 187–8.
19. I follow H. Williams, *The Text of Gulliver's Travels* (Cambridge: Cambridge University Press, 1952) and *IE*, vol. 3, pp. 493–5.
20. See *CW*, vol. 3, pp. 9–14 and nn.
21. Teerink, *Bibliography of the Writings of Jonathan Swift*, pp. 192–207.
22. *CW*, vol. 3, p. 44.
23. *PW*, vol. 11, pp. 19–20.
24. *CW*, vol. 3, p. 47.
25. See M. Treadwell, 'Benjamin Motte, Andrew Tooke and *Gulliver's Travels*', in H. J. Real and H. J. Vienken (eds), *Proceedings of the First Münster Symposium on Jonathan Swift* (Munich: W. Fink, 1985), pp. 287–304, and Williams, *Text*, pp. 31–61. Faulkner feared, for example, that a reference to German mercenary armies might offend the Hanoverian king; see *PW*, vol. 11, pp. 247, 315 and Williams, *Text*, p. 57.
26. With *PW*, vol. 11, p. 191, cf. vol. 11, p. 311.
27. With *PW*, vol. 11, pp. 309–10, cf. Lock, *Politics of Gulliver's Travels*, pp. 101–2.
28. *PW*, vol. 11, p. 48.
29. Pillars of the allegorical tradition include C. H. Firth, 'The Political Significance of *Gulliver's Travels*', *Proceedings of the British Academy*, 9 (1919–20), pp. 237–59, and A. E. Case, *Four Essays on Gulliver's Travels* (Gloucester, MA: Peter Smith, 1958), pp. 69–96; principals in its demolition include P. Harth, 'The Problem of Political Allegory in *Gulliver's Travels*', *Modern Philology*, 73:4 (May 1976), pp. S40–S47, Lock, *Politics of Gulliver's Travels*, pp. 94–111, and Downie, 'Political Significance of *Gulliver's Travels*', pp. 1–19, the last of whom takes his title from Firth.

30. *PW*, vol. 11, p. 48.

31. *PW*, vol. 11, p. 107.

32. *PW*, vol. 11, p. 134.

33. J. Swift, *Gulliver's Travels: Complete, Authoritative Text with Biographical and Historical Contexts, Critical History, and Essays from Five Contemporary Critical Perspectives*, ed. C. Fox (Boston, MA, and New York: Bedford-St Martin's, 1995), p. 5.

34. *PW*, vol. 11, p. 53.

35. The references are, again, to Lock, *Politics of Gulliver's Travels*, and Lock, *Swift's Tory Politics*; to Downie, *Jonathan Swift*, which devotes a chapter to *Travels*; and to Higgins, *Swift's Politics*, which does the same.

36. Swift, *Gulliver's Travels*, ed. Rawson, pp. 278–362.

37. *PW*, vol. 11, pp. 103–4.

38. On Gulliver as spectacle, see A. M. Taylor, 'Sights and Monsters in Gulliver's *Voyage to Brobdingnag*', *Tulane Studies in English*, 7 (1957), pp. 29–82.

39. *PW*, vol. 11, p. 71.

40. *PW*, vol. 11, p. 122.

41. *PW*, vol. 11, pp. 229–30.

42. *PW*, vol. 11, p. 265.

43. *PW*, vol. 11, p. 177.

44. *PW*, vol. 11, p. 176.

45. *PW*, vol. 11, p. 196.

46. *PW*, vol. 11, p. 55.

47. *PW*, vol. 11, p. 53.

48. *PW*, vol. 11, p. 56.

49. *PW*, vol. 11, p. 65.

50. *PW*, vol. 11, p. 165.

51. *PW*, vol. 11, p. 124.

52. *PW*, vol. 11, p. 107.

53. *PW*, vol. 11, p. 267.

54. *PW*, vol. 11, p. 68.

55. *PW*, vol. 11, pp. 118–19.

56. See Higgins's remarkably concise summary of the debate, in Swift, *Gulliver's Travels*, ed. Rawson, pp. 340–1.

57. Orwell, 'Politics Vs. Literature', p. 217; cf. 218 ('the Yahoos ... occupy rather the same place ... as the Jews in Nazi Germany'), p. 217 ('the highest stage of totalitarian organisation'), p. 215 ('a sort of caste system which is racial in character').

58. Rawson, *God, Gulliver, and Genocide*, p. 366, n. 10, a critique of Wilding, 'Politics of Gulliver's Travels'.

59. *PW*, vol. 11, p. 268.

60. *PW*, vol. 11, pp. 278–9.

61. *Tale*, p. 5; italic and roman reversed.

62. *CW*, vol. 2, p. 642.

63. *CW*, vol. 2, pp. 606–7.

64. *Correspondence*, vol. 5, pp. 228–9. Kennet may have been the model for Corusodes in Swift's *Intelligencer* no. 7; see Woolley's informed assessment, *Intelligencer*, pp. 93–4; Swift's humanity did not extend to conspicuous tolerance of enemies.

65. Oakleaf, '*Trompe l'Oeil*', p. 169.

66. *PW*, vol. 11, p. 247.

67. *PW*, vol. 11, pp. 134–5.

68. *PW*, vol. 11, pp. 294–5.

69. Rawson discusses Swift's tirade on colonialism briefly in Swift, *Gulliver's Travels*, ed. Rawson, pp. xxiii–xxvii, more fully in Rawson, *God, Gulliver, and Genocide*, pp. 17–24. But reluctance to be more particular has arguably marred Swift criticism; see A. Stewart, 'The Yahoo and the Discourse of Racialism in *Gulliver's Travels*', *Lumen: Selected Proceedings from the Canadian Society for Eighteenth-Century Studies*, 12 (1993), pp. 35–43.

70. As on his return from England in 1726 or his return from Market Hill in 1729 (*IE*, vol. 3, pp. 495–6, 627).

71. *PW*, vol. 13, p. 135.

72. *IE*, vol. 3, p. 575 and n. 1.

73. *PW*, vol. 12, p. 11.

74. *PW*, vol. 12, pp. 135–6. Cf. the *Proposal for Giving Badges*: 'this is the only Christian Country where People contrary to the old Maxim, are the Poverty and not the Riches of the Nation' (*PW*, vol. 13, p. 135).

75. J. L. McCracken, 'The Social Structure and Social Life, 1714–60', in Moody and Vaughan (eds), *New History of Ireland IV*, pp. 31–56; p. 34; Connolly, *Religion, Law, and Power*, p. 48. On the intersection of poor harvests with other economic conditions, see L. M. Cullen, 'Economic Development, 1691–1750', in Moody and Vaughan (eds), *New History of Ireland IV*, pp. 123–58; pp. 145–7.

76. *PW*, vol. 12, p. 122.

77. *PW*, vol. 11, p. 116.

78. J. Swift, *Swift's Irish Pamphlets: An Introductory Selection*, ed. J. McMinn, Ulster Editions and Monographs 2 (Gerrards Cross: Colin Smythe, 1991), p. 149, n. 8; McMinn's annotated 'Checklist of Swift's writings on Irish Affairs', pp. 179–86, is useful despite the inclusion of some dubious items.

79. *PW*, vol. 11, p. 281.

80. *PW*, vol. 12, p. 111.

81. On this theme, see Rawson, *God, Gulliver, and Genocide*, pp. 183–255 (ch. 3).

82. *PW*, vol. 12, p. 117.

83. *PW*, vol. 2, p. 15.

84. *PW*, vol. 7, pp. 109, 123–4.

85. Hoppit, *Land of Liberty?*, pp. 265–9; cf. C. Hill, *1530–1780: Reformation to Industrial Revolution*, The Penguin Economic History of Britain (London: Penguin, 1992), p. 227, which quotes Joshua Gee speaking in 1729.

86. J. Richardson, 'Swift, *A Modest Proposal* and Slavery', *Essays in Criticism*, 51:4 (2001), pp. 404–23.

WORKS CITED

Primary Sources

Addison, J. et al., *The Spectator*, 5 vols, ed. D. F. Bond (Oxford: Clarendon Press, 1965).

Ali, C., *The History of Timur-Bec, Known by the Name of Tamerlain the Great. Being an Historical Journal. Written in Persian by Cherefeddin Ali. Now Faithfully Render'd Into English*, trans. F. P. de la Croix, 2 vols (London: J. Darby and others, 1723).

[Anon.], *A Letter to Isaac Bickerstaff, Esq; Occasion'd by the Letter to the Examiner* (1710), in *Swiftiana II: Bickerstaffiana and Other Early Materials on Swift 1708–1715* (New York: Garland, 1975).

—, *The Perils of False Brethren: Set Forth in the Fable of the Boy and the Wolf* (London: n.p., 1710).

—, *Remarks on a False, Scandalous, and Seditious Libel Intituled The Conduct of the Allies and of the Late Ministry, andc.* (1711), in *Swiftiana III: On Swift's Remarks on the Barrier Treaty and His Conduct of the Allies 1711–1712* (New York: Garland, 1974).

—, *Remarks Upon Remarks; or, The Barrier-Treaty and the Protestant Succession Vindicated. In Answer to the False and Treasonable Reflections of the Author of The Conduct of the Allies* (1711), in *Swiftiana III: On Swift's Remarks on the Barrier Treaty and His Conduct of the Allies 1711–1712* (New York: Garland, 1974).

—, *The Fatal Effects of Arbitrary Power and the Dangerous Condition of Court Favourites Demonstrated by the Wicked Intrigues of the Court of Philip II. King of Spain* (London: Jonas Brown and J. Richardson, 1715)

—, *Hibernia's Passive Obedience Strain to Britannia* (Dublin: n.p., 1720).

—, *Gulliver Decypher'd; or, Remarks on a Late Book Intitled, Travels Into Several Remote Nations of the World. By Capt. Lemuel Gulliver. Vindicating the Reverend Dean on Whom It is Maliciously Father'd. With Some Probable Conjectures on the Real Author* (London: J. Roberts, 1726).

Arbuthnot, J., *The History of John Bull*, ed. A. W. Bower and R. A. Erickson (Oxford: Clarendon Press, 1976).

Benson, W., *A Letter to Sir J— B—, by Birth a Swede, but Naturaliz'd, and a M—r of the Present P—t: Concerning the Late Minehead Doctrine, Which Was Establish'd by a Certain Free Parliament of Sweden, to the Utter Enslaving of That Kingdom* (London: A. Baldwin, 1711).

Boccalini, T., *Advices from Parnassus, in Two Centuries. With the Political Touchstone, and an Appendix Translated by Several Hands* (London: L. Stokoe, 1705).

Burnet, G., *Bishop Burnet's History of His Own Time: With Notes by the Earls of Dartmouth and Hardwicke, Speaker Onslow, and Dean Swift*, 2nd edn enlarged, 6 vols (Oxford: Oxford University Press, 1833)

Burnet, T. *Essays Divine, Moral, and Political. By the Author of the Tale of a Tub, sometime the Writer of the examiner, and the Original Inventor of the Band-Box Plot* (London, 1714).

A Collection of State Tracts, Publish'd on Occasion of the Late Revolution in 1688. And During the Reign of King William III, 3 vols (London: n.p., 1705–7).

Defoe, D., *The True-Born Englishman* (1700–1), in G. de F. Lord (gen. ed.), *Poems on Affairs of State: Augustan Satirical Verse, 1660–1715: Vol. 6: 1697–1704*, ed. F. H. Ellis (New Haven, CT: Yale University Press, 1970), pp. 259–309.

—, *The Scots Nation and Union Vindicated, from the Reflections Cast on Them in an Infamous Libel Entitl'd, The Publick Spirit of the Whigs* (London: A. Bell, 1714).

Dryden, J., *Mac Flecknoe*, in *The Works of John Dryden II: Poems 1681–1684*, ed. H. T. Swedenberg, Jr and V. A. Dearing (Berkeley and Los Angeles, CA: University of California Press, 1972), pp. 54–60.

—, *Absalom and Achitophel*, in *The Works of John Dryden II: Poems 1681–1684*, ed. H. T. Swedenberg, Jr and V. A. Dearing (Berkeley and Los Angeles: University of California Press, 1972), pp. 2–36.

Filmer, R., *Patriarcha* [1679], in *Patriarcha and Other Political Works of Sir Robert Filmer*, ed. P. Laslett (Oxford: Blackwell, 1949), pp. 33–48.

Fleetwood, W., *A Sermon Preach'd August the 4th 1700* (London: C. Harper, 1700).

Hamilton, D., *The Diary of Sir David Hamilton*, ed. P. Roberts (Oxford: Clarendon Press, 1975).

Hare, F., *The Allies and the Late Ministry Defended Against France and the Present Friends of France* (1711), in *Swiftiana III: On Swift's Remarks on the Barrier Treaty and His Conduct of the Allies 1711–1712* (New York: Garland, 1974).

—, *The Allies and the Late Ministry Defended Against France, and the Present Friends of France, Part II* (London: A. Baldwin, 1711).

—, *The Allies and the Late Ministry Defended Against France, and the Present Friends of France, Part IV* (London: E. Sanger, 1712).

Hobbes, T., *Leviathan*, ed. C. B. Macpherson (Harmondsworth: Penguin, [1651] 1968).

King, W., *The State of the Protestants of Ireland Under the Late King James's Government, in Which Their Carriage Towards Him is Justified, and the Absolute Necessity of Their*

Endeavouring to be Freed from His Government, and of Submitting to Their Present Majesties is Demonstrated (London: Robert Clavell, 1691).

—, *An Answer to All that Has Ever Been Said, or Insinuated in Favour of a Popish Pretender. Exhibited in an Abstract of The State of the Protestants in Ireland Under King James the 2d's Government. Written by Dr. King, Now Lord Archbishop of Dublin* (London: A. Baldwin, 1713).

Leslie, C., *The Snake in the Grass; or, Satan Transform'd Into an Angel of Light. Discovering the Deep and Unsuspected Subtilty Which is Couched Under the Pretended Simplicity of Many of the Principal Leaders of Those people Call'd Quakers* (London: Charles Brome, 1696).

—, *The Case Stated, Between the Church of Rome and the Church of England. Wherein is Shewed, That the Doubt and the Danger is in the Former, and the Certainty and Safety in the Latter Communion* (London: G. Strahan, 1713).

Locke, J., *Two Treatises of Government: A Critical Edition with an Introduction and Apparatus Criticus*, ed. P. Laslett, rev. edn (New York: Mentor-New American Library, 1963).

Mandeville, B., *The Fable of the Bees; or, Private Vices, Publick Benefits*, ed. F. B. Kaye, 2 vols (Oxford: Clarendon Press, 1924; fac. repr. Indianapolis, IN: Liberty Fund, 1988).

Molyneux, W., *The Case of Ireland's Being Bound by Acts of Parliament in England Stated* (Dublin: Joseph Ray, 1698).

P., W., *The Jamaica Lady: Or, The Life of Bavia. Containing An Account of Her Intrigues, Cheats, Amours in England, Jamaica, and the Royal Navy. A Pleasant Relation of the Amours of the Officers of a Fourth Rate Man of War with Their Female Passengers, in a Voyage from Jamaica to England. With The Diverting Humours of Capt. Fustian, Commander of the Said Ship. And the Character of His Irish Surgeon; the Reason of His Preferment, and Manner of Obtaining His Warrant* (London: Tho. Bickerton, 1720).

Pétis de la Croix, F., *The History of Genghizcan the Great, First Emperor of the Antient Moguls and Tartars; in Four Books*, trans. P. Aubin (London: J. Darby and others, 1722).

Pope, A., *The Dunciad* (1742), in *The Poems of Alexander Pope: A One-Volume Edition of the Twickenham Text with Selected Annotations*, ed. J. Butt (London: Methuen, 1963).

Pope, A., et al., *Memoirs of the Extraordinary Life, Works, and Discoveries of Martinus Scriblerus: Written in Collaboration by the Members of the Scriblerus Club* (1741), ed. C. Kerby-Miller (New York: Russell and Russell, [1950] 1966).

Roberts, G., *The Four Years Voyages of Capt. George Roberts. Written by Himself* (London: A. Bettesworth and J. Osborn, 1726).

Spenser, E., *A Present View of the State of Ireland*, ed. W. L. Renwick (Oxford: Clarendon, [1633] 1970)

Steele, R., *The Publick Spirit of the Tories, Manifested in the Case of the Irish Dean, and His Man Timothy* (London: J. Roberts, 1714).

—, *The Crisis; or, A Discourse Representing, from the Most Authentick Records, the Just Causes of the Late Happy Revolution* (London: n.p., 1714).

Steele, R., et al., *The Guardian*, ed. J. C. Stephens (Lexington, KY: University Press of Kentucky, 1982).

—, *The Tatler*, ed. D. F. Bond, 3 vols (Oxford: Clarendon Press, 1987).

Swift, J., *Seasonable Advice. Since a Bill is Preparing for the Grand Jury, to Find Against the Printer of the Drapier's Last Letter* ([Dublin]: n.p., 1724).

—, *The Drapier's Letters to the People of Ireland Against Receiving Wood's Halfpence*, ed. H. Davis (Oxford: Clarendon Press, 1935).

—, *Prose Works*, ed. H. Davis and others, 14 vols (Oxford: Blackwell, 1939–74).

—, *Journal to Stella*, ed. H. Williams, 2 vols [vol. 1: pp. 1–368; vol. 2, pp. 369–801] (Oxford: Clarendon, 1948).

—, *An Enquiry Into the Queen's Last Ministry*, ed. I. Ehrenpreis (Bloomington, IN: Indiana University Press, 1956).

—, *A Tale of a Tub; To Which is Added The Battle of the Books and the Mechanical Operation of the Spirit*, ed. A. C. Guthkelch and D. N. Smith, 2nd edn (Oxford: Clarendon Press, 1958).

—, *The Correspondence of Jonathan Swift*, ed. H. Williams, 5 vols (Oxford: Clarendon Press, 1963–5).

—, *A Discourse of the Contests and Dissentions Between the Nobles and the Commons in Athens and Rome With the Consequences They Had Upon Both Those States*, ed. F. H. Ellis (Oxford: Clarendon Press, 1967).

—, *The Complete Poems*, ed. P. Rogers (New Haven, CT, and London: Yale University Press, 1983).

—, *Gulliver's Travels*, ed. P. Turner (Oxford: Oxford University Press, 1986).

—, *Swift's Irish Pamphlets: An Introductory Selection*, ed. J. McMinn, Ulster Editions and Monographs 2 (Gerrards Cross: Colin Smythe, 1991).

—, *Gulliver's Travels: Complete, Authoritative Text with Biographical and Historical Contexts, Critical History, and Essays from Five Contemporary Critical Perspectives*, ed. C. Fox (Boston, MA, and New York: Bedford-St Martin's, 1995).

—, *The Correspondence of Jonathan Swift, D.D*, ed. D. Woolley, 4 vols in 5 (Frankfurt am Main: Peter Lang, 1999–).

—, *Gulliver's Travels*, ed. C. Rawson, annot. I. Higgins (Oxford: Oxford University Press, 2005).

Swift, J., and T. Sheridan, *The Intelligencer*, ed. J. Woolley (Oxford: Clarendon Press, 1992).

—, *Swift Vs. Mainwaring: The Examiner and The Medley* ed., F. H. Ellis (Oxford: Clarendon Press, 1985).

Temple, Sir J., *The Irish Rebellion; or, An History of the Beginnings and First Progresse of the General Rebellion Raised Within the Kingdom of Ireland, Upon the Three and Twentieth Day of October, in the Year, 1641. Together with the Barbarous Cruelties and Bloody Massacres Which Ensued Thereupon* (London: Samuel Gellibrand, 1646).

Temple, Sir W., *An Introduction to the History of England* (London: Richard Simpson at the Three Trouts, and Ralph Simpson at the Harp in St. Paul's Church-Yard, 1695).

—, *Miscellanea. The Third Part*. Published by Jonathan Swift, A.M. Prebendary of St Patrick's, Dublin (London: Benjamin Tooke, 1701).

—, *Letters to the King, the Prince of Orange, the Chief Ministers of State, and Other Persons*, ed. J. Swift (London: Tim. Goodwin and Benj. Tooke, 1703).

—, 'Some Thoughts upon Reviewing the Essay of Ancient and Modern Learning', in *Five Miscellaneous Essays by Sir William Temple*, ed. S. H. Monk (Ann Arbor, MI: University of Michigan Press, 1963), pp. 72–97.

Trenchard, J., and T. Gordon, *Cato's Letters; or, Essays on Liberty, Civil and Religious, and Other Important Subjects*, 6th edn, 2 vols (1755), ed. R. Hamowy (Indianapolis, IN: Liberty Fund, 1995).

Ward, E., *A Trip to Jamaica. With a True Character of the People and Island. By the Author of Sot's Paradise* (London: n.p., 1698).

—, *A Trip to New-England with a Character of the Country and People, Both English and Indians* (London, 1699).

Secondary Sources

Anderson, B., *Imagined Communities: Reflections on the Origin and Spread of Nationalism*, rev. edn (London: Verso, 1991).

Auden, W. H., *W. H. Auden: A Selection*, ed. R. Hoggart (London: Hutchinson Educational, 1961)..

Backscheider, P. R., *Daniel Defoe: His Life* (Baltimore, MD, and London: Johns Hopkins University Press, 1989)

Ballaster, R., *Seductive Forms: Women's Amatory Fiction from 1684 to 1740* (Oxford: Clarendon Press, 1992).

Barnard, T., *A New Anatomy of Ireland: The Irish Protestants, 1649–1770* (New Haven, CT, and London: Yale University Press, 2003).

—, *The Kingdom of Ireland, 1641–1760* (Houndsmills: Palgrave Macmillan, 2004).

Beckett, J. C., 'Literature in English 1691–1800', in T. W. Moody and W. E. Vaughan (eds), *A New History of Ireland IV: Eighteenth-Century Ireland 1691–1800* (Oxford: Clarendon, 1986), pp. 424–70.

Bertelsen, L., 'Ireland, Temple, and the Origins of the Drapier', *Papers on Language and Literature*, 13:4 (Autumn 1977), pp. 413–19

—, 'Popular Entertainment and Instruction, Literary and Dramatic: Chapbooks, Advice Books, Almanacs, Ballads, Farces, Pantomimes, Prints and Shows', in J. Richetti (ed.), *The Cambridge History of English Literature, 1660–1780* (Cambridge: Cambridge University Press, 2005), pp. 61–86.

Black, J., *The English Press in the Eighteenth Century* (Philadelphia, PA: University of Pennsylvania Press, 1987).

Bond, R. P., *The Tatler: The Making of a Literary Journal* (Cambridge, MA: Harvard University Press, 1971).

Bottigheimer, K. S., 'The Glorious Revolution and Ireland', in L. G. Schwoerer (ed.), *The Revolution of 1688–1689: Changing Perspectives* (Cambridge: Cambridge University Press, 1992), pp. 234–43.

Boyle, F. T., 'Ehrenpreis's "Swift and the Date of *Sentiments of a Church-of-England Man*"', *Swift Studies*, 6 (1991), pp. 3–37.

Brady, F., 'Vexations and Diversions: Three Problems in *Gulliver's Travels*', *Modern Philology*, 75:4 (May 1978), pp. 346–67.

Braverman, R., *Plots and Counterplots: Sexual Politics and the Body Politic in English Literature, 1660–1730* (Cambridge: Cambridge University Press, 1993).

Bredvold, L. I., 'The Gloom of the Tory Satirists', in J. L. Clifford and L. A. Landa (eds), *Pope and His Contemporaries: Essays Presented to George Sherburn* (Oxford: Clarendon Press, 1949), pp. 1–19.

Brewer, J., *The Sinews of Power: War, Money and the English State, 1688–1783*, 1st American edn (New York: Alfred A. Knopf, 1989).

Brückmann, P. C., *A Manner of Correspondence: A Study of the Scriblerus Club* (Montreal and Kingston, ON: McGill-Queen's University Press, 1997).

Canny, N., *From Reformation to Restoration: Ireland, 1534–1660*, Helicon History of Ireland (Dublin: Helicon, 1987).

Case, A. E., *Four Essays on Gulliver's Travels* (Gloucester, MA: Peter Smith, [1945] 1958).

Clark, J. K., 'Wharton, Thomas, First Marquess of Wharton, First Marquess of Malmesbury, and First Marquess of Catherlough (1648–1715)', in *ODNB*, article 29175.

Clark, J. R., *Form and Frenzy in Swift's Tale of a Tub* (Ithaca, NY: Cornell University Press, 1970).

Clegg, J., 'Swift on False Witness', *Studies in English Literature, 1500–1900*, 44:3 (Summer 2004), pp. 461–85.

Coleborne, B., 'Parnell, Thomas (1679–1718)', in *ODNB*, article 21390.

Colley, L., *In Defiance of Oligarchy: The Tory Party 1714–1760* (Cambridge and New York: Cambridge University Press, 1982).

—, *Britons: Forging the Nation 1707–1837* (New Haven, CT, and London: Yale University Press, 1992).

—, *Captives* (New York: Pantheon-Random House, 2002).

Connolly, S. J., *Religion, Law, and Power: The Making of Protestant Ireland 1660–1760*. (Oxford: Clarendon Press, 1992).

—, 'Swift and Protestant Ireland: Images and Reality', in A. Douglas, P. Kelly, and I. C. Ross (eds), *Locating Swift: Essays from Dublin on the 250th Anniversary of the Death of Jonathan Swift 1667–1745* (Dublin: Four Courts Press, 1998), pp. 28–46.

—, 'The Glorious Revolution in Irish Protestant Political Thinking', in S. J. Connolly (ed.), *Political Ideas in Eighteenth-Century Ireland* (Dublin: Four Courts Press, 2000), pp. 27–63.

—, 'Religion in Ireland', in H. T. Dickinson (ed.), *Companion to Eighteenth-Century Britain* (Oxford: Blackwell Publishing, 2002), pp. 271–80.

Cook, R. I., *Jonathan Swift as a Tory Pamphleteer* (Seattle, WA, and London: University of Washington Press, 1967).

Corish, P. J., 'The Rising of 1641 and the Catholic Confederacy, 1641–5', in T. W. Moody, F. X. Martin, and F. J. Byrne (eds), *A New History of Ireland III: Early Modern Ireland 1534–1691* (Oxford: Clarendon, 1976), pp. 289–316.

Cruickshanks, E., and H. Erskine-Hill, *The Atterbury Plot* (Houndmills: Palgrave Macmillan, 2004).

Cullen, L. M., 'Economic Development, 1691–1750', in T. W. Moody and W. E. Vaughan (eds), *A New History of Ireland IV: Eighteenth-Century Ireland 1691–1800* (Oxford: Clarendon Press, 1986), pp. 123–58.

DePorte, M., 'Swift, God, and Power', in C. Fox and B. Tooley (eds), *Walking Naboth's Vineyard: New Studies of Swift* (Notre Dame, IN: University of Notre Dame Press, 1995), pp. 73–97.

—, 'Riddles, Mysteries, and Lies: Swift and Secrecy', in H. Real and H. Stover-Leidig (eds), *Reading Swift: Papers from the Fourth Munster Symposium on Jonathan Swift* (Muncih: Fink, 2003), pp. 115–31.

Dickinson, H. T., *Bolingbroke* (London: Constable, 1970).

—, *Liberty and Property: Political Ideology in Eighteenth-Century Britain* (London: Weidenfeld and Nicolson, 1977).

Dickson, D., *New Foundations: Ireland 1660–1800*, Helicon History of Ireland (Dublin: Helicon, 1987).

Dickson, P. G. M., *The Financial Revolution in England: A Study in the Development of Public Credit 1688–1756* (London: Macmillan, 1967)

Doherty, R., *The Williamite War in Ireland 1688–1691* (Dublin: Four Courts Press, 1998).

Doody, M. A., 'Swift and Women', in C. Fox (ed.), *The Cambridge Companion to Jonathan Swift* (Cambridge: Cambridge University Press, 2003), pp. 87–111.

Downie, J. A., 'The Commission of Public Accounts and the Formation of the Country Party', *English Historical Review*, 91 (January 1976), pp. 33–51.

—, '*The Conduct of the Allies*: The Question of Influence', in C. T. Probyn (ed.), *The Art of Jonathan Swift* (London: Vision Press, 1978), pp. 108–28.

—, *Robert Harley and the Press: Propaganda and Public Opinion in the Age of Swift and Defoe* (Cambridge: Cambridge University Press, 1979).

—, *Jonathan Swift: Political Writer* (London and Boston, MA: Routledge, 1984).

—, 'The Political Significance of *Gulliver's Travels*', in J. I. Fischer, H. J. Real and J. Woolley (eds), *Swift and His Contexts* (New York: AMS Press, 1989), pp. 1–19.

—, 'Swift and Jacobitism', *English Literary History*, 64:4 (1997), pp. 887–901.

Eagleton, T., *The Function of Criticism: From The Spectator to Post-Structuralism* (London: Verso, 1984).

Ehrenpreis, I., 'The Date of Swift's "Sentiments"', *Review of English Studies*, 3 (1952), pp. 272–4.

—, *Swift: The Man, His Works, and the Age*, 3 vols (Cambridge, MA: Harvard University Press, 1962–83).

Elias Jr, A. C., *Swift at Moor Park: Problems in Biography and Criticism* (Philadelphia, PA: University of Pennsylvania Press, 1982).

Elliott, R. C., 'Swift's "I"', *Yale Review*, 62:3 (March 1973), pp. 372–91.

Ellis, S. G., *Ireland in the Age of the Tudors 1447–1603: English Expansion and the End of Gaelic Rule*, Longman History of Ireland (London and New York: Longman, 1998).

Fabricant, C., 'Swift as Irish Historian', in C. Fox and B. Tooley (eds), *Walking Naboth's Vineyard: New Studies of Swift* (Notre Dame, IN: University of Notre Dame Press, 1995), pp. 40–72.

Ferguson, O. W., *Jonathan Swift and Ireland* (Urbana, IL: University of Illinois Press, 1962).

Firth, C. H., 'The Political Significance of *Gulliver's Travels*', *Proceedings of the British Academy*, 9 (1919–20), pp. 237–59.

Gandhi, M., 'Letter to Maganlal Gandhi, *Vaisakh Vad 5 [May 8, 1911]*', in *Collected Works of Mahatma Gandhi*, 90 vols (Delhi: Publications Division, Ministry of Information and Broadcasting, Government of India, 1958–84), vol. 11, pp. 77–8.

Gilbert, J. G., 'The Drapier's Initials', *Notes and Queries*, 10 (June 1963), pp. 217–18.

Goldie, M., 'The Roots of True Whiggism 1688–94', *History of Political Thought*, 1:2 (Summer 1980), pp. 195–236.

Goodwin, A., 'Wood's Halfpence', *English Historical Review*, 51 (October 1936), pp. 647–74.

Gordimer, N., 'Lust and Death [Review of *Everyman*, by Philip Roth (Boston, MA: Houghton, 2006)]', *New York Times Book Review*, 7 May 2006, p. 10.

Hammond, B. S., *Pope and Bolingbroke: A Study in Friendship and Influence* (Columbia, MO: University of Missouri Press, 1984).

—, 'Scriblerian Self-Fashioning', *Yearbook of English Studies*, 18 (1988), pp. 108–24.

—, *Professional Imaginative Writing in England, 1670–1740: 'Hackney for Bread'* (Oxford: Clarendon Press, 1997).

—, 'The Satirist and His Faith: An Overview', The Satirist and His Faith. A Symposium on Jonathan Swift and Christianity, St Patrick's Cathedral, Dublin, 12 October 2002, http://www.iol.ie/~rjtechne/swift/2002/hammond.htm.

—, 'Swift's Reading', in C. Fox (ed.), *The Cambridge Companion to Jonathan Swift* (Cambridge: Cambridge University Press, 2003), pp. 73–86.

Hanham, A., '"So Few Facts": Jacobites, Tories, and the Pretender', *Parliamentary History*, 19:2 (2000), pp. 233–57.

Harris, T., *Politics under the Later Stuarts: Party Conflict in a Divided Society 1660–1715* (London and New York: Longman, 1993).

Harth, P., 'The Problem of Political Allegory in *Gulliver's Travels*', *Modern Philology*, 73:4 (May 1976), pp. S40–S47.

Hawes, C., 'Three Times Round the Globe: Gulliver and Colonial Discourse', *Cultural Critique*, 18 (Spring 1991), pp. 187–214.

Haydon, C., 'Religious Minorities in England', in H. T. Dickinson (ed.), *A Companion to Eighteenth-Century Britain* (Oxford: Blackwell Publishing, 2002), pp. 241–51.

Hayes-McCoy, G. A., 'The Completion of the Tudor Conquest and the Advance of the Counter-Reformation, 1571–1603', in T. W. Moody, F. X. Martin, and F. J. Byrne (eds), *A New History of Ireland III: Early Modern Ireland 1534–1691* (Oxford: Clarendon, 1976), pp. 119–36.

Hayton, D. W., 'Anglo-Irish Attitudes: Changing Perceptions of National Identity Among the Protestant Ascendancy in Ireland *c.* 1690–1750', *Studies in Eighteenth-Century Culture*, 17 (1987), pp. 145–57.

Herman, R. A., 'The Dean and the Dissenters', Dean Swift: The Satirist and His Faith. A Symposium on Jonathan Swift and Christianity, St Patrick's Cathedral, Dublin, 19 October 2002, http://www.iol.ie/~rjtechne/swift/2002/herman.htm.

—, *The Business of a Woman: The Political Writings of Delarivier Manley* (Newark, DE: University of Delaware Press; London: Associated University Presses, 2003).

Higgins, I., *Swift's Politics: A Study in Disaffection* (Cambridge: Cambridge University Press, 1994).

Hill, B. W., *Robert Harley: Speaker, Secretary of State and Premier Minister* (New Haven, CT, and London: Yale University Press, 1988).

Hill, C., *1530–1780: Reformation to Industrial Revolution*, The Penguin Economic History of Britain (London: Penguin, 1992).

Holmes, G., 'Religion and Party in Late Stuart England', in *Politics, Religion and Society in England 1679–1742* (London and Ronceverte, WV: Hambledon Press, [1975] 1986), pp. 181–215.

—, 'Harley, St. John and the Death of the Tory Party', in *Politics, Religion and Society in England 1679–1742* (London and Ronceverte, WV: Hambledon Press, 1986), pp. 139–60.

Hoppit, J., *A Land of Liberty? England 1689–1727*, The New Oxford History of England (Oxford: Clarendon Press, 2000).

Hudson, N., 'From "Nation" to "Race": The Origin of Racial Classification in Eighteenth-Century Thought', *Eighteenth-Century Studies*, 29 (1996), pp. 247–64.

Hunter, J. P., *Before Novels: The Cultural Contexts of Eighteenth-Century English Fiction* (New York: Norton, 1990).

Ingrassia, C., *Authorship, Commerce, and Gender in Early Eighteenth-Century England: A Culture of Paper Credit* (Cambridge: Cambridge University Press, 1998).

Johnson, J. W., *The Formation of English Neo-Classical Thought* (Princeton, NJ: Princeton University Press, 1967).

Kelly, A. C., 'Swift's Explorations of Slavery in Houynhnmland and Ireland', *PMLA*, 91 (1976), pp. 846–55.

—, *Jonathan Swift and Popular Culture: Myth, Media, and the Man* (New York: Palgrave, 2002).

Kramnick, I., *Bolingbroke and His Circle: The Politics of Nostalgia in the Age of Walpole* (Cambridge, MA: Harvard University Press, 1968).

Landa, L. A., *Swift and the Church of Ireland* (Oxford: Clarendon Press, 1954).

Leavis, F. R., 'The Irony of Swift', in E. Tuveson (ed.), *Swift: A Collection of Critical Essays* (Englewood Cliffs, NJ: Prentice-Hall, 1964), pp. 15–29.

Lock, F. P., *The Politics of Gulliver's Travels* (Oxford: Clarendon Press, 1980).

—, *Swift's Tory Politics* (Newark, DE: University of Delaware Press, 1983).

Lowe, N. F., 'Why Swift Killed Partridge', *Swift Studies*, 6 (1991), pp. 71–82.

McClintock, A., *Imperial Leather: Race, Gender and Sexuality in the Colonial Contest* (New York and London: Routledge, 1995).

McCracken, J. L., 'The Political Structure, 1714–60', in T. W. Moody and W. E. Vaughan (eds), *A New History of Ireland IV: Eighteenth-Century Ireland 1691–1800* (Oxford: Clarendon Press, 1986), pp. 57–83.

—, 'Protestant Ascendancy and the Rise of Colonial Nationalism, 1714–1716', in (eds) T. W. Moody and W. E. Vaughan *A New History of Ireland IV: Eighteenth-Century Ireland 1691–1800* (Oxford: Clarendon, 1986), pp. 105–22.

—, 'The Social Structure and Social Life, 1714–60', in T. W. Moody and W. E. Vaughan (eds) *A New History of Ireland IV: Eighteenth-Century Ireland 1691–1800* (Oxford: Clarendon Press, 1986), pp. 31–56.

MacDermott, K., 'Literature and the Grub Street Myth', in P. Humm, P. Stigant and P. Widdowson (eds), *Popular Fictions: Essays in Literature and History* (New York: Methuen, 1986), pp. 16–28.

McInnes, A., *Robert Harley, Puritan Politician* (London: Victor Gollancz, 1970).

McKeon, M., *The Origins of the English Novel 1600–1740* (Baltimore, MD: Johns Hopkins University Press, 1987).

—, *The Secret History of Domesticity: Public, Private, and the Division of Knowledge* (Baltimore. MD: Johns Hopkins University Press, 2005).

McMinn, J., *Jonathan's Travels: Swift and Ireland*, foreword by M. Foot (Belfast: Appletree Press, 1994).

Mayhew, G. P., 'Swift's Bickerstaff Hoax as an April Fools' Joke', *Modern Philology*, 61:2 (May 1964), pp. 270–80.

Monod, P. K., *Jacobitism and the English People 1688–1788* (Cambridge: Cambridge University Press, 1989).

Murdoch, A., 'Scotland and the Union', in H. T. Dickinson (ed.), *A Companion to Eighteenth-Century Britain* (Oxford: Blackwell, 2002), pp. 380–91.

Nokes, D., *Jonathan Swift, A Hypocrite Reversed: A Critical Biography* (Oxford: Oxford University Press, 1985).

Oakleaf, D., '*Trompe l'Oeil*: Gulliver and the Distortions of the Observing Eye', *University of Toronto Quarterly*, 53 (1983–4), pp. 166–80.

—, 'Politics and History', in C. Fox (ed.), *The Cambridge Companion to Jonathan Swift* (Cambridge: Cambridge University Press, 2003), pp. 31–47.

Orwell, G., 'Jonathan Swift, an Imaginary Interview by George Orwell', in *Orwell: The War Broadcasts*, ed. W. J. West (London: Duckworth and the British Broadcasting Corporation, [1942] 1985), pp. 112–16.

—, 'Politics Vs. Literature: An Examination of *Gulliver's Travels*', in *The Collected Essays, Journalism and Letters of George Orwell*, ed. S. Orwell and I. Angus, 4 vols (New York: Harcourt, Brace & World, 1968), vol. 4, pp. 205–23.

Passman, D. F., and H. J. Vienken, *The Library and Reading of Jonathan Swift: A Bio-Bibliographical Handbook. Part I*, 4 vols (Frankfurt am Main: Peter Lang, 2003).

Paulson, R., *Theme and Structure in Swift's Tale of a Tub*, Yale Studies in English No. 143 (New Haven, CT: Yale University Press, 1960).

—, *The Fictions of Satire* (Baltimore, MD: Johns Hopkins University Press, 1967).

Plumb, J. H., *Sir Robert Walpole*, 2 vols (London: Allen Lane-Penguin, [1956–60] 1972).

Pocock, J. G. A., *The Machiavellian Moment: Florentine Political Thought and the Atlantic Republican Tradition* (Princeton, NJ: Princeton University Press, 1975).

—, 'Protestant Ireland: The View from a Distance', in S. J. Connolly (ed.), *Political Ideas in Eighteenth-Century Ireland* (Dublin: Four Courts Press, 2000), pp. 221–30.

—, 'The Varieties of Whiggism from Exclusion to Reform: A History of Ideology and Discourse', in *Virtue, Commerce, and History: Essays on Political Thought and History, Chiefly in the Eighteenth Century* (Cambridge: Cambridge University Press, 1985), pp. 213–310.

—, 'The Mobility of Property and the Rise of Eighteenth-Century Sociology', in *Virtue, Commerce, and History: Essays on Political Thought and History, Chiefly in the Eighteenth Century* (Cambridge: Cambridge University Press, 1985), pp. 103–23.

Porter, R., *English Society in the Eighteenth Century*, rev. edn (London: Penguin, 1991).

Prest, W., *Albion Ascendant: English History, 1660–1815* (Oxford: Oxford University Press, 1998).

Rankin, D., *Between Spenser and Swift: English Writing in Seventeenth-Century Ireland* (Cambridge: Cambridge University Press, 2005).

Rawson, C., 'Addison and the Parnell Brothers', *Notes and Queries*, 6:10 (1959), p. 396.

—, *God, Gulliver, and Genocide: Barbarism and the European Imagination, 1492–1945* (Oxford: Oxford University Press, 2001).

Richardson, J., 'Swift, *A Modest Proposal* and Slavery', *Essays in Criticism*, 51:4 (2001), pp. 404–23.

Rogers, P., 'Gulliver's Glasses', in C. T. Probyn (ed.), *The Art of Jonathan Swift* (London: Vision Press, 1978), pp. 179–88.

Rose, C., *England in the 1690s: Revolution, Religion and War*, A History of Early Modern England (Oxford: Blackwell Publishers, 1999).

Rosenhiem, Jr, E., 'Swift and the Atterbury Case', in H. K. Miller, E. Rothstein and G. S. Rousseau (eds), *The Augustan Milieu: Essays Presented to Louis A. Landa* (Oxford: Clarendon Press, 1970), pp. 174–204.

Rowlands, M. B., 'Wood, William (1671–1730), Ironmaster', in *ODNB*, article 29898.

Sachse, W. L., *Lord Somers: A Political Portrait* (Manchester: Manchester University Press, 1975).

Said, E., 'Swift's Tory Anarchy', in *The World, the Text, and the Critic* (Cambridge, MA: Harvard University Press, 1983), pp. 54–71.

—, 'Swift as Intellectual', in *The World, the Text, and the Critic* (Cambridge, MA: Harvard University Press, 1983), pp. 72–89.

—, *Culture and Imperialism* (New York: Vintage-Random House, 1993).

Schworer, L. G., *The Declaration of Rights, 1689* (Baltimore, MD, and London: Johns Hopkins University Press, 1981).

Sedgwick, R., *The House of Commons 1715–1754*, The History of Parliament, 2 vols (New York: Oxford University Press for the History of Parliament Trust, 1970).

Shapiro, J., *A Year in the Life of William Shakespeare: 1599* (New York: Harper-Perennial, [2005] 2006).

Simms, J. G., 'The War of the Two Kings, 1685–91', in T. W. Moody, F. X. Martin, and F. J. Byrne (eds), *A New History of Ireland III: Early Modern Ireland 1534–1691* (Oxford: Clarendon, 1976), pp. 478–87.

Speck, W. A., 'Social Status in Late Stuart England', *Past and Present*, 34 (July 1966), pp. 127–9.

—, 'From Principles to Practice: Swift and Party Politics', in B. Vickers (ed.), *The World of Jonathan Swift: Essays for the Tercentenary* (Oxford: Blackwell, 1968), pp. 69–86.

—, '*The Examiner* Examined: Swift's Tory Pamphleteering', in C. J. Rawson (ed.), *Focus: Swift* (London: Sphere Books, 1971), pp. 138–54.

—, *Reluctant Revolutionaries: Englishmen and the Revolution of 1688* (Oxford: Oxford University Press, 1988).

—, *The Birth of Britain: A New Nation 1700–1710* (London: Blackwell, 1994).

Stewart, A., 'The Yahoo and the Discourse of Racialism in *Gulliver's Travels*', *Lumen: Selected Proceedings from the Canadian Society for Eighteenth-Century Studies*, 12 (1993), pp. 35–43.

Szechi, D., *Jacobitism and Tory Politics 1710–14* (Edinburgh: John Donald Publishers, 1984).

—, *The Jacobites: Britain and Europe 1688–1788* (Manchester and New York: Manchester University Press, 1994).

—, *1715: The Great Jacobite Rebellion* (New Haven, CT, and London: Yale University Press, 2006).

Taylor, A. M., 'Sights and Monsters in Gulliver's *Voyage to Brobdingnag*', *Tulane Studies in English*, 7 (1957), pp. 29–82.

Teerink, H., *A Bibliography of the Writings of Jonathan Swift*, 2nd edn, ed. A. H. Scouten (Philadelphia, PA: University of Pennsylvania Press, 1963).

Treadwell, M., 'Swift, William Wood, and the Factual Basis of Satire', *Journal of British Studies*, 15:2 (Spring 1976), pp. 76–91.

—, 'Swift's Relations with the London Book Trade to 1714', in R. Myers and M. Harris (eds), *Author/Publisher Relations During the Eighteenth and Nineteenth Centuries* (Oxford: Oxford Polytechnic Press, 1983), pp. 1–36.

—, 'Benjamin Motte, Andrew Tooke and *Gulliver's Travels*', in H. J. Real and H. J. Vienken (eds), *Proceedings of the First Münster Symposium on Jonathan Swift* (Munich: W. Fink, 1985), pp. 287–304.

Wilding, M., 'The Politics of *Gulliver's Travels*', in *Studies in the Eighteenth Century II: Papers Presented at the Second David Nichol Smith Memorial Seminar Canberra 1970*, ed. R. F. Brissenden (Toronto and Buffalo, ON: University of Toronto Press, 1973), pp. 303–22.

Williams, H., *The Text of Gulliver's Travels* (Cambridge: Cambridge University Press, 1952).

Williams, K. (ed.), *Swift: The Critical Heritage* (New York: Barnes and Noble, 1970).

Yeats, W. B., *The Variorum Edition of the Plays of W. B. Yeats*, ed. R. K. Alspach, assisted by C. C. Alspach (London: Macmillan, 1966).

INDEX

Works by Swift (JS) appear directly under title; works by others under author's name.